THE SOCIAL
AND POLITICAL
THOUGHT
OF AMERICAN
PROGRESSIVISM

THE AMERICAN HERITAGE SERIES

The American Heritage Series

THE SOCIAL
AND POLITICAL
THOUGHT
OF AMERICAN
PROGRESSIVISM

Edited, with an Introduction, by
Eldon J. Eisenach

Hackett Publishing Company, Inc.
Indianapolis/Cambridge

Copyright © 2006 by Hackett Publishing Company, Inc.

12 11 10 09 08 07 06   1 2 3 4 5 6 7

For further information, please address:

   Hackett Publishing Company, Inc.
   P.O. Box 44937
   Indianapolis, IN   46244-0937

   www.hackettpublishing.com

Cover design by Rick Todhunter and Abigail Coyle
Text design by Meera Dash
Composition by Brighid Willson
Printed at Edwards Brothers, Inc.

Library of Congress Cataloging-in-Publication Data

The social and political thought of American progressivism / edited, with
introduction, by Eldon J. Eisenach.
      p. cm. — (American heritage series)
Includes bibliographical references and index.
ISBN 0-87220-785-4 (cloth) — ISBN 0-87220-784-6 (pbk.)
  1. Political science—United States—History. 2. Progressivism (United States
politics) 3. United States—Social conditions—1865-1918. 4. United States—
Politics and government. I. Eisenach, Eldon J. II. Series: American heritage
series (New York, N.Y.)
  JA84.U5S573 2006
  324.2732'7—dc22

                                       2005029206

The paper used in this publication meets the minimum requirements of
American National Standard for Information Sciences—Permanence of Paper
for Printer Library Materials, ANSI Z39.48–1984.

∞

Contents

Introduction

It is important to understand Progressivism—the political and social reform movement that began at the end of the nineteenth century—correctly. After all, the movement's leading minds founded the modern American university and created the modern academic disciplines and journals; they created the ligaments of the national administrative and regulatory state and founded and supplied a mass national journalism independent of political parties and churches; and they witnessed and helped legitimate the creation of a national financial and industrial corporate economy that soon became the engine driving the international economy. In short, they helped transform America into the dominant world power it is today. If we cannot understand the Progressives' influence on the shaping of modern American political life, we have little hope of understanding ourselves or our country's place in the world; nor can we equip ourselves to play a constructive role in shaping its future.

To discover what legitimated, energized, and drove the Progressive reforms, one must consider the Progressives' ideas and the institutions that embodied those ideas. The ideas and ideals of national Progressivism originated well before most national reform legislation was enacted, and they persisted well after the movement's national electoral energies had dissipated. The earliest selection in this collection of Progressive writings is an election pamphlet written in 1844; the latest selection is an analysis of industrial society penned by Richard Ely in 1938. The ideas and institutions of the Progressives outlasted, and had a much greater influence on American political institutions and culture than, their efforts in the party-electoral and legislative arenas; these coherent, enduring ideals will be the focus of this collection.

The Progressive Era in American national political life began in the mid-1890s and lasted through 1920. The election of William McKinley to the presidency in 1896 broke a twenty-year electoral stalemate and provided an opening for Progressives in the Republican Party to begin to restructure the relationship of the national government to the new industrial economy. By the presidential election of 1912, the candidates from all three contending parties were Progressive in varying degrees, with the victory going to Woodrow Wilson, who ran on the Democratic ticket. Eight years later, however, James M. Cox, a Wilsonian Progressive from Ohio, was decisively defeated by Republican Warren G. Harding, who was by no means a Progressive reformer. In 1924, John W. Davis—who later became (in)famous as the lead attorney defending segregation in southern schools in *Brown v. Board of Education of Topeka* (1954)—was defeated by Calvin Coolidge, the conservative Republican candidate; the electoral energies of Progressivism were spent.[1]

The first national wave of reform was both Progressive and populist: the Interstate Commerce Act of 1887 regulated railroad rates and outlawed discriminatory pricing practices; the Sherman Anti-Trust Act of 1890 put an end to business monopolies and pricing. Although both enactments were initially contradictory in their aims, and though they were often rendered ineffectual through court decisions, they symbolized a new national commitment to responsible oversight of the flourishing industrial economy.

Reforms in states and localities began even earlier. The prevailing political party system that seemed to privilege local and special interests over the national interest (and, indeed, over the very idea of a consciously willed common good) was attacked by a series of reforms undertaken at the state and city level. Beginning in the 1880s, the patronage system was assailed through civil service reform. Later, especially in the north and midwest, political parties became tightly regulated; they were transformed from unregulated private and voluntary organizations into something like public corporations. Voter registration acts, mandatory party primaries (held in thirty-one states by 1908), and the almost universal introduction of official ballots (based on the Australian model) printed and controlled by governments—all of these innovations eroded the control political parties held over their electorates. Among these antiparty reforms were initiative and referenda provisions whereby citizens themselves could pass laws through direct vote, thereby circumventing the party-dominated state legislatures. A companion measure gave citizens the power, through petition and vote, to recall a standing elected official from office.

Still other reforms hastened the decline of the major political parties. Elections of nonpartisan city governments and school boards were held independently of state and national elections. Regulatory bodies and increasingly powerful political executives drained the strength of party-

---

1. Link, "What Happened to the Progressive Movement?" (1959). One could date the beginnings of Progressive politics earlier than this by looking at northern and midwestern state and municipal elections. One could also extend Progressivism into the 1930s, in New Deal liberalism, a position defended in Stettner, *Shaping Modern Liberalism* (1993), but most historians would maintain that the election of Franklin Roosevelt in 1932 inaugurated a distinctly new era in American politics in terms of constituencies, interests, and policies.

dominated state legislatures and city councils. The loss of the political parties' autonomous power and prestige was accompanied by a decline in the influence of the party press. An increase in national advertising and distribution paved the way for the rise of a more nationally oriented and officially nonpartisan form of journalism that offered both an alternative to local partisan newspapers and a new model of journalistic profession-alism. The ability to vote freely—for "the best man"—instead of along party lines was increasingly viewed as a right guaranteed by the ideal of American "citizenship."

The long-standing alliance between political party machines and "special interests" was also attacked from the business side. Between 1903 and 1908, twenty-two states made it illegal for business corpora-tions to contribute to political campaigns. Some cities, having achieved a measure of home rule and the capacity to create their own municipal charters, formed their own municipal corporations to supply transporta-tion, water, gas, and electricity; many other cities created nonpartisan commissions to regulate these industries. More importantly, private business itself was increasingly regulated. Among the many campaigns to restrict the freedom of private industry, three stand out: the outlaw-ing or strict regulation of child labor, first by most non-southern states (twenty-five states by 1901), and then by national legislation; the regu-lation of employment, hours, and minimum wages for women and girls; and the establishment of workers' compensation for injuries or death suffered in the workplace.

All three of these successful campaigns were based largely on the argument that the family—with its responsibility for raising healthy and competent children—must be protected from the depredations of big business. Similar reforms, not addressed to business practices, included the establishment of compulsory school attendance laws and state wid-ows' pensions, and the raising of the age of female sexual consent and marriage. Along with this recognition of the family came a politically influential movement to give women a greater voice in national poli-tics. Many cities and states had already granted women the right to vote long before the constitutional amendment for woman suffrage was passed in 1920; other states permitted women to hold appointive public office. Moreover, much of the political power held by women derived from nonparty and nonelectoral sources. Although women had long exerted great influence in reform-minded Protestant churches, the dra-matic increase throughout the late 1880s and 1890s in women's clubs, reform-minded newspapers, and reform organizations founded and run by women significantly increased the power and influence of their antiparty and reform campaigns.

Nowhere was the voice of politically active women clearer and more insistent for reform than in the temperance movement. The Prohibition Party—founded in 1869 on the platform that alcoholic drinks should be prohibited in order to protect women, children, and the family from its corrupting influence—was the first to call for compulsory schooling for all children (1876) and for woman suffrage (1888).[2] With the help of the Woman's Christian Temperance Union (WCTU), antialcohol education became part of the curriculum in every public school in every state. As early as 1887, twenty-seven state Republican Party platforms urged some form of prohibition, and the preparedness campaign for World War I included strict national regulation of alcohol. In short, by the time the national prohibition amendment was passed in 1919 (by an aggregate state legislative majority of more than 80 percent), most Americans were already living in dry states and counties—a change brought about, in large part, through the efforts of the Prohibition Party and the WCTU.

Understanding Progressivism correctly is not as easy as it may first appear. In the 1970s, historians began to question whether the Progressive movement actually possessed any intellectual, ideological, or political coherence—and their answer was largely negative.[3] In the 1980s, a review article attempting to systematize this interpretive disarray concluded that Progressives "did not share a common creed or a string of common values"; instead, they spoke in three incommensurable "languages of discontent": antimonopolism, social bonds, and social efficiency.[4] This ongoing argument among historians is nicely documented in a recent collection that charts these disagreements from the 1950s until 2002.[5]

The scholarship produced by the generation of historians trained by the Progressives themselves stands in striking contrast to these current interpretive muddles. The now classic histories of American economic thought (Joseph Dorfman), American philosophy (Herbert Schneider),

---

2. To give an indication of the depth of support for prohibition among the educated, a straw poll of University of Chicago undergraduates in the election of 1892 had the Populist candidate (Weaver) receiving 3 votes; the Democrat (Cleveland), 52 votes; and the Republican (Harrison), 151 votes—but the winner was John Bidwell, running on the Prohibition ticket, with 164 votes.

3. Buenker, Burnham, and Crunden, *Progressivism* (1977) contains three essays responding to a seminal article by Filene, "An Obituary for the 'Progressive Movement'" (1970).

4. Rodgers, "In Search of Progressivism" (1982).

5. Gilmore, *Who Were the Progressives?* (2002). This collection of Progressive historiography includes selections from Richard Hofstadter, *Age of Reform* (1955) and Robert Wiebe, *Search for Order* (1967).

and American democratic thought (Ralph Henry Gabriel)[6] written by
the Progressives' intellectual heirs evidence a clear understanding of
Progressivism as a positive and coherent body of political and social
thought set within, but deeply critical of, prevailing forms of American
thought. Because they read American political history through the nar-
rative of a history of ideas (including religious ideas) these scholars
helped us see Progressivism as both reform and national fulfillment.

The difference between these earlier historians and later ones is
partly an artifact of emphasis and timing. Progressivism as a developing
body of *ideas*—ideas that presented Americans with a clear alternative
to the economic dislocations produced by the stalemated and confused
political arena of the "Gilded Age"—can be dated from the mid-1880s
onward.[7] When Progressive alternatives entered the political arena
with the hegemonic victory of the Republican Party in 1896, many
obstacles lay in their path. Personal ambitions, internal party divisions,
regional economic interests, and rapidly changing economic and
social conditions all contributed to a rhythm of progress and retreat
and a series of the policy shifts and compromises that typified reform
politics in the first two decades of the twentieth century. Studying the
ideas that developed in the late nineteenth and early twentieth century—instead of the local, state, and national election campaigns,
party platforms and policies, social protests and movements, and political tensions that developed as reform ideas began to take hold—allows
us to study the Progressive movement through a much more coherent
body of literature.

Selection Criteria

This collection is consciously structured to stress those elements of Progressivism that display both its coherence and its long-range influence
on American political life and culture. Three interconnected criteria

---

6. Dorfman, *Economic Mind of American Civilization* (1949); Schneider, *History of American Philosophy* (1946); Gabriel, *Course of American Democratic
Thought* (1940). Studies that relate pragmatism to Progressive political economy (Livingston, *Pragmatism and Political Economy*, 1994) and to Protestantism and the social sciences (Feffer, *Chicago Pragmatists*, 1993) recapture
some of this same understanding, as does Ross, *Origins of American Social Science* (1990).

7. Although the term Gilded Age was made famous as the title of a novel co-
written by Mark Twain and Charles Dudley Warner in 1873, it came to characterize the robust and reckless economic expansion from the end of the Civil
War through the 1880s.

guide the selections. First, this collection is focused on Progressive social and political *thought*, especially in its first articulations, locations, and inspirations. These early Progressives spoke to the entire nation — the American people conceived as one body — expecting that, whatever the scope and locations of individual activity, national ends would be paramount. The criterion of relatively durable sets of ideas is best evidenced in indices of their duration — and even the institutionalization — of influence. Many of the selections collected here are taken from books that remained in print for two decades or more, from articles in academic journals, and from the widely read periodicals that transformed American political and social thought in the decades that followed. These writings informed the thinking of generations of university and college faculty and students and came to represent a growing reform community that included journalists, social workers, members of the clergy, and leaders of national business, labor, reform, and professional associations. This same focus will emphasize the kinds of deep-seated forms of political, economic, and moral thinking the Progressives sought to displace.

Almost all of the selections collected here are simultaneously "academic" and "popular": the same ideas and arguments appeared in textbooks, popular magazines, church and reform society publications, and even government reports. Because the academic disciplines had not yet become clearly defined and somewhat isolated from each other, contributors to specialized academic journals often worked in other academic fields; contributors also regularly included members of the larger reform community working outside of academia — for example, labor leaders, settlement house workers, clergy members, and social and moral reform leaders. It's worth noting that a handful of universities produced more than their fair share of Progressive ideas: Johns Hopkins, Cornell, Michigan, Wisconsin, and Chicago achieved the earliest prominence, closely followed by Harvard, Yale, and Columbia. This prominence was at once intellectual and institutional.

The second criterion is to focus on Progressive *institution building*. I selected Progressive writings that stress the powerful potential in public opinion and nonpartisan journalism, in the universities and the emerging professions of social work, education, and business and public administration, and even in new models of school, church, and family life. These writings demonstrate the Progressives' belief in the reformist potential inherent in these new forms of institutional power. Conversely, I include Progressive warnings about the antireformist practices of "politics as usual," those long-standing political traditions that often resulted in illicit collusions of business and party organizations

and legislatures and even extended into courts and the legal profession. At the root of these antireformist institutions and practices were
corrupting forms of competitive individualism encouraged by weak
government and by markets designed to support earlier forms of isolated communities and small-producer capitalism. Prevailing constitutional interpretation was implicated in all of these institutions and
practices because such antireformist interpretations privileged local
and individual rights over collective purpose and action.

A third criterion for selection lies in the way Progressive political
thought can be understood—and how the Progressives themselves
understood it—within the reigning *party-political context*. The Progressive writers included here were, almost without exception, from the
northeast and midwest, of Puritan ancestry, and educated in Protestant
colleges and universities in both America and Germany; their immediate forebears were staunch Republicans and abolitionists. Drawing on
current scholarship on realigning elections of Presidents whose authority consists in their repudiation of the previous party-electoral regime,[8] I
situate many of the writings in this collection in terms of their location
in this electoral periodicity. Special attention, therefore, is paid to the
place and role of Theodore Roosevelt, both as Vice President and President in a realigning electoral moment (1900–1908) and as the Progressive Party presidential candidate in 1912. Roosevelt served for almost two
decades as a "magnet" who attracted Progressive reformers of almost
every stripe from locations as diverse as Wall Street, labor, and Christian
socialism.

Organization

In addition to the three selection criteria, which help us to appreciate
the depth and reach of Progressive social and political thought, this collection has a structure that provides context. Preceding each selection
is a biographical sketch of its author; such biographical information
reveals the range of activities and experiences that motivated the leaders of Progressive reform. Moreover, these biographies show the scale
and intensity of the relationships within this reform community. The
Progressives reviewed each others' books. They helped each other
establish professional and reform associations and succeeded each
other in leadership positions at these institutions. Some of the authors
represented here were teachers, some were pupils; many leading

---

8. Burnham, *Critical Elections* (1970); Skowronek, *Building a New American State* (1982).

Progressives mentored those who sought to join and contribute to the common cause. These institutional and personal connections help explain the energy and focus that marked Progressive reform, giving it a reach and durability that extended far beyond the vicissitudes of electoral and party politics and the changing interest group alliances that caused them. As their institutional innovations and personal ties spread across and penetrated the larger culture—especially through education, religion, the professions, journalism, and philanthropy—Progressivism became much more than a political reform movement. It became a new political culture—a new way of seeing America and, therefore, of seeing ourselves as Americans.

Chapter 1 of this collection—a selection of materials related to the Whig and national Republican background, to Progressivism, and to the signal importance of Lincoln—serves as a preface to Progressive ideas. Chapters 2, 3, and 4 address the ways in which the Progressives sought to reconstitute American national identity. The writings in these chapters assert that America's political institutions were not prepared for the momentous challenges that confronted the country at the end of the nineteenth century. The selections in Chapter 2 show how these new challenges required Americans to consolidate their political, social, and moral ideals around distinctly national principles and purposes.

The selections in Chapter 3 support this argument by discussing the ways in which American material prosperity and international power were linked by a new industrial economy that integrated labor and capital, science and management, and private and public purposes. This political economy required the creation of new values and new institutions to harness it to the service of national democracy. The writings in Chapter 4 extend the political-economy argument into a general theory of modern society. Just as the new industrial economy integrated economic producers and consumers on a nationwide basis, so it created networks of social and psychological interdependence that had to be legitimated and directed. Interdependence required an ethic of interconnectedness and cooperation as the basis for a new and self-conscious public. Programs of civic and moral education had to be formulated in order to create a public willing to serve democratic ends.

The Progressives saw many barriers to the achievement of their vision of America. Chief among these obstacles was a constitutional system mandating state and local jurisdictions radically at odds with the spatial organization of the economy and culture. This asymmetry of political

authority and economic power was worsened by the prevailing understanding of the contractual and property rights guaranteed by the Constitution; the current thinking on such rights had its origins in the
previous generations' economic system based on small-producer capitalism with local and isolated markets. The judiciary provided powerful
institutional support for such narrow constitutional interpretations, and
the larger legal profession sustained this thinking. In Chapter 5, selections from the writings of academically trained social and political economists present the Progressives' early critique of the prevailing
relationship between law and economics; the effects of this critique are
then discussed in writings by legal reformers, both inside and outside
the legal profession.

The most notable change wrought by the new financial and industrial economy was the creation of a permanent class of wage-earning
workers. This new industrial working class was the energy source
powering the industrial dynamo; without this class's willing cooperation and consent, the industrial economy would have been a force
working against the achievement of a democratic society. While
hourly or daily wage-workers had always existed in the American
economy, this condition was seen as a temporary way station on the
road to becoming one's own boss as a farmer, small proprietor, or artisan. The writings in Chapter 6 examine the Progressives' understanding of the labor question and the political, legal, and moral changes
this new situation required. Immigration and assimilation informed
the Progressives' consideration of the labor question: their call for
social justice was also a call for the assimilation of the immigrant
working class into both American democratic culture and American
material prosperity.

Most of the early Progressive academics and intellectuals were brought
up in an intense and demanding evangelical Protestant religious culture.
As the biographical sketches of the contributors will attest, many of these
early Progressive thinkers felt a religious calling to redeem American
democracy. They chose to use their energies and talents not within the
church denominations of their upbringing, however, but in the more
ecumenical settings of universities and colleges, reform journalism, and
reform organizations. But the difference between these two worlds should
not be overstated: large numbers of clergy members and nonclerical Progressives contributed equally in shaping a liberal-evangelical Protestant
theology in support of social reform. Thus, it was often difficult to distinguish a Progressive theological textbook from a sociological one, or a
reforming minister from a reforming professor. In both cases, "social

Christianity"—later termed the "Social Gospel"—was an integral part of Progressive social and political thought. Biographically, institutionally, and philosophically, the fortunes of Progressivism and the fortunes of liberal-evangelical Protestantism were linked. The selections in Chapter 7 come from the writings of some of the most prominent of these "social Christians."

Thanks to the proliferation of studies in women's history, we can now appreciate more than ever before the critical role that women played in Progressive social and political thought; they contributed to both the theory and practice of the movement. Indeed, most Progressives quite consciously argued that their aspirations for a new America necessarily incorporated values typically ascribed to women, and that the demands of the new economy and society required outlooks and virtues they felt women possessed in greater abundance than men. Not only were women streaming into colleges and universities during this period (especially in the midwest), they were carving out new public roles and professions for themselves, especially in the settlement house movement and the emerging profession of social work. Equally important were their calls for the reconfiguration of marriage and the family in light of new economic opportunities and new moral imperatives. The selections in Chapter 8 highlight writings that address all of these dimensions.

It will be evident, by this stage of the collection, that Progressive political and social thinkers were "historicist" in their approach to psychological, social, economic, and political knowledge. The Progressives held that such knowledge must be grounded in historical time marked by major shifts or "moments" in historical direction. But their historicism took many forms. Chief among these was a Hegelian view that humankind was lifted ever closer to the achievement of universal ideals through the victories and defeats among peoples and states that defined each historical period. This Hegelian perspective, learned in German universities, often incorporated religious and millennial values native to American Protestantism: the progress of social knowledge charted God's Progressive revelation to humankind and signaled the coming of a kingdom of brotherhood and justice. Another form of historicism had its origins in English and Scottish political economy. Although these scientific theories of social evolution preceded Darwin's theories of biological evolution, they too rested on notions of competitive struggle leading to higher forms of life. With the addition of Darwin's concept of "survival of the fittest," unremitting suffering and loss became the necessary price to pay for progress. American Progressives, however, rejected this "social Darwinist" reading. By assuming the heritability of acquired social and moral learning, they held that struggle would be increasingly replaced by cooperation as interdependence replaced competitive individualism in the provision of material needs. This new interdependence would lead people to replace their narrowly self-interested moral standards with nobler, more altruistic ones. Needless to say, the increasing role of women in the larger society was seen as a mark of this progress.

The presidential election of 1912 pitted three Progressive reform candidates against each other: William Howard Taft (the Republican incumbent), Woodrow Wilson (the Democratic challenger), and ex-president Theodore Roosevelt (who ran on a third-party Progressive ticket). The selections in Chapter 9 record the sense of confidence and triumph felt by three younger Progressive intellectuals in the period 1912–1915. It is remarkable that these celebratory books include no discussion of foreign policy or international relations. When the Great War finally broke out, and as America was increasingly drawn into the conflict, Progressives led the charge. Progressive nationalism was, from the start, a kind of internationalism as well, not only in its economic analysis, but also in the larger sense of seeing America as the vanguard nation leading the world in advancing social justice and political democracy. With the outbreak of hostilities in Europe, Progressive academics flocked to George Creel's wartime committee on public information, Progressive clergy members rallied their churches, and Progressive journalists and publicists flooded the media with the message of preparedness. The selections in Chapter 10 address the general ideals of Progressive internationalism as well as some specific calls to America to prepare for entry into the Great War.

Import

Whereas interest in the social and political thought of the Progressives has waxed and waned, two periods stand out as times of renewed interest. The republication of writings by Herbert Croly, Simon Patten, Walter Weyl, Benjamin De Witt, Florence Kelley, and Charlotte Perkins Gilman in the 1960s, for example, signaled attempts to relate the wave of "Great Society" reforms undertaken by President Lyndon Johnson to those of the Progressive Era. More recently, a spate of books by political theorists and public intellectuals has reasserted the relevance of the Progressive tradition for our

own times.[9] These commentators see the era beginning in the 1980s—
with that decade's economic restructurings and dislocations, its growing inequalities of wealth and income, and its explosive growth of
immigration—as a new "gilded age" calling for an intellectual and
political response modeled on that of the previous century's Progressive generation. Moreover, the collapse of the Soviet Empire and the
sudden emergence of America as the unchallenged world power
evoked the America of the nineteenth century, a nation just starting to
flex its economic, cultural, and military muscle on a global scale.

While these parallels are interesting and suggestive, it may be more
important to reflect on the Progressives' achievement in creating
"The American Century" in the first place. The "institutional matrix"
of business corporations, finance, research universities, and national
government was forged under the auspices of Progressive ideas, policies, and leadership. As new elements were added to this matrix—
foundations, organized labor, the military—the alliance of knowledge,
wealth, and power proved successful almost beyond reckoning.[10] This
alliance of national institutions created a new pluralistic political
order that not only overcame the previous governing order of "courts
and parties";[11] it mobilized and coordinated American talents and
energies on an unprecedented scale. The Great Depression and the
rebirth of the Democratic Party through the New Deal did not appre-
ciably change this dynamic; indeed, by assimilating new regions, eth-
nicities, interests, and values into this matrix, America grew even
stronger.

Whether the Progressives' achievement is to be praised for its
undoubted successes or damned for its exclusions, hierarchies, and
complacencies, we are required to fully understand its ideas and ideals
before we can fully understand our contemporary society and, perhaps,
even ourselves.

---

9. Dawley, *Struggles for Justice* (1991) and *Changing the World* (2003);
Dionne, *They Only Look Dead* (1996); Hansen, *Lost Promise of Patriotism*
(2003); Lind, *Next American Nation* (1995); McGerr, *A Fierce Discontent*
(2003); Rorty, *Achieving Our Country* (1998); and Tomasky, *Left for Dead*
(1996). There is already a book by Isaac, *Poverty of Progressivism* (2003), that critiques some of this literature. Johnston, "Re-Democratizing the Progressive
Era" (2002) is the most complete overview of historiography in the contemporary period.

10. Zunz, *Why the American Century?* (1998); and see Zunz, *Making America
Corporate* (1990).

11. Skowronek, *Building a New American State* (1982).

Bibliography and Further Reading

Buenker, John D., John C. Burnham, and Robert M. Crunden, *Progressivism* (Schenkman, 1977).

Burnham, Walter Dean, *Critical Elections and the Mainsprings of American Politics* (Norton, 1970).

Crunden, Robert M., *Ministers of Reform: The Progressives' Achievement in American Civilization 1889–1920* (University of Illinois Press, 1984).

Dawley, Alan, *Changing the World: American Progressives in War and Revolution* (Princeton University Press, 2003).

———. *Struggles for Justice: Social Responsibility and the Liberal State* (Harvard University Press, 1991).

Dionne, E. J., *They Only Look Dead: Why Progressives Will Dominate the Next Political Era* (Simon and Schuster, 1996).

Dorfman, Joseph, *The Economic Mind of American Civilization, Volume Three, 1865–1918* (Viking, 1949).

Eisenach, Eldon J., *The Lost Promise of Progressivism* (University Press of Kansas, 1994).

Feffer, Andrew, *The Chicago Pragmatists and American Progressivism* (Cornell University Press, 1993).

Filene, Peter, "An Obituary for the 'Progressive Movement,'" *American Quarterly* 22 (1970): 20–34.

Gabriel, Ralph Henry, The *Course of American Democratic Thought* (Roland Press, 1956/1940).

Gilmore, Glenda Elizabeth, ed., *Who Were the Progressives?* (St. Martin's, 2002).

Hansen, Jonathan, *The Lost Promise of Patriotism: Debating American Identity, 1890–1920* (University of Chicago Press, 2003).

Hofstadter, Richard, *The Age of Reform: From Bryan to FDR* (Knopf, 1955).

Isaac, Jeffrey C., *The Poverty of Progressivism: The Future of American Democracy in a Time of Decline* (Rowman & Littlefield, 2003).

Johnston, Robert D., "Re-Democratizing the Progressive Era: The Politics of Progressive Era Political Historiography," *Journal of the Gilded Age and Progressive Era*, vol. 1, issue 1 (2002).

Kloppenberg, James, *Uncertain Victory: Social Democracy and Progressivism* (Oxford University Press, 1986).

Lasch, Christopher, *The New Radicalism in America, 1889–1963: The Intellectual as a Social Type* (Knopf, 1965).

Lind, Michael, *The Next American Nation: The New Nationalism and the Fourth American Revolution* (Free Press, 1995).

Link, Arthur S., "What Happened to the Progressive Movement in the 1920s?" *American Historical Review*, vol. 64 (1959): 833–51.

Livingston, James, *Pragmatism and the Political Economy of Cultural Revolution, 1850–1940* (University of North Carolina Press, 1994).

McCormick, Richard, *Party Period and Public Policy: American Politics from the Age of Jackson to the Progressive Era* (Oxford University Press, 1986).

McGerr, Michael, A *Fierce Discontent: The Rise and Fall of the Progressive Movement in America, 1870–1920* (Free Press, 2003).

Mott, Luther, *A History of American Magazines, Volume 4* (Harvard University Press, 1957).

Rodgers, Daniel T., *Atlantic Crossings: Social Politics in a Progressive Age* (Harvard University Press, 1998).

———. "In Search of Progressivism," *Reviews in American History* 10 (December 1982): 113–32.

Rorty, Richard, *Achieving Our Country: Leftist Thought in Twentieth-Century America* (Harvard University Press, 1998).

Ross, Dorothy, *Origins of American Social Science* (Cambridge University Press, 1990).

Schneider, Herbert W., *A History of American Philosophy* (Columbia University Press, 1946).

Skowronek, Stephen, *Building a New American State: The Expansion of National Administrative Capacities, 1877–1920* (Cambridge University Press, 1982).

Stettner, Edward A., *Shaping Modern Liberalism: Herbert Croly and Progressive Thought* (University Press of Kansas, 1993).

Thomas, John, *Alternative America: Henry George, Edward Bellamy, Henry Demarest Lloyd, and the Adversary Tradition* (Harvard University Press, 1983).

Tomasky, Michael, *Left for Dead: The Life, Death, and Possible Resurrection of Progressive Politics in America* (Free Press, 1996).

Wiebe, Robert, *The Search for Order, 1877–1920* (Hill and Wang, 1967).

Zunz, Olivier, *Why the American Century?* (University of Chicago Press, 1998).

———. *Making America Corporate, 1870–1920* (University of Chicago Press, 1990).

1

A Preface to Progressivism

Herbert Croly was Progressivism's foremost spokesman. His seminal book, *The Promise of American Life* (1909), was simultaneously a summary of the fruits of twenty years of Progressive scholarship in political science, political economy, and sociology, and an original synthesis of that scholarship into a new and compelling story of American national development and destiny. Central to that story was Abraham Lincoln. Unlike all of his political peers, says Croly, Lincoln saw that prevailing political practices and constitutional understandings could not adequately resolve the problem of slavery. And because slavery was, at the time, the single barrier standing in the path of America's democratic destiny—a behavioral and ethical barrier that spawned many more such barriers—only a reconstituted America could fulfill its promise. Croly argued that new barriers to America's promise had since arisen, barriers that could be overcome only by the kind of political intelligence and moral courage Lincoln displayed.

To Croly's audience, Lincoln was something of a sacred symbol. Croly's readers were the children of Unionism and national Republicanism, with all of the regional, cultural, and religious resonances carried by that genealogy. This political culture had its origins in northern anti-Jacksonian Whiggery; it perceived slavery and states rights as barriers to American national purpose. An election manifesto of the Whig Party said it best:

> We wish, fully and entirely, TO NATIONALIZE THE INSTITUTIONS OF OUR LAND AND TO IDENTIFY OURSELVES WITH OUR COUNTRY; to become a single great people, separate and distinct in national character, political interest, social and civil affinities from any and all other nations, kindred and people on the earth. (*American Republican*, November 7, 1844)

The nationalism of the Whig, and then of the Republican, Party paralleled other nationalist features of their core constituencies. First among these constituencies were the liberal evangelical churches and their colleges and universities. Through their churches, intellectual journals, popular magazines, institutions of higher education, and many ecumenical reform organizations, these Republicans saw themselves as uniquely responsible for the shaping of America's future. By the late nineteenth century, Lincoln had become a talisman and inspiration for this growing reform constituency, and a series of articles and books venerating Lincoln spurred the reformers to action. Chief among these

1

books was *The Life of Abraham Lincoln* (1900) by Ida Tarbell, a notable "muckraking" journalist.

1. *Progressive Democracy*, David Francis Bacon (1813–1866)

If one were to search pre-Civil War America for a "proto-Progressive," it would be difficult to find a better example than Bacon. He was born in New Haven, Connecticut, home of Yale College, the center of liberal evangelical theology that produced the founding presidents of three major research universities (Cornell, Johns Hopkins, and Chicago). Bacon wrote books and pamphlets on the slave trade, Christ's apostles, missionary enterprises, and "eminently pious women of Britain and America." In addition to the election pamphlet excerpted here, he also wrote a political pamphlet exposing election fraud and municipal corruption in New York City.

— 1844 —

It is most evident that, in this age of revolutions, while the mass of human mind is in motion, not only throughout Christendom, but throughout vast portions of the Mahommedan and heathen world,—the mental, moral and physical power of America is not, is not to be, and cannot be, STATIONARY. A movement in some direction is a necessity involved not only in its sympathies with mankind, but in the very existence of liberty—liberty of motion, with perfect, free choice of direction, whether forward or backward, upward or downward. Into the boundless ever-heaving ocean of the world of mind, the American Republic has hitherto poured an Amazonian Stream, like a torrent and like a flood, changing the currents of the mighty deep, rolling back its tides, coloring its waves, setting them in a new swell upon the shores of other continents. Until the sources are dried, that movement can never cease.

DEMOCRACY, "the people's power," can never be inactive; for it is only by the continual exercise of their strength that the people are assured of its continued possession. The attempt to resist or check that spontaneous use of power, to lull the people into quietude and indifference, is futile—is antidemocratic. ACTION is an inevitable condition of liberty; and judgment and philosophy can do no more than decide whether that activity shall degenerate into wild and fitful restlessness, or shall be harmonized, directed and concentrated into healthful, beneficial MOVEMENT. The course of liberty is not only onward but upward. The way to national happiness, power and glory, is a long and steep ascent, on which a pause is but the beginning of a swift downward movement. Progress is labor; repose or effective resistance to progress is revolution and destruction. The history of all governments is summed in this fact.

The true democratic party therefore is the party of *progress*—laborious, uniform progress *upward*. The governmental measures necessary to the useful exercise of the people's power, to the development of their capacities of happiness, and to their improvement and elevation in the scale of being, always naturally encounter a two-fold opposition. They are opposed, *first*, by those who wish the present to be the future, who are satisfied with the good now in possession, who feel no need of the influences which cherish the infancy of enterprise, which protect laborious poverty from the malign agencies of associated wealth, and which raise the mass, or the active portions of the mass, to the large possession of the blessings of life, to the acquisition of knowledge, respectability, property, and all the means of happiness and power. These are the true CONSERVATIVES, properly so called. . . . The party of progress are opposed, *secondly*, by those who, despairing of their own improvement and benefit by the action of a beneficent system of government—incapable by ignorance, indolence or vice, of appreciating and enjoying the advantages which such a system offers to intelligent and honest enterprise and envious of the success of those who profit thus by gifts free to all as the air which they breathe—devote the energies which they should have employed for their own good, to the injury of others. . . .

Those who "hold this truth to be self-evident—that they were endowed by their Creator with an inalienable right to the pursuit of happiness, and that FOR THIS PURPOSE GOVERNMENTS WERE INSTITUTED, deriving their just powers from the consent of the governed," and deriving their security from the happiness of the governed —these, being of the people, first desire that the people's power be exercised in government for the people's good. To this end, their political action is instinctively, uniformly directed. They aid and share the upward movement of the age. They demand and enforce the beneficent, protective influences of government, by which alone they can rise, and raise their co-evals with them.

In a *Republic*, (and to some extent under any government,) the PARTY OF PROGRESS is the true Democracy, whose antagonists are the PARTY OF REPOSE, the men of possession, who desire to limit possession to themselves, who would be an aristocracy in exclusive enjoyment of honor, wealth, knowledge and political power; in which undertaking, being naturally few and sluggish, they necessarily depend upon the massive strength and malignant ferocity of the third party—THE PARTY OF RETROGRESSION, the ignorant and obstinate and the vicious, who can enjoy their power of numbers only by exercising it to the injury of those that seek to improve and reform themselves and the community.

While the party of progress and reform, and intelligent laborious enterprise, strive to direct the movements of the political and social system in "the ways of wisdom and pleasantness," in "the paths of peace," they are beset behind and before by these two opposite hostile agencies—those who are UP striving to *push* them down as they mount with toilsome energy—and those who are DOWN—too lazy, stupid or vicious to rise—struggling to *pull* them down before they can ascend above the reach of their envious malignity.

Such is the testimony of philosophy and history, of nations living and dead, of instinctive human sense of good—as to the purposes of our political organization as a republican people. This is the mystic circle of the social and political system, THE COMMONWEALTH, in which wherever we begin, we return to the same end—the personal objects of the individual, meeting and combining with the good of all and the glory of the democratic whole, and the glory of democracy consisting and resulting in the good of each—patriotism and liberty boasting and rejoicing in the happiness of each citizen, while even the selfish pursuit of gain is ennobled and hallowed by the prosperity which it attests, partakes and diffuses, to the honor of the republican system, its source and PROTECTION.

And in the higher view which looks beyond the bounds of our own range of action, this magnificent circle still widens with the swell of time into the cycle of ages, the series of movements which make the PROGRESS of the world and mankind in the development of the gifts designed for the good of all, of the least as well as the greatest. [David Francis Bacon, *Progressive Democracy, A discourse on the history, philosophy and tendency of American Politics* (New York: Central Clay Committee, 1844), 11–3]

2. *On Lincoln*, Herbert Croly (1869–1930)[1]

Croly's The Promise of American Life *(1909) was Progressivism's most notable and influential book. Croly was something of an anomaly among Progressives in that he did not trace his ancestry to New England. His religious background was unique: his father was a leading American disciple of August Comte (1798–1857), the French*

---

1. More biographical information on Croly prefaces his selections in Chapters 2, 5, and 6.

sociologist, and a follower of Comte's "Religion of Humanity."
Educated intermittently at Harvard University, Croly pursued careers in
architectural, and then reform, journalism. He was close friends with
Theodore Roosevelt and founded The New Republic — *a journal that*
immediately became the chief organ of Progressive, and then liberal,
politics and opinion — with Walter Lippmann in 1914.

— 1909 —

Both the Whig and the Democratic parties betrayed the insufficiency of
their ideas by their behavior towards the problem of slavery. Hitherto I
have refrained from comment on the effect which the institution of
slavery was coming to have upon American politics because the increasing importance of slavery, and of the resulting anti-slavery agitation,
demand for the purpose of this book special consideration. Such a consideration must now be undertaken. The bitter personal and partisan
controversies of the Whigs and the Democrats were terminated by the
appearance of a radical and a perilous issue; and in the settlement of
this question the principles of both of these parties, in the manner in
which they had been applied, were of no vital assistance.

The issue was created by the legal existence in the United States of
an essentially undemocratic institution. The United States was a
democracy, and however much or little this phrase means, it certainly
excludes any ownership of one man by another. Yet this was just what
the Constitution sanctioned. Its makers had been confronted by the
legal existence of slavery in nearly all of the constituent states; and a
refusal to recognize the institution would have resulted in the failure
of the whole scheme of Constitutional legislation. Consequently they
did not seek to forbid negro servitude; and inasmuch as it seemed at
that time to be on the road to extinction through the action of natural
causes, the makers of the Constitution had a good excuse for refusing
to sacrifice their whole project to the abolition of slavery, and in
throwing thereby upon the future the burden of dealing with it in
some more radical and consistent way. Later, however, it came to pass
that slavery, instead of being gradually extinguished by economic
causes, was fastened thereby more firmly than ever upon one section
of the country. The whole agricultural, political, and social life of the
South became dominated by the existence of negro slavery; and the
problem of reconciling the expansion of such an institution with the
logic of our national idea was bound to become critical. Our country
was committed by every consideration of national honor and moral

integrity to make its institutions thoroughly democratic, and it could not continue to permit the aggressive legal existence of human servitude without degenerating into a glaring example of political and moral hypocrisy. . . .

Mr. Theodore Roosevelt in his addresses to the veterans of the Civil War has been heard to assert that the crisis teaches us a much needed lesson as to the supreme value of moral energy. It would have been much pleasanter and cheaper to let the South secede, but the people of the North preferred to pay the cost of justifiable coercion in blood and treasure than to submit to the danger and humiliation of peaceable rebellion. Doubtless the foregoing is sometimes a wholesome lesson on which to insist, but it is by no means the only lesson suggested by the event. The Abolitionists had not shirked their duty as they understood it. They had given their property and their lives to the anti-slavery agitation. But they were as willing as the worst Copperheads to permit the secession of the South, because of the erroneous and limited character of their political ideas. While the crisis had undoubtedly been, in a large measure, brought about by moral lethargy, and it could only be properly faced by a great expenditure of moral energy, it had also been brought about quite as much by political unintelligence; and the salvation of the Union depended primarily and emphatically upon a better understanding on the part of Northern public opinion of the issues involved. Confused as was the counsel offered to them, and distracting as were their habits of political thought, the people of the North finally disentangled the essential question, and then supported loyally the man who, more than any other single political leader, had properly defined the issue.

That man was Abraham Lincoln. Lincoln's peculiar service to his countrymen before the war was that of seeing straighter and thinking harder than did his contemporaries. No doubt he must needs have courage, also, for in the beginning he acted against the advice of his Republican associates. But in 1858 there were plenty of men who had the courage, whereas there were very few who had Lincoln's disciplined intelligence and his just and penetrating insight. Lincoln's vision placed every aspect of the situation in its proper relations; and he was as fully competent to detect the logical weakness of his opponent's position as he was to explain his own lucidly, candidly, and persuasively. It so happened that the body of public opinion which he particularly addressed was that very part of the American democracy most likely to be deluded into allowing the Southern leaders to have their will, yet whose adhesion to the national cause was necessary to the preservation of the Union. It was into this mass of public opinion, after the announcement of his senatorial candidacy, that he hammered a new and a hard truth. He was the first responsible politician to draw the logical inference from the policy of the Republican party. The Constitution was inadequate to cure the ills it generated. By its authorization of slavery it established an institution whose legality did not prevent it from being anti-national. That institution must either be gradually reduced to insignificance, or else it must transform and take possession of the American national idea. The Union had become a house divided against itself; and this deep-lying division could not be bridged merely by loyal Constitutionalism or by an anti-national interpretation of democracy. The legal Union was being threatened precisely because American national integrity was being gutted by an undemocratic institution. The house must either fall or else cease to be divided. Thus for the first time it was clearly proclaimed by a responsible politician that American nationality was a living principle rather than a legal bond; and Lincoln's service to his country in making the Western Democracy understand that living Americans were responsible for their national integrity can scarcely be over-valued. The ground was cut from under the traditional point of view of the pioneer—which had been to feel patriotic and national, but to plan and to agitate only for the fulfillment of local and individual ends.

The virtue of Lincoln's attitude may seem to be as much a matter of character as of intelligence; and such, indeed, is undoubtedly the case. My point is, not that Lincoln's greatness was more a matter of intellect than of will, but that he rendered to his country a peculiar service, because his luminous and disciplined intelligence and his national outlook enabled him to give each aspect of a complicated and confused situation its proper relative emphasis. At a later date, when he had become President and was obliged to take decisive action in order to prevent the House from utterly collapsing, he showed an inflexibility of purpose no less remarkable than his previous intellectual insight. For as long as he had not made up his mind, he hesitated firmly and patiently; but when he had made up his mind, he was not to be confused or turned aside. Indeed, during the weeks of perplexity which preceded the bombardment of Fort Sumter, Lincoln sometimes seems to be the one wise and resolute man among a group of leaders who were either resolute and foolish or wise (after a fashion) and irresolute. The amount of bad advice which was offered to the American people at this moment is appalling, and is to be explained only by the bad moral and intellectual habits fastened upon our country during forty years of national turpitude. But Lincoln never for an instant allowed his course to be diverted.

If the Union was attacked, he was prepared actively to defend it. If it was let alone, he was prepared to do what little he could towards the denationalization of slavery. But he refused absolutely to throw away the fruits of Republican victory by renewing the policy of futile and unprincipled compromises. Back of all his opinions there was an ultimate stability of purpose which was the result both of sound mental discipline and of a firm will. His was a mind, unlike that of Clay, Seward, or even Webster, which had never been cheapened by its own exercise. During his mature years he rarely, if ever, proclaimed an idea which he had not mastered, and he never abandoned a truth which he had once thoroughly achieved. . . .

The average Western American of Lincoln's generation was fundamentally a man who subordinated his intelligence to certain dominant practical interests and purposes. He was far from being a stupid or slow-witted man. On the contrary, his wits had been sharpened by the traffic of American politics and business, and his mind was shrewd, flexible, and alert. But he was wholly incapable either of disinterested or of concentrated intellectual exertion. His energies were bent in the conquest of certain stubborn external forces, and he used his intelligence almost exclusively to this end. The struggles, the hardships, and the necessary self-denial of pioneer life constituted an admirable training of the will. It developed a body of men with great resolution of purpose and with great ingenuity and fertility in adapting their insufficient means to the realization of their important business affairs. But their almost exclusive preoccupation with practical tasks and their failure to grant their intelligence any room for independent exercise bent them into exceedingly warped and one-sided human beings. . . .

Some of my readers may protest that I have over-emphasized the difference between Lincoln and his contemporary fellow countrymen. In order to exalt the leader have I not too much disparaged the followers? Well, a comparison of this kind always involves the risk of unfairness; but if there is much truth in the foregoing estimate of Lincoln, the lessons of the comparison are worth its inevitable risks. The ordinary interpretation of Lincoln as a consummate democrat and a "Man of the People" has implied that he was, like Jackson, simply a bigger and a better version of the plain American citizen; and it is just this interpretation which I have sought to deny and to expose. . . . Yet [Lincoln's] very qualities of high intelligence, humanity, magnanimity and humility are precisely the qualities which Americans, in order to become better democrats, should add to their strength, their homogeneity, and their innocence; while at the same time they are just the qualities which Americans are prevented by their individualistic practice and tradition from attaining or properly valuing. Their deepest convictions make the average unintelligent man the representative democrat, and the aggressive successful individual, the admirable national type; and in conformity with these convictions their uppermost ideas in respect to Lincoln are that he was a "Man of the People" and an example of strong will. He was both of these things, but his great distinction is that he was also something vastly more and better. He cannot be fully understood and properly valued as a national hero without an implicit criticism of these traditional convictions. Such a criticism he himself did not and could not make. In case he had made it, he could never have achieved his great political task and his great personal triumph. But other times bring other needs. It is as desirable today that the criticism should be made explicit as it was that Lincoln himself in his day should preserve the innocence and integrity of a unique unconscious example. [Herbert Croly, *The Promise of American Life* (Macmillan, 1909), 72–3, 86–91, 98–9]

3. *Lincoln*, John S. Phillips

The poem below prefaced In the Footsteps of the Lincolns *(1908), one of Ida Minerva Tarbell's (1857–1944) many books on Lincoln. The first woman to graduate from Allegheny College in Pennsylvania, Tarbell went on to become one of America's most successful reform journalists. Many of her serial articles for the new mass-circulation magazines were collected into notable books. Although she is perhaps best known today for her exposé of the misdeeds of Rockefeller's Standard Oil trust, she was equally known in her own time for her many books on Abraham Lincoln and his circle, new societal roles for women, and progressive business corporations and their leaders. As indicated by its prefatory poem, Tarbell's* In the Footsteps of the Lincolns *is a history of the Lincoln family in America. The book begins in Massachusetts in 1637 and ends with Abraham Lincoln's election to the presidency in 1860. Tarbell writes the Lincoln family history as a sacred story of American hardship, struggle, and triumph.*

— 1908 —

In him distilled and potent the choice essence of a race!
Far back the Puritans—stern and manful visionaries,
Repressed poets, flushed with dreams of glowing theologies!
Each new succession, out of border hardship,

Refined to human use the initial rigor of the breed,
Passing to the next the unconscious possession of a perfecting
*   soul!*
Each forest clearing gave something of neighborly grace,
The rude play of cabin-bred natural people something of
*   humor,*
Each mountain home something of inner daring,
Each long-wandering life something of patience and of hope!
In the open, far-seen nature gradually chiseled
The deepening wistful eyes.
Each ax man and each plowman added
Another filament of ruggedness;
Unknowing minds dumbly cried for liberty;
Mute hearts strove against injustice. . . .

At last was ready the alembic, where Nature stored and set
*   apart*
Each generation's finest residue,
Waiting for the hour of Perfect mixture
And then the Miracle!

[John S. Phillips, in Ida Tarbell, *In the Footsteps of the Lincolns* (Harper & Brothers, 1908), xiv]

4. *On the Civil War,* Vida Dutton Scudder (1866–1954)[2]

Born in India to Congregational missionaries, Vida Dutton Scudder graduated from Smith College and attended Oxford University. Before serving as a professor of literature at Wellesley College (1892–1928), she helped establish Denison House, a Boston branch of the College Settlements Association. Always active in reform politics, she was a founding member and lecturer for the Society of Christian Socialists (1889), an organization founded by W.D.P. Bliss, another child of Congregational missionaries. She was also active in promoting labor rights and co-founded the Women's Trade Union League in 1903. Her textbook, Social Ideals in English Letters, *from which this selection is taken, was published continuously from 1898 to 1923.*

---

2. More biographical information on Scudder prefaces her selection in Chapter 8.

— 1898—

The American idea of freedom was not stationary. Nobly dramatic phases marked its evolution. New England had been colonized by men who counted civilization well lost for spiritual liberty; and the tradition of their severe unworldliness remained long, as it should remain today, a vital inspiration. The revolutionary struggle had formed the image of the Nation, and added to the religious conception of freedom a political idea definite and highly intellectualized. The religious and the political idea had alike carried with them a corollary clearly assumed though not stated. If the founders of the nation did not grasp in its entirety the modern thought of social democracy—as indeed no man at their time could grasp it—they at least expected that America should have no privileged class with a monopoly of luxuries, and that fair opportunity to enter the struggle of life on equal terms should be open to all citizens. A plutocracy was assuredly the last result of their hopes contemplated either by our Puritan forefathers, or by the great statesmen of the Revolution.

To all the splendid conditions of our early years—a fine tradition of unworldliness, a simple social life free from material preoccupations, personal types singularly pure and high—came the last and chief aid to idealism, a noble cause to fight for. The anti-slavery conflict, in that long history of which the Civil War is the climax, was the third great episode in the national struggle for freedom. It confronted men with a clear-cut issue. A dark subject race, avowedly deprived of even the simulacrum of liberty, stood visibly mocking in its bondage the ideal of the founders of the nation. To destroy slavery, and at the same time to assert and finally establish that national unity which had been somewhat hastily assumed, was the obvious task of the America of 1860. With such a cause to summon, with almost complete blindness to the complexity of the growing national life, with faith undimmed by disillusion and upheld by purest religious fervor, fortunate indeed were the men of the North in that generation. They saw

Truth forever on the scaffold, Wrong forever on the throne.[3]

No perception of a less simple antithesis bewildered them; and, confident that "that scaffold ruled the Future," they marched bravely up its steps with a song upon their lips. For Truth demanded martyrs: real soldier-martyrs, inspired by simple, obvious, glorious heroism, by that

---

3. From the American poet and abolitionist James Russell Lowell (1819–1891).

readiness to lay down the life of the body which forever makes the blood leap and renews the youth of the spirit of man. During the slow gathering and great outburst of the anti-slavery struggle, one feels pulsing through all the written words of our idealists the exultant sense of hope and power, the conviction that mighty, and terrible though the task may be, intrusted by Freedom to America, the young nation shall prove itself worthy even unto death. Nor was their faith disappointed. It was the "plain people" of President Lincoln who fought the Civil War.

This ringing note of American optimism was slow to die from our literature. It echoes many years later in Lowell's fine essay on "Democracy," and its high conviction, its beautiful confidence in Freedom, its assurance of victory, sound courage to our more uncertain age. Well may we be thankful for that early struggle against obvious slavery: we, children of a new world already old, immersed in questions agonizing from their confusion, facing the most intricate problems of race and class, with no means to solve them except an idea pitilessly and sublimely simple.

For the social situation developed as the anti-slavery conflict receded. Peace was not yet to be the inheritance of a land protagonist among the nations in the frank assertion of a new ideal. To achieve Democracy was no light task that a hundred years and two great wars could finish. New difficulties unfolded: the struggle for freedom was seen to involve wider and more complex issues than our first Americans had dreamed. . . .

That she will bear it, that she may lead it if she will, who, loving her, can doubt? If the work awaiting us is greater than the work achieved, we have great strength with which to meet it. If our conditions are in some respects even more complex than those of Europe, we have an immense advantage over her in the different foundations on which our national life is laid; in our assumption of social equality, and in the absence among us of solidified class feeling, such as removes all possibility of unconsciousness from social advance in the Old World. Ours not to create a tradition of freedom; ours only to maintain and apply a tradition, the chief glory of our inheritance. The Spirit of the American people— an invisible Presence such as Cardinal Newman[4] loved to picture presiding over the destiny of nations—bends over us and beckons us on.

To realize a spiritual democracy for the victims and outcasts of the Old World is a task before which we may indeed quail, unless we

---

4. John Henry Newman (1801–1890), a leader of the high church party of the Church of England who converted to Catholicism, and author of *The Idea of the University* (1852).

believe it to be God-given. But, turning back to the lives of our fathers, surely we see in the warfare against the slavery of the negro a prophecy of our larger conflict against evil less evident, but more deeply imbedded in the social body. The Civil War lies behind us as a great symbol, and its limited and clear-cut struggle may well inspire our generation as we face the more confused and widespread forces of industrial bondage that hold our laboring classes in a spiritual deprivation as complete in some ways as that of the slave. Indeed, the same relation binds our present to all the episodes of our great history, even to that most recent episode which lies too close behind us for discussion. Noble and of vast import they have been; yet we begin to question whether they were not all alike the preludes to a vaster conflict for which the forces are slowly gathering: the conflict against industrial slavery, the class-war that threatens the civilized world. We need all the courage the past can give us; we need all the consecration it can inspire. Well is it for us if the idealism of our first poets of freedom can still tingle on our lips, and the assurance of their faith cheer us. Well also if those soldier-martyrs who visibly laid down their lives for freedom can beckon and nerve those modern martyrs of the spirit, whom no physical excitement helps to sustain through that long agony in which their hearts hold up to God the victims of the modern slavery of trade. If our earlier struggles have bequeathed to us purpose, strength, and hope for that impending test of our idealism, then the splendid cheer, the tenacity and simplicity of faith in our early American literature need not be lost. [Vida Dutton Scudder, *Social Ideals in English Letters* (Houghton Mifflin, 1898), 204–7, 210–1]

5. *The Influence of Lincoln,* Jane Addams (1860–1935)[5]

One of the most famous Progressive reformers in America, Jane Addams is best known for founding Hull House, one of America's first neighborhood settlements, in Chicago in 1889. The most influential of her many books and magazine articles on reform was Democracy and Social Ethics *(1902).* Twenty Years at Hull House *(1910), from which the selection below is taken, was her most popular book and remained in print for almost forty years. Jane Addams' father was active in Republican Party politics; he was an Illinois state senator and organized and led a military company in the Civil War. While a student at*

---

5. More biographical information on Addams prefaces her selections in Chapters 4 and 8.

*Rockford College in Illinois, Jane Addams toured Europe and visited
Toynbee Hall, an early settlement house in London run by volunteer
university men. Hull House became something of an academic
laboratory and showcase for urban reform. A list of the House's
volunteers (mostly college educated young women) and visitors reads like
a "who's who" of notable Progressive reform leaders. She was a founding
member of the American Sociological Society (1905) and seconded
Theodore Roosevelt's nomination as the Progressive Party's candidate for
President in 1912. Unlike most Progressive leaders, she opposed entry
into World War I and remained active in the peace movement following
the war. She received the Nobel Peace Prize in 1931.*

— 1910 —

My father always spoke of the martyred President as Mr. Lincoln, and I
never heard the great name without a thrill. I remember the day—it
must have been one of comparative leisure, perhaps a Sunday—when
at my request my father took out of his desk a thin packet marked "Mr.
Lincoln's Letters," the shortest one of which bore unmistakable traces
of that remarkable personality. These letters began, "My dear Double-
D'ed Addams," and to the inquiry as to how the person thus addressed
was about to vote on a certain measure then before the legislature, was
added the assurance that he knew that this Addams "would vote according to his conscience," but he begged to know in which direction the
same conscience "was pointing." As my father folded up the bits of
paper I fairly held my breath in my desire that he should go on with the
reminiscence of this wonderful man, whom he had known in his comparative obscurity, or better still, that he should be moved to tell some
of the exciting incidents of the Lincoln-Douglas debates. There were at
least two pictures of Lincoln that always hung in my father's room, and
one in our old-fashioned upstairs parlor, of Lincoln with little Tad. For
one or all of these reasons I always tend to associate Lincoln with the
tenderest thoughts of my father.

I recall a time of great perplexity in the summer of 1894, when
Chicago was filled with federal troops sent there by the President of
the United States, and their presence was resented by the governor of
the state, that I walked the wearisome way from Hull-House to Lincoln Park—for no [street]cars were running regularly at that moment
of sympathetic strikes—in order to look at and gain magnanimous
counsel, if I might, from the marvelous St. Gaudens statue which
had been but recently placed at the entrance of the park. Some of

Lincoln's immortal words were cut into the stone at his feet, and never did a distracted town more sorely need the healing of "with charity towards all" than did Chicago at that moment, and the tolerance of the man who had won charity for those on both sides of "an irrepressible conflict.". . .

Of the many old friends of my father who kindly came to look up his daughter in the first days of Hull-House, I recall none with more pleasure than Lyman Trumbull, whom we used to point out to the members of the Young Citizens' Club as the man who had for days held in his keeping the Proclamation of Emancipation until his friend President Lincoln was ready to issue it. I remember the talk he gave at Hull-House on one of our early celebrations of Lincoln's birthday, his assertion that Lincoln was no cheap popular hero, that the "common people" would have to make an effort if they would understand his greatness, as Lincoln painstakingly made a long effort to understand the greatness of the people. There was something in the admiration of Lincoln's contemporaries, or at least of those men who had known him personally, which was quite unlike even the best of the devotion and reverent understanding which has developed since. In the first place they had so large a fund of common experience; they too had pioneered in a western country, and had urged the development of canals and railroads in order that the raw prairie crops might be transported to market; they too had realized that if this last tremendous experiment in self-government failed here, it would be the disappointment of the centuries and that upon their ability to organize self-government in state, county and town depended the verdict of history. These men also knew, as Lincoln himself did, that if this tremendous experiment was to come to fruition, it must be brought about by the people themselves; that there was no other capital fund upon which to draw. . . .

It is perhaps fitting to record in this chapter that the very first Christmas we spent at Hull-House, in spite of exigent demands upon my slender purse for candy and shoes, I gave to a club of boys twenty-five copies of the then new Carl Schurz's "Appreciation of Abraham Lincoln."

In our early effort at Hull-House to hand on to our neighbors whatever of help we had found for ourselves, we made much of Lincoln. We were often distressed by the children of immigrant parents who were ashamed of the pit whence they were digged, who repudiated the language and customs of their elders, and counted themselves successful as they were able to ignore the past. Whenever I held up Lincoln for their admiration as the greatest American, I invariably pointed out his marvelous power to retain and utilize past experiences; that he never forgot how the plain people in Sangamon County thought and felt when he himself had moved to town; that this habit was the foundation for his marvelous capacity for growth; that during those distracting years in Washington it enabled him to make clear beyond denial to the American people themselves, the goal towards which they were moving. I was sometimes bold enough to add that proficiency in the art of recognition and comprehension did not come without effort, and that certainly its attainment was necessary for any successful career in our conglomerate America. . . .

Is it not Abraham Lincoln who has cleared the title to our democracy? He made plain, once for all, that democratic government, associated as it is with all the mistakes and shortcomings of the common people, still remains the most valuable contribution America has made to the moral life of the world. [Jane Addams, "The Influence of Lincoln," in *Twenty Years at Hull House* (Macmillan, 1926), 31–2, 34–7, 42]

Further Reading

Beecher, Lyman, *A Plea for the West* (Arno Press, 1977/1835).

Cohen, Nancy, *The Reconstruction of American Liberalism, 1865–1914* (University of North Carolina Press, 2002).

Elshtain, Jean, *Jane Addams and the Dream of American Democracy* (Basic Books, 2002).

Furner, Mary, "The Republican Tradition and the New Liberalism: Social Investigation, State Building, and Social Learning in the Gilded Age," in Michael J. Lacey and Mary O. Furner, eds., *The State and Social Investigation in Britain and the United States* (Cambridge University Press, 1993).

Gienapp, William E., *The Origins of the Republican Party, 1852–1856* (Oxford University Press, 1987).

Howe, Daniel Walker, *The Political Culture of the American Whigs* (University of Chicago Press, 1978).

Keller, Morton, *Affairs of State: Public Life in Late Nineteenth Century America* (Harvard University Press, 1977).

Kelley, Robert Lloyd, *The Cultural Pattern in American Politics: The First Century* (Knopf, 1979).

Kohl, Lawrence Frederick, *The Politics of Individualism: Parties and the American Character in the Jacksonian Era* (Oxford University Press, 1989).

Levy, David W., *Herbert Croly of "The New Republic"* (Princeton University Press, 1985).

McClay, Wilfred M., *The Masterless: Self and Society in Modern America* (University of North Carolina Press, 1994).

McPherson, James M., *The Abolitionist Legacy* (Princeton University Press, 1975).

Skocpol, Theda, *Protecting Soldiers and Mothers: The Political Origins of Social Policy in the United States* (Harvard University Press, 1992).

Sproat, John G., *The Best Men: Liberal Reformers in the Gilded Age* (Oxford University Press, 1968).

Stevenson, Louise, *Scholarly Means to Evangelical Ends: The New Haven Scholars and the Transformation of Higher Learning in America, 1830–1890* (Johns Hopkins University Press, 1986).

Strong, Josiah, *Our Country* (Harvard University Press, 1963/1885).

Thomas, John, *Alternative America: Henry George, Edward Bellamy, Henry Demarest Lloyd, and the Adversary Tradition* (Harvard University Press, 1983).

2

A Democratic People with
Common National Goals

An overriding feature of Progressive political and social thought was its ardent nationalism. By this I do not mean "patriotism" in a chauvinistic or militarist sense, but rather a commitment to thinking of America as a whole, as one people confronting common problems and sharing a common destiny. In contrast to prevailing constitutional and legal self-understandings, Progressive thinkers wanted their audiences to see the nation's interconnectedness: the connections between the many forms and layers of America's governments, the nation's regions and ethnic and religious cultures, its economic institutions, and even its families and individual citizens. Although theirs was a militant nationalism, it was militancy in service to a common good.

In the words of Theodore Roosevelt, the Progressives called for a "new nationalism" that would pull Americans away from abstract patriotism and narrow constitutional self-understanding by leading them to undertake, together, substantive national projects that would both ameliorate their differences and make possible the sharing of a common life. These calls were made in the face of an America that Progressives saw as increasingly divided by wealth and income, social class, specialization and division of labor, regional inequalities, and access to cultural and educational resources. Progressives felt that these differences and inequalities should not be flattened by homogenization but rather harmonized by a coordinated effort toward shared democratic goals. To be sure, Progressive nationalism had a strongly pluralistic component. But it was pluralism designed to assimilate rather than separate and divide.

The Progressives' nationalism is clearly reflected in two major areas of their thinking: in their ruminations on the meaning of America as a single nation-state (as opposed to a series of constitutionally defined local, state, and federal governments) and in their vision of specific political, social, and economic reforms that would create common bonds of democratic citizenship.

Pervading the following selections is a common historical consciousness, the idea that the nation-state is the bearer of historical progress — and that America was destined to be in the vanguard of that progress. The theories of social evolution then being promulgated in the social sciences supported this idea. The question, then, was not whether America was to be part of this evolutionary process, but rather how America could shape this process to serve its democratic and humanistic ends. Evolutionary processes both create and destroy; Progressives held that nations unable to adapt would cease to drive human history and destiny. These themes were at once Hegelian in philosophical spirit, Protestant millennialist in their religious expression, and Enlightened in their codification in the new social sciences.

6. *The American Democracy and Its National Principle,* Herbert Croly (1869–1930)[1]

Croly's proposal to unite "Hamiltonian" belief in strong and authoritative national institutions to "Jeffersonian" democratic ends — a kind of conflation of matter and spirit — is the defining idea of his Promise of American Life. *Although Lincoln was a short-lived exemplar of this alliance, Croly saw a dangerous conflict between Hamiltonian means and Jeffersonian ends developing in the postwar period and believed that the victory of either side on their original terms would lead to chaos. Most of his writings and reform energies were placed in service to this democratic-nationalist ideal, making it a leading feature of general Progressive thought. His increasing reliance on the new social sciences to buttress his arguments is especially evident in his book* Progressive Democracy *(1914).*

— 1909 —

The American democracy can trust its interest to the national interest, because American national cohesion is dependent, not only upon certain forms of historical association, but upon fidelity to a democratic principle. A nation is a very complex political, social, and economic product — so complex that political thinkers in emphasizing one aspect of it are apt to forget other and equally essential aspects. Its habits and traditions of historical association constitute an indispensable bond; but they do not constitute the only bond. A specific national character is more than a group of traditions and institutions. It tends to be a formative idea, which defines the situation of a country in reference to its

------

1. More biographical information on Croly prefaces his selections in Chapters 1, 5, and 6.

neighbors, and which is constantly seeking a better articulation and understanding among the various parts of its domestic life. . . .

Americans are tied together by certain political, social, and economic habits, institutions, and traditions. From the political point of view these forms of association are at once constitutional, Federal, and democratic. They are accustomed to some measure of political centralization, to a larger measure of local governmental responsibility, to a still larger measure of individual economic freedom. This group of political institutions and habits has been gradually pieced together under the influence of varying political ideas and conditions. It contains many contradictory ingredients, and not a few that are positively dangerous to the public health: Such as it is, however, the American people are attached to this national tradition; and no part of it could be suddenly or violently transformed or mutilated without wounding large and important classes among the American people, both in their interests and feelings. . . .

During the past generation, the increased efficiency of organization in business and politics, the enormous growth of an irresponsible individual money-power, the much more definite division of the American people into possibly antagonistic classes, and the pressing practical need for expert, responsible, and authoritative leadership,—these new conditions and demands have been by way of upsetting once more the traditional national balance and of driving new wedges into American national cohesion. New contradictions have been developed between various aspects of the American national composition; and if the American people wish to escape the necessity of regaining their health by means of another surgical operation, they must consider carefully how much of a reorganization of traditional institutions, policy, and ideas are necessary for the achievement of a new and more stable national balance. . . .

A balance is not to be struck merely by the process of compromise in the interest of harmony. Our forbears tried that method in dealing with the slavery problem from 1820 to 1850, and we all know with what results. American national cohesion is a matter of national integrity; and national integrity is a matter of loyalty to the requirements of a democratic ideal. For better or worse the American people have proclaimed themselves to be a democracy, and they have proclaimed that democracy means popular economic, social, and moral emancipation. The only way to regain their national balance is to remove those obstacles which the economic development of the country has placed in the path of a better democratic fulfillment. The economic and social changes of the past generation have brought out a serious and a glaring contradiction between the demands of a constructive democratic ideal and the machinery of methods and institutions, which have been considered sufficient for its realization. This is the fundamental discrepancy which must be at least partially eradicated before American national integrity can be triumphantly re-affirmed. The cohesion, which is a condition of effective nationality, is endangered by such a contradiction, and as long as it exists the different elements composing American society will be pulling apart rather than together. The national principle becomes a principle of reform and reconstruction, precisely because national consistency is constantly demanding the solution of contradictory economic and political tendencies, brought out by alterations in the conditions of economic and political efficiency. Its function is not only to preserve a balance among these diverse tendencies, but to make that balance more than ever expressive of a consistent and constructive democratic ideal. Any disloyalty to democracy on the part of American national policy would in the end prove fatal to American national unity.

The American democracy can, consequently, safely trust its genuine interests to the keeping of those who represent the national interest. It both can do so, and it must do so. Only by faith in an efficient national organization, and by an exclusive and aggressive devotion to the national welfare, can the American democratic ideal be made good. If the American local commonwealths had not been wrought by the Federalists into the form of a nation, they would never have continued to be democracies; and the people collectively have become more of a democracy in proportion as they have become more of a nation. Their democracy is to be realized by means of an intensification of their national life just as the ultimate moral purpose of an individual is to be realized by the affirmation and intensification of its own better individuality. Consequently the organization of the American democracy into a nation is not to be regarded in the way that so many Americans have regarded it, — as a necessary but hazardous surrender of certain rights and liberties in order that other rights might be preserved, — as a mere compromise between the democratic ideal and the necessary conditions of political cohesion and efficiency. Its nationalized political organization constitutes the proper structure and veritable life of the American democracy. No doubt the existing organization is far from being a wholly adequate expression of the demands of the democratic ideal, but it falls equally short of being an adequate expression of the demands of the national ideal. The less confidence the American people have in a national organization, the less they are willing to surrender themselves to the national spirit, the worse democrats they will be. The most stubborn impediments which block the American national advance issue from the imperfections in our democracy. The American people are not prepared for a higher form of democracy, because they are not prepared for a more coherent and intense national life. When they are prepared to be consistent, constructive, and aspiring democrats, their preparation will necessarily take the form of becoming consistent, constructive, and aspiring nationalists. . . .

The nationalizing of American political, economic, and social life means something more than Federal centralization and something very different therefrom. To nationalize a people has never meant merely to centralize their government. . . .

The process of centralization is not, like the process of nationalization, an essentially formative and enlightening political transformation. When a people are being nationalized, their political, economic, and social organization or policy is being coordinated with their actual needs and their moral and political ideals. Governmental centralization is to be regarded as one of the many means which may or may not be taken in order to effect this purpose. Like every other special aspect of the national organization, it must be justified by its fruits. There is no presumption in its favor. Neither is there any general presumption against it. Whether a given function should or should not be exercised by the central government in a Federal system is from the point of view of political logic a matter of expediency with the burden of proof resting on those who propose to alter any existing Constitutional arrangement.

It may be affirmed, consequently, without paradox, that among those branches of the American national organization which are greatly in need of nationalizing is the central government. Almost every member of the American political body has been at one time or another or in one way or another perverted to the service of special interests. The state governments and the municipal administrations have sinned more in this respect than the central government; but the central government itself has been a grave sinner. The Federal authorities are responsible for the prevailing policy in respect to military pensions,[2] which is one

---

2. The Civil War pension system, which began as a modest program to aid wounded or disabled Union soldiers and the widows of those who died in service, became a patronage-driven fiscal feeding frenzy during the Gilded Age. It absorbed more than one-third of the federal budget (the budget itself was a vehicle for patronage, swollen by tariff revenues). In the mid-1880s, 40 percent of all legislation in the House and 55 percent in the Senate concerned private bills to award pensions. Some 60,000 pension attorneys and claims agents and 4,000 examining surgeons battened off of the pension system's loosely monitored standards for eligibility.

of the most flagrant crimes ever perpetrated against the national interest. The Federal authorities, again, are responsible for the existing tariff schedules, which benefit a group of special interests at the expense of the national welfare. The Federal authorities, finally, are responsible for the Sherman Anti-Trust Law,[3] whose existence on the statute books is a fatal bar to the treatment of the problem of corporate aggrandizement from the standpoint of genuinely national policy. These instances might be multiplied, but they suffice to show that the ideal of a constructive relation between the American national and democratic principles does not imply that any particular piece of legislation or policy is national because it is Federal. The Federal no less than the state governments has been the victim of special interests; and when a group of state or city officials effectively assert the public interest against the private interests, either of the machine or of the local corporations, they are acting just as palpably, if not just as comprehensively, for the national welfare, as if their work benefited the whole American people. The process of nationalization in its application to American political organization means that political power shall be distributed among the central, state, and municipal officials in such a manner that it can be efficiently and responsibly exerted in the interest of those affected by its action.

Be it added, however, in the same breath, that under existing conditions and simply as a matter of expediency, the national advance of the American democracy does demand an increasing amount of centralized action and responsibility. . . .

To be sure, any increase in centralized power and responsibility, expedient or inexpedient, is injurious to certain aspects of traditional American democracy. But the fault in that case lies with the democratic tradition; and the erroneous and misleading tradition must yield before the march of a constructive national democracy. The national advance will always be impeded by these misleading and erroneous ideas, and, what is more, it always should be impeded by them, because at bottom ideas of this kind are merely an expression of the fact that the average American individual is morally and intellectually inadequate to a serious and consistent conception of his responsibilities as a democrat. An American national democracy must always

---

3. This Act was passed in 1890 by huge majorities in the Senate and House. Because it criminalized so many acts that large firms were, more or less, forced to commit in order to survive, the courts undercut many of its strictures.

prove its right to a further advance, not only by the development of a policy and method adequate for the particular occasion, but by its ability to overcome the inevitable opposition of selfish interests and erroneous ideas. The logic of its position makes it the aggressor, just as the logic of its opponents' position ties them to a negative and protesting or merely insubordinate part. If the latter should prevail their victory would become tantamount to national dissolution, either by putrefaction, by revolution, or by both.

The ideal of a constructive relation between American nationality and American democracy is in truth equivalent to a new Declaration of Independence. It affirms that the American people are free to organize their political, economic, and social life in the service of a comprehensive, a lofty, and far-reaching democratic purpose. At the present time there is a strong, almost a dominant, tendency to regard the existing Constitution with superstitious awe, and to shrink with horror from modifying it even in the smallest detail; and it is this superstitious fear of changing the most trivial parts of the fundamental legal fabric which brings to pass the great bondage of the American spirit. If such an abject worship of legal precedent for its own sake should continue, the American idea will have to be fitted to the rigid and narrow lines of a few legal formulas; and the ruler of the American spirit, like the ruler of the Jewish spirit of old, will become the lawyer. But it will not continue, in case Americans can be brought to understand and believe that the American national political organization should be constructively related to their democratic purpose. Such an ideal reveals at once the real opportunity and the real responsibility of the American democracy. It declares that the democracy has a machinery in a nationalized organization, and a practical guide in the national interest, which are adequate to the realization of the democratic ideal; and it declares also that in the long run just in so far as Americans timidly or superstitiously refuse to accept their national opportunity and responsibility, they will not deserve the names either of freemen or of loyal democrats. There comes a time in the history of every nation, when its independence of spirit vanishes, unless it emancipates itself in some measure from its traditional illusions; and that time is fast approaching for the American people. They must either seize the chance of a better future, or else become a nation which is satisfied in spirit merely to repeat indefinitely the monotonous measures of its own past. [Herbert Croly, *The Promise of American Life* (Macmillan, 1909), 267–71, 273–7, 278]

7. *The Bonds of Nationality,* Albion Small (1854–1926)[4]

Albion Small's father was a Congregational clergyman in Maine; his mother, Thankful Lincoln Small, was a descendent of Samuel Lincoln, Abraham Lincoln's earliest American ancestor. After receiving degrees from Colby College and Newton Theological Institute, Albion Small studied in Germany. He returned to receive his PhD from the German-trained social science faculty at Johns Hopkins University. He became a professor of sociology at the University of Chicago at its founding in 1892 and taught there until his death. Small was a founding member of the American Sociological Society, serving as the Society's president from 1912 to 1914, and the founder and editor of the American Journal of Sociology *(1895–1926), a leading venue for Progressive scholarship and reform causes. Small wrote extensively on "social economy"—the relationship of the new industrial society to moral, social, and political life—and on the role of religion in American life. Small was more of a synthesizer than an original thinker; his articles can almost be read as "proof texts" in the Progressive social sciences.*

— 1915 —

The resources for promoting the human process are, on the one hand, the developed and undeveloped natural values; on the other hand, developed and undeveloped personal values. These personal, or human or moral values, as we may call them interchangeably in the present connection, consist, first, in the control which men have gained and may gain over nature; secondly, in the control which they have gained and may gain over themselves as individuals; thirdly in the types of co-operation which they have achieved and may achieve, for more effective control of nature, and for more effective correlation of moral forces, to the end of progressive sublimation of human qualities, in progressively efficient combinations of activities for progressively higher ranges of achievement in cycles to which our knowledge can assign no end. . . .

We may point to all this necessary moral side of the personal equation by using the blanket term "loyalty." By this term I would call attention to all those qualities of individuals which hold them *by influence*

---

4. More biographical information on Small prefaces his selections in Chapters 3 and 5.

from within to fidelity at their posts in doing what their fellows have a right to expect of them there. The difference between large and small social assets under this head is the difference between adequate and defective individual working ideals of responsibility to the group. A population in which the individuals are under no inward restraint from lying, or stealing, or violating their promises, so long as the odds are in favor of not getting caught, is a population with a materially and morally high cost of living. Everyone has to pay more for what he gets, and he gets less for what he pays, than in a population otherwise in the same stage of technical development, but made up of people who have a high degree of regard for one another's rights. This is true, not of pecuniary cost alone, but of all the effort, both active and passive, which must be charged to the overhead cost of life. . . .

We must observe in passing that the individual type which is best adapted to one stage of social achievement may not be equally adapted to another later stage. Indeed, traits which may have been most in demand in an earlier stage may even be the chief hindrances to the distinctive work of a later stage. A foremost social task then, in every transition period, consists in reconstructing the individual type which bore the brunt of bringing the group to its accomplished condition, and in substituting a type better fitted to the work of the next stage in the social process.

The illustration which most readily suggests itself to Americans is the one to which thoughtful Americans have to refer on so many occasions, viz.: throughout the formative period of our national life thus far, individual initiative has been the most distinctive of American traits. In economic matters particularly, less so in political action, and still less so in the realms of higher thought and religious belief, we have until recently been individualists in theory, and to a relatively high degree in practice. Even in the spheres in which we have most mechanically followed bellwethers, we have blatantly professed our independence. This supposed independence in these latter spheres was really, as De Tocqueville[5] detected, merely the class bias of some minor group defying conflicting groups in terms of the assumed independence of the individual. While we have been cowed into some curious slaveries to conventionality in matters which were not our first concern, we have been the most persistent individualists in the world in our struggle for economic gain.

---

5. Alexis de Tocqueville (1805–1859), a French politician and historian, wrote his two-volume study, *Democracy in America*, following an extended tour of America in 1831.

Self-reliance, fighting one's own battle, thrift, every man for himself, every man the architect of his own fortune, God helps those that help themselves—such standards as these have been the mothers' milk and the last will and testament of the prevailing American type. Today the circumstances of life press for transformation of these standards and corresponding remolding of individuals. While it is not probable that individual initiative will ever be undesirable as a factor in the social process, it is evident that it will be differently orchestrated in the social harmony of the future. The perceptions of our present social outlook are reflected in substitutes for the older standards. We are remodeling the older type of self-reliance into self-reliance in executing team-plays. Instead of stimulating one another to fight each his own battle, we are demanding that each shall fall into the ranks of the social battle. We are broadening the principle of thrift into the program of social conservation. Instead of being content with the savage half-truth every man for himself, we are trying to see steadily within the wider view that in the long run men cannot make the most of themselves unless each is for all. We are trying to take in the discovery of a few, that "every man the architect of his own fortune" builds at last a few sightly structures, in a wilderness of many failures and much débris and wreckage. We are becoming conscious of the task of converting the ideal "Every man the architect of his own fortune" into that of "every man in his place in building the city efficient and the city beautiful." We are facing the problem of convincing ourselves that "God helps those that help themselves" much less than he helps those who most systematically help one another.

Accordingly, the most dependable social asset in any period is a population of individuals whose personal equation is adaptable to the processes which must be carried on at that stage of progress.

In the era of teamwork which we have already entered, the typical individualist, even if equipped with the choicest of the individualistic virtues, is as unavailable as the sails and rigging of an old-fashioned clipper ship would be on a modern liner. Attention to the type of individual unit that must be developed in order to meet the demands of present stages of the social process, and invention of ways and means for supplying that type of individual unit to the process, must become increasingly urgent items in the program of every advancing society. . . .

We turn particularly to . . . the *types of association* which a group has become able to sustain, including all the instrumentalities and activities which are means of maintaining those sorts of association.

All that is included here is sometimes symbolized by the omnibus phrase "the social tradition," which phrase may or may not be used to include the agencies employed to pass along the tradition.

Again I shall make no attempt even to name all the social resources which may be styled institutional, in distinction from those of the previous type, which are relatively individual. By way of familiarizing the two conceptions "social achievements" and "social bonds," I shall discuss a selection from the cardinal institutional resources primarily contributing to national stability, and in the second place most efficiently sustaining national functions. . . .

A. Common Language. It is no wonder that conquering peoples have always tried to impose their language upon the conquered. Community of language is the most spontaneous means of social assimilation. It is no wonder that Americans believe almost fanatically in the efficiency of the American language in making Americans. While there is doubtless a great deal of credulity in American minds about the sufficiency of language alone to accomplish stages of socialization which must be otherwise achieved, we have probably on the other hand failed to make full use of our language as a national bond. It is not merely true that common language for all the people of the country makes the technique of our intercourse more capable, just as connecting railroad, telegraph and telephone lines do the same thing. It is still further true that language carries the valuations of the group that uses it, and that adoption of a national language is followed, more directly than would otherwise be the case, by adoption of the mental and moral attitudes which language implies. . . .

B. Race Solidarity. I am deliberately using this phrase now in a sense which physical anthropology would outlaw. I do not mean literally physical amalgamation, at least not as the exclusive or even the principal factor in the achievement now to be discussed. I mean such a sort and degree of like-mindedness, such "consciousness of kind," that differences of ancestry cease to be mischievous in partitioning the population. This qualification applies throughout the section. . . .

Without venturing to assert that there is an invariable ratio between different factors which compose national strength or weakness, we are safe in reckoning that "blood will tell" in the future as it has in the past, as a bond or a barrier among social relations. On the other hand, we must observe at once that race assimilation, first in the physical sense and then still more in the psychological sense, is also a progressive social phenomenon, and that the social blending of racial strains becomes at last a cardinal factor of national strength.

That is . . . a population made up of successfully blended racial elements will have a high degree of social strength; but until this process of blending has been accomplished, by way of cross-breeding physically, intellectually, and morally, one or all, diversity of racial elements is in itself a national weakness. The very task of blending heterogeneous stocks is in itself an element of weakness, and it may be the most critical weakness in a given nation.

By way of expanding the qualification already made, it should be added that when the word "race," or any of its derivatives, appears in this section, the facts referred to may not, in the strict sense, be very largely racial at all. In moral effect, it is enough that they stand out in the reactions of the people as race peculiarities. Thus there would doubtless be friction of a very intense sort between a group of Kentucky mountain whites, and a group of the purest English stock that could be found in Connecticut or Vermont, if the two groups were suddenly thrown together in a single area. The racial ancestry would be very nearly the same. Accidental differences in environment and experience have molded the one type in one way, the other type in another; so that it would be easy for each group to confuse the differences with differences of race, and for each group to react toward the other as though the supposed racial differences were actual. The same mistake is often involved when an actual difference of language confirms the appearance of racial diversity. The marks that pass as race differences might be to the anthropologist mere variations in nonessential mannerisms within the same race. When these nonessentials are the marks of a distinct group, however, especially if they include difference of language, or even of dialect, or sometimes only of pronunciation, they may amount socially to differences of race, and for our present purpose are properly so considered. . . .

Returning to our main proposition, while I repeat that race solidarity in the strictly ethnic sense is largely imaginary, I must also repeat that the sort of social likeness which passes for race solidarity is in itself a prime condition of national strength. The myth that Americans today are Anglo-Saxons is so generous that, under favorable circumstances, only one or two generations are required to assimilate citizens of the most heterogeneous origins to the amiable fiction that we are all of one blood. In the degree in which we develop such likenesses that the fiction escapes our attention we are strong. Since starting to write this section I have heard one of my colleagues tell of a recent visit to a vocational school in Illinois, some distance from Chicago. On the platform was a choir of one hundred voices. The principal of the school stated that these one hundred pupils represented thirty-five nationalities. No nationality was discoverable, however, in their rendering of "My country 'tis of thee." The incident is unfortunately less symbolic of our national success than of our national task. . . .

C. A Coherent Family Type. For our immediate purpose it will be useful to detach our evaluation of the family from all higher considerations, and to consider domestic institutions in their lowest functions, merely as parts of the national machinery. The family is the mechanism which delivers over to the nation the raw material, or the partially improved material, out of which the nation must be composed—the adolescent individuals. To what extent one of these individuals shall prove fit to work into the national processes depends in large measure upon the type of process in the family of which he is a product. Perhaps it depends, in the greater number of cases, more largely upon the family influence than upon any other single factor. A nation is relatively strong if the prevailing type of relationship in its families predisposes the individuals produced by the families to the sort of social co-operation upon which the nation relies, or needs to rely, for its progress. A nation is weak if its families do not contribute individuals predisposed to such co-operation. . . .

Not all good things are modern. Some social attainments of many centuries ago are still standard for wholesome life. Among these is the Hebrew conception of family loyalty. Long before the Hebrew family became monogamous, its customary law presented a social unit which is far above the ideal practiced or professed by large sections of Americans. The conjugal fidelity, parental priesthood, the filial piety of the Hebrew family in patriarchal times, have survived in a degree which makes the typical family life of modern Jews a salutary factor in American society. "Honor thy father and thy mother" was not merely a precept of juvenile discipline. It was a standard of honor that welded the Hebrew family together into a hierarchy of respect and deference from the youngest child to the oldest grandparent or great-grandparent. The Jewish family was thus, in embryo, a pattern society. The Jewish ideal of the Kingdom of God could hardly have sprung up in a society with a different quality of family relation. No society is likely to approach very close to realization of that which is most vital in the Kingdom of God idea, unless it can build upon a customary family institution which realizes the moral essentials of the Hebrew family ideal. . . .

The most dangerous enemy to the coherence of the family of the economic middle class in the United States is the comparative freedom and desire to pursue individual interests. No one can tell whether this trait is more cause or effect of our individualistic conception of life in general. The fact that the individualistic theory was earlier in the order of time than this type of individualistic practice in America does not settle the question; and indeed the question is not of first-rate importance. The fact is that the members of the middle-class family in the United

States have as a rule relatively less use for one another than the members of any other type of family in a corresponding class in the civilized world. It is not true that this fact is in every respect an element of social weakness. In certain respects it sets free a tremendous volume of force to bring things to pass. At the same time this very release of a flood of energy is again like that regime of economic individualism which in the past century has resulted in combinations of certain overdeveloped individualists into trusts that are a menace to the whole social process. In the fundamental matter of group loyalty the American middle-class family is a dubious social asset. As compared with the homogeneity of many types of families, or with the family of a lower social stratum in our own society, in which parents and children form an offensive and defensive alliance for bread-winning and savings-hoarding and mutual insurance again the accidents of life, the middle class family is a notoriously unstable combination. It is easy and common to caricature the centrifugal motions of this middle-class family. Beyond the boarding-house clubbing arrangements for the essential commonplaces of bed and board, the members of this family tend to a relation like that of guests in a hotel. Each goes his or her own way, for employment, for friends, for amusement. The same family may be represented in half a dozen different churches, clubs, lodges, and social sets. The extent of this family disintegration is a never-failing source of astonishment to observing foreigners. No European can believe that the strata of our society in which these phenomena occur can be as strong and reliable for social ends as the corresponding strata in Europe, in which the family is a relatively compact unit. Other elements, of course, enter into the comparison on both sides, so that the balance cannot be struck in that summary way. It remains true, however, that the gain of individual independence in the middle-class American family is at the expense of a rudimentary training in loyalty which, in ordinary circumstances, cannot be replaced by any means equal in efficiency to the traditional group type of domestic interest. Other things being equal, the man or woman or child who treats the family as the lodger treats his lodging-house is presumably the same unstable member of every other social group, whenever it does not appear to give him more than it costs. . . .

D. A Convincing Religion. My proposition is that *there is no more energetic fusing agent in a nation than unity of religion.* So far as homogeneity of the nation is an element of strength, or a factor of national solidarity for better or for worse, no combining force is more effective than a common religion. . . .

In every modern community a large fraction of religious energy is consumed in efforts to make people with one type of experience, and consequently with a corresponding impression about the make-up of the world, adopt the religious interpretations of people whose experience and interpretations have been of a different order. These efforts may to a certain extent secure conformity, but they may not produce conviction. That sort of religious harmony may be effective for repression. It is a poor substitute for the spur and lure of a faith which blends all one's mental and moral insights. . . .

The crucial problem at the present stage of religious development is not whether this, that, or the other doctrinal formula or system is correct; but the incalculably more radical problem is whether religion is a hand-out from an external authority or a deposit of the evolving output of men's objective experience and subjective interpretations and valuations. . . .

The situation affords another outlook upon the service which the sociologists are trying to perform. Modern men have been gaining experience so fast and within so many ranges . . . that no individual would be competent even to edit the complete returns, so as to show how the totality of the world's latest experience supplements and transforms the visions of life dramatized into the religions of earlier men. A few men calling themselves sociologists have been so bold as to say that this knowledge is not merely an accumulation of disconnected snapshots at reality, but in proportion as it is distinct in its several partial views, and not a blur, it is knowledge each part of which would convey more of its meaning if composed into a representation of the whole which modern experience has encountered. Some of these sociologists have dared to say, and many more have probably believed, that there is only one hope of going very far beyond merely mending our religious manners, in the direction of reaching a religion that will convince modern men generally. This hope is in such organization of the world's knowledge that there cannot permanently be a dualism in men's minds between this composite rendering of reality and any other version which might propose itself as an alternative under the name of religion. Accordingly the sociologists have volunteered to represent among scholars the conviction that the world's knowledge, in the degree in which it approaches objectivity, must be capable of demonstrating its objectivity in part by its composability into an organization of knowledge, each portion of which shall corroborate and vitalize every other portion. Nothing less than this is conceivably adequate intellectual support for a religion that should convince all men. Given this organism of present experience, consisting of course in part of a distillation of all past experience, there is lacking only dramatic vision of the incomparable worth of conforming conduct to the implications of this knowledge, to give a religion eager with youth, in place of the senile religions of past men's partial experience.

This program then gives the ultimate forelook of the sociologists. They aim to perform a necessary portion of the work of constructing a *Weltanschauung*, a positive cosmic philosophy, which will do justice to every fraction of human experience. Such a composite representation of life, so far as it has been explored and recorded and audited in the experiences of all men, is the only conceivable creedal basis for social unity at its highest power. The sociologists have voiced as well as they could the implicit human demand for such a conspectus, and their objective is nothing short of the achievement of such a conspectus. [Albion Small, "The Bonds of Nationality," *American Journal of Sociology*, vol. 20 (1915), 632, 635–9, 641, 643–4, 647–9, 651, 655–6, 668, 673, 675–6]

8. *The New State*, Mary Parker Follett (1868–1934)[6]

Born in Boston and educated at Radcliffe College with additional study in England, Follett came late to recognition as a major Progressive thinker. Following the example of Jane Addams, she did social work in Roxbury, a poor Boston neighborhood. During her early membership in the Women's Municipal League, Follett advocated the use of public school buildings as "social centers" during evenings and weekends in order to strengthen social services and educate the residents in the practices of citizenship and self-government. With the publication of The New State *(1918), her ideas of local democracy and national reform received powerful advocacy.*

— 1918 —

Democracy has meant to many "natural" rights, "liberty" and "equality." The acceptance of the group principle defines for us in truer fashion those watchwords of the past. If my true self is the group-self, then my only rights are those which membership in a group gives me. The old idea of natural rights postulated the particularist individual; we know now that no such person exists. The group and the individual come into existence simultaneously: with this group-man appear group-rights. Thus man can have no rights apart from society or independent of society or against society. Particularist rights are ruled out as everything particularist is ruled out. When we accept fully the principle of

---

6. More biographical information on Follett prefaces her sections in Chapters 4 and 10.

rights involved in the group theory of association, it will change the decisions of our courts, our state constitutions, and all the concrete machinery of government. The truth of the whole matter is that our only concern with "rights" is not to protect them but to create them. Our efforts are to be bent not upon guarding the rights which Heaven has showered upon us, but in creating all the rights we shall ever have.

As an understanding of the group process abolishes "individual rights," so it gives us a true definition of liberty. We have seen that the free man is he who actualizes the will of the whole. I have no liberty except as an essential member of a group. The particularist idea of liberty was either negative, depending on the removal of barriers, or it was quantitative, something which I had left over after the state had restrained me in every way it thought necessary. But liberty is not measured by the number of restraints we do not have, but by the number of spontaneous activities we do have. Law and liberty are not like the two halves of this page, mutually exclusive — one is involved in the other. One does not decrease as the other increases. Liberty and law go hand in hand and increase together in the larger synthesis of life we are here trying to make. . . .

But liberty on the popular tongue has always been coupled with equality, and this expression too needs revaluation. The group process shows us that we are equal from two points of view: first, I am equal to everyone else as one of the necessary members of the group; secondly, each of these essential parts is the tap from an infinite supply — in every man lives an infinite possibility. But we must remember that there are no mechanical, no quantitative equalities. Democracy in fact insists on what are usually thought of as inequalities. Of course I am not "as good as you" — it would be a pretty poor world if I were, that is if you were no better than I am. Democracy without humility is inconceivable. The hope of democracy is in its inequalities. The only real equality I can ever have is to fill my place in the whole at the same time that every other man is filling his place in the whole.

Much of our present class hatred comes from a distorted view of equality. This doctrine means to many that I have as much "right" to things as anyone else, and therefore if I see anyone having more things than I have, it is proper to feel resentment against that person or class. Much legislation, therefore, is directed to lopping off here and there. But such legislation is a negative and therefore non-constructive interpretation of equality. The trouble with much of our reform is that it is based on the very errors which have brought about the evils it is fighting. The trade-unionists say that the courts give special privileges to employers and that they do not have equal rights. But this is just the complaint of the employers: that the unionists are doing them out of their time-honored equal rights.

Our distorted ideas of rights and liberty and equality have been mixed up with our false conception of the state, with the monstrous fallacy of man *vs.* the state. But as we now see that the individual and society are different aspects of the same process, so we see that the citizen and the state are one, that their interests are identical, that their aims are identical, that they are absolutely bound up together. Our old political dualism is now disappearing. The state does not exist for the individual or the individual for the state: we do not exalt the state and subordinate the individual or, on the other hand, apotheosize the individual and give him the state as his "servant." *The state is not the servant of the people.* The state must *be* the people before it can reach a high degree of effective accomplishment. The state is one of the collective aspects of the individual; the individual is from one point of view the distributive aspect of the state. The non-existence of self-sufficing individuals gives us the whole of our new theory of democracy. Those who govern and those who are governed are merely two aspects of the common will. When we have a state truly representative of our collective citizenship, then the fear of the state will disappear because the antithesis between the individual and the state will have disappeared.

To sum up: our present idea of the state is that it is not something outside ourselves, that it must flow out from ourselves and control our social life. But it must "control" our life by expressing it. The state is always the great Yes, not the great No. Liberty and restraint are not opposed, because ideally the expression of the social will in restraint *is* our freedom. The state has a higher function than either restraining individuals or protecting individuals. It is to have a great forward policy which shall follow the collective will of the people, a collective will which embodied through our state, in our life, shall be the basis of a progress yet undreamed of. . . .

If many people have defined democracy as liberty and equal rights, others have defined it as "the ascendancy of numbers," as "majority rule." Both these definitions are particularistic. Democracy means the will of the whole, but the will of the whole is not necessarily represented by the majority, nor by a two-thirds or three-quarters vote, nor even by a unanimous vote; majority rule is democratic when it is approaching not a unanimous but an integrated will. We have seen that the adding of similarities does not produce the social consciousness; in the same way the adding of similar votes does not give us the political will. We have seen that society is not an aggregation of units, of men considered one by one; therefore we understand that the will of the state is not discovered by counting. This means a new conception of politics: it means that the organization of men in small, local groups must be the next form which democracy takes. Here the need and will of every man and woman can appear and mingle with the needs and wills of all to produce an all-will. Thus will be abolished the reign of numbers. . . .

Even now so far as a majority has power it is not by the brute force of numbers; it is because there has been a certain amount of unifying; it has real power directly in proportion to the amount of unifying. The composition of a political majority depends at present partly on inheritance and environment (which includes sentiment and prejudice), partly on the mass-induced idea (the spread of thought and feeling throughout a community by suggestion), and partly on some degree of integration of the different ideas and the different forces of that particular society. Its power is in proportion to the amount of this integration. When we use the expression "artificial majority" we mean chiefly one which shows little integration, and we have all seen how quickly such majorities tend to melt away when the artificial stimulus of especially magnetic leadership or of an especially catchy and jingoistic idea is withdrawn. Moreover a majority meaning a preponderance of votes can easily be controlled by a party or an "interest"; majorities which represent unities are not so easily managed. Group organization is, above everything else perhaps, to prevent the manipulation of helpless majorities. . . .

But all talk of majority and minority is futile. It is evident that we must not consider majority versus minority, but only the methods by which unity is attained. Our fetich of majorities has held us back, but most of the plans for stopping the control of majorities look to all kinds of bolstering up of minorities. This keeps majorities and minorities apart, whereas they have both one and only use for us—their contribution to the all-will. Because such integration must always be the ideal in a democracy, we cannot be much interested in those methods for giving the minority more power on election day. The integration must begin further back in our life than this. . . .

The philosophy of the all is supposed, by its advocates, to be opposed to the philosophy of the individual, but it is interesting to notice that the crowd theory and the particularistic theory rest on the same fallacy, namely, looking on individuals one by one: the crowd doctrine is an attempt to unite mechanically the isolated individuals we have so ardently believed in. This is the danger of the crowd. The crowd idea of sovereignty is thoroughly atomistic. This is sometimes called an era of crowds, sometimes an era of individuals: such apparent opposition of judgment need not confuse us, the crowd spirit and the particularistic spirit are the same; that spirit will continue to corrupt politics and disrupt society until we replace it by the group spirit. . . .

The promise for the future is that there now is in associations of men an increasing tendency for the laws of the group rather than the laws of the crowd to govern. Our most essential duty to the future is to see that that tendency prevail. As we increase the conscious functioning of the group we shall inevitably have less and less of the unconscious response, chauvinists will lose their job, and party bosses will have to change their tactics. People as a matter of fact are not as suggestible as formerly. Men are reading more widely and they are following less blindly what they read. . . .

The enthusiasts of democracy today are those who have caught sight of a great spiritual unity which is supported by the most vital trend in philosophical thought and by the latest biologists and social psychologists. It is, above all, what we have learnt of the psychical processes of association which makes us believe in democracy. Democracy is every one building the single life, not my life and others, not the individual and the state, but my life bound up with others, the individual which *is* the state, the state which *is* the individual. . . .

Thus democracy, although often considered a centrifugal tendency, is rather a centripetal force. Democracy is not a spreading out: it is not the extension of the suffrage—its merely external aspect—it is a drawing together; it is the imperative call for the lacking parts of self. It is the finding of the one will to which the will of every single man and woman must contribute. We want women to vote not that the suffrage may be extended to women but that women may be included in the suffrage: we want what they may have to add to the whole. Democracy is an infinitely including spirit. We have an instinct for democracy because we have an instinct for wholeness; we get wholeness only through reciprocal relations, through infinitely expanding reciprocal relations. Democracy is really neither extending nor including merely, but creating wholes. . . .

Today . . . we have many evidences of the steadily increasing appreciation of the individual and a true understanding of his place in society, his relation to the state. Chief among these are: (1) the movement towards industrial democracy, (2) the woman movement, (3) the increase of direct government, and (4) the introduction of social programs into party platforms. These are parallel developments from the same root. What we have awakened to now is the importance of every single man. [Mary Parker Follett, *The New State: Group Organization the Solution of Popular Government* (Longmans, Green, 1918), 137–42, 144–6, 151, 153, 156–7, 171]

Further Reading

Crunden, Robert M., *Ministers of Reform: The Progressives' Achievement in American Civilization, 1889–1920* (University of Illinois Press, 1984).

Dibble, Vernon K., *The Legacy of Albion Small* (University of Chicago Press, 1975).

Elshtain, Jean, *Jane Addams and the Dream of American Democracy* (Basic Books, 2002).

Herbst, Jurgen, "From Moral Philosophy to Sociology: Albion Woodbury Small," *Harvard Educational Review* 29 (1959).

Levy, David W., *Herbert Croly of "The New Republic"* (Princeton University Press, 1985).

McGerr, Michael, *A Fierce Discontent: The Rise and Fall of the Progressive Movement in America, 1870–1920* (Free Press, 2003).

Quandt, Jean D., *From Small Town to Great Community: The Social Thought of Progressive Intellectuals* (Rutgers University Press, 1970).

Wilson, R. Jackson, *In Quest of Community: Social Philosophy in the United States, 1860–1920* (Wiley, 1968).

3

The New Social and Political Economy

By establishing the organization of material life as the most objective, most easily charted indicator of historical change—and by asserting that the organization of the economy occurs within national political boundaries—the new German-trained political and social scientists claimed a primary role in laying the foundation for the Progressives' nationalist reform projects.

Although English political economy, beginning with Adam Smith's *Wealth of Nations* (1776), had dominated American economic thinking in the early and mid-nineteenth century, the new German political economy caught on quickly in America's new research universities. The establishment of the American Economic Association—whose founding members were primarily German-trained academic economists and Protestant clergy—ratified this new political economy. The shared power between the academics and clergy illustrated the ethical component of social and political economy; the most influential works in American social and political economy were written not just by economists and sociologists based in the universities, but also by social reformers, labor leaders, settlement house directors, social workers, and clergy members.

The capaciousness of social and political economy was made possible precisely because of its ethical, national, and historical orientation. Because the organization of material life was only one piece of external evidence for social evolution, the less obvious markers—found in the family, the growth of cities, the formation of distinct economic classes, labor migration patterns, and even the psychic dimensions of evolutionary progress—were all legitimate subjects for study and commentary. A recent study of Progressive political economy nicely captured the spirit of this new economic thinking:

> In reconceiving market society as a culture rather than a contract, modern social economics and sociology set the stakes for a new kind of social struggle: a struggle over inclusion instead of independence, over self-identity instead of self-interest. The old ideal of a commercial republic united by a common class of self-employed households, steeped in the political economy of the Revolutionary Era, slowly lost ground to the new vision of an industrial order united—or divided—along racial, ethnic, and national lines, a vision steeped in the social psychology of the Progressive Era.[1]

---

1. Sklansky, *The Soul's Economy* (2002), 178.

Edwin Seligman (1861–1939), a professor of political economy at
Columbia University and a co-founder of the American Economic
Association, even appropriated a de-radicalized Karl Marx into Progressive reform along social-evolutionary lines. Marx's enduring legacy was
his assertion of the lawlike character of social progress. Discounting all
Marxist elements of class warfare and violent revolution, Seligman drew
this conclusion:

> With every improvement in the material condition of the great mass of
> the population there will be an opportunity for the unfolding of a higher
> moral life; but not until the economic conditions of society become far
> more ideal will the ethical development of the individual have a free
> field for limitless progress.

If proper reforms are undertaken to reap the rewards and avoid the pit-
falls of the new industrial society, then "progress in the individual and
the race [will] be possible without any conflict except one for unselfish
ends, and when the mass of the people shall live as do today its noblest
members." [2]
  This chapter offers selections from the writings of some of the most
innovative social and economic thinkers in America. Richard Ely's
analysis of industrial society, Simon Patten's analysis of the emerging
consumption economy, and John Bates Clark's revisions of classical
economic theories of profits, wages, and rents not only were recognized
as major advances in the social sciences but also showed the close connection between intellectual innovation and social reform and between
the professionalization of knowledge and national political power. The
selections in this chapter also shed light on the different facets of Progressive political economy: its ties to "new" women like Charlotte
Perkins Gilman[3] (a precursor of the feminist movement), churches and
divinity schools, reform journalism, and the nascent labor movement.
The expertise of economists and their felt professional calling was not

---

2. Seligman, *The Economic Interpretation of History* (1907), 132, 155. Seligman was the only Jewish co-founder of the American Economics Association
(there were no Catholics). His writings strongly influenced the historical and
political writings of Charles Beard, his colleague at Columbia University. Seligman was born into a prominent German-Jewish international private banking
family with strong ties to the Republican Party. His father turned down Lincoln's offer to appoint him Secretary of the Treasury. Seligman's given name,
Edwin Robert Anderson, was the full name of the first Union soldier to die in
the defense of Fort Sumter.
  3. A selection from Gilman's writings and her biography are found in Chapter 8.

to be exercised from the top down, but in and through the other institutions of civil society that gave meaning and voice to the larger American public.

9. The Establishment of the American Economic Association, Richard Ely (1854–1943)[4]

Ely, a professor of economics first at Johns Hopkins University and then at the University of Wisconsin, was born in upstate New York; his stern Presbyterian family traced its roots to followers of Oliver Cromwell who emigrated to Connecticut in 1660. After completing his undergraduate education at Dartmouth College and Columbia University, Ely, like so many of his peers, set off to Germany for further study in philosophy. While there, he met Simon Patten and others who were studying political economy, a discipline that—as taught by the Germans— included ethical, historical, and philosophical perspectives. Most notably, however, Ely was instrumental in founding and leading the American Economic Association. In 1962, the American Economic Association established the Richard Ely Lectures, delivered at their annual meetings in honor of distinguished economic thinkers.

— 1938 —

We, who had tasted the new and living economics which was taught in the German universities, were depressed with the sterility of the old economics which was being taught in the American colleges. We became weary of the controversies, the wordy conflicts over free trade and protection, and the endless harangues over paper money which seemed to us to savor more of political partisanship than of scientific inquiry. We had little patience with a press which preached conceptions of orthodoxy, and we were prepared to fight these conceptions as not belonging to the realm of science. There was a pugnacious element in our attitude, for we were young and had the pugnacity of youth. We felt that men, who thought as we did, were denied the right to exist scientifically, and this denial we believed to proceed from certain older men able to exercise a very large influence over thought, particularly thought in university circles. Therefore we felt called upon to fight those who we

---

4. More biographical information on Ely prefaces his other selections in this chapter and in Chapter 6.

believed stood in the way of intellectual expansion and of social growth. We were determined to inject new life into American economics.

Two aspects of the early history of the American Economic Association should be stressed: First, it represented a protest against the system of laissez faire, as expounded by writers of the older school of "orthodox" American economics. Several of the founders of our association, particularly Simon N. Patten, wished to register their protest against this aspect of orthodox economic theory. The second aspect, and the one on which we were all in complete agreement, was the necessity of uniting in order to secure complete freedom of discussion; a freedom untrammeled by any restrictions whatsoever. It was this second point that came, in final analysis and after much debate, to be accepted as the foundation stone of our association. . . .

AMERICAN ECONOMIC ASSOCIATION
Objects of This Association

I. The encouragement of economic research.
II. The publication of economic monographs.
III. The encouragement of perfect freedom in all economic discussion.
IV. The establishment of a bureau of information designed to aid all members with friendly counsels in their economic studies.

Platform

1. We regard the state as an educational and ethical agency whose positive aid is an indispensable condition of human progress. While we recognize the necessity of individual initiative in industrial life, we hold that the doctrine of laissez faire is unsafe in politics and unsound in morals; and that it suggests an inadequate explanation of the relations between the state and the citizens.

2. We do not accept the final statements which characterized the political economy of a past generation; for we believe that political economy is still in the first stages of its scientific development, and we look not so much to speculation as to an impartial study of actual conditions of economic life for the satisfactory accomplishment of that development. We seek the aid of statistics in the present, and of history in the past.

3. We hold that the conflict of labor and capital has brought to the

front a vast number of social problems whose solution is impossible without the united efforts of church, state, and science.

4. In the study of the policy of government, especially with respect to restrictions on trade and to protection of domestic manufactures, we take no partisan attitude. We are convinced that one of the chief reasons why greater harmony has not been attained is because economists have been too ready to assert themselves as advocates. We believe in a progressive development of economic conditions which must be met by corresponding changes of policy. . . .

Even in its modified and more conservative form, our platform met with a certain amount of friendly criticism. A mimeographed circular was distributed among all the economists who might be supposed to be in sympathy with the general ideas expressed in the new constitution; and it was proposed to gather at Saratoga in September, 1885, in connection with the American Historical Association, to which nearly all the economists belonged. The response to the invitation was general. On September 8, 1885, a call signed by H. C. Adams,[5] J. B. Clark,[6] and R. T. Ely was read at a public meeting of the Historical Association. All those interested were invited to meet at the Bethesda Parish Building at 4 P.M. on that same day to take into consideration plans for the formation of an American Economic Association. Among those present at this first meeting, besides the original sponsors of the project (E. J. James and H. C. Adams, and I), were John B. Clark, Edwin R. A. Seligman, Davis R. Dewey, Andrew D. White, C. K. Adams, Katherine Coman, and E. Benjamin Andrews, to mention only a few. . . .

In the end, it was decided to refer our platform to a committee of five, consisting of H. C. Adams, the Reverend Washington Gladden,[7] Professor Alexander Johnston, and Professor J. B. Clark and me. The committee decided that it was desirable to make it plain that the founders of the American Economic Association did not intend to formulate any creed which should restrict freedom of inquiry or independence of thought. With this end in view, the following note was appended to the "statement of principles" which was finally adopted: "This statement was

---

5. Henry Carter Adams. A selection of his writings and his biography are found in Chapter 5.

6. John Bates Clark. A selection of his writings and his biography are found in the next selection.

7. Washington Gladden (1836–1918) was a prominent Social Gospel clergyman in Ohio and author of *Applied Christianity* (1886), the most influential of his many books.

proposed and accepted as the general indication of the views and the purposes of those who founded the American Economic Association, but it is not to be regarded as binding upon individual members." The statement of principles read as follows:

1. We regard the state as an agency whose positive assistance is one of the indispensable conditions of human progress.
2. We believe that political economy as a science is still in an early stage of its development. While we appreciate the work of former economists, we look, not so much to speculation as to the historical and statistical study of actual conditions of economic life for the satisfactory accomplishment of that development.
3. We hold that the conflict of labor and capital has brought into prominence a vast number of social problems, whose solution requires the united efforts, each in its own sphere, of the church, of the state, and of science.
4. In the study of the industrial and commercial policy of governments we take no partisan attitude. We believe in a progressive development of economic conditions, which must be met by a corresponding development of legislative policy. . . .

Rightly or wrongly to many, the statement of principles seemed like a proclamation of emancipation. At this time the enthusiasm with which we were greeted may appear a little difficult to comprehend. . . .

Why this jubilation? Why this feeling of emancipation? It was felt by many that political economy was opposed to the recognition of any ethical element in our economic life, that it opposed all social reforms for social uplift as futile, that it exalted into a principle of economic righteousness the individual and unrestrained pursuit of self-interest, that it almost deified a monstrosity known as the economic man, that it looked upon laissez faire as a law of beneficent providence, and held that free trade must be received as an ethical dogma, being a practical application of the command, "Thou shalt not steal," for here inconsistently an ethical principle was admitted as all-controlling. Now let it be said that no support, or at any rate very little support, for such views could be found in the writings of the great economists of England or any other country; but a false and undue emphasis of certain teachings of the masters had led to this misapprehension; and for this one-sided development, popularization and the exigencies of practical politics were largely responsible. Hence when the recognition of evils was proclaimed as in harmony with science, when it was proposed to examine the actual situation of the wage-earner and to reason on the basis of

observation, when it made known that a body of economists was prepared to examine free trade and protection scientifically and not dog-
matically, and that economics embraced the whole of the economic
life; the simple message, which now no one would think it necessary to
proclaim, produced an impression and aroused an enthusiasm which
can be understood only by those who by the aid of the scientific
imagination work their way back to the situation of 1885. [Taken from
Carl Resek, ed., *The Progressives* (Bobbs-Merrill, 1967), 21–2, 24–6,
28–9, 31]

10. *The New Economics,* John Bates Clark (1847–1938)

*Clark was born in Rhode Island to a family with a long history in the
clergy. After completing his studies at Brown University and Amherst
College, he received his PhD from the University of Heidelberg and
went on to become a professor of economics at Columbia University.
Clark's scholarship on marginal utility theory, written just as the
economics profession was establishing itself in America, closed the gap
between English classical economics and German political economy.
With the help of Franklin Giddings,[8] his colleague in sociology at
Columbia University, Clark translated marginal utility theory into a
larger evolutionary theory of social and moral progress. The highest
annual award given by the American Economic Association is the John
Bates Clark Medal, established in 1947.*

— 1886 —

That mankind as a whole shall become richer does not, of necessity,
involve an increase of human welfare. That is dependent, not only on
the quantity of wealth accumulated, but on the mode in which it is
shared. A better division of the results of industry might atone for some
diminution in the amount produced. As bearing on the prospects of
mankind, there are three practical problems to he solved; of these the
first is how to create, with the least sacrifice, the largest aggregate of utilities; the second is how to justly divide the gain; and the third is how to
ensure in the product that quality which shall cause it to minister to permanent rather than to transient well being. We are now to consider the
second of these problems. The quantity of wealth created is, in fact,

---

8. A selection from Giddings and his biography are found in Chapter 4.

increasing faster than population; are the equities of distribution also increasing?

The mode of dividing the proceeds of social industry is changing, under our eyes, at a rate so rapid that it is difficult for a scientific system to keep pace with it. Demand and supply are the regular agents of distribution, and have divided the stream of social production into three channels, containing respectively Rent, Gross Profits, and Wages. Of these, the first has been traditionally regarded as determined by a more or less independent law; and it will be convenient for our purposes to accept this theory, and confine our attention to the division which determines the amount of wages and of profits.

Vital as are the interests centering in the law of wages, the subject is full of unsettled theoretical questions of a kind that, as one would suppose, ought to be forever decided by a little clear and candid thought. There is, moreover, a moral element in these questions. Points of fact suggest problems in equity. What are wages? From what source do they come? What determines their amount? These questions suggest the inquiry whether, in nature, source, and amount, they are what they ought to be, or whether there is, in the present transactions of class with class, a series of wrongs which demand a reform, and, as an alternative, threaten a revolution.

In the absence of a scientific answer to the points of equity at issue, and of one so clearly proven as to compel belief, interest dictates the replies given in the greater number of cases; and this fact arrays one social class against another, and makes it possible for each to claim a moral basis for its action. The contests of interest between capitalists and laborers are intensified by counter-claims in equity; and the problem thrust upon society is not merely how to divide a sum, but how to adjust rights and obligations.

Politics cannot escape the dominant influence of these ethico-economic issues. The solidarity of capital on the one hand, and of labor on the other, are things of which the founders of our republic thought as little as the founders of our system of economics. The strain to which this influence is about to subject our institutions would be indefinitely less if the counter claims in equity could be in so far settled that men not biased by belligerent feeling might be in substantial agreement concerning them. If it is humanly possible to thus settle the questions at the basis of the law of wages, no scientific work can be more immediately and widely beneficent. These questions tend, if rightly answered, to public order; if wrongly answered, to communism; and, if unanswered, to agitation and peril. . . .

The action of demand and supply is systematic and capable of clear analysis. It proceeds in one way in the case of products ready for social consumption, in another in the case of the specific utilities which workers in the producing series impart, and in still another in the case of the shares of capitalists and laborers who jointly create a particular utility. To fix the value of clothing ready for use is one thing; to divide that value among agriculturists, transporters, manufacturers and tailors, is another; and to adjust the proportions falling to capitalists and to laborers in each of these producing groups is still another. The entire distributing process consists of a division, a subdivision and a farther subdivision of the general product of social industry. Demand and supply have a primary, a secondary and a ternary field of action.

Social production takes place, as already noticed, not by a single operation, but by a succession of many. One producing agency begins with crude nature, and so modifies it as but partially to prepare it for rendering its service to men; another and another continue the operation. The ultimate result of the action of all is a completed product, and the particular change effected by each may be distinguished as a sub-product. . . .

In each of these provinces of action there may exist three more or less distinct conditions in respect to competition. There may be, first, the conservative competition in which economists of a few years ago were able to see realized a general harmony of social interests. There may be, secondly, the fiercer contest in which eventual success comes to a participant through the extermination of rivals, the process well named "cut-throat" competition. There may be, thirdly, a combination of parties in the strife, which produces a monopoly, tempered, as we shall hereafter see, by a certain latent competition. The first two conditions would seem to shade into one another by easy gradations, while the second and the third would appear to be the antitheses of each other. The competitive struggle might, seemingly, progress in fierceness from a rivalry conducted on a live-and-let-live principle to a war of extermination; while between such a war and the combination which excludes all strife there would appear to be nothing in common. Yet the first process is the result of a distinct set of industrial conditions, while the second and third are the product of another set. Easy and tolerant competition is the antithesis of monopoly; the cut-throat process is the father of it.

At the time when economic science was in process of formulating, the functions of manufacturer and of merchant were merged in a large number of productive groups. The word "shop," as signifying a place for retail dealing, is, in itself, a record of a comparatively primitive, industrial system in which manufactures were conducted in a multitude of little shops, whose owners often retailed their products. Large remnants of this system exist in every European country; but in America it is a thing of the past. . . .

The first effect of the industrial change was the extermination of the general class of artisan retailers. The survivors of the guild-brethren whose shuttles wrought all fine fabrics for our ancestors are now crowded into a few fields where hand work is prized for its own sake. The utility of hand-worked laces and embroideries, as badges of social caste, still insures their production on a limited scale. Handicraftsmen hold, mainly under the protection of fashion, a few other fields in precarious tenure.

The method by which the machine has, in many cases, displaced the artisan has been by appealing to his own interest as a retailer; it is by offering to him, in his capacity of shopkeeper, goods for less than they would cost him as an artificer. The machine, the enemy of the tradesman in one of his capacities, is his friend in another. . . .

Competition is no longer adequate to account for the phenomenon of social industry. What was once assumed as a universal law is now but partial in its operation. . . . There is something deeper than competition in the economic life of men; and the relation of competition to the underlying law has not been analyzed. The principle whereby the struggle of many men, each for himself, to secure wealth is made to work out the general good of all, has all the beauty that is claimed for it. We have noticed . . . the moral limitations that hedge about this struggle. The contest is never unrestricted. A Spirit of Justice is ever standing over the contestants, and bidding them compete only thus and thus. This they may do; that they may not do; and the prohibitions increase with time. Competition at best exists by sufferance, and the power that tolerates and controls it is moral.

We have now to notice a still more decisive manner in which the moral sovereignty asserts itself. It not only regulates competition in its modes, but, at will, it thrusts the whole process aside. It is because there have long been departments of practical economy not left to competition, that there has always been, in science, some need of a province of non-competitive economics. It is because these activities are increasing apace with the rapid developments of the past century, that the need is now pressing.

We have seen that the ultimate end of political economy is not, as is generally assumed, the mere quantitative increase of wealth. Society, as an organic unit, has a higher economic end. That end is the attainment of the greatest quantity, the highest quality, and the most just distribution of wealth. It is the true subjection of matter, the placing of it in the most rational condition, absolute and relative. The matter and force of external nature are to be brought into that state which, in itself, is best, and they are to be brought into that relation of ownership which best promotes the general happiness. Matter modified by labor in accordance with enlightened reason may be termed rational wealth; it is this that society is pursuing, and partially realizing. . . .

The competitive mode of production and distribution has been adopted by society because, in its day, it has given the nearest practical approximation to the standard of rational wealth. Imperfect as are its results those of any other system would have been more imperfect; they would have rendered the wealth of society less, worse, or worse distributed. As compared with them, the principle of competition has increased, improved, and with rude equity divided the products of industry; and for this reason only has it been tolerated. . . .

Society does not and will not completely abandon the competitive principle; it is still needed as an agent of distribution, and it is the sole means on which we can rely for the securing of a large product to distribute. Yet, if what we have claimed be true, society should hold this agent in abeyance within limited fields of industry, whenever, within those limits, a better system is available. This it actually does. Sometimes, as in railroad operations, competition works sluggishly, interruptedly, or not at all; sometimes, as in the transactions of labor and capital, it works, for a time, one-sidedly and cruelly, and then almost ceases to do its work. It may happen that, in exactly that field in which competition operates unusually ill, another method may operate especially well, and the comparison of results may be in favor of the latter. If once society becomes conscious that this is the fact, farewell to one particular form of competition.

That the future field of non-competitive economics will be vast is less surprising than that its present field is considerable. Arbitration promises to replace the former agent of distribution in a comprehensive way. Cooperation is the antithesis of competition; wherever it exists the competitive struggle is held, to some extent, in abeyance. In practice cooperation is most frequently of an incomplete kind, and a greater or less residuum of competition remains; but any realization of the one principle means the elimination of somewhat of the other; and, moreover, whatever is done by a public or governmental agency is done, in a sense, cooperatively. What we have now to consider is a certain displacement of competition which is of long standing, and which, therefore, serves to show that society has always been ready to set the process aside, whenever it has been able, by other means, to better attain the rational end which it has had in view. . . .

As thus apprehended, there is no apotheosis of selfishness in the theory of political economy, and there is no necessarily corrupting effect from the practical outworking of its principles. Recognizing the competitive struggle, wherever it survives, the imperfect agent of moral law, a man may participate in it without taint. The bad effects of the contest he does not need to suffer; and to the lower levels where the golden calf-worship is unhindered and blighting, he does not need to descend. It is his privilege to live on the mountainous slope at the summit of which moral law reigns. He may buy, sell, and get gain, as well as give thanks and worship, with his eyes uplifted to the hills whence cometh his help. [From *The Philosophy of Wealth* (Ginn & Company, 1886), 107–9, 111, 120–1, 123, 203–8, 219–20]

11. *The Evolution of Industrial Society,* Richard Ely (1854–1943)[9]

Like Vida Scudder before him, Richard Ely was active in early Christian socialist groups led by W.D.P. Bliss and maintained a continued interest in the church's role in achieving social justice. With John Commons, a prominent reformer and labor economist based at the University of Wisconsin, Ely co-founded and served as the first president of the American Association for Labor Legislation. Ely's early book on industrial society was first published as part of a "home reading series" of the Chautauqua Movement, a Methodist-inspired summer camp and series of national lecturerships dedicated to melding together Christianity, family life, ethical values, and responsible citizenship. At the Movement's peak in 1924, traveling Chautauqua lectures had reached 10,000 communities and were attended by more than 40,000,000 people. Prior to becoming the founding president of the University of Chicago, William Raney Harper was educational director of the national Chautauqua organization.

— 1903 —

The use of power manufacture, made possible by the great mechanical inventions in the latter part of the eighteenth century, brought about that far-reaching and rapid change in our industrial life which is known as the Industrial Revolution. It ushered in the era of capitalism, the

---

9. More biographical information on Ely prefaces his other selections in this chapter and in Chapter 6.

wage system, and the extensive use of credit. It now became necessary for the laborers to leave their homes and assemble in factories to use the expensive machinery which each one could not own for himself. To an increasing extent, those supplying the factors of production become separated. In a particular business one set of persons might furnish the capital, an entirely different set the labor, and still a third the land. Under such conditions, the organizer, the *entrepreneur*, receives a new importance, and *captains of industry* are made possible. . . .

The reason that the evils of the change were not so great in this country was partly in the fact that there was a great supply of free land to which any who were dissatisfied with the changing conditions could turn, and partly in the fact that we had as yet not established a great economic system of any kind that could be overthrown. With us the change was an evolution rather than a revolution. The existence of a great body of unoccupied land has, indeed, been one of the most characteristic facts of our economic development. It has served as a constant force tending to keep up wages in the older regions and to furnish an outlet for the discontented element. Timothy Dwight speaks of this fact in his "Travels in New England and New York in 1821." They had many troubles in the older regions, he says, but they would have had many more if this discontented element had remained at home. Our free land has almost disappeared, and we shall in the future have to find a new way to deal with those who are dissatisfied. That this will be no easy matter is evident when we consider that if the mainland of the United States were only half as densely populated as the German Empire is today, we should have over four hundred millions of people under one government.

The abuses that appeared with the factory system led, in both England and America, to a twofold reaction against the *laissez-faire* policy. Competition has been regulated by a series of factory acts and other legislation, and workmen have been stimulated to more thorough organization to secure for themselves, in the shape of higher wages, a part of the increasing wealth. But at best, a change from one stage to another must always mean loss and suffering to a part of society. The methods which were compatible with success in the slow-going handicraft stage became inappropriate in a more strenuous competitive period; and those who could not make the change lingered behind, and became what has been expressively called "the rubbish heap of the competitive system." There was once a strong feeling that those who had learned a trade had a sort of vested interest in it, and ought not to be turned out immediately when some other man could be found who might do the work more cheaply. Custom protected the incompetent to some extent

from the ruthless force of competition, but later they were turned adrift
to shift for themselves. In many ways, too, our habits of thought have to
be changed as we pass from one stage to another. This is irksome, and
we resist it for a time. The idea that a business is a man's own and ought
not to be interfered with by the public is one that belongs to this early
part of the industrial stage, and it has been only with extreme slowness
and obstinacy that it is coming to be recognized by business men that
such an attitude is an anachronism. Unquestionably the dispute
between labor and capital has been aggravated by this fact. . . .

Within the last two or three decades a new movement has been taking place. The marked concentration of production in large establishments, commonly called the trust movement, may be regarded as a
second phase of the industrial stage. It is seen in almost every line of
production, although less markedly in some than in others. It is to be
observed least of all in the farming and mercantile business. To illustrate the movement, we may take the manufacture of agricultural
implements. From the table

AGRICULTURAL IMPLEMENTS					
		AVERAGE PER ESTABLISHMENT			
			Wage Earners		
	NUMBER OF		Average		Value of
YEAR	ESTABLISHMENTS	Capital	Number	Wages	Product
1900	715	$220,571	65	$31,400	$141,549
1890	910	159,686	43	19,898	89,310
1880	1,943	31,966	20	7,905	35,327
1870	2,076	16,780	12	5843	25,080
1860	2,116	6,553	8	2,800	9,845
1850	1,333	2,674	5	1,626	5,133

notice an absolute decrease in the number, and a marked increase in
the average size, of the establishments.

But a third phase, quite distinct from the preceding, has been attract-
ing attention recently. It is the movement toward the integration of
allied industries. For illustration, take the case of the United States Steel
Corporation. Here we have united under one management the American Bridge Company, the American Sheet Steel Company, the American Steel Hoop Company, the American Steel and Wire Company, the
American Tin Plate Company, the Federal Steel Company, the Lake

Superior Consolidated Iron Mines, the National Steel Company, the National Tube Company, and the Carnegie Steel Company. Of the last itself, Mr. Charles M. Schwab says, in his testimony before the Industrial Commission (Vol. XIII, p. 448): "The Carnegie Company were large miners of ore—mined all the ore that they required themselves, to the extent of over 4,000,000 tons per year. They transported a large percentage of it in their own boats over the lakes; they carried a large percentage of it over their own railroad to their Pittsburgh works, and manufactured it there, by the various processes, into a great variety of iron and steel articles—I think perhaps a larger general variety of steel articles than almost any other manufacturing concern." . . .

In the earliest of the economic stages; we have seen, the idea is wanting, not merely of private, but also of public property. The idea of ownership does not exist. In the pastoral stage, ownership in movable goods is recognized, and in the agricultural stage, landownership makes its appearance. Today the idea of property is so thoroughly ingrained in our habits of thought that it must be regarded as one of the fundamental facts in our economic life. But it has reached no final form. It is continually being modified; and we may note here some of the present tendencies along this line. In the first place, there is an increasing mass of free goods, especially free intellectual goods. Every year sees an addition to the number of great ideas that may be utilized by anyone who cares to appropriate them. To be sure, we grant patents and copyrights, but they are but temporary. In a very true sense there exists a body of knowledge that is a social heritage handed down from one generation to another, constantly increasing, and free to all. A second tendency is the restriction of the extent of private property, and, generally speaking, an extension of public property. The world over we notice an increase in public property in forest lands. The increase in play-grounds for children, in public parks, in public libraries, and in the municipal ownership of "public utilities," affords other illustrations. In the third place, there is a clear development in the social side of private property. More and more the idea that private property is a social trust has made its way, and it is now recognized that the arguments in favor of private property are based chiefly upon the benefits which society derives therefrom. Again, new forms of property are continually appearing. Patents and copyrights are comparatively recent in the world's history. Good will in business is often bought and sold. Certain new rights very much akin to private property are also being recognized, such as the right to be protected against injury, which seems to be implied in the employer's liability acts. We are hearing more, also, of the right to work. Finally, we notice changes in the mode of acquisition of private property. In earlier

times, force played a larger part in the acquisition of property, but we
are coming to insist more and more that it shall be won by service.
There is a general movement to restrict the sources of unearned
incomes, such as monopoly profits, and the increasing taxation of
inheritances has some significance in this connection. . . .

But perhaps the one fact in the evolution of society that becomes
clearer and clearer as time passes, is that cooperation is the great law of
social life growth. Men learn to act together in increasingly large numbers for increasingly numerous purposes. Individualism in production,
exchange, distribution, and even consumption, gradually yields to
cooperation. Early man produces for himself, and in his own group
consumes that which has been produced and worked up in the household. He goes his way with economically little regard to the activities of
other households. Every step forward in his progress means an increasing number of relations with other households, until we come to a time
when very little which the ordinary individual consumes is produced by
him, but reaches him as a result of the activities of thousands and hundreds of thousands, and even millions of men, who are working for him,
while he serves them. The whole world becomes a vast network, in
which each serves all and all serve each.

Another great social law which becomes apparent in the course of
evolution is this: *we pass over from unconscious social cooperation to conscious social cooperation.* At first, men act together because each one is
pursuing his own ends, and they are scarcely aware that they are coop-
erating with each other. But this changes with a growth in the complexity and magnitude of the industrial units of society. Conscious
cooperation in industry is only one part of the developing self-consciousness of society. Society sets before itself purposes, and attempts to
achieve them through social action. As our life becomes social, this
method for the achievement of our purposes, namely, social action, is
inevitable. We have in this an explanation of many modern phenomena
which seem strange to those who do not have the right clue for their
explanation. At first, social efforts for the attainment of social purposes
are necessarily crude, and failures are more common than successes.
Society, like a child, must learn to walk without stumbling. We have our
Granger movements[10] in our attempts to regulate those agencies of

---

10. A protest movement led primarily by southern and western farmers. Beginning soon after the Civil War and reaching its height in the mid-1870s, the
Movement sought higher commodity prices, debt relief, and expanded agricultural credits. The Movement influenced various states' attempts to regulate railroad rates.

social cooperation which we call the railways. A failure of early move-ments does not, and cannot, lead to an abandonment of social efforts. The Granger legislation makes way for state railway commissions and the Interstate Commerce Commission. This represents a higher form of social effort, but by no means a final form. These various commissions must receive a much higher development, or make way for something else, possibly even public ownership, but this remains to be seen.

That which is especially characteristic of the most modern phase of social evolution is the effort to secure harmony and unity of action among great industrial establishments, in order to achieve thereby the largest results with the least output of energy. The avoidance of waste of economic energy is, in other words, the great underlying principle of the present phase of industrial evolution. In the earlier phase of the industrial stage a marvellous order was achieved in a single industrial establishment; but each establishment went its own way with little regard to other industrial establishments. The result was disharmony and loss. The critics of society found many points of attack in this con-tradiction between the harmonious cooperation of all the parts of a sin-gle establishment, and the lack of organized and harmonious working among the various establishments. It was this particular aspect of pro-duction which led the socialists to speak of the planlessness of private capitalistic production. Planlessness is, indeed, one of the great words in the socialist critique, but one heard somewhat less frequently since the trust era began. Each one, they said, is dependent upon all others who are producing for the same market the things which he is produc-ing. All manufacturers of shoes are dependent upon all other manufac-turers of shoes, inasmuch as all these others are competitors. But no one, it was argued, knows what his competitors are doing, and each one is therefore working in the dark. The result of this unorganized produc-tion of competitors must therefore be overproduction, stagnation, and industrial ruin brought about by the economic crisis. This is but a rough sketch of the criticism, and takes up but a single line. Nowadays, the socialists insist more upon bad distribution as the cause of crises. Unquestionably, this lack of harmony was a weakness which intelligent men, desiring progress, must endeavor to correct. To secure harmo-nious action among producers and to avoid needless waste, two meth-ods have been followed: the first, the method of public action; the second, the method of private action. . . .

In the United States, clear-sighted and long-headed men, powerful personalities like Commodore Vanderbilt, saw, with equal clearness, the advantages of unity; and, through his own private effort, seconded by able lieutenants, Vanderbilt began a movement for consolidation and unification which yielded him one of the largest fortunes up to that time known in the history of the world. . . .

The efforts to secure unity and harmony in the relations of manufacturing establishments to one another have, however, been almost altogether private in this country as well as in other countries. The United States leads the world in the trust movement, and the most gigantic, perhaps one should say colossal, achievement along this line is found in the United States Steel Corporation. The industrial question which overshadows in importance all other questions is this: Is industrial evolution naturally leading to the domination of substantially all the great fields of industry by monopoly? . . . Marx predicted that the business units in production would continually increase in magnitude, until in each branch of industry monopoly would emerge from the struggle of interests. When this happened he thought that private monopoly would be replaced by public monopoly; in other words, that pure social ownership and operation of all great industries would be substituted for private ownership and operation, and thus would dawn the era of socialism. . . .

The advocates of the trust frequently use arguments precisely like these of the socialists in pointing out the benefits of trust production, and maintain that the advantages of system and unity are so vast that in the end the trust method will dominate every great industrial field.

A discussion of the various aspects of this question brings before us, as subordinate questions, nearly all the pressing economic problems of our day. It is hard to see how we can have any clear opinions in regard to public policy, until we have satisfied ourselves in regard to the question whether or not there are natural laws in the industrial world governing industrial evolution, and bringing about inevitably a reign of monopoly, either private or public.

In considering this question, we must first of all sharply distinguish between large-scale production and monopolistic production. This is something which the author has been iterating, and reiterating, for the past fifteen years, or more. Many others have also been saying the same thing, and it seems now to be generally understood. It is, indeed, strange that it should ever have been difficult to understand the difference between vast production and monopolistic production. One of our great retail stores, like Marshall Field's, or Mandel Brothers', in Chicago, or Wanamaker's, in Philadelphia or New York City, represents very large scale production, but along with this large scale production there is the sharpest kind of competition.

Competition is the foundation of our present social order. Our legal system rests upon competition as a basis. The great legal decisions in England and America assume, either implicitly or explicitly, that competition is a pillar of the social order. Competition, along with large scale production, brings its own problems, but they are easy of solution as compared with the problems of monopoly, because competition is compatible with private property in capital, and with private production. Where competition exists, the problem is its regulation in such a manner as to secure its benefits, and to remove, where it is possible, and where it is not possible, to mitigate, its evils. What is needed for competition, especially, is to raise its moral and ethical level.

But we find among us widespread monopoly as a result of industrial evolution, and this has brought evils of another sort. . . . There seems to be something inevitable in all these general tendencies that we have been sketching. When we have said all that we can about the power of the individual will, we still find that there are great social forces which compel us to act along certain lines. The steady growth of population brings with it new problems, more complex social relations, and we are forced to adjust ourselves accordingly. The momentous changes resulting from the industrial revolution have come about without the anticipation or express will of society; we could not turn back now to former conditions if we would; all that we can do is to attempt to control and take advantage of these new forces. The most general statement of our industrial problem is this: How shall we retain the advantages of associated effort with freedom of movement and a socially desirable distribution of products? This is a task which demands all our best powers and our best purposes, with a willingness to sacrifice private ease and comfort for the public good.

Reference has been made to the growing cooperation among men. This means at the same time increasing dependence of man upon man, but this increasing dependence is not burdensome, provided it is mutual. If it is one-sided dependence, it may become virtually slavery under the name of freedom. Dependence must mean interdependence. The multiplying relations of men with one another give us a new economic world. These relations require regulation, in order to preserve freedom. The regulation by the power of the state of these industrial and other social relations existing among men is an essential condition of freedom. Herbert Spencer,[11] looking at the political regulation of economic relations, speaks of a coming slavery, but he overlooks

---

11. Herbert Spencer (1820–1903) was an English social philosopher influential in translating evolutionary ideas from biology into "social Darwinism," in which individual economic competition is viewed as the engine of natural selection and social progress. This theory is best illustrated in his books, *Social Statics* (1851) and *The Man Versus the State* (1884).

the fact that with the increasing dependence of man upon man in modern society, this dependence becomes one-sided, and results in slavery if these relations are not regulated. This is the explanation of the fact that every civilized nation in the world finds it necessary to regulate to an increasing extent the industrial relations existing among men. Free contract alone, that is to say, unregulated, can only result in a degrading dependence of some men upon others, and consequently social degradation. On the other hand, through regulated association come freedom and individuality. [From *Studies in the Evolution of Industrial Society* (Chautauqua Press, 1903), 57–61, 63–4, 87–99]

12. *Social Gradations of Capital,* Albion Small (1854–1926)[12]

Albion Small was far more influential as the founding editor of the American Journal of Sociology *than as a major sociological thinker in his own right. For more than thirty years, Small used his journal as a sort of clearinghouse for Progressive ideas, welcoming Jane Addams, Florence Kelley, and Charlotte Perkins Gilman—none of whom were trained sociologists—to its pages. Small carried this interest in integrating women into sociology and reform into his academic career as well. The sociology department at the University of Chicago produced the first female PhDs in America and, by 1900, was turning out one-third of all female social science doctorates in America. One of these students, Sophonisba Breckenridge (1866–1948), went on to help found that university's school of social work; another, Katharine Bement David (1860–1935), became the first woman to hold a cabinet-level position in New York City, as Commissioner of Correction. The fact that half of the undergraduates in this period were women had a major effect on the university's political culture. In a straw poll of University of Chicago undergraduates in the presidential election of 1892, the Populist candidate received 3 votes; the Democrat, 52; and the Republican, 151. But the winner was John Bidwell, the Prohibition candidate, with 164 votes. The Prohibition Party platforms in this early period combined moral and social reform—including female suffrage—in a way that the other parties did not.[13]*

---

12. More biographical information on Small prefaces his selections in Chapters 2 and 5.

13. Eisenach, *Lost Promise* (1994), 118–31.

— 1914 —

The real thing which it is up to modern men to realize, by some means or other, is that in the last hundred and fifty years, and especially in the last fifty years, civilized people have changed their ways of doing their work. The kinds of work that they do have changed. Meanwhile our thoughts about the work to be done and about ways of doing it have also changed. Many of us see that the ways of thinking about the work of the world, which were fairly satisfactory a century and a half or even a half-century ago, have to a considerable extent lost their plausibility. They do not seem to us now to cover the facts with which we are familiar, as they seemed to our predecessors to cover the facts with which they were familiar. Every day new people are passing through a mental conversion which they report in some equivalent of the confession: "For a long time I've had a sort of feeling that something is out of whack in our economic institutions; but I kept still, because I couldn't make out just what is the matter. I've come to the idea now that this very keeping still is a good deal of the matter. We know our present economic system doesn't convince us any longer, but we keep still, instead of speaking out that much, and then comparing notes about why it isn't convincing. The longer we keep still, the more different kinds of twinges it will cost us to make the changes which we shall find to be necessary. The moral is that it is time to take stock of our fundamental social ideas, and to find out how much must be written off for depreciation."

Another fact about the present phase of social transition is that social unrest can no longer be sneered out of court by the plea that it is merely the envy of the unsuccessful toward the successful. Since the present economic traditions began to take shape, there have always been leaders of protest against the system of whom this charge surely would not hold. The number of such who have no private complaint against the present economic order, who admit that it has treated them better than they deserve, if measured by the average of men of similar merit, is daily gaining recruits. They do not join the ranks of destroyers. They have no bombs hidden in their clothes. They are not subsidizing dynamiters. They have waked up, however, to the fact that as a sheer matter of clear thinking, it is necessary for them to find out whether the economic ideas which are supposed to be here to stay are truths or myths. . . .

This paper has to do with a single illustration of these propositions. The particular thesis to be developed is that *a large part of the confusion in the present stage of transition is due to our acquiescence in conceptions of capital as an exclusively economic phenomenon, and in corollaries from those conceptions which act as automatic adjusters of conduct to*

those unmoral conceptions. Conflicts centering around capital press for
convincing analysis of capital as a social phenomenon. . . .

The clue to a primary analysis of capital from the social standpoint
may be found in the question: To what extent is the effectiveness of capital in the economic process due to unaided acts of the owner; and to
what extent is its effectiveness conferred by acts of others than the
owner?

When the answer to this question is partially made out, it shows that
there are three distinct types of capital, considered as a social phenomenon, viz., first, capital which is used solely by the owner; second, capital which is used by the owner in some sort of dependence upon the
acts of others; third, capital which is employed, as such, wholly by others than the owner, and under conditions which he does not and could
not maintain by his individual power. . . .

The relations between capital and labor, as represented by the farmer
and his hoe, are thus settled on a basis that is as little open to question as
the propriety of leaving his hand free to convey food to his mouth. If
all capital were literally a tool in the hands of its owner, and if there
were no questions about accidental shiftings of the products of one tool-
capitalist's work into the hands of another, it is hard to see how there could
be any dubious questions of moral principle in the field of industry.

Let us now suppose a neighboring claim, through which a stream
flows. Let us suppose that it has a fall sufficient to develop a considerable amount of power. Let us suppose that the settler has saved enough
to build and equip a small grist mill, and that he presently becomes a
miller as well as a farmer. As owner and operator of the mill, are his relations to the community in any way different in kind from his neighbor's
social relations as owner and operator of the hoe? The customary economic presumption is that they are not, and this presumption may be
taken as marking the beginnings of all the differences of opinion about
the ethics of capitalistic society.

If we confine attention simply to the fact that the miller is still working, let us say just as industriously as the farmer, if we think of the mill
as his tool, just as literally as the hoe is the farmer's tool, the capitalistic
presumption is apparently in strict accordance with the facts. But if we
press our analysis a little farther, we find that another factor must now
be taken into the account. . . . That factor is the *co-operation of others
beside the owner* in making the capital efficient. On the technical side,
this has of course been one of the commonplaces of economics, since
Adam Smith's masterly exposition of division of labor. In the aspect here
emphasized, it has been almost totally ignored. . . .

The crucial matter about this class of capital is that it cannot be a part of the personality of the owner, in the same intimate and literal and complete sense as in the case of the hoe. . . . Given the mill in running order, the owner cannot be in all parts of it at once. He must have one or more helpers. One of them may be needed to keep the gearings in repair, while another tends the hoppers, and the owner deals with the customers. At times the owner must leave the premises for food, or sleep, or bargaining with his neighbors. At those times the mill has to be left in charge of others. That is, the owner is forced to rely upon actual co-operation with others, in order to make his management-capital effective; and the ratio between his own literal operation of the capital and that of the other co-operators varies with the volume and form of this sort of capital. Moreover, another kind of co-operation is involved, both as condition and consequence of the existence and efficiency of this sort of capital. This is the co-operation of the surrounding community in maintaining the conditions without which this type of capital would be impossible. . . .

Thus the management-capitalist is not, like the man with the hoe, chiefly a self-sufficient individual. On the contrary, the management-capitalist is chiefly a social product. Measured by the ratio of his powers as a literal tool-wielder, and the influence which he actually exerts as a wielder of other men who actually use the bulk of the tools, he is in a very small fractional degree himself, and he is in a very large degree what his community has enabled him to be. The community has gone before him, and stood behind him and around him, and has potentially or actually exercised a collective power for his benefit, in comparison with which the most capable man is puny. . . .

We do not doubt that the idea of a managerial function is made to go as far as it can in many cases to conceal the fact of exploitation. The laborer will be his own worst enemy, however, until he educates himself out of the notion that there is "no such thing as a managerial function." The laborer has really a larger stake than anybody else in competent discharge of the managerial function. If it is not well performed, it may mean the loss of his job and indirectly of his life and the life of his family. At the same time, it might mean to the capitalist only the loss of a fraction of his property. . . .

It begs the question at the outset to assume that the management-capitalist is simply an individual, like the man with the hoe; to regard him as exercising solely his own personal faculties; as acting merely in the enjoyment of indubitable natural rights; as possessing and using only those things and those powers which belong to him strictly as a person, which are to all intents and purposes his own proper self, just as the hoe is the extended arms of the man who uses it. On the contrary, the management-capitalist is a highly artificialized social contrivance. A large part of the efficiency which is credited to him is in fact merely symbolized by him. It is really the working of other men, first in the immediate economic organization of which he is the head, second, in the entire legal and social community whose institutions make the industrial operations possible. . . .

But there is now a third grade of capital. It is still further removed from the literal productive activity of the owner. It is capital which might be just as productive as it is, if the owner had never lived. It is capital to which the owner has no functional relation at all, so far as the process of economic production is concerned. It is capital the owner's possession of which is a purely conventional arrangement. He does not hold it literally. He could not retain it by the utmost exertion of his individual power. It might be sterile in his hands if he could. All his competence in connection with it is conferred by the agreement of civic society to sustain him as owner, and to sanction his exercise of those property rights which the morals of that society associate with ownership. We have called this grade finance-capital.

Our analysis of the intermediate grade of capital has gone far toward showing that *private property is progressively social endowment.* . . .

Every person who has opened a savings-bank account by depositing a dollar is a finance-capitalist. The three, four, or five cents payable on that deposit at the end of the year have not been produced by any effort of the depositor. They would have accrued just the same if he had dropped dead before he passed out of the bank door. Year after year the interest would be credited to that account, whether or not an heir put in an appearance to collect it. The dollar goes on "earning," utterly irrespective of the further actions of the finance-capitalist, but by virtue of two co-operating organizations; the business organization on the one hand, which forwards the dollar to some point where workers convert it into more than a dollar, and the legal organization on the other hand, which puts every man in the business organization under liability to punishment—from the bank window, out through the business system, and back again to another bank window—if he fails to do what the law requires of him in the process which makes that deposit safe and profitable. . . .

We must keep calling attention to the fact that we are not arguing that finance-capital is wrong. We are pointing out that it is artificial. The simple fact that it is artificial keeps the question eternally open whether the artificial elements in the arrangement correspond with a relatively belated or a relatively advanced stage of social intelligence. The legal system which supports the artificial adjustments is the expression of a complicated body of *opinions,* one resting upon another in the most involved fashion, about what ought to be, in the relationships of all concerned with this type of property. It should go without saying that the banking functions must be performed by someone, somehow, in any society that continues the process of civilization. No one capable of conducting an analysis like this could have any doubts about that point. On the other hand, finance-capital when aggregated, and held in large masses by a few owners or their agents, is such a different social factor from anything that could be imagined from the standpoint of the depositor of a dollar, that the theory and practice of finance-capital present perhaps the central sociological problem of our time. The whole hierarchy of opinions, upon which our present system of finance-capital rests, must be re-examined from premise to premise, and from conclusion to conclusion, in the light of the enormous visible anomalies that have developed in the operation of the system. . . .

By generations of stultifying habit we have deadened our minds to the anomaly of a system, professedly democratic, which permits individuals, through the sheer irrelevancy of blood relationship to other individuals, to take over and exercise the ownership of millions of capital, without even counterbalancing conditions requiring a corresponding return to the community. We gratuitously present to some men the privilege for life of levying on the earnings of other men, and of passing along the same gratuitous privilege to someone in the next generation, without the slightest assurance, beyond a paltry inheritance tax, that an effort will be made by the grantee to compensate either the persons directly under tribute or the general public. Not only this, but by placing the powers of finance-capital at the disposal of these privileged persons we give them large scope to influence the social conditions which affect the lives and fortunes of their fellow-citizens. . . .

The present vagueness in our conceptions of the morals of capitalism is due in part to crude credulity that a relation which is morally wholesome in a relatively simple social situation is necessarily wholesome in a highly complex social situation. . . .

This paper began with a reference to the current social transition. The change may be described on its subjective side as an unorganized and largely instinctive effort of adjustment to a new attitude toward life. From the men whose adjustments are of the most particular and concrete sorts to those who attempt to philosophize the universe, the modern temper is no longer conformity to models, but inclination to understand and obey or control laws of cause and effect. The farmer no longer figures on a harvest because he has performed the prescribed ritual to the gods of the fields. He counts on a harvest because he has used information that came from his own experience, supplemented perhaps by the agricultural experiment station. The citizen will not always believe that the best civic conditions possible are those given up to date by the spontaneous historical processes, and sanctified by conventional social doctrine. He is already beginning to believe that the best possible civic conditions will be the result of men's desire and will to find out whether they are co-operating toward the most intelligent ends, and with the highest attainable degree of efficiency. That is, our thinking and our feeling are no longer merely historical, or merely syllogistic; they are finally and chiefly functional. We believe in a thing, or disbelieve in it, because it works or does not work up to a standard set by our growing sense of what ought to be. Theories pro or con may hold what they will about criticism and reconstruction of capitalistic institutions. Those institutions are merely provisionally adopted means toward certain incidental ends. So sure as humanity remains virile, transition after transition will follow, in experiment with modified institutions, until our economic machinery gets into stable equilibrium with the implications of human needs.

The capitalistic ultimatum is that property is property, whether it is a hoe or a house or a railroad, a dollar or a thousand dollars or a thousand million dollars. The dictum belongs in the "important-if-true" class. With only the rudiments of objective social analysis, one may discover that it is not true. On the contrary, it would seem to be axiomatic that in the degree in which the partnership of other men besides the proprietor is necessary to make a type of capital possible and efficient, corresponding partnership of those other men in control of that capital is indicated. This logic is making the social transition. Men are applying this analysis and making this discovery. The result appears in gathering momentum of the movement to retire those accidents of our social order which make large sections of capital chiefly pretexts for privilege, and to substitute control which shall tend to make capital, from least to greatest, a consistent means of human service. [From "The Social Gradations of Capital," *American Journal of Sociology*, vol. 19 (1914): 721–2, 725–31, 733, 739–40, 742–3, 747–8, 751]

13. *Economics and the New Basis of Civilization,*
Simon N. Patten (1852–1922)[14]

Patten, a descendant of eighteenth-century Scotch Irish settlers in New York, was born in Illinois. Educated at Northwestern University and at the University of Halle-Wittenberg, where he received his PhD, Patten was another German-trained founder and early president of the

---

14. More biographical information on Patten prefaces his selection in Chapter 6.

American Economic Association. Along with Albion Small, as well as six of his own doctoral students, Patten was also one of the founders and presidents of the American Sociological Society. Patten followed Edmund J. James, another son of Illinois and a University of Halle-Wittenberg PhD, to the University of Pennsylvania, where they taught together in the Wharton School, the first professional business school in America to offer a curriculum that combined economics, public finance, and business studies. Together, Patten and James founded and led the American Academy of Social and Political Science and edited the Academy's journal, the Annals. *This journal became a repository for important ideas from German-trained American academics as well as leaders in business, finance, and government. Called an "economic theologian" for his highly speculative ideas about human destiny, Patten also wrote and published hymns and a didactic novel. Despite a somewhat mystical side to his economic writings, Patten's many students (called "Patten Men") included Walter Weyl of* The New Republic, *Edward Devine (general secretary of the New York Charity Organization Society), and Scott Nearing.[15] Rexford Tugwell and Frances Perkins, two of Patten's former students, made major contributions to the New Deal. Perkins became FDR's Secretary of Labor and was the first woman to hold a cabinet-level position in the Federal Government. Patten is credited with inventing and popularizing the term "social work."*

— 1907 —

There can be no permanent progress until poverty has been eliminated, for then only will the normally evolving man, dominant through numbers and keen mental powers, force adjustments, generation by generation, which will raise the general level of intellect and character. And when poverty is gone, the last formidable obstacle to the upward movement of the race will have disappeared. Our children's children may learn with amazement how we thought it a natural social phenomenon that men should die in their prime, leaving wives and children in terror of want; that [workplace] accidents should make an army of maimed dependents; that there should not be enough houses for workers; and that epidemics should sweep away multitudes as autumn frost sweeps away summer insects. They will wonder that the universal sadness of such a world should have appealed to our transient sympathies but did not absorb our widest interests. They will ask why there was some hope of succor for those whose miseries passed for a moment before the eyes of the tenderhearted, but none for the dwellers beyond the narrow horizon within which pity moves. And they will be unable to put themselves in our places, because the new social philosophy which we are this moment framing will have so moulded their minds that they cannot return to the philosophy that moulds ours.

It is for us to unite the social activities—whose motive forces are charity, religion, philanthropy, revolt, and unrest—into a philosophy that is social and not sectional, in that it gives to them all a reorganized rational body of evidence upon which to proceed. They will then understand each other while doing the work that transforms the world into a place worth living in. It was a perception that to sympathy and charitable impulse must be added knowledge and skill which founded the school of philanthropy. If the social worker would be a social philosopher and the reformer a builder as well as a destroyer, he must know how to use the matter and the spirit that make the philanthropies, the trades unions, the settlements, the institutional churches, and the theatres. Economists groping among the formulæ of deficit are surprised and overtaken by the new world, and statesmen are bewildered by the surge of the new democracy of industrial liberty against the barriers of class. But these difficulties only prove that the new civilization will be ready as soon as social work has been made a science and is practised with knowledge and ideals which make clear to the statesman who directs and the workman who produces the treasures in health and happiness and safety of the new time. . . .

The striking aspect of the recent development of thought is the changing concept concerning the part heredity plays in life. Men have been trained from the earliest times to attach great importance to the influence of blood descent upon racial and individual character. Some families and peoples are said to be inherently superior to others, because they have possessed, generation after generation, well-marked qualities which others did not have. The differences between them were readily explained by heredity, so readily, in fact, that more influence was soon given to ancestry than to the environment into which a man was born. This unequal division of power seems to be destroyed by recent discoveries in biology, which are establishing a new equilibrium between natural or inherited qualities and those acquired after birth. Many qualities are inherited, but the number is smaller than it was thought to be, and many of them may be readily suppressed by the action of the environment in which men live, so that they do not show themselves for long periods in a particular family or a given race. This curtailment of the force of physical heredity gives more power to the acquired qualities handed on from generation to generation as a social tradition. A physical inheritance, simpler than we thought, is ours at birth; but there is a larger and increasingly important social heredity which must be constantly renewed through the conscious efforts of parents and teachers.

The recognition of man's power over heredity is equalled by the perception of his power over nature as it is shown by his achievements in industry. Food is abundant, income grows, and machines do the old drudgeries. That work is pleasant, the environment is good, and human nature is a group of ennobling qualities are now axioms that contrast the new thought with the old philosophy of deficit so long taught and so ardently defended. The depraved man is not the natural man; for in him the natural is suppressed beneath a crushing load of misfortunes, superstitions, and ill-fitting social conventions. But in spite of the good hope that follows, elation is replaced by dejection as soon as we remember that poverty is scarcely mitigated by prosperity. The normal qualities of human nature are modified so slowly and under such complex conditions that the reformer often believes himself helpless to make the improvements he longs for. The biologists do not encourage him, if he looks to them for help, for they say it is a matter of ages to engraft a new characteristic upon humanity. If this indeed is true we can create neither virtues nor heroes nor genius. We can be no more than watchers of changes as slow and inevitable as the subsidences and elevations of the earth's surfaces.

Now look at the brighter side. It is, without doubt, more difficult than was once believed to lift a man with normal faculties to a higher plane of existence; but it is far easier than we have thought to raise a man below the general level of humanity up to it. There are no differences between him and his normal neighbors which cannot be rapidly obliterated. He does not lack their blood, but their health, their vigor, their good fortune, their culture, and their environment. The doctrine which teaches that evolution is the slowest of moving forces also teaches that the distinctions between men on the two sides of the line of poverty are frailer than we have been led to believe. The faculties and social qualities of human nature were implanted in it before the beginnings of history; but health, vigor, and good fortune are determined by today's environment. Poverty is not rooted in a debased heredity nor in a worldwide lack of work. The motives of the unfortunate have weakened while the inclinations of standard men to labor have remained strong enough to lead them to efficient activity. The men in whom energy is sapped, or who have been the victims of misfortune, are a class in which the normal race stimuli are failing to act. The loaf of bread, the cigar, the theatre ticket held before men as rewards to work remain inducements only until they have been consumed. Zeal wanes as they are used up, and will not steadily flow again except from a fund of surplus energy that in its exit sharpens imagination and revives the drooping faculties. Give rain and crops grow; give surplus energy and men become spontaneously efficient. Land is the slow accumulations of past ages as the faculties of men are the sum of the slow changes in heredity. Both are what the past has bequeathed, and both are useless unless vitalized by material within the present. . . .

It therefore becomes the social worker's first task to discover how faculties may be made active, how industry may be stimulated, and how men may be surrounded—rich and poor alike—with conditions that shall renew energy and after every expenditure of it bring it back greater than it went out. The measure of increase is the freshness of imagination and the keenness of motive. There is, moreover, another task of equal magnitude. The social worker must examine himself to learn whether or no his own motives and emotions are powerful enough to break the traditions that bind him. Does not he also neglect the distant good, and treat superficial symptoms of disorder? And, most futile attempt of all, does he not struggle to create new traits and to construct new social conventions when he should be striving to make men free by removing the pressure that stifles feeling and disintegrates motive? Let us have more confidence in what nature has implanted in heredity and less in what we as individuals can add to it. Our own forms of culture, our own religion, and our own system of morality seem to be the embodiment of fixed ideals which alone can lift men above the common-place level of their fellows. Therefore we are urgent in transferring this body of practice to the poor in the hope that it will affect their lives as it has ours. But have we first aroused the imagination and trained it so that these ideals will attract and hold them? Have they the energy, functioning in a proper environment, which will start them toward remote rewards that are not at the moment very desirable? The means of progress are material; its ends are ideal. We will reach the ends only when we lose sight of them in the struggle for material improvements.

The truth of this is partially seen by social workers, but they do not yet see as clearly as they should the distinction between the regeneration of the poverty class and the progress of normal men. The aim of social work is democracy rather than culture; energy rather than virtue; health rather than income; efficiency rather than goodness; and social standards for all rather than genius and opportunity for the few. It may be shocking to put these contrasts so forcefully; I do it, not to depreciate the old ideals closely associated with progress, but to make emphatic the means by which they are reached. In whatever direction progress may seem to lie, an ideal has been erected as the prize to be striven for which shines forth in our thoughts; but the means of reaching it are not also made vivid. And therefore we honor the herculean toilers who strive to cut direct roads toward the goal of the ideal. We encourage self-denial when we should encourage self-expression. We try to suppress vices when we should release virtues. We laud country life when we should strive for the improvement of cities. We judge the poor by their family history when we should judge them by their latent powers. We impose penalties when we should offer rewards. We ask for the gratitude of the poor when we ought to point out their rights to them. We dwell too long upon the weaknesses of the man who drinks and too little upon why the saloon remains at the corner. Too heavy stress is laid on the duties of parents to children and too little upon the obligations of teachers, authors, editors, and doctors, who do, in fact, exercise a stronger influence on the health and character of a city child than its parents can. We also over-estimate the power of the home to mould its members, and in consequence neglect to utilize the institutions of city life. We rely on restraint to shape the characters of boys when we should be thinking of their recreations. As the city home becomes smaller its unity is interfered with. The functions it loses are taken over by the growing town, and in their exercise is to be found the process of character making which was carried on in the older form of the isolated home. . . .

The new morality does not consist in saving, but in expanding consumption; not in draining men of their energy, but in storing up a surplus in the weak and young; not in the process of hardening, but in extending the period of recreation and leisure; not in the thought of the future, but in the utilization and expansion of the present. We lack efficiency, not capital; pleasures, not goods; keen present interests, not solemn warnings of future woes; courage to live joyous lives, not remorse, sacrifice, and renunciation. The morality of restraint comes later than the morality of activity; for men need restraint only after poverty disappears. And hence we must return with renewed emphasis to the thought that social work has to do with the means of progress and not with its ends. But the ideals of progress have become so incorporated into our thought that we instinctively place them in the foreground and neglect the activity which must open the way to them.

Progress in thought is obtained by a change from conventional standards to ideal standards. Conventions are a weight that the distant past has placed on us. Ideals project us into an equally distant future. There are ideals but no ideal activities, because the ideal is thought projected into the future while activity is in the present and must always go out toward the next thing, not toward the distant thing. Activities are either self-centred or social. We can have a selfish programme or we can have a social programme, but we cannot have an ideal programme; for programmes relate to activities and not to thought. "Hitch your wagon to a star" is a great thought well expressed, but no one can work out a programme by which it can be done. We often see well-deserving movements start out with flying banners, happy phrases, and great enthusiasm, only to find the road to the stars blocked at the first hillside. To be effective ideal constructive thought must be transferred into practical social work, and hence the need of the contrast between ideal ends and the indirect means by which they are reached. [From *The New Basis of Civilization* (Macmillan, 1907), 197–9, 204–7, 211–6]

Further Reading

Bensel, Richard Franklin, *The Political Economy of American Industrialization, 1877–1900* (Cambridge University Press, 2000).

Chandler, Alfred, *Scale and Scope: The Dynamics of Industrial Capitalism* (Harvard University Press, 1990).

Dorfman, Joseph, *The Economic Mind of American Civilization, Volume Three, 1865–1918* (Viking, 1949).

Eisenach, Eldon J., *The Lost Promise of Progressivism* (University Press of Kansas, 1994).

Fox, Daniel M., "Editor's Introduction," in Simon N. Patten, *The New Basis of Civilization* (Belknap/Harvard University Press, 1968).

Galambos, Louis, and Joseph Pratt, *The Rise of the Corporate Commonwealth: U.S. Business and Public Policy in the Twentieth Century* (Basic Books, 1988).

Glickman, Lawrence B., *A Living Wage: American Workers and the Making of Consumer Society* (Cornell University Press, 1997).

James, Scott Curtis, *Presidents, Parties, and the State: A Party System Perspective on Democratic Regulatory Choice, 1884–1936* (Cambridge University Press, 2000).

Livingston, James. *Pragmatism and the Political Economy of Cultural Revolution, 1850–1940* (University of North Carolina Press, 1994).

Lustig, R. Jeffrey, *Corporate Liberalism: The Origins of Modern American Political Theory, 1890–1920* (University of California Press, 1982).

Rodgers, Daniel T., *Atlantic Crossings: Social Politics in a Progressive Age* (Harvard University Press, 1998), Chapter 3.

Seligman, Edwin Robert Anderson, *The Economic Interpretation of History*, second edition (Columbia University Press, 1907).

Sklansky, Jeffrey, *The Soul's Economy: Market Society and Selfhood in American Thought, 1820–1920* (University of North Carolina Press, 2002).

Sklar, Martin, *The Corporate Reconstruction of American Capitalism, 1890–1916* (Cambridge University Press, 1988).

Zunz, Olivier, *Making America Corporate, 1870–1920* (University of Chicago Press, 1990).

4

Creating an Ethic of Interconnectedness
and a Democratic Public

Just as the boundaries between social economy and political economy
blurred in the selections in Chapter 3, the boundaries separating sociology, social psychology, psychology, and philosophy are permeable in
the selections collected in this chapter. John Dewey considered himself
as much a psychologist as a philosopher; his theories of pragmatism
offered a psychological account of human experience as well as a philosophical account of its methods and system of ideas. Charles Horton
Cooley, Dewey's colleague and collaborator at the University of Michigan, is considered the "father" of American academic social psychology.
Franklin Giddings, Dewey's colleague at Columbia University, wrote
sociology textbooks that incorporated elements of political economy,
sociology, and social psychology. What bound these academic specialists together—and connected them so strongly to the larger reform community—was a shared social ethic. The selections in this chapter
illustrate the ethical dimension of Progressivism as voiced by academics
from a variety of disciplines and by reform activists and publicists—the
kinds of prominent figures we might call "public intellectuals" today.

In these selections, the Progressives directly confront the relationship
between social reform and social control—a thorny issue that became
the basis of a vigorous indictment of Progressivism first launched by left-
leaning intellectuals in the 1960s and 1970s. A parallel critique of the
Progressives' take on the issue, advanced by some historians today, considered these new social sciences both potentially manipulative—especially when social knowledge was annexed to bureaucratic structures of
power—and emancipatory. These critiques tended to group the Progressives into "good" ones and "bad" ones—those deeply dedicated to extending democracy and those more concerned with their own institutional
power and professional prestige.[1] While there is little evidence that
Progressives actually divided themselves in these ways—any more than
they divided themselves into "professional" academics and "amateur"
clergy members, social workers, and activists—there was a recognizable

---

1. Dawley, *Struggles for Justice* (1991); Hansen, *Lost Promise of Patriotism*
(2003); Taylor, *Citizenship and Democratic Doubt* (2004).

tension between reform and control and between bottom-up and top-down methods of reform. These tensions, however, were more often expressed by a single writer and did not engender much debate between Progressive authors until the 1920s.

An astute student of the social-psychological dimension of Progressive thought defined social control this way: "Always an elusive concept, social control meant essentially a system of power founded upon control of human instincts, desires, and habits rather than upon ownership and rulership as they were conceived in political economy."[2]

One result of this turn to social psychology was a new stress on the critical role "public opinion" must play in shaping a better society. Progressive writers drew sharp contrasts between external and legal modes of social coordination and internal, self-generated modes of cooperation. And, as was intimated in Chapter 2, they drew a further distinction between judgments of an "authentic" public opinion and decisions reached in party-dominated elections. To them, public opinion was the product of a collective, even organic, process of interaction and communication while voting decisions only aggregated individual preferences. Mere aggregation of preferences resulted in government manipulated by party machines and special interests. As we shall see in Chapter 5, this same reliance on opinion and influence—"spirit," if you will—was also reflected in their views of law and coercion. To the Progressives, government by lawyers and courts only reinforced rule by party and the treatment of politics as a sort of amoral "game."

14. *Democratic Ethics*, John Dewey (1859–1952)[3]

John Dewey was a descendant of longtime Vermont farmers. Soon after he was born, his father, then fifty years old, sold his grocery store and enlisted in the Union Army; he remained a soldier until 1867. John Dewey began his studies at the University of Vermont and completed his PhD at Johns Hopkins University. His interests combined philosophy and psychology; indeed, he became one of the early presidents of both the American Psychological Association (1899) and the American Philosophical Association (1904). After a brief period teaching at the University of Michigan, where he collaborated with the social psychologist Charles Horton Cooley, he spent eight years at the University of Chicago; he then left for Columbia University, where he

---

2. Sklansky, *The Soul's Economy* (2002), 201.

3. More biographical information on Dewey prefaces his selection in Chapter 5.

taught for almost fifty years. Equally known for his writings in
philosophy and education, his theories in both fields are still influential
today. His co-authored book, Ethics, *was continuously published from*
1908 to 1942; his book Democracy and Education *stayed in print even*
longer, from 1916 to 1953.

— 1888 —

What gives the democracy more than other forms of government the
appearance of being a mere rule of a mass or multitude is, without
doubt, the use which it makes of individual suffrage on the one hand
and majority rule on the other. Since it thus appears to decide all questions of policy and of men by mere weighing of numbers, it is easy to
represent democracy as concerned for the most part with a problem in
arithmetic. Analytic abstraction, having perchance already deprived
men of all their qualities due to their social relations, now proceeds further to reduce them into merely numerical individuals, into ballot-
projecting units. Then the mere accident of a few bare units more or
less on this side or that, seems, by bare numerical preponderance, to
form the will of the people in this direction or that. Such is the theoretical analysis of democracy most often presented to us. Many of its
upholders have no more adequate idea of it than this, and rest for their
final support on the fact that after all the numerical majority would
have, in case of an appeal to arms, the brute force to coerce the minority. Such presentations come off very poorly when compared with the
sketch of an ideal aristocracy, where not mere stress of numbers, but
superiority in wisdom, elevation in goodness, enable the few having
these qualities to guide the mass without them. . . .

But the student of society has constantly to be on his guard against
the abstract and purely mechanical notions introduced from the physical sciences. If he will beware of such abstractions, he will remember
that men cannot be reduced for political purposes, any more than for
any other, to bare figure ones, marks to be placed in rows set over
against one another. A man when he comes to vote does not put off
from him, like a suit of old clothes, his character, his wealth, his social
influence, his devotion to political interests, and become a naked unit.
He carries with him in his voting all the influence that he should have,
and if he deserves twice as much as another man, it is safe to say that he
decides twice as many votes as that other man. Even if his character is
corrupt, and his devotion to politics is from motives of pelf, it yet
remains true that he votes, not as a mere unit, but as a representative of
the social organism. It is only because society allows him, nay, grants

him power on such grounds, that he can use it. His very corruption is the expression of society through him. A vote, in other words, is not an impersonal counting of one; it is a manifestation of some tendency of the social organism through a member of that organism.

But this only touches the matter. There still appears to be in majority rule an instrument for putting all on a dead level, and allowing numerical surplus to determine the outcome. But the heart of the matter is found not in the voting nor in the counting the votes to see where the majority lies. It is in the process by which the majority is formed. The minority are represented in the policy which they force the majority to accept in order to be a majority; the majority have the right to "rule" because their majority is not the mere sign of a surplus in numbers, but is the manifestation of the purpose of the social organism. Were this not so, every election would be followed by a civil war; there would be no need of writing concerning the weakness of popular government; it would be the only striking fact about democracy. . . .

We must now turn to the other side of the picture. The theory which makes of democratic society a mere mass, makes, on the other hand, the democratic citizen a mere minced morsel of this mass, a disorganized fragment. If, however, society be truly described as organic, the citizen is a member of the organism, and, just in proportion to the perfection of the organism, has concentrated within himself its intelligence and will. Disguise it as we may, this theory can have but one result, that of the sovereignty of the citizen. There are various theories which have served to keep this in the background, and to hide the fact that the ordinary American expression of the sovereignty of every elector is not a mere exaggerated burst of individualistic feeling, fostered through crude Fourth of July patriotism, but is the logical outcome of the organic theory of society. . . .

If then, society and the individual are really organic to each other, then the individual is society concentrated. He is not merely its image or mirror. He is the localized manifestation of its life. And if, as actually happens, society be not yet possessed of one will, but partially is one and partially has a number of fragmentary and warring wills, it yet follows that *so far* as society has a common purpose and spirit, *so far* each individual is not representative of a certain proportionate share of the sum total of will but is its vital embodiment. And this is the theory, often crudely expressed, but none the less true in substance, that every citizen is a sovereign, the American theory, a doctrine which in grandeur has but one equal in history, and that its fellow, namely, that every man is a priest of God.

In conception, at least, democracy approaches most nearly the ideal of all social organization; that in which the individual and society are organic to each other. For this reason democracy, so far as it is really democracy, is the most stable, not the most insecure, of governments. In every other form of government there are individuals who are not organs of the common will, who are outside of the political society in which they live, and are, in effect, aliens to that which should be their own commonwealth. Not participating in the formation or expression of the common will, they do not embody it in themselves. Having no share in society, society has none in them. . . .

Government does not mean one class or side of society set over against the other. The government is not made up of those who hold office, or who sit in the legislature. It consists of every member of political society. And this is true of democracy, not less, but more, than of other forms. The democratic formula that government derives its powers from the consent of the governed, like the theory of the sovereignty of the political citizen, has suffered as much at the hands of its friends as of its enemies; but its true significance is not thereby destroyed. It means that in democracy, at all events, the governors and the governed are not two classes, but two aspects of the same fact—the fact of the possession by society of a unified and articulate will. It means that government is the organ of society, and is as comprehensive as society. . . .

Democracy does not differ from aristocracy in its goal. . . . Personal responsibility, individual initiation, these are the notes of democracy. Aristocracy and democracy both imply that the actual state of society exists for the sake of realizing an end which is ethical, but aristocracy implies that this is to be done primarily by means of special institutions or organizations within society, while democracy holds that the ideal is already at work in every personality, and must be trusted to care for itself. There is an individualism in democracy which there is not in aristocracy; but it is an ethical, not a numerical individualism; it is an individualism of freedom, of responsibility, of initiative to and for the ethical ideal, not an individualism of lawlessness. In one word, democracy means that *personality* is the first and final reality. It admits that the full significance of personality can be learned by the individual only as it is already presented to him in objective form in society; it admits that the chief stimuli and encouragements to the realization of personality come from society; but it holds, none the less, to the fact that personality cannot be procured for anyone, however degraded and feeble, by anyone else, however wise and strong. It holds that the spirit of personality indwells in every individual and that the choice to develop it must proceed from that individual. From this central position of personality result the other notes of democracy, liberty, equality, fraternity,—words which are not mere words to catch the mob, but symbols of the highest ethical idea which humanity has yet reached—the idea that personality is the one thing of permanent and abiding worth, and that in every human individual there lies personality. . . .

Democracy and the one, the ultimate, ethical ideal of humanity are to my mind synonyms. The idea of democracy, the ideas of liberty, equality, and fraternity, represent a society in which the distinction between the spiritual and the secular has ceased, and as in Greek theory, as in the Christian theory of the Kingdom of God, the church and the state, the divine and the human organization of society are one. But this, you will say, is idealism. In reply, I can but quote James Russell Lowell once more and say that "it is indeed idealism, but that I am one of those who believe that the real will never find an irremovable basis till it rests upon the ideal"; and add that the best test of any form of society is the ideal which it proposes for the forms of its life, and the degree in which it realizes this ideal.

— 1908 —

Individualism has been so successful in asserting rights that it is now apt to forget that there are no rights morally except such as express the will of a good *member of society*. But in recognizing possible excesses we need not forget the value of the idea of rights as a weapon in the struggle in which the moral personality has gradually won its way. The other side of the story has been the growth of responsibility. The gain in freedom has not meant an increase in disorder; it has been marked rather by gain in peace and security, by an increasing respect for law, and an increasing stability of government. The external control of force has been replaced by the moral control of duty. . . .

The genuinely moral person is one, then, in whom the habit of regarding all capacities and habits of self from the social standpoint is formed and active. Such an one forms his plans, regulates his desires, and hence performs his acts with reference to the effect they have upon the social groups of which he is a part. He is one whose dominant attitudes and interests are bound up with associated activities. Accordingly he will find his happiness or satisfaction in the promotion of these activities irrespective of the particular pains and pleasures that accrue. . . .

We now see what is meant by a distinctively *moral* happiness, and how this happiness is supreme in quality as compared with other satisfactions, irrespective of superior intensity and duration on the part of the latter. It *is* impossible to draw any fixed line between the *content* of the moral good and of natural satisfaction. The end, the right and only right end, of man, lies in the fullest and freest realization of powers in their appropriate objects. The good consists of friendship, family and political relations, economic utilization of mechanical resources, science, art, in all their complex and variegated forms and elements. There is no separate and rival moral good; no separate empty and rival "good will.". . .

Consequently the true or final happiness of an individual, the happiness which is not at the mercy of circumstance and change of circumstance, lies not in objective achievement of results, but in the supremacy within character of an alert, sincere, and persistent interest in those habits and institutions which forward common ends among men. . . .

For all alike, in short, the chief thing is the discovery and promotion of those activities and active relationships in which the capacities of all concerned are effectively evoked, exercised, and put to the test. It is difficult for a man to attain a point of view from which steadily to apprehend how his own activities affect and modify those of others. It is hard, that is, to learn to accommodate one's ends to those of others; to adjust, to give way here, and fit in there with respect to our aims. But difficult as this is, it is easy compared with the difficulty of acting *in such a way* for ends which are helpful to others as will call out and make effective their activities. . . .

If the vice of the criminal, and of the coarsely selfish man is to disturb the aims and the good of others; if the vice of the ordinary egoist, and of every man, upon his egoistic side, is to neglect the interests of others; the vice of the social leader, of the reformer, of the philanthropist and the specialist in every worthy cause of science, or art, or politics, is to seek ends which promote the social welfare in ways which fail to engage the active interest and cooperation of others. The conception of conferring the good upon others, or at least of attaining it for them, which is our inheritance from the aristocratic civilization of the past, is so deeply embodied in religious, political, and charitable institutions and in moral teachings, that it dies hard. Many a man, feeling himself justified by the social character of his ultimate aim (it may be economic, or educational, or political), is genuinely confused or exasperated by the increasing antagonism and resentment which he evokes, because he has not enlisted in his pursuit of the "common" end the freely cooperative activities of others. This cooperation must be the root principle of the morals of democracy. . . .

But in truth a common end which is not made such by common, free voluntary cooperation in process of achievement is common in name only. It has no support and guarantee in the activities which it is supposed to benefit, because it is not the fruit of those activities. Hence, it does not stay put. It has to be continually buttressed by appeal to external, not voluntary, considerations; bribes of pleasure, threats of harm, use of force. It has to be undone and done over. There is no way to escape or evade this law of happiness, that it resides in the exercise of the active capacities of a voluntary agent; and hence no way to escape or evade the law of a common happiness, that it must reside in the congruous exercise of the voluntary activities of all concerned. The inherent irony and tragedy of much that passes for a high kind of socialized activity is precisely that it seeks a common good by methods which forbid its being either common or a good. . . .

The evolution of democratically regulated States, as distinct from those ordered in the interests of a small group, or of a special class, is the social counterpart of the development of a comprehensive and common good. Externally viewed, democracy is a piece of machinery, to be maintained or thrown away, like any other piece of machinery, on the basis of its economy and efficiency of working. Morally, it is the effective embodiment of the moral ideal of a good which consists in the development of all the social capacities of every individual member of society. [John Dewey, "The Ethics of Democracy," *Philosophical Papers*, Second Series, No. 1 (University of Michigan, 1888): 8–12, 14–5, 21–3, 28; and John Dewey (with James Tufts), *Ethics* (Henry Holt, 1908), 153, 298, 300–1, 303–4, 474]

15. *The Subjective Necessity of Social Settlements,* Jane Addams (1860–1935)[4]

Jane Addams was revered as a religious figure in America for her philanthropic endeavors, symbolized by Hull House, and her strong ethical commitments. Her book Democracy and Social Ethics *made the powerful case that social ethics—which Addams also termed "righteousness"—must hold primacy over individual ethics in the emerging historical era. This argument was, in part, an analysis of an emerging "spirit" that was manifested in the felt calling to social service on the part of morally serious and well-educated young men and women, most prominently Addams herself. Like her essay "The Objective Value of a Social Settlement," the following selection links Progressive social economy to Progressive social psychology. "Subjective Necessity" was first published in a collection of papers, edited by the*

---

4. More biographical information on Addams prefaces her selections in Chapters 1 and 8.

economist Henry Carter Adams (see Chapter 5), delivered at a
conference by five American and English reformers in 1892. Anthony
Giddings, whose selection immediately follows Addams', was one of the
participants in the conference. By the early 1890s, publishing
companies like Thomas Y. Crowell and Macmillan saw a lucrative
market in reform publications. For example, Henry Carter Adams'
collection was one of twenty-one books already published as part of the
"Library of Economics and Politics" series that included volumes on
Hull House and on issues such as socialism and social reform, criminal
punishments, proportional representation, railroad regulation,
municipal ownership, and workers' insurance.

— 1893 —

This paper is an attempt to treat of the subjective necessity for Social
Settlements, to analyze the motives which underlie a movement based
not only upon conviction, but genuine emotion. Hull House of
Chicago is used as an illustration, but so far as the analysis is faithful, it
obtains wherever educated young people are seeking an outlet for that
sentiment of universal brotherhood which the best spirit of our times is
forcing from an emotion into a motive.

I have divided the motives which constitute the subjective pressure
toward Social Settlements into three great lines: the first contains the
desire to make the entire social organism democratic, to extend democracy beyond its political expression; the second is the impulse to share
the race life, and to bring as much as possible of social energy and the
accumulation of civilization to those portions of the race which have little; the third springs from a certain *renaissance* of Christianity, a movement toward its early humanitarian aspects. . . .

It is constantly said that because the masses have never had social
advantages they do not want them, that they are heavy and dull, and that
it will take political or philanthropic machinery to change them. This
divides a city into rich and poor; into the favored, who express their sense
of the social obligation by gifts of money, and into the unfavored who
express it by clamoring for a "share"—both of them actuated by a vague
sense of justice. This division of the city would be more justifiable, however, if the people who thus isolate themselves on certain streets and use
their social ability for each other gained enough thereby and added sufficient to the sum total of social progress to justify the withholding of the
pleasures and results of that progress from so many people who ought to
have them. But they can not accomplish this. "The social spirit discharges
itself in many forms, and no one form is adequate to its total expression."

We are all uncomfortable in regard to the sincerity of our best phrases, because we hesitate to translate our philosophy into the deed.

It is inevitable that those who feel most keenly this insincerity and partial living should be our young people, our so-called educated young people who accomplish little toward the solution of this social problem, and who bear the brunt of being cultivated into unnourished, over-sensitive lives. They have been shut off from the common labor by which they live and which is a great source of moral and physical health. They feel a fatal want of harmony between their theory and their lives, a lack of co-ordination between thought and action. I think it is hard for us to realize how seriously many of them are taking to the notion of human brotherhood, how eagerly they long to give tangible expression to the democratic ideal. These young men and women, longing to socialize their democracy, are animated by certain hopes.

These hopes may be loosely formulated thus: that if in a democratic country nothing can be permanently achieved save through the masses of the people, it will be impossible to establish a higher political life than the people themselves crave; that it is difficult to see how the notion of a higher civic life can be fostered save through common intercourse; that the blessings which we associate with a life of refinement and cultivation can be made universal and must be made universal if they are to be permanent; that the good we secure for ourselves is precarious and uncertain, is floating in mid-air, until it is secured for all of us and incorporated into our common life. . . .

I find it somewhat difficult to formulate the second line of motives which I believe to constitute the trend of the subjective pressure toward the Settlement. There is something primordial about these motives, but I am perhaps over-bold in designating them as a great desire to share the race life. We all bear traces of the starvation struggle which for so long made up the life of the race. Our very organism holds memories and glimpses of that long life of our ancestors which still goes on among so many of our contemporaries. Nothing so deadens the sympathies and shrivels the power of enjoyment as the persistent keeping away from the great opportunities for helpfulness and a continual ignoring of the starvation struggle which makes up the life of at least half the race. To shut one's self away from that half of the race life is to shut one's self away from the most vital part of it; it is to live out but half the humanity which we have been born heir to and to use but half our faculties. We have all had longings for a fuller life which should include the use of these faculties. These longings are the physical complement of the "Intimations of Immortality" on which no ode has yet been written. To portray these would be the work of a poet, and it is hazardous for any but a poet to attempt it.

You may remember the forlorn feeling which occasionally seizes you when you arrive early in the morning a stranger in a great city. The stream of laboring people goes past you as you gaze through the plate-glass window of your hotel. You see hard-working men lifting great burdens; you hear the driving and jostling of huge carts. Your heart sinks with a sudden sense of futility. The door opens behind you and you turn to the man who brings you in your breakfast with a quick sense of human fellowship. You find yourself praying that you may never lose your hold on it all. A more poetic prayer would be that the great mother breasts of our common humanity, with its labor and suffering and its homely comforts, may never be withheld from you. You turn helplessly to the waiter. You feel that it would be almost grotesque to claim from him the sympathy you crave. Civilization has placed you far apart, but you resent your position with a sudden sense of snobbery. Literature is full of portrayals of these glimpses. They come to shipwrecked men on rafts; they overcome the differences of an incongruous multitude when in the presence of a great danger or when moved by a common enthusiasm. They are not, however, confined to such moments, and if we were in the habit of telling them to each other, the recital would be as long as the tales of children are, when they sit down on the green grass and confide to each other how many times they have remembered that they lived once before. If these tales are the stirring of inherited impressions, just so surely is the other the striving of inherited powers. . . .

We have in America a fast-growing number of cultivated young people who have no recognized outlet for their active faculties. They hear constantly of the great social mal-adjustment, but no way is provided for them to change it, and their uselessness hangs about them heavily. Huxley[5] declares that the sense of uselessness is the severest shock which the human system can sustain, and that, if persistently sustained, it results in atrophy of function. These young people have had advantages of college, of European travel and economic study, but they are sustaining this shock of inaction. They have pet phrases, and they tell you that the things that make us all alike are stronger than the things that make us different. They say that all men are united by needs and sympathies far more permanent and radical than anything that temporarily divides them and sets them in opposition to each other. If they affect art, they say that the decay in artistic expression is due to the decay in ethics, that art when shut away from the human interests and from the great mass of humanity is self-destructive.

---

5. Thomas Henry Huxley (1825–1895) was an English evolutionary biologist and essayist who speculated widely on society, philosophy, and religion.

They tell their elders with all the bitterness of youth that if they expect success from them in business, or politics, or in whatever lines their ambition for them has run, they must let them consult all of humanity; that they must let them find out what the people want and how they want it. It is only the stronger young people, however, who formulate this. Many of them dissipate their energies in so-called enjoyment. Others, not content with that, go on studying and go back to college for their second degrees, not that they are especially fond of study, but because they want something definite to do, and their powers have been trained in the direction of mental accumulation. Many are buried beneath mere mental accumulation with lowered vitality and discontent. Walter Besant[6] says they have had the vision that Peter had when he saw the great sheet let down from heaven, wherein was neither clean nor unclean. He calls it the sense of humanity. It is not philanthropy nor benevolence. It is a thing fuller and wider than either of these. This young life, so sincere in its emotion and good phrases and yet so undirected, seems to me as pitiful as the other great mass of destitute lives. One is supplementary to the other, and some method of communication can surely be devised. Mr. Barnett, who urged the first Settlement,—Toynbee Hall, in East London,—recognized this need of outlet for the young men of Oxford and Cambridge, and hoped that the Settlement would supply the communication. It is easy to see why the Settlement movement originated in England, where the years of education are more constrained and definite than they are here, where class distinctions are more rigid. The necessity of it was greater there, but we are fast feeling the pressure of the need and meeting the necessity for, Settlements in America. Our young people feel nervously the need of putting theory into action, and respond quickly to the Settlement form of activity.

The third division of motives which I believe make toward the Settlement is the result of a certain *renaissance* going forward in Christianity. The impulse to share the lives of the poor, the desire to make social service, irrespective of propaganda, express the spirit of Christ, is as old as Christianity itself. We have no proof from the records themselves that the early Roman Christians, who strained their simple art to the point of grotesqueness in their eagerness to record a "good news" on the walls of the catacombs, considered this "good news" a religion. Jesus had no set of truths labelled "Religious." On the contrary, his doctrine was that

---

6. Sir Walter Besant (1836–1901), an Englishman, was a prolific novelist, reformer, and surveyor of life in London. William T. Stead quotes him in his selection in Chapter 10.

all truth is one, that the appropriation of it is freedom. His teaching had no dogma to mark it off from truth and action in general. He himself called it a revelation—a life. These early Roman Christians received the Gospel message, a command to love all men, with a certain joyous simplicity. The image of the Good Shepherd is blithe and gay beyond the gentlest shepherd of Greek mythology; the hart no longer pants, but rushes to the water brooks. The Christians looked for the continuous revelation, but believed what Jesus said, that this revelation to be held and made manifest must be put into terms of action; that action is the only medium man has for receiving and appropriating truth. "If any man will do His will, he shall know of the doctrine.". . .

I believe that there is a distinct turning among many young men and women toward this simple acceptance of Christ's message. They resent the assumption that Christianity is a set of ideas which belong to the religious consciousness, whatever that may be, that it is a thing to be proclaimed and instituted apart from the social life of the community. They insist that it shall seek a simple and natural expression in the social organism itself. The Settlement movement is only one manifestation of that wider humanitarian movement which throughout Christendom, but pre-eminently in England, is endeavoring to embody itself, not in a sect, but in society itself. . . .

I cannot, of course, speak for other Settlements, but it would, I think, be unfair to Hull House not to emphasize the conviction with which the first residents went there, that it would simply be a foolish and an unwarrantable expenditure of force to oppose or to antagonize any individual or set of people in the neighborhood; that whatever of good the House had to offer should be put into positive terms; that its residents should live with opposition to no man, with recognition of the good in every man, even the meanest. I believe that this turning, this *renaissance* of the early Christian humanitarianism, is going on in America, in Chicago, if you please, without leaders who write or philosophize, without much speaking, but with a bent to express in social service, in terms of action, the spirit of Christ. Certain it is that spiritual force is found in the Settlement movement, and it is also true that this force must be evoked and must be called into play before the success of any Settlement is assured. There must be the over-mastering belief that all that is noblest in life is common to men as men, in order to accentuate the likenesses and ignore the differences which are found among the people whom the Settlement constantly brings into juxtaposition. . . .

The Settlement, then, is an experimental effort to aid in the solution of the social and industrial problems which are engendered by the modern conditions of life in a great city. It insists that these problems are not confined to any one portion of a city. It is an attempt to relieve, at the same time, the over-accumulation at one end of society and the destitution at the other; but it assumes that this over-accumulation and destitution is most sorely felt in the things that pertain to social and educational advantage. . . .

[The Settlement] must be grounded in a philosophy whose foundation is on the solidarity of the human race, a philosophy which will not waver when the race happens to be represented by a drunken woman or an idiot boy. Its residents must be emptied of all conceit of opinion and all self-assertion, and ready to arouse and interpret the public opinion of their neighborhood. They must be content to live quietly side by side with their neighbors until they grow into a sense of relationship and mutual interests. Their neighbors are held apart by differences of race and language which the residents can more easily overcome. They are bound to see the needs of their neighborhood as a whole, to furnish data for legislation, and use their influence to secure it. In short, residents are pledged to devote themselves to the duties of good citizenship and to the arousing of the social energies which too largely lie dormant in every neighborhood given over to industrialism. They are bound to regard the entire life of their city as organic, to make an effort to unify it, and to protest against its over-differentiation. . . .

The Settlement movement is from its nature a provisional one. It is easy in writing a paper to make all philosophy point one particular moral and all history adorn one particular tale; but I hope you forgive me for reminding you that the best speculative philosophy sets forth the solidarity of the human race; that the highest moralists have taught that without the advance and improvement of the whole no man can hope for any lasting improvement in his own moral or material individual condition. The subjective necessity for Social Settlements is identical with that necessity which urges us on toward social and individual salvation. [Jane Addams, "The Subjective Necessity of Social Settlements," in Henry Carter Adams, ed., *Philanthropy and Social Progress* (Thomas Y. Crowell, 1893), 2, 5–7, 10–2, 15–23, 26]

16. *Democracy and Social Organization,* Franklin Giddings (1855–1931)

Giddings, a descendant of seventeenth-century English settlers, was the son of a Congregational minister in Connecticut. After receiving his bachelor's and master's degrees from Union College in New York, and following a brief stint as a reforming journalist, Giddings was invited to

join the newly formed department of sociology at Columbia University.
He remained at Columbia for the rest of his career. He edited the
journals of both the American Economic Association and the American
Academy of Political and Social Science and went on to help found,
and then lead, the American Sociological Society. Since Giddings was
best known for his coining of the term "consciousness of kind" to denote
the increasingly powerful role of shared consciousness—or deep
structures of "public opinion"—in modern society, his writings
encompassed elements of economics, sociology, and psychology. Simon
Patten dedicated his Theory of Prosperity *to Giddings; Giddings, in*
turn, thanked Patten for his help with his Principles of Sociology—*an*
early indication of the ways in which Progressive academics created
networks of influence. Principles of Sociology, *which charted these*
interdisciplinary connections, remained in print for thirty years. Richard
Ely enlists "consciousness of kind" in The Evolution of Industrial
Society, *selections from which appear in Chapter 3.*

—1898—

The Rational Origin of Public Opinion. No error is more common
than one which confounds popular beliefs with the social judgments
that constitute true public opinion. Public belief . . . is essentially emotional; while judgments are a product of critical thinking, and are essentially rational in character. Where two or more individuals, each of
whom is capable of subjecting his ideas and inherited beliefs to a critical examination, come to the same conclusion, so that their critically
tested judgments are identical, the result is a rational like-mindedness,
and is properly to be spoken of as public opinion. Another way of stating the same truth is to say that public opinion comes into existence
only when a sympathetic like-mindedness or an agreement in belief is
subjected to criticism, started by some sceptical individual who doubts
the truth of the belief or the wisdom of the agreement; and an opinion
is then thought out to which many communicating minds can yield
their rational assent.

It is obvious that not all members of a community are equally competent to share in the creation of the critical judgments that constitute
true public opinion. Yet, nearly every individual of ordinary intelligence
may share in it to some extent. All that is necessary is that his beliefs
should be assailed by doubt, and that, after passing through the experience of questioning and uncertainty, he should arrive at judgments for
which he can give reasons rather than at convictions which he merely
feels. . . .

Public opinion, then, develops in any community just to the extent that free discussion develops, just to the extent that men are in the habit of asking searching questions and compelling one another to prove their assertions.

Public opinion, therefore, can exist only where men are in continual communication, and where they are free to express their real minds, without fear or restraint. Wherever men are forbidden by governmental or other authority to assemble, to hold meetings, to speak or write freely, or wherever they stand in fear of losing social position, or employment, or property, if they freely speak their minds, there is no true public opinion; there is only a mass of traditional beliefs or outbursts of popular feeling. . . .

Social Values. Belief and tradition are products of intellectual activity in combination with emotion. Public opinion is almost wholly an intellectual product. The combinations of public opinion with tradition . . . are largely intellectual in character, though not altogether so. All these products become further complicated by the combination with them of the ever-changing moods of desire. In these combinations, and certain resulting products now to be described, we have the final and most complex integration of the elements and products of the social mind. . . .

From this fact it follows that the first category of objects of social value, comprises these; namely, the companion or socius, companionship or association, like-mindedness, and that state of mind which has been called the consciousness of kind. These are the objects for which society exists. They directly yield the supreme satisfaction of the social relation. All other social products, all forms of social organization, are secondary objects of social value, because they are merely means to the attainment of ulterior ends. . . .

Laws of Social Choice. Social values are the grounds of rational social choice, and of all action of the social will that is deliberate rather than impulsive.

There have been writers on sociology who have denied that masses of men ever act rationally. They have argued that as men differ less in feeling than in intelligence, and as men in crowds are peculiarly susceptible to emotion and suggestion, the intellectual processes have, under such circumstances, very little opportunity to manifest themselves.

Nevertheless, there is abundant historical proof that communities do oftentimes arrive at rational decisions, after many years of persistent discussion of the merits of the question. Among excellent examples have been most of the amendments to the Constitution of the United States, and to the constitutions of the several commonwealths. . . .

When the conditions favourable to rational social choice exist, the choice itself is determined by the scale of social values, just as individual choices are determined by the scale of ethical and economic values in individual minds. . . .

In all social choice, the most influential ideal is that of personal force or of virtue in the original sense; the second in influence is the hedonistic or utilitarian ideal, namely, the ideal of pleasure; the third is self-conservation, or the Puritan ideal; the least influential is the ideal of self-realization or self-development. But if mental evolution continues, the higher ideals become increasingly influential. . . .

To make this clear, it is necessary to begin with an explanation of a simple case.

In choosing our pleasures, we have to modify some indulgences so that they will combine well with others; or, failing to do that, we have to sacrifice some pleasures altogether. As a rule, many moderate pleasures that combine well will make up a larger total of satisfaction than a few pleasures, each of which is intense. Therefore, it is necessary to correct each subjective value as individually considered, by reference to its probable relation to other values. . . .

As soon as the individual has acquired the intellectual power to make such corrections, he attempts to bring his subjective values into a consistent whole; but the composition of the whole, and his success in making it harmonious throughout, depend very much upon his own experiences. If his experiences have been of few kinds, and each has often been repeated, his consciousness has become identified with a total of subjective values that is thoroughly consistent as far as it goes, but that is very simple in its make-up. His few pleasures are relatively intense, and he pursues each further than he would if they were varied.

Suppose, now, that some new element or new mode of good is introduced into his life — a new pleasure, more intense than any that he has hitherto enjoyed; or that suddenly he sees opened to him possibilities of many new modes of good which, however, are more or less incompatible with those to which he has been accustomed. His group of subjective values becomes at once larger and more complex than it was before, but also less organized. A long time will elapse before the readjustment is made. It will involve many sacrifices and self-denials. Meanwhile, the chances are that he will choose crudely and radically. He will substitute oftener than he will combine. He will destroy when he might conserve. He will go wholly over to the new way of life, enjoying as before a few modes of experience intensely, instead of learning that he might get a greater total of satisfaction from a large number of less intense experiences harmoniously put together.

Let these principles now be applied to a population. It is usual to speak of the elements, modes, and means of good collectively as interests. A population map of a country may be made, showing the distribution of the people according to their interests. In one region is discovered a marked predominance of those who have lived for generations in a circumscribed way—the people of narrow experiences and of few interests. In another region are discovered large numbers of those who have suddenly found themselves face to face with possibilities of which they had not dreamed. Elsewhere are discovered those who have so long enjoyed varied experiences and have cultivated manifold interests that their subjective values make up totals that are highly complex and yet, at the same time, harmonious.

The people of these different regions in their industry, their law-making, their educational and religious undertakings, and their organization of institutions, choose, select, or decide, strictly in accordance with the mental characteristics that these different experiences have developed.

The law of combination and of means which their choices exemplify is as follows:

A population that has only a few interests, which, however, are harmoniously combined, is conservative in its choices. A population that has varied interests, which are as yet inharmoniously combined, is radical in its choices. Only the population that has many, varied, and harmoniously combined interests is consistently progressive in its choices. . . .

Democracy. Democracy is more than a form of government; and those who see in it nothing else have hardly made a beginning towards understanding it. Scientifically, democracy is a form of government, or a form of the state, or a form of society, or a combination of all three.

As a form of government, democracy is the actual administration of political affairs through universal suffrage. Completely carried out, democracy as a form of government would be the actual decision of every question of legal and executive detail, no less than of every question of right and policy, by a direct popular vote. Something closely approaching this has been accomplished in the New England town meeting and in some of the cantonal governments of Switzerland. There has never been any such thing, however, as a strictly democratic form of government on a large scale.

Democracy as a form of the state is popular sovereignty. It is a popular distribution of formal political power. It is the right of the masses of the people to participate in the creation of the government or machinery of administration. It may act through representative institutions as well as directly.

Democracy as a form of society is, in the first place, a democratic organization and control of the non-political forms of association. In a perfectly democratic society, not only must the state be democratic, but the church, the industrial organization, and the educational organization likewise must be democratic. Democracy as a form of society is, in the second place, a distribution among the entire people of that indefinite, unformed, but actual political power which lies back of the formal power that registers its decisions through the act of voting. . . . The state is democratic when all its people, without distinction of birth, class, or rank, participate in the making of legal authority. Society is democratic only when all people without distinction of rank or class participate in the making of public opinion and of moral authority.

Character of Democracy. — When these distinctions are perceived, it is easily understood that the state may be democratic while society is yet aristocratic or oligarchic. Universal suffrage may give to every adult male member of the community the right to vote; and yet, in all except political relations, a majority of the voters may be living under a system of social organization that is essentially aristocratic or even monarchical. In their industrial relations, and in their schools and churches, voters may have practically no voice whatever in determining organization or policy. Moreover, although voting in the political organization, they may be contributing nothing whatever to public opinion or moral authority, because their intellectual development is too slight to enable them to take an independent attitude on any question, or to add anything to the sum total of new thought.

While, therefore, it is conceivable that ignorant masses, when given the right to vote, may actually attempt in their voting to give expression to their own ignorant notions, there is evidently no necessity for thinking that a general election registers a really popular judgment. It is quite as likely that tradition, custom, imitation, industrial conditions, indefinite modes of economic and social pressure, may conspire to make a popular election nothing more than an endorsement of the policy of a few individuals.

Therefore, whether democracy is the rule of ignorance or not, is a question that depends upon the sort of leadership to which the majority of all voters in any commonwealth yield their allegiance. For unless society is no less democratic than the state,—a condition of things that can exist only when all socii are educated, thoughtful men,—the majority do not independently rule at all, but merely endorse the policy of their leaders. . . .

The Success or Failure of the democratic experiment . . . therefore turns upon this relation of the many who imitate, accept guidance, and yield allegiance, to the comparatively few who invent, who think independently, who have the gift of leadership, and the ability to organize their fellow-men. This relationship, which has always existed in human society, must, unless humanity in the future becomes totally unlike the humanity of the past and of today, continue to be one of the fundamental facts of the social system. In other words, we shall never get rid of that natural aristocracy which is made up of the talented, the wise, the unselfish and generous, who have the ability and the wish to plan, to organize, and to lead. If we are wise we shall never wish to get rid of it. The only aristocracy that the people should wish to destroy is that which is constituted by artificial distinctions, by inherited titles, and inherited privileges. No community can make a more fatal mistake than that of confounding natural with artificial superiority. Democracy is fatal to the latter. Without the former, democracy itself cannot hope long to exist. . . .

The Safe-guarding of Democracy. Let us not suppose, however, that these dangers . . . are so serious as to destroy our faith in the permanence of civilization or of popular government. Intelligent and brave men are not dismayed by danger. The good citizen sees in the perils that threaten society only an occasion for more active effort, more earnest thought, and more unselfish devotion to duty. . . . That influence is a growing ethical spirit, and the formation of the highest mode of like mindedness, namely, the ethical.

The Ethical Spirit. — The limitations and reactions of progress arrest public attention. Sympathy for the unfortunate is quickened by the spectacle of misery in the midst of splendour; and the conscience of society begins to demand that systematic efforts shall be made to mitigate suffering and thus to minimize the dangers that threaten the community. Private philanthropy vies with legislation in attempts to diminish poverty and crime, and ultimately in attempts to improve the general life conditions of the masses. Much of this endeavour is sentimental; and not a little of it is mischievous. Gradually, however, intelligence is enlisted. In a measure, philanthropic passion is brought under the direction of reason and made more efficient for good. The social mind undergoes a profound moral experience. It begins to develop an ethical character. It is this awakening of the moral reason which prevents any serious undoing of the work of social evolution. It is the rational-ethical consciousness that maintains social cohesion in a progressive democracy. . . .

The Real Demands of Democracy. What, then, are the real and legitimate demands of the many? What are the satisfactions that must continually be thought about, devised, and secured by the intelligence and unselfish activity of the few?

They are demands for the satisfaction of certain fundamental needs, in respect of which all men are born equal.

In recent years there has been among the educated a tendency to scoff at this famous phrase from eighteenth century thought and the American Declaration of Independence. In many respects men are so obviously unequal—in physical strength, in intelligence, in moral qualities—that when all allowances and modifications have been made, it has seemed that very little meaning has remained in the assertion that men are born equal.

If, however, we look a little more deeply into the matter, we discover that, after all, there is still in these words a meaning which it behooves us to understand and to respect.

Wherein All Men are Equal. — All men are born substantially equal, and throughout life remain substantially equal in respect of all the following needs:

1. The need of such material necessaries of existence as food, clothing, and shelter. The amount needed and even the quality needed differ with different individuals; but the poorest and the weakest, equally with the richest and the strongest, experience the fundamental need for all these things.

2. The need of satisfaction of the family instinct; the need of affection, of the love of husband and wife, of parent and child. There are, of course, individuals who seem devoid of this need; but in most cases the appearance is not the reality, and where it is, it is pathological.

3. The need of opportunity for expansion and development of life. The desire to satisfy not merely one appetite of the body or craving of the mind, but by activity to satisfy every organ, and by free play every faculty, is the fundamental ethical motive—the source of all that we call conscience, of all aspiration for enlargement and growth. This need is common to all mankind.

4. The need of human sympathy and companionship, especially in suffering. After having shown so fully that the love of companionship is the fundamental passion of society, we need not stop here to prove that

it is a fundamental human need. Perhaps nothing that Abraham Lincoln ever said so clearly revealed the trait that endeared him to the American people, and at the same time so perfectly demonstrated his wonderful insight into the nature of popular government, as his remark, in defence of the doctrine that all men are born equal, that whatever disparity of fortune or of ability may exist among human beings, all are substantially equal in their capacity for suffering, and in the certainty that during the years of their earthly life they will be obliged to encounter and endure it. In this equality of capacity for suffering, Lincoln saw one of the strongest bonds that unite a democratic people.

5. The need of emancipation from fear. Primitive men have found alleviation in their crude religious beliefs and in their rude forms of social organization. Civilized men have found it in more elaborate and efficient forms of social organization, in nobler forms of religion, in philosophy, and in science. Indeed, so effective in our own day have been these means of relief that many of us now fail to realize how terribly fear has oppressed mankind in the past, and how absolutely equal men are in their deep need of emancipation from its bondage.

In all these needs, men are substantially equal. Throughout time, men will insist that wants like these shall be appeased; and they will not tolerate any form of social organization or of government that fails to meet this fundamental demand.

As a matter of historical fact, the popular insistence upon this truth is, and has ever been, the very essence of the democratic movement; for, in truth, democracy has been far more an insistence that, government shall be *for* the people who are governed, than that it shall be *by* the people. Insistence that it shall be by the people has been in order that it might more certainly be for the people.

Accordingly, the social system that is thought about, perfected, maintained, and administered by those who have the ability to plan and to lead, must be one that meets these fundamental demands of democracy. Any system of laws that endangers material subsistence, that diminishes comfort, that makes the struggle for life an increasingly hard one for the masses, that attacks the essential features of family life, that seems to curtail the opportunity for mental and moral expansion, that weakens the bonds of sympathy, or that attacks the social organization and the knowledge that emancipate men from the curse of fear, will be resisted by the masses of the people, and ultimately will be overthrown. . . .

Necessary Modes of Equality. — Some of the modes of equality upon which fraternity and liberty depend, and which therefore must be sedulously maintained in a democratic community are the following:

1. Political equality; universal and equal suffrage.

2. Equality before the law; neither wealth, nor privilege, nor vice, nor ignorance to control legislation or to receive consideration in the courts.

3. Equality of opportunity to serve the public according to the measure of ability; men of equal ability to have absolutely equal chances of appointment to office under impartial civil service rules, irrespective of party service or allegiance.

4. Equality of rights in public places and in public conveyances.

5. Equality of sanitary conditions; all streets to be equally cleaned and cared for, tenement houses to be made decent and wholesome.

6. Equality of opportunity to enjoy certain means of recreation and culture; in public parks, libraries, museums, and galleries of art.

7. Equality of elementary educational opportunities through a well-administered public school system.

8. Equality of fair play; especially in all bargaining, between employer and employé, and in the relations of workingmen to one another.

9. Equality of courtesy; rich and poor to be treated with equal politeness.

10. Equality of good will to all men.

Other modes of equality that, in addition to the above, are essential to fraternity, are those which assure the supremacy of rational over impulsive social action. They are, namely:

1. Equality of regard for certain fundamental social values, especially (*a*) respect for law, (*b*) respect for expert knowledge.

2. Equality of sobriety and calmness of judgment, and of common sense.

These modes of equality can be approximately established by the perfection of an efficient system of public school education, but not by any other means.

Finally, there must be maintained also that mode of equality on which progress depends; namely, equality of opportunity for potential inventiveness, greatness, and leadership to become actual.

Democracy is Ethical Like-Mindedness. Appreciation of these truths by the community and a practical application of them involve both intellectual agreement and a unity of purpose which, while containing elements of sympathy, contain also the judgments born of rational criticism of the social problem. Such unity is a mode of like-mindedness in which reason and conscience predominate.

Democracy, then, in terms of sociological theory, is the outworking or expression of ethical like-mindedness. [Franklin Giddings, *Elements of Sociology* (Macmillan, 1898), 155–7, 159–61, 167–71, 314–7, 320–1, 324–9]

17. *The Democratic Mind,* Charles Horton Cooley (1864–1929)

By now, readers should not be surprised to learn that Cooley, the founder of the field of social psychology in America, was also a professor of economics and sociology. Cooley studied at the University of Michigan and then at the University of Munich, returning to complete his PhD at Michigan, where he remained as a professor. He was strongly influenced by John Dewey; as a graduate student, Cooley enrolled in many of Dewey's courses and later married one of Dewey's former undergraduate psychology students. Unlike most Progressive authors, he had a relatively well-known father, Thomas McIntyre Cooley (1824–1898), who was the founding dean of the University of Michigan's law school and the first chair of the Interstate Commerce Commission. Charles Cooley always maintained a close relationship with Dewey and, like so many other writers included in this collection, was a founding member and president of the American Sociological Society. His groundbreaking textbook in sociology, Social Organization: A Study of the Larger Mind *(1909), stayed in print for twenty years.*

— 1909 —

The present epoch . . . brings with it a larger and, potentially at least, a higher and freer consciousness. In the individual aspect of life this means that each one of us has, as a rule, a wider grasp of situations, and is thus in a position to give a wider application to his intelligence, sympathy and conscience. In proportion as he does this he ceases to be a blind agent and becomes a rational member of the whole. . . .

The new conditions demand also a thorough, yet diversified and adaptable, system of training for the individual who is to share in this freer and more exigent society. While democracy as a spirit is spontaneous, only the fullest development of personal faculty can make this spirit effectual on a great scale. Our confidence in our instincts need not be shaken, but our application of them must be enlarged and enlightened. We must be taught to do some one thing well, and yet never allowed to lose our sense of the relation of that one thing to the general endeavor.

The general or public phase of larger consciousness is what we call Democracy. I mean by this primarily the organized sway of public opinion. It works out also in a tendency to humanize the collective life, to make institutions express the higher impulses of human nature, instead of brutal or mechanical conditions. That which most inwardly distinguishes modern life from ancient or mediæval is the conscious power of the common people trying to effectuate their instincts. All systems rest, in a sense, upon public opinion; but the peculiarity of our time is that this opinion is more and more rational and self-determining. It is not, as in the past, a mere reflection of conditions believed to be inevitable, but seeks principles, finds these principles in human nature, and is determined to conform life to them or know why not. In this all earnest people, in their diverse ways, are taking part. . . .

May we not say, speaking largely, that there has always been a democratic tendency, whose advance has been conditioned by the possibility, under actual conditions, of organizing popular thought and will on a wide scale? Free cooperation is natural and human; it takes place spontaneously among children on the playground, among settlers in new countries, and among the most primitive sorts of men—everywhere, in short, where the secondary and artificial discipline has not supplanted it. The latter, including every sort of coercive or mechanical control is, of course, natural in the larger sense, and functional in human development; but there must ever be some resistance to it, which will tend to become effective when the control ceases to be maintained by the pressure of expediency. Accordingly we see that throughout modern history, and especially during the past century, there has been a progressive humanism, a striving to clear away lower forms of cooperation no longer essential, and to substitute something congenial to natural impulse. . . .

Public opinion is no mere aggregate of separate individual judgments, but an organization, a cooperative product of communication and reciprocal influence. It may be as different from the sum of what the individuals could have thought out in separation as a ship built by a hundred men is from a hundred boats each built by one man.

A group "makes up its mind" in very much the same manner that the individual makes up his. The latter must give time and attention to the question, search his consciousness for pertinent ideas and sentiments, and work them together into a whole, before he knows what his real thought about it is. In the case of a nation the same thing must take place, only on a larger scale. Each individual must make up his mind as before, but in doing so he has to deal not only with what was already in his thought or memory, but with fresh ideas that flow in from others whose minds are also aroused. Every one who has any fact, or thought, or feeling, which he thinks is unknown, or insufficiently regarded, tries to impart it; and thus not only one mind but all minds are searched for pertinent material, which is poured into the general stream of thought for each one to use as he can. In this manner the minds in a communicating group become a single organic whole. Their unity is not one of identity, but of life and action, a crystallization of diverse but related ideas.

It is not at all necessary that there should be agreement; the essential thing is a certain ripeness and stability of thought resulting from attention and discussion. There may be quite as much difference of opinion as there was before, but the differences now existing are comparatively intelligent and lasting. People know what they really think about the matter, and what other people think. Measures, platforms, candidates, creeds and other symbols have been produced which serve to express and assist cooperation and to define opposition. There has come to be a relatively complete organization of thought, to which each individual or group contributes in its own peculiar way.

Take, for instance, the state of opinion in the United States regarding slavery at the outbreak of the Civil War. No general agreement had been reached; but the popular mind had become organized with reference to the matter, which had been turned over and regarded from all points of view, by all parts of the community, until a certain ripeness regarding it had been reached; revealing in this case a radical conflict of thought between the North and the South, and much local diversity in both sections. . . .

It is not unreasonable, then, to combine a very slight regard for most of what passes as public opinion with much confidence in the soundness of an aroused, mature, organic social judgment.

There is a widespread, but as I believe a fallacious, idea that the public thought or action must in some way express the working of an average or commonplace mind, must be some kind of a mean between the higher and lower intelligences making up the group. It would be more correct to say that it is representative, meaning by this that the preponderant *feeling* of the group seeks definite and effectual expression through individuals specially competent to give it such expression. Take for instance the activities of one of our colleges in intercollegiate athletics or debates. What belongs to the group at large is a vague desire to participate and excel in such competitions; but in realizing itself this desire seeks as its agents the best athletes or debaters that are to be found. A little common-sense and observation will show that the expression of a group is nearly always superior, for the purpose in hand, to the average capacity of its members.

I do not mean morally superior, but simply more effective, in a direction determined by the prevalent feeling. If a mob is in question, the brutal nature, for the time being ascendant, may act through the most brutal men in the group; and in like manner a money-making enterprise is apt to put forward the shrewdest agents it can find, without regard for any moral qualities except fidelity to itself. . . .

One who ponders these things will see that the principles of collective expression are the same now as ever, and that the special difficulties of our time arise partly from confusion, due to the pace of change, and partly from the greater demands which a free system makes upon human capacity. The question is, whether, in practice, democracy is capable of the effective expression to which no very serious theoretical obstacle can be discerned. It is a matter of doing a rather simple thing on a vaster and more complicated scale than in the past. . . .

In politics communication makes possible public opinion, which, when organized, is democracy. The whole growth of this, and of the popular education and enlightenment that go with it, is immediately dependent upon the telegraph, the newspaper and the fast mail, for there can be no popular mind upon questions of the day, over wide areas, except as the people are promptly informed of such questions and are enabled to exchange views regarding them.

Our government, under the Constitution, was not originally a democracy, and was not intended to be so by the men that framed it. It was expected to be a representative republic, the people choosing men of character and wisdom, who would proceed to the capital, inform themselves there upon current questions, and deliberate and decide regarding them. That the people might think and act more directly was not foreseen. The Constitution is not democratic in spirit, and, as Mr. Bryce has noted, might under different conditions have become the basis of an aristocratic system.

That any system could have held even the original thirteen states in firm union without the advent of modern communication is very doubtful. . . .

Popular education is an inseparable part of all this: the individual must have at least those arts of reading and writing without which he can hardly be a vital member of the new organism. And that further development of education, rapidly becoming a conscious aim of modern society, which strives to give to every person a special training in preparation for whatever function he may have aptitude for, is also a phase of the freer and more flexible organization of mental energy. The same enlargement runs through all life, including fashion and other trivial or fugitive kinds of intercourse. And the widest phase of all, upon whose momentousness I need not dwell, is that rise of an international consciousness, in literature, in science and, finally, in politics, which holds out a trustworthy promise of the indefinite enlargement of justice and amity. . . .

The relations between persons or communities that are without mutual understanding are necessarily on a low plane. There may be indifference, or a blind anger due to interference, or there may be a good-natured tolerance; but there is no consciousness of a common nature to warm up the kindly sentiments. . . .

The aim of all organization is to express human nature, and it does this through a system of symbols, which are the embodiment and vehicle of the idea. So long as spirit and symbol are vitally united and the idea is really conveyed, all is well, but so far as they are separated the symbol becomes an empty shell, to which, however, custom, pride or interest may still cling. It then supplants rather than conveys the reality.

Underlying all formalism, indeed, is the fact that it is psychically cheap; it substitutes the outer for the inner as more tangible, more capable of being held before the mind without fresh expense of thought and feeling, more easily extended, therefore, and impressed upon the multitude. Thus in our own architecture or literature we have innumerable cheap, unfelt repetitions of forms that were significant and beautiful in their time and place.

The effect of formalism upon personality is to starve its higher life and leave it the prey of apathy, self-complacency, sensuality and the lower nature in general. A formalized religion and a formalized freedom are, notoriously, the congenial dwelling-place of depravity and oppression. . . .

In America and western Europe at the present day there is a great deal of formalism, but it is, on the whole, of a partial and secondary character, existing rather from the inadequacy of vital force than as a ruling principle. The general state of thought favors adaptation, because we are used to it and have found it on the whole beneficial. We expect, for example, that a more vital and flexible form of organization will supplant the rigid systems of Russia and the Orient, and whatever in our own world is analogous to these.

But dead mechanism is too natural a product of human conditions not to exist at all times, and we may easily find it today in the church, in politics, in education, industry and philanthropy; wherever there is a lack of vital thought and sentiment to keep the machinery pliant to its work. . . .

The apparent opposite of formalism, but in reality closely akin to it, is disorganization or disintegration, often, though inaccurately, called "individualism." One is mechanism supreme, the other mechanism going to pieces; and both are in contrast to that harmony between human nature and its instruments which is desirable.

In this state of things general order and discipline are lacking. Though there may be praiseworthy persons and activities, society as a whole wants unity and rationality, like a picture which is good in details but does not make a pleasing composition. Individuals and special groups appear to be working too much at cross purposes; there is a "reciprocal struggle of discordant powers" but the "harmony of the universe" does not emerge. As good actors do not always make a good troupe nor brave soldiers a good army, so a nation or a historical epoch—say Italy in the Renaissance—may be prolific in distinguished persons and scattered achievements but somewhat futile and chaotic as a system.

Disorganization appears in the individual as a mind without cogent and abiding allegiance to a whole, and without the larger principles of conduct that flow from such allegiance. The better aspect of this is that the lack of support may stimulate a man to greater activity and independence, the worse that the absence of social standards is likely to lower his plane of achievement and throw him back upon sensuality and other primitive impulses: also that, if he is of a sensitive fibre, he is apt to be over strained by the contest with untoward conditions. . . .

It looks at first sight as if formalism and disorganization were as far apart as possible, but in fact they are closely connected, the latter being only the next step after the former in a logical sequence—the decay of a body already dead. Formalism goes very naturally with sensuality, avarice, selfish ambition, and other traits of disorganization, because the merely formal institution does not enlist and discipline the soul of the individual, but takes hold of him by the outside, his personality being left to torpor or to irreverent and riotous activity. . . .

In the same way a school whose discipline is merely formal, not engaging the interest and good-will of the scholar, is pretty certain to turn out unruly boys and girls, because whatever is most personal and vital in them becomes accustomed to assert itself in opposition to the system. And so in a church where external observance has been developed at the expense of personal judgment, the individual conforms to the rite and then feels free for all kinds of self-indulgence. In general the lower "individualism" of our time, the ruthless self-assertion which is so conspicuous, for example, in business, is not something apart from our institutions but expresses the fact that they are largely formal and unhuman, not containing and enlarging the soul of the individual.

The real opposite of both formalism and disorder is that wholesome relation between individuality and the institution in which each supports the other, the latter contributing a stable basis for the vitality and variation of the former. . . .

In the writings of one of the most searching and yet hopeful critics of our times [Jane Addams] we find that "individualism" is identified primarily with an isolation of sentiment, like that of the scholar in his study, the business man in his office or the mechanic who does not feel the broader meaning of his work. The opposite of it is the life of shoulder-to-shoulder sympathy and cooperation , in which the desire for separate power or distinction is lost in the overruling sense of common humanity. And the logical remedy for "individualism" is sought in that broadening of the spirit by immediate contact with the larger currents of life, which is the aim of the social settlement and similar movements.

This is, indeed, an inspiring and timely ideal, but let us hold it without forgetting that specialized and lonesome endeavor, indeed even individual pride and self-seeking, have also their uses. If we dwell too exclusively upon the we-feeling and the loss of the one in the many, we may lapse into a structureless emotionalism. Eye-to-eye fellowship and the pride of solitary achievement are both essential, each in its own way, to human growth, and either is capable of over-indulgence. We need the most erect individual with the widest base of sympathy. [Charles Horton Cooley, *Social Organization: A Study of the Larger Mind* (Charles Scribner's Sons, 1909), 116–24, 126, 85–8, 342–5, 347–51]

18. *Public Opinion and Social Control,* Edward Alsworth Ross (1866–1951)

Like Charles Horton Cooley, Edward Alsworth Ross was a professor of economics and sociology—first at the University of Nebraska, where he met Roscoe Pound, then at Stanford University and the University of Wisconsin. And, like Cooley, Ross was a co-founder and president of the American Sociological Society. Born in Illinois, Ross attended Coe College in Iowa and studied in Germany before returning to Johns Hopkins University for his PhD. One of the most prominent American social theorists of his day, he actively associated his scholarship with social reform, most notably in Sin and Society (1907). He argued that most personal moral failing in America is caused by social conditions, and he recast social reform as a battle against immorality. After reading Ross' Social Control (1901) on the recommendation of Justice Oliver Wendell Holmes, Theodore Roosevelt wrote a prefatory letter to

Sin and Society *in which he said, "You insist, as all healthy-minded patriots should insist, that public opinion, if only sufficiently enlightened and aroused, is equal to the necessary regenerative tasks and can yet dominate the future."[7] In the 1920s, Ross became enamored of scientific theories of race and the eugenics movement[8] and crusaded against further immigration of inferior racial stock into America. Although he saw his pursuit of eugenics as a logical continuance of his early efforts to purify and perfect American society, this dubious allegiance greatly harmed his reputation. Nonetheless, his two major books,* Social Psychology *and* Social Control, *remain classics in the field. He dedicated* Social Psychology *to Franklin Henry Giddings, "Bold Seeker and Valiant Proclaimer of Truth."* Social Control *was part of "The Citizen's Library," a series sponsored by Macmillan and edited by Richard Ely. In addition to Ross' work, this series included three books by Ely, two by Jane Addams, and one by Florence Kelley.*

—1901—

Let us . . . examine the merits and demerits of public opinion, comparing it especially with law, the most formidable engine of control employed by society. Public opinion has the advantage of a *wide gamut* of influences. By thus supplementing the coarse and rough sanctions of the law, society avoids putting itself into such undisguised opposition to a man's wishes, and is not so likely to raise the spirit of rebellion. Its blame does not exclude moral suasion, and its ban does not renounce all appeal to the feelings. Public opinion is *less mechanical* in operation than law. The public can weigh provocation better, and can take into account condoning or aggravating circumstances of time, place, motive, or office. The blade of the law playing up and down in its groove with iron precision is hardly so good a regulative instrument as the flexible lash of public censure. . . .

Public opinion guards the social peace *by enforcing moral claims* that law, with its rigid definitions and stern self-consistency, dares not support. The law frequently upholds the right of summary eviction, grants the widow's cow to the rich creditor, permits a railway company to turn adrift an employee crippled in its service, and confirms the right of a

---

7. Ross, *Sin and Society* (1907), xi.

8. Members of this movement believed that the human race could be improved through controlled breeding for desirable inherited characteristics.

husband to administer moderate castigation to his wife. But the public will not tolerate such things. . . .

In most cases, the law must wait till the "overt act." Public opinion, on the other hand, can act in anticipation of an offence, interfere at any moment, and apply a gradually increasing pressure. Its premonitory growl is more *preventive* than the silent menace of Justice.

The action of public opinion has the virtue of *immediacy*. If not deliberate, it is at least prompt, and it brooks not the delay so conspicuous in the pursuit of leaden-footed law. . . .

Finally, the sanctions of public opinion are *cheap*. Marvellous is the economy of praise and blame. To regulate a man merely by letting him know your opinion of him is as much cheaper than legal process, as faith-cure is simpler than surgery. The economy of reward is especially great. . . .

These, then, are the merits of public opinion. It has a wide gamut of sanctions. It is flexible. It is penetrating. It is preventive. It is prompt. It is cheap. Let us now review its defects.

The requirements of one's neighbors are *not clear and precise*. They are not codified, and their uncertainty weakens the deterrent power of their sanctions. Moreover, these sanctions likewise are not *definite*, and not proportioned to the gravity of the offence. . . .

Again, to utilize the temper of the community, it is necessary to strike while the iron is hot. The ministers of the law, if they have a slow foot, have a firm clutch and, like the gods, are known by their long memories. But the public has a short wrath and a poor memory, and the offender, if he dodges into obscurity and waits till the gust of public indignation is over, often goes unpunished. . . .

The might of public wrath is destroyed by any thing that diverts it from an individual and spreads it harmlessly over a network of administrative responsibility. The common indignation, always confused by a shifting responsibility, is most baffled when responsibility on being traced back is found to be lodged in a body of men. It is this fact that accounts for the increasing disregard of public opinion in the management of business. . . .

Mindful of these defects—its indefiniteness, its passional character, its short memory, its divided jurisdiction, and its frequent impotence— we must recognize that public opinion is far from satisfactory as to technique. The only way in which society can profit by the excellences of its coercion without suffering too much from the shortcomings, is to hand over to specialized organs all those harsh physical penalties that ought to be used only in grave cases and after careful inquisition. Moreover, all the major behests of society must be enforced by long-memoried agents that have feet for pursuing and hands for gripping. The waste of energy in securing the effective cooperation of the amorphous public is too great. . . .

The place reserved to public opinion in the system of social control should depend, furthermore, on its competency to coerce in the right direction; for it must not only drive men, but drive them along the paths it is necessary they should go in. Now, in respect to technique, public opinion is, as we have seen, primitive. It is vague as to requirements. It is indefinite as to kind and quantity of sanction. It is crude as to procedure. It is evidently not a product fashioned for the purpose of regulation, but the *original plasm* out of which various organs of discipline have evolved.

Now equally primitive is the public as to the *purposes* of its coercion. A statute, moral standard, or ideal is several removes from raw human sentiment. Time and the influence of the wise have purged it of whim and prejudice and made it a matter of social hygiene. It has detached itself from persons and become a semi-independent factor in control. But public opinion cannot go through such a process without ceasing to be public opinion. . . .

Primitive public opinion, therefore, far from being a wise disciplinarian, meddles when it ought to abstain, and blesses when it ought to curse. Now, how does this ignorant, despotic patron of conservatism and stagnation become a respectable agent for the righteous protection of the social welfare? The processes are three:

1. A general improvement in character and intelligence. The feeling of the many reflects the feeling of the average person, and if he is cool and reasonable in his private resentments, he will be so in his sympathetic and corporate resentments. . . .

2. A general acceptance of principles of law or right which guide opinion and cause it to play smoothly in certain grooves. These slow-won, time-hallowed maxims are bits in the mouth of the mob and reins in the hands of the wise. They virtually endow the multitude with memory and equip it with experience. . . .

3. The ascendency of the wise. A scrutiny of the source of public opinion in a healthy community shows us not an amorphous crowd, but an organic combination of people. Not only is there a reciprocal influence of man on man, but in this universal give-and-take we find some men giving out many impulses and receiving few, while others receive many impulses and give out few. Thus arises the contrast of influencers and influenced, leaders and led, which does so much toward explaining how minds of weight and worth come to their own

under a popular regime. These knots of influential men, which in time spontaneously arrange themselves into higher and lower, constitute the nerve centres or ganglia of society. They are the rallying points of public opinion, and although even these leaders may be bad or addle-pated, the mere existence of such a psychic organization shows that the popular consensus is by no means the Walpurgis-night of feeling and folly it is often said to be.

Such a guidance being possible, the remedy for the abuses of public opinion is not to discredit it but to instruct it. . . .

Signs are not wanting that in the future an increasing restraint will be exercised through public opinion, and that this kind of control will gain at the expense of other kinds. For one thing, this form of coercion is suited to the type of man created by modern life. Only the criminal or the moral hero cares not how others may think of him. The growing rage for publicity and the craving for notoriety shows that the men of today respond warmly to praise and wilt quickly under general disap-proval. Then, too, certain social developments favor the ascendancy of the public. The growing economic interdependence and the closer interweaving of private interests mean that the individual gives hostages to the community for his good behavior. Liable as he is to have his pros-perity blighted and his course of life changed by the resentful action of others, he will think twice before flying in the face of common senti-ment. The more frequent contacts of men and the better facilities for forming and focussing the opinion of the public tend in the same direc-tion. Similar in effect is the modern emphasis on *publicity* instead of positive regulation. We are more and more insisting on the complete transparency of industry and business.

With a democratic, forward-looking people like ours, opinion, no longer split up into small currents by class lines or broken in force by masses of family, sect, or caste tradition, the debris of the past, acquires a tidal volume and sweep. In such a stream all oaks become reeds. The day of the sturdy backwoodsman, settler, flat-boatman, or prospector, defiant not alone of law but of public opinion as well, is gone never to return. We are come to a time when ordinary men are scarcely aware of the coercion of public opinion, so used are they to follow it. They can-not dream of aught but acquiescence in an unmistakable edict of the mass. It is not so much the dread of what an angry public may do that disarms the modern American, as it is sheer inability to stand unmoved in the rush of totally hostile comment, to endure a life perpetually at variance with the conscience and feeling of those about him. [Edward A. Ross, *Social Control: A Survey of the Foundations of Order* (Macmil-lan, 1901), 93–105]

19. *Training Democratic Citizens*, Mary Parker Follett (1868–1934)[9]

Follett believed that government ought to be organized from the ground up—in this respect, her thinking was not unlike Thomas Jefferson's when he proposed to base all government in America on a system of community wards (or "hundreds"). According to Jefferson's plan, the leaders of each level of government would elect the leaders of the next higher level; Jefferson believed that this grassroots, self-maintaining government would leave the central state with almost nothing to do except provide for external defense. While Follett thought that organization should begin with the neighborhood, she also believed that "the neighborhood groups must then be integrated, through larger intermediary groups, into a true state" (New State, 245). She tapped into small group psychology in the name both of reform and of social efficiency as a way to link citizens at the bottom to public policy experts at the top. Her plan to turn every neighborhood school into an evening Hull House—what she termed the "School Centre" movement—best expresses her ideal.

—1918—

Early psychology was based on the study of the individual; early sociology was based on the study of society. But there is no such thing as the "individual," there is no such thing as "society"; there is only the group and the group-unit—the social individual. Social psychology must begin with an intensive study of the group, of the selective processes which go on within it, the differentiated reactions, the likenesses and unlikenesses, and the spiritual energy which unites them. . . .

The acceptance and the living of the new psychology will do away with all the progeny of particularistic psychology: consent of the governed, majority rule, external leadership, industrial wars, national wars etc. From the analysis of the group must come an understanding of collective thought and collective feeling, of the common will and concerted activity, of the true nature of freedom, the illusion of self-and-others, the essential unity of men, the real meaning of patriotism, and the whole secret of progress and of life as a genuine interpenetration which produces true community. . . .

---

9. More biographical information on Follett prefaces her selections in Chapters 2 and 10.

The fundamental reason for the study of group psychology is that no one can give us democracy, we must learn democracy. To be a democrat is not to decide on a certain form of human association, it is to learn how to live with other men. . . .

The training for the new democracy must be from the cradle—through nursery, school and play, and on and on through every activity of our life. Citizenship is not to be learned in good government classes or current events courses or lessons in civics. It is to be acquired only through those modes of living and acting which shall teach us how to grow the social consciousness. This should be the object of all day school education, of all night school education, of all our supervised recreation, of all our family life, of our club life, of our civic life.

When we change our ideas of the relation of the individual to society, our whole system of education changes. What we want to teach is interdependence, that efficiency waits on discipline, that discipline is obedience to the whole of which I am a part. Discipline has been a word long connected with school life—when we know how to teach *social* discipline, then we shall know how to "teach school."

The object of education is to fit children into the life of the community. Every cooperative method conceivable, therefore, must be used in our schools for this end. It is at school that children should begin to learn group initiative, group responsibility—in other words social functioning. The group process must be learnt by practice. We should therefore teach subjects which require a working together, we should have group recitations, group investigations, and a gradual plan of self-government. Every child must be shown his place in the life that builds and his relation to all others who are building. All the little daily and hourly experiences of his interrelations must be constantly interpreted to him. Individual competition must, of course, disappear. All must see that the test of success is ability to work with others, not to surpass others.

Group work is, indeed, being introduced into our more progressive schools. Manual training, especially when the object made is large enough to require the work of two or more, cooking classes, school papers, printing classes etc., give opportunity for organization into groups with the essential advantage of the group: coordinated effort. . . .

Again, every good teacher teaches her pupils to "assemble" his different thoughts, shows them that a single thought is not useful, but only as it is connected with others. The modern teacher is like the modern curator who thinks the group significance of a particular classification more important than the significance of each isolated piece. The modern teacher does not wish his pupils' minds to be like an old-fashioned museum—a hodge-podge of isolated facts—but a useful workshop.

Again, to learn genuine discussion should be considered an essential part of our education. Every child must be trained to meet the clash of difference—difference of opinion, difference of interest—which life brings. In some universities professors are putting aside one hour a week for a discussion hour. This should be done in all colleges and schools, and then it should be seen to that it is genuine discussion that takes place in that hour.

Moreover, in many schools supervised playground and gymnasium activities are being established, athletic clubs encouraged, choruses and dramatic leagues developed, not only because of their value from the health or art point of view, but because they teach the social lesson.

The question of self-government in the schools is too complicated a subject and has met with too many difficulties, notwithstanding its brilliant successes, to take up here, but undoubtedly some amount of self-control can be given to certain groups, and in the upper grades to whole schools, and when this can be done no training for democracy is equal to the practice of democracy.

The aim is to create such a mental atmosphere for children that it is natural for them to wish to take their part, to make them understand that citizenship is not obeying the laws nor voting, nor even being President, but that all the visions of their highest moments, all the aspirations of their spiritual nature can be satisfied through their common life, that only thus do we get "practical politics."

In our industrial schools it is obviously easier to carry further the teaching of coordinated effort than in the regular day schools.

Our evening schools must adopt the methods of the more progressive day schools, and must, as they are doing in many cases, add to the usual activities of evening schools.

The most conscious and deliberate preparation for citizenship is given by the "School Centres" now being established all over the United States. The School Centre movement is a movement to mould the future, to direct evolution instead of trusting to evolution. The subject of this book has been the necessity for community organization, but the ability to meet this necessity implies that we know how to do that most difficult thing in the world—work with other people: that we are ready to sacrifice individual interests to the general good, that we have a fully developed sense of responsibility, that we are trained in initiative and action. But this is not true. If the School Centres are to fill an important place in neighborhood life, they must not only give an opportunity for the development of neighborhood consciousness and neighborhood organization, but they must train up young people to be ready for neighborhood organization. We who believe in the School Centre as one of the most effective means we have for reconstructing city life believe that the School Centre can furnish this training. We hear everywhere of the corruption of American municipal politics, but why should the next generation do any better than the present unless we are training our young men and women to a proper understanding of the meaning of good citizenship and the sense of their own responsibility? The need of democracy today is a trained citizenship. We must deliberately train for citizenship as for music, art or trade. The School Centres are, in fact, both the prophecy of the new democracy and a method of its fulfilment. They provide an opportunity for its expression, and at the same time give to men and women the opportunity for the training needed to bring it to its highest expression.

The training in the School Centres consists of: group-activities, various forms of civic clubs and classes, and practice in self-government.

First, we have in the Centres those activities which require working together, such as dramatic and choral clubs, orchestras and bands, civic and debating clubs, folk-dancing and team-games. We want choral unions and orchestras, to be sure, because they will enrich the community life at the same time that they emphasize the neighborhood bond, we want civic and debating clubs because we all need enlightenment on the subjects taken up in these clubs, but the primary reason for choosing such activities is that they are group activities where each learns to identify himself with a social whole. This is the first lesson for all practical life. Take two young men in business. One says of his firm, "*They* are doing so and so": his attitude is that the business is a complete whole, without him, to which he may indeed be ministering in some degree. Another young man who has been a few weeks with an old-established firm says "*We* have done so and so for years," "*Our* policy is so and so." You perhaps smile but you know that he possesses one of the chief requirements for rising.

In our group the centre of consciousness is transferred from our private to our associate life. Thus through our group activities does neighborhood life become a preparation for neighborhood life; thus does it prepare us for the pouring out of strength and strain and effort in the common cause.

Then the consciousness of the solidarity of the group leads directly to a sense of responsibility, responsibility in a group and for a group. Sooner or later every one in a democracy must ask himself, what am I worth to society? Our effort in the Centres is to help the birth of that moment. This is the social lesson: for people to understand that their every act, their work, their home-life, the kind of recreation they demand, the kind of newspapers they read, the bearing of their children, the bringing up of their children—that all these so-called private acts create the city in which they live. It is not just when we vote, or meet together in political groups, or when we take part in some charitable or philanthropic or social scheme, that we are performing our duty to society. Every single act of our life should be looked at as a social act.

Moreover, we learn responsibility for our group as well as to our group. We used to think, "I must do right no matter what anyone else does." Now we know how little that exhausts our duty; we must feel an equally keen responsibility for our whole group.

These then are the lessons which we hope group activities will teach—solidarity, responsibility and initiative,—how to take one's place worthily in a self-directed, self-governing community. . . .

But the Centres prepare for citizenship not only by group activities but also by direct civic teaching. This takes the form not only of lectures, classes in citizenship, but also of societies like the "junior city councils" or the "legislatures" where municipal and state questions are discussed, and young men's and young women's civic clubs. And it must be remembered that the chief value of these clubs is not the information acquired, not even the interest aroused, but the lesson learned of genuine discussion with all the advantages therefrom.

We have many forms of adult education: extension courses, continuation and night schools, correspondence schools, courses in settlements, Young Men's Christian Associations etc. And yet all these take a very small per cent of our adult population. Where are people to get this necessary education? Our present form of industry does not give enough. Tending a machine all day is not conducive to thought; a man thus employed gets to rely entirely on his foreman. The man who lets his foreman do his thinking for him all day tends to need a political boss at night. We must somehow counteract the paralyzing effect of the methods of modern industry. In the School Centre we have an opportunity for adult education in the only forms in which many people, tired out with the day's work, can take it: discussion, recreation, group activities and self-governing clubs. . . .

Self-government in the Centres then means not only the election of officers and the making of a constitution, but a real management of club and Centre affairs, the opportunity to take initiative, to make choices and decisions, to take responsibility. The test of our success in the Centres will always be how far we are developing the self-shaping instinct. But we must remember that we have not given self-government by allowing the members of a club to record their votes. Many people think a neighborhood association or club is self-governing if a question is put to them and every one votes upon it. But if a club is to be really self-governed it must first learn collective thinking. This is not a process which can be hurried, it will take time and that time must not be grudged. Collective thinking must be reverenced as an act of creation. The time spent in evolving the group spirit is time spent in creating the dynamic force of our civilization.

Moreover each Centre should be begun, directed and supported (as far as possible) by the adult people of a community acting together for that end. A Centre should not be an undertaking begun by the School Committee and run by the School Committee, but each Centre should be organized by local initiative, to serve local needs, through methods chosen by the people of a district to suit that particular district. The ideal School Centre is a Community Centre. A group of citizens asks for the use of a schoolhouse after school hours, with heat, light, janitor, and a director to make the necessary connection between the local undertaking and the city department. Then that group of citizens is responsible for the Centre: for things worthwhile being done in the schoolhouse, and for the support of the activities undertaken. By the time such a School Centre is organized by such an association of citizens, neighbors will have become acquainted with one another in a more vital way than before, and they will have begun to learn how to think and to act together as a neighborhood unit.

We are coming to a more general realization of this. In the municipal buildings in the parks of Chicago, the people are not given free lectures, free moving pictures, free music, free dances etc.; they are invited to develop their own activities. To the Recreation Centres of New York, operated by the Board of Education, are being added the Community Centres controlled by local boards of neighbors. In Boston we have under the School Committee a department of "The Extended Use of School Buildings," and the aim is to get the people of each district to plan, carry out and supervise what civic, educational and recreational activities they wish in the schoolhouses.

A Chicago minister said the other day that the south side of Chicago was the only part of the city where interest in civic problems and community welfare could be aroused, and this he said was because of the South Park's work in field houses, clubrooms and gymnasiums for the last ten or twelve years.

When the chairman of the Agricultural Council of Defense of Virginia asked a citizen of a certain county what he thought the prospects were of being able to rouse the people in his county in regard to an increased food production, the prompt reply was, "On the north side of the county we shall have no trouble because we have several Community Leagues there, but on the south side it will be a hard job."

The School or Community Centre is the real continuation school of America, the true university of true democracy. [Mary Parker Follett, *The New State: Group Organization the Solution of Popular Government* (Longmans, Green, 1918), 21–2, 363–70, 372–3]

Further Reading

Cohen, Marshall J., *Charles Horton Cooley and the Social Self in American Thought* (Garland, 1982).

Crunden, Robert M., *Ministers of Reform: The Progressives' Achievement in American Civilization, 1889–1920* (University of Illinois Press, 1984).

Dawley, Alan, *Struggles for Justice: Social Responsibility and the Liberal State* (Harvard University Press, 1991).

Elshtain, Jean, *Jane Addams and the Dream of American Democracy* (Basic Books, 2002).

Hansen, Jonathan, *The Lost Promise of Patriotism: Debating American Identity, 1890–1920* (University of Chicago Press, 2003).

Kestenbaum, Victor, *The Grace and the Severity of the Ideal: John Dewey and the Transcendent* (University of Chicago Press, 2002).

Livingston, James, *Pragmatism and the Political Economy of Cultural Revolution, 1850–1940* (University of North Carolina Press, 1994).

Quandt, Jean D., *From Small Town to Great Community: The Social Thought of Progressive Intellectuals* (Rutgers University Press, 1970).

Ross, Dorothy, *G. Stanley Hall: The Psychologist as Prophet* (University of Chicago Press, 1972).

Ross, Edward Alsworth, *Sin and Society: An Analysis of Latter-Day Iniquity* (Houghton Mifflin, 1907).

Ryan, Alan, *John Dewey and the High Tide of American Liberalism* (Norton, 1995).

Sklansky, Jeffrey, *The Soul's Economy: Market Society and Selfhood in American Thought, 1820–1920* (University of North Carolina Press, 2002).

Stettner, Edward, *Shaping Modern Liberalism: Herbert Croly and Progressive Thought* (University Press of Kansas, 1993).

Taylor, Bob Pepperman, *Citizenship and Democratic Doubt: The Legacy of Progressive Thought* (University Press of Kansas, 2004).

Thelen, David Paul, *The New Citizenship: The Origins of Progressivism in Wisconsin, 1885–1900* (University of Missouri Press, 1972).

Westbrook, Robert, *John Dewey and American Democracy* (Cornell University Press, 1991).

Wilson, R. Jackson, *In Quest of Community: Social Philosophy in the United States, 1860–1920* (Wiley, 1968).

5

The Law, the State, and the Economy

It would be an understatement to say that most Progressive thinkers held lawyers and contemporary constitutional jurisprudence in low regard. Not only was the American legal mind resistant to the new thinking in political economy and sociology, the leading practitioners of law were considered to be part of the long-standing "regime of courts and parties"[1] Progressive reform sought to supplant. Just as the "political specialists"—Herbert Croly's term for political party bosses—worked to maintain the old, corrupt political status quo, the "legal specialists" employed in the new corporate law firms were working to protect large business and financial institutions from public scrutiny and control. With the exception of Justice Oliver Wendell Holmes (1841–1935), whom Theodore Roosevelt appointed to the Supreme Court in 1902, judges and the upper bar were seen as barriers to work around rather than as potential allies in reform.

By the second decade of the twentieth century, however, instructors at law schools around the country had begun to pick up on Progressive ideas and legal formalism soon began to lose its grip on the profession.[2] While the terms "sociological jurisprudence" and, later, "legal realism" were coined to describe this shift in legal thinking, the real change lay in the introduction of historical and evolutionary perspectives from economics and the social sciences into legal conceptual thinking. The result was a frontal attack on "mechanical jurisprudence," the idea that the court's rulings on any given social or political conflict ought to be dictated by a set of fixed and immutable legal and constitutional principles. The Progressives, who extended their attack to include the court's general role in the larger political system, were especially interested in those cases in which the court was required to address regulatory and other economic issues. They considered political executives, legislatures, and expert administrative commissions to be more democratically accountable than the court system—and, therefore, better equipped to decide

---

1. Skowronek, *Building a New American State* (1982).

2. For the larger intellectual context of antiformalism, see White, *Social Thought in America* (1957), stressing the writings of Charles Beard, John Dewey, and Oliver Wendell Holmes.

many public issues that the court had previously claimed as its exclusive domain.[3]

This new legal thinking—premised on the assumption that the constitution was an organic document constantly evolving in response to historical, societal, and economic changes—had a profound effect on constitutional jurisprudence. The political science textbook that Charles Beard first published in 1910 (and that would dominate collegiate instruction in American politics throughout the 1920s and 1930s) offered the following description of the new legal thinking:

> No longer do statesmen spend weary days over finely spun theories about strict and liberal interpretations of the Constitution, about the sovereignty and reserved rights of states. No longer are men's affections so centered in their own commonwealths that they are willing to take up the sword . . . to defend state independence. It is true that there are still debates on such themes as federal encroachments on local liberties, and that admonitory volumes on "federal" usurpation come from the press. It is true also that conservative judges, dismayed at the radical policies reflected in new statutes, federal and state, sometimes set them aside in the name of strict interpretation. But one has only to compare the social and economic legislation of the last decade with that of the closing years of the nineteenth century, for instance, to understand how deep is the change in the minds of those who have occasion to examine and interpret the Constitution bequeathed to them by the Fathers. Imagine Jefferson . . . reading Roosevelt's autobiography affirming the doctrine that the President of the United States can do anything for the welfare of the people which is not forbidden by the Constitution! Imagine Chief Justice Taney[4] . . . called upon to uphold a state law fixing the hours of all factory labor. . . . Imagine James Monroe[5] . . . called upon to sign bills appropriating federal money for roads, education, public health . . . and other social purposes! . . . Why multiply examples?[6]

---

3. The most striking example is labor law. See Orren, *Belated Feudalism* (1992).

4. Roger Brook Taney (1777–1864), a firm believer in narrowly construing constitutional powers granted to the federal and state governments, was appointed chief justice of the Supreme Court by Andrew Jackson in 1836, where he served until his death.

5. James Monroe (1758–1831) was the fifth President of the United States (1816–1824), who, on constitutional grounds, vetoed bills that authorized the building of national roads.

6. Beard, *American Government and Politics* (1928), 100–1. This part was probably introduced into the textbook around 1914.

While some Progressive writings, notably Edward Alsworth Ross' *Social
Control*, held a pessimistic view of human perfectibility and thus
believed that law—especially criminal law and punishment—would
remain important despite growing humanitarian sentiments, most Progressives thought that public opinion and moral coercion would gradually supplant legal control of human behavior. This shift would most
certainly be true in cases regarding property and contract law and labor-
management conflicts. Put another way, the Progressives believed that
"administration" would expand as the realm of adversarial adjudication
constricted.

20. *The State and Large Business Corporations,* Albion Small (1854–1926)[7]

*The essay from which this selection is taken appeared in the inaugural
volume of the* American Journal of Sociology, *a journal founded and
edited by Small. The essay set the tone and spirit for economic regulation and protective labor legislation by stressing the interdependence of
the new industrial economy and the state, thereby blurring the lines
between private and public and changing the very meaning of property
as a legal right. Sociologists like Small, Franklin Giddings, and Charles
Horton Cooley tended to be somewhat more radical in their economic
thinking than those academics who were formally trained in economics
and the role of markets.*

—1895—

Corporations are presumptively servants, not masters, of the public.
They are to be judged by their performances, and should be treated
accordingly. A corporation which is deficient in the discharge of its delegated function should be restored to usefulness by vigorous measures,
if necessary, just as the proper public authority should repair a bad road.
This principle was assumed by congress, when it passed the interstate
commerce bill in 1886, in view of the eighteen distinct classes of delin-
quencies on the part of the railroads, recited by the Cullom committee
of the senate. A corporation that has turned its social office into a personal "snap" should be abated like any other nuisance.

---

7. More biographical information on Small prefaces his selections in Chapters
2 and 3.

These opinions are sustained by the law of the land, as interpreted by our courts. At the same time, it must be confessed that the complexity of our administrative and judicial system has been a stumbling block to many persons of large intelligence who have not been specially instructed in constitutional law. The interlocking state and federal juris-dictions, the curiously distributed powers of regulating commerce, of enforcing police regulations, of sanctioning and interpreting and enforcing contracts, etc., seem to the uninitiated to furnish easy means of nullifying the popular will as expressed in the laws. It is hard for the ordinary man to understand that a railroad corporation is not held to be above the law-making power, when a state law regulating railroads within the state is declared unconstitutional by a United States court, on the ground that the law is a regulation of commerce. Yet, in spite of such afflictions to the lay mind, the accepted rules of law are sufficiently explicit to leave no proper doubt that in theory corporations are held to be accountable to the people for their stewardship of public trusts. . . .

It would be trite and commonplace to multiply illustrations of the reversal by corporation managers of the functional and ethical relation upon which society predicates corporate privileges. The morbid and extreme suspicion of corporations, and especially of trusts as such . . . is the natural consequence of corporate defiance of obligation to the sanc-tioning and sustaining public. The popular mind is at present tending to the view that capitalistic organizations are inherently and necessarily evil. Innumerable corporations are acting on the presumption that the public is a mine, to be worked for all it is worth till the lead runs out. A change of public opinion is unlikely, therefore, until there is an evident change of front in corporate management.

We have to ask then what shall we do about it?

I answer: First and foremost, the thing at which the "practical" men smile, which professional "reformers" sneer at as an evasion of the issue, viz., teach the fundamental principles of corporate and state relation-ship to all sorts and conditions of men. . . . Men must be taught to dis-tinguish between these devices, as controllable social agencies, and on the other hand the unsocial personal volition, which at present often acts the role of a possessing devil perverting the agency. Men must be taught to study the social adaptabilities of capitalistic organization as expectantly as we study the applications of electrical energy. Everybody except the anarchist anticipates the next grand social gain through some manner of extension of the principles of industrial organization. Let us promote this gain by spreading intelligence about actual and possible economy of effort through organization of organizations.

In the second place, let us encourage *legislation* that shall prescribe

the lines within which corporate action must recognize public interest.
I admit that this is only another way of saying: Let us face the necessity
of evolving superior citizens in order that there may be superior legislators. In other words let public opinion register itself in authoritative
public standards as rapidly as the social consciousness becomes intelligent. Let there be careful study of the developing needs and opportunities of society, and let the results of study declare themselves in
developing legal principles of social self-control. . . .

Third, let us by all means fit ourselves to assume direct public control of many properties which belong by nature to the public; properties
which we have hitherto farmed out at enormous public sacrifice. I do
not fix a limit to the number of these properties, for I do not know where
the limit will be found, and so far as any fears are concerned about consequences of public proprietorship as authorized by the principles cited,
I do not care. I am sure of this, that so long as men agree to maintain
society, they will more and more agree that the question of private or
corporate or public control of the industrial opportunities upon which
the good of all depends is in the last resort a question of administration.
Is the public welfare most likely to be subserved by public or by proxy
management? . . .

We are just fairly entering upon the observing and describing and
analyzing stage of social relations. Our national and state and municipal governments have already done an enormous amount of necessary
preliminary work in gathering and organizing essential information.
Popular and systematic thought is asserting its freedom from arbitrary
conventional philosophies. A quickened social consciousness is assuming the right, the privilege, the duty of life — "life more abundant," in
the individual and in society. As never before in the history of society,
we are anticipating problems of social order, and proposing solutions,
instead of being satisfied to explain solutions after the centuries have
worked them out. We are learning to formulate what we want as freely
in civics as in mechanics. We are learning to set ourselves in as busi-
nesslike fashion in the one field as in the other to the task of getting our
wants supplied. Better than all, some of the choice and master spirits of
our age are showing by word and deed that in these tasks of peace there
is service to be rendered and renown to be won not less splendid than
the victories and laurels of war. We are already within the line of operations of a campaign for human improvement. The end will not be till
every toiler with hand or brain has secured social guarantee of more
secure industrial status. The coming lot of the capable and faithful
laborer will be as superior to his present condition of industrial dependence and insecurity as the political status of citizens in a democratic

republic is to that of the unprivileged class in ancient oligarchies. I cal-
culate confidently upon progressive public absorption of corporate and
monopolistic advantages as a certain incident of this glorious gain.
[Albion Small, "The State and Semi-Public Corporations," *American
Journal of Sociology* 1 (1895): 403–10]

21. *Economics and Jurisprudence*, Henry Carter Adams (1851–1921)

*Like John Bates Clark, Henry Carter Adams was major innovator in
American economic thinking. Adams graduated from Iowa (now
Grinnell) College, an institution co-founded by his father, who was a
member of the "Iowa Band" of New England evangelicals (most of
whom graduated from Yale University) dedicated to erecting a Christian
commonwealth in the midwest. After attending Andover Theological
School, Adams studied for two years in Heidelberg and Berlin before
receiving his PhD from Johns Hopkins University. He spent his entire
career as a professor of political economy at the University of Michigan,
where he was deeply influenced by his colleague John Dewey. Adams
was a co-founder and, eventually, president, of the American Economic
Association (AEA). This selection is taken from his presidential address
to the AEA in 1897.*

—1897—

Now, it is clear that jurisprudence . . . must be subject to a development corresponding to that of a society whose ethical ideals it is
designed to express. . . . Thus, every change in the social structure,
every modification of the principle of political or industrial association,
as well as the acceptance of a new social ideal, must be accompanied
by a corresponding change in those rights and duties acknowledged
and enforced by law. Should this development in jurisprudence be
arrested or proceed sluggishly, as compared with that of some particular phase of associated action, serious mischief will inevitably follow.
This is true because such unequal development would evidence the
general appreciation by men that the law fails to express rights which
they hold to be fundamental; and it is the universal testimony of history that every desire for a right or a privilege common to any considerable number of men, yet of such a sort that it is opposed by the
common law of conduct, will find expression through an appeal to a
higher law, a divine law, a natural law, an ethical claim, an historic

necessity, or some other phrase pressed into the service of agitators whenever an appeal is taken from that which is to that which should be. If, now, this desire, asserted as a natural right merely because it is not acknowledged by the philosophy of jurisprudence, be in reality an historic product, and, therefore, an enduring force, it is futile to expect the restoration of harmony until either the established system of jurisprudence shall assert its authority and repress the aspiration of those who seek the orderly expression of unusual rights, or until, this aspiration being acknowledged as just, the interest which it represents is incorporated in a reformed system of jurisprudence. . . .

Corporations originally were regarded as agencies of the state. They were created for the purpose of enabling the public to realize some social or national end without involving the necessity of direct governmental administration. They were in reality arms of the state, and in order to secure efficient management, a local or private interest was created as a privilege or property of the corporation. A corporation, therefore, may be defined in the light of history as a body created by law for the purpose of attaining public ends through an appeal to private interests.

A corporation, as it appears in this latter half of the nineteenth century, differs in every essential particular, from the original conception out of which it grew. Its public purpose and its dependence on government have been lost to view, while its character as a private industrial concern has been especially emphasized. Three points respecting the modern corporation should be noted in order to appreciate the influences which emanate from it.

First. The growth of the corporation and the consequent centralization of industrial power is only limited by the market for the goods which it produces or the services which it renders. This is true because the credit of corporations is practically without limit. The bearing of this fact may easily be perceived. It was assumed by those who formulated the doctrine that the principle of competition was an adequate guarantee of justice and equity in business affairs, that any particular business would be represented by a large number of independent and competing organizations. . . .

Second. Corporations are coming to conceive of themselves as business associations of perpetual life. The contracts which they enter into bind not only the present but the future, and, when it is understood that gain in the present is the motive directing these contracts, it is easy to see that the best interests of the future may be jeopardized. I cannot suggest even, at this time, the far reaching consequences of this peculiarity of corporate organization, but must content myself with the remark, that the considerations which led reasonable men of half a century ago to approve the philosophy of industrial individualism, did not include the observation that a body of men organized for the purpose of private gain should ever plead the interests of a perpetual existence. Such a plea, it was assumed, pertained to the state alone.

Third. Corporations do not recognize the principle of righteousness, candor, courtesy, or indeed, any of the personal virtues, except energy and enterprise, which, according to the old English economists, are assumed to be essential to continued business success. I do not say that the common virtues may not be appreciated by men entrusted with the management of corporate enterprises, or that they do not practice such virtues in their personal affairs; but such is the nature of intercorporate competition, especially for industries in which success is measured by the volume of business transacted, that the managers of corporations are obliged to recognize a dual code of ethics,—one for the business, one for the home. Whether or not a man ought to choose defeat rather than success under such conditions does not concern the present argument. Your attention was called to this peculiarity of corporate organization for the purpose of presenting yet another reason why the old rules of business conduct are not pertinent to the latest phase of industrial development. The old theory of society which assumes identity between personal interests and social morality, may possibly have been true when industries stood forth in the person of those who conducted them; but to claim that this is true as business is at present organized, is to ignore the influence which corporations have exerted upon the character of business. If it be true that the growth of a corporate enterprise is only limited by the world's demands, that its life is only limited by that of the civilization to which it pertains, and that it is deprived of those restraining influences which work so powerfully upon the individual, is it not clear that a new theory of industrial relations becomes a necessity? . . .

The mistake of English political economy, as it seems to me, does not lie in the emphasis it gives to competition as a regulator of commercial conduct, but in its assumption that the *bourgeois* conception of property was ordained by nature and on that account, lay outside the influence of evolutionary forces. But I must set aside for a moment the consideration of this point.

It is also necessary for the satisfactory working of a society whose moral code is expressed in the formula of rights, that responsibility should attach itself to the exercise of liberty. The nature of responsibility must, of course, conform to the nature of the liberty it is designed to control, and dealing as we are with industrial forces, our analysis must content itself, in the application of this principle, with a consideration of industrial responsibility. As already remarked, wherever the system of English jurisprudence holds sway, the details of associated action are the result of voluntary contract, and provided the terms of the contract do not jeopardize any public interest, the state concerns itself only with the task of enforcement.

At this point, however, the analysis must proceed with great care. The word, "enforcement," as employed in English legal procedure, has no thought of arbitrary action. It consists rather in the exacting of the penalty recognized in the contract, (either expressly stated, or implied in the common law under which the contract is drawn) and voluntarily assumed by both parties to the agreement. This exacting of the penalty is the means by which responsibility is brought to the support of voluntary association. Every contract, to be effective, must state or imply not alone the advantages to be secured by the consummation of the agreement, but also the nature and extent, of the loss to be sustained or reparation to be made, in case the agreement is not carried out. The application of this generalization to the industrial controversies of the present time leads to a most important conclusion. It is evident from the nature of the responsibility upon which reliance is placed for the enforcement of contracts, that all parties to an agreement must be commercially responsible; that is to say, they must be in the possession of some property, privilege, or advantage that may be placed in jeopardy as surety for their conduct. The great body of workmen, however, have no property, privilege, or advantage that they can place in jeopardy as a pledge for the fulfillment of a labor contract, from which it follows that labor contracts, on one side at least, are bereft of responsibility, and consequently incapable of enforcement by the orderly procedure of English jurisprudence.

In the situation thus portrayed, do we find the explanation, first, of the reckless manner in which workmen frequently urge their claims; and second, of the tendency on the part of employers to appeal to force. The workmen are reckless because in the evolution of modern industry they have been bereft of all proprietary interest in the plant that gives them employment; the employers appeal to force because there is nothing else to which they can appeal for the restraint of propertyless men. Such is the explanation of the belligerent condition in which the industrial world at present finds itself.

Two or three thoughts are suggested by the above presentation of the situation. In the first place, this turning of the mind toward authority is proof of an incipient infidelity respecting the claims of a free society. It is an admission that the law of property has reached the limit of its evolution, and that it is incapable of giving expression to that refinement of rights which results from differentiation in the industrial process. Its logical outcome is the abandonment of the English system of jurisprudence. He who appeals to force turns his back upon a society whose moral code is expressed in the language of rights, and turns his face toward a society whose moral code is expressed in the language of duty.

The second suggestion is, in a sense, the reverse of the one just mentioned. If it be true that the difficulty in the industrial situation arises from the fact that all men come into the industrial order by voluntary agreement, while the majority of men are in no way commercially responsible for the fulfillment of agreement, it is clear that one way of solving the difficulty would be to diffuse commercial responsibility. This, indeed, would be the conservative solution of the problem, for it demands a development within the accepted scheme of jurisprudence rather than a reversal of the established principles of jurisprudence. The truth is, the *régime* of contract cannot work unless all men are in substantially the same condition concerning property; not, I hasten to say, in the amount of property held, but in the relation which proprietorship establishes between the proprietor and industry. To demand, therefore, the diffusion of property, a phrase that I shall explain more fully in a moment, is a conservative demand, for the process it contemplates is essential to the conservation of the *régime* of contract which is the vital principle of liberty in the industrial world. . . .

It follows from this line of argument that in the industrial world the possession of property is essential to industrial liberty.

The assertion that property is essential to liberty should be the occasion of no apprehension. It is as old as the conception that the essence of liberty consists in a proper correlation of rights and responsibilities. He who reads with a discerning mind those writers who developed the theory of industrial individualism, will perceive that the ability of a careful and energetic man to acquire property, and through property to control the conditions under which he works, was an assumed, though frequently an unexpressed premise of all their arguments. The same thought underlies the theories of prosperity incorporated into the writings of professed economists. By reference also to the proposals of industrial reformers which have claimed, or are claiming, the attention of our own time, it will be discovered that they all agree in the assertion that it is impossible for a man to become master of himself without acquiring control over the opportunities of labor. What else can the doctrine of the English economists respecting the importance of personal savings imply? What other meaning can be given to the theory of co-operation, the aim of which is to make all laborers capitalists, if it be not that by becoming a proprietor one becomes his own master? How are we to understand the arguments for profit sharing, which urge that one of the perquisites of proprietorship be granted to the worker, except it be assumed that in this manner the worker is made a co-partner with his employer? The same thought lies at the basis of communism, collectivism, and socialism, all of which seek to guarantee men industrial liberty by converting the communal or political organization into an industrial corporation in which all men shall be share holders by virtue of being citizens. We are not concerned with the feasibility of these programmes of reform. They are referred to in this connection because the persistence of an idea is presumptive evidence that it pertains to the conditions out of which it springs; and it is indeed significant that the only ground common to all writers upon social affairs (with the single exception of those who believe in the Tory idea of society) is found in the phrase, that industrial liberty is impossible without industrial property. All recognize, in principle at least, the necessity of a property which shall become an universal possession in order that the character of the worker and the technique of production may conform to the motives of independence and the conditions of self-possession. In no other way can the sense of independence and the sense of responsibility be made universal. In no other way can the fruits of liberty in industry be realized. . . .

My second thought respecting that which, by courtesy of your imagination I have termed the workmen's property, is that its clarification will take place through the evolution of collective bargaining and the formal labor contract. . . .

My third suggestion respecting property rights adjusted to the needs of modern industry is, that the sociology of the industrial process renders it necessary, wherever the interests of society at large are concerned, to lay increased stress upon the theory of industrial agency. This concept is not strange to English jurisprudence, although it has been overgrown, in late years, by the assertions of self-aggrandizement. There is no necessity for the development of a new principle, but rather for the return of an old principle well recognized by common law. The problem to which this thought leads is forced upon our attention by the evolution of corporations, trusts, and great industries; and it is referred to in this connection for the purpose of saying, that the theory of property adjusted to the needs of our time is of a dual character. It must first express the rights of individuals associated together in an industrial unit; it must, next, express the duties of these industrial units to the public at large. The former constitutes the labor problem and the test of its solution should be freedom for the individual to realize himself. The latter constitutes the monopoly problem and the aim of its solution should be the attainment of a just price and the preservation of industrial mobility. Provided these rights can be discovered and expressed in such a manner that they may be incorporated in a contract, on the one hand, and in legislative enactment, on the other, there is no reason in the nature of the case, why harmony cannot be restored to the industrial world, and why the science of Political Economy may not recover that symmetry and form of which it has been deprived by the trenchant criticisms of the last fifty years. [Henry Carter Adams, "Economics and Jurisprudence," *Economic Studies*, Vol. II, No. 1 (American Economic Association by Macmillan, 1897): 8–10, 16–9, 22–5, 27–9, 31–5]

22. *The People and the Law*, Herbert Croly (1869–1930)[8]

In The Promise of American Life *(1909), Croly began a critique of the American upper bar for its role in shaping and protecting modern business corporations and its lack of regard for the larger public interest. In* Progressive Democracy *(1914), from which this selection is taken, Croly expanded on this critique by asking his readers to rethink the entire relationship between political democracy, constitutionalism, and the rule of law. With this rethinking, Croly hoped to lay the groundwork for a shift away from the current reliance on "mechanical jurisprudence" and toward an increased reliance on the power of popular sovereignty, executive power, and administrative law shaped by expert commissions.*

—1914—

Public opinion can no longer be hypnotized and scared into accepting the traditional constitutionalism, as the final word in politics. . . .

The Federal Constitution even more than the state constitutions was supposed to embody a social contract and a Higher Law—a code of righteous political behavior, any violation of which formed a justification of revolution. It was theoretically subject to popular control; popular control was seldom exercised as it was in the case of the state constitutions. The authority which the Higher Law ought to exercise, according to the political philosophy of the period, was reinforced by

---

8. More biographical information on Croly prefaces his selections in Chapters 1, 2, and 6.

the authority which, as a result of its comparative independence, it actually did exercise. The Law in the shape of the Federal Constitution really came to be a monarchy of the Word. It had been imposed upon the popular will, which was the only power capable of disputing its authority; and its friends came more and more to assume that the imposition was wise and beneficent. A systematic attempt was made to justify the supremacy of the Law. The people were warned that, if they rebelled, the just and awful judgment of the Lord would overtake them. Thus the aspirations and the conviction of the early democrats that popular political authority should be righteously expressed hardened into a system, which consecrated one particular machinery of possibly righteous expression. Reverence for law was made to mean reverence for one specific formulation of Law. Reverence for order was made to mean reverence for an established order. All that the American people had to do to insure their political salvation was vigilantly to safeguard the specific formulation of law and order which was found in the sacred writing. . . .

The Constitution was really king. Once the kingdom of the Word had been ordained, it was almost as seditious to question the Word as it was to plot against the kingdom. A monarch exists to be obeyed. In the United States, as in other monarchies, unquestioning obedience was erected into the highest of political virtues.

That the American people should have submitted so readily and so patiently to the kingdom of the Constitution is certainly an extraordinary fact. They were predisposed to insubordination rather than subordination, and the centrifugal political forces were insistent, pervasive and powerful. A complete explanation of this fact would afford the guiding clue to American political history, and would carry us far beyond the necessary limits of the present discussion; but the decisive importance of one agency of reconciliation seems sufficiently clear. The American people were reconciled to obedience partly as a consequence of the admirable administration of the new kingdom. By virtue of such administration the possibly remote, rigid and arid monarchy of the Word was converted into a benevolent human dominion, in such wise that this government by Law really became government by a peculiarly qualified body of men. Government by Law, it is true, was supposed to dispense with the need of any such highly responsible human agency. In theory all officials and even all citizens were both equally the servants of the Law, and equally free to place their own interpretation upon its meaning. But in practice this interpretation of the system deprived obedience of its essential quality. The monarchy of the Law could not be worked without the assistance of an administrative aristocracy, who made an exposition of the Law the excuse for mediating between its rigors and prevailing popular needs and opinions. . . .

The desire of the legal profession to protect the property of their clients from damage by adverse legislative action had much to do with the particular development of American jurisprudence; but no such economic motive affords any complete explanation of it. There was logic in it and good intentions as well as special economic interests. There was logic in it, because the unchecked assumption by the legislature of such a considerable discretionary authority would have made that branch of the government paramount over the other branches; and this result would have been wholly obnoxious to the principle of the separation of the powers. The traditional system was not intended to permit the exercise of a paramount legislative authority. There were good intentions in it, because this curb on legislative authority was at least in part desired for the purpose of rationalizing and moralizing the political behavior of the state. In case legislatures had possessed the legal power to commit flagrant acts of economic injustice, all the guarantees of the American system would have been meaningless. For these reasons American public opinion sustained the courts in the assertion of their authority. The manner in which the legislatures actually employed the police power of the state[9] convinced public opinion that its unrestrained exercise was dangerous, and should be checked by a free use of both an executive veto and that of the courts. The American people have never respected and trusted their legislative bodies to anything like the extent that the Englishmen have trusted Parliament; and our American legislatures have rarely deserved the trust.

No matter, consequently, how much such phrases as due process of law and the equal protection of the laws were tortured in order to serve as legal pretexts for judicial control over legislation, the logic of traditional political system demanded that they should be broken upon the rack. That system, according to its original presuppositions, could not survive unless it were rationalized and moralized. The attempt had been made to rationalize it by embodying what were supposed to be fundamental principles of right in the very constitution of the system;

---

9. Police power is the plenary power of state governments to regulate the health, morals, and general welfare of the community. This power, which was frequently used to grant favors to locally based economic interests by interfering in national market competition, was often overruled by the courts under the federal power to regulate interstate commerce and the due process clause of the Fourteenth Amendment.

and it necessarily followed that the active branches of the government, such as the executive and the legislature, must somehow be subordinated to these rules of justice. When it was found that the specific phrases which were supposed comprehensively to define essential individual liberties, still left to the legislatures so much discretionary authority that the exercise of it would erect them into the paramount branch of the government, it became necessary both to check their tendency to self-aggrandizement and to find warrant for the interference in the bill of rights. The warrant was found, but only with some difficulty and only by trusting to the courts a discretionary power almost equal to that which the legislatures had assumed: The angel of due process of law hovered over the dragon of the police power and prevented him from becoming the scourge of the land.

In this way the American system escaped the threat of legislative omnipotence, but only at the expense of making another branch of the government preponderant. The courts could not be said to be omnipotent, because they were a passive branch of government, and were supposed to decide particular cases rather than to establish general rules binding on the legislature. But they could not live up to the responsibility which they had assumed without attempting to develop constructive principles, to which subsequent legislative and executive action would in practice have to conform. As a consequence of their power to establish these principles and of the acquiescence therein by public opinion and the active branches of the government, the American judiciary began to exercise a positive political function. In relation to all matters of fundamental importance their opinions came to have a decisive influence on the policy of the state. Of course their political influence was exercised in the name of the Law and was supposed to possess the higher sanction which the Law in its majesty possesses over the arbitrary action of the human will; but in point of fact the American people were not living under a government of laws. What they had done was to prefer government by one class of men, viz. the class of lawyers, to that of another class, viz. the political leaders. This choice was made in obedience to the real necessities of their political system, which bestowed upon the legally trained man a privileged political position and a latently representative character. There is much to be said in its favor; but well as in certain respects it has worked, government by lawyers must not be confused with government by Law. In so far as it was successful, its success was due to the fact, not that it reduced the personal element in government to a minimum, but that it bestowed enormous political power upon a group of specially qualified men.

That so grave a political responsibility should have been intrusted in a democracy to a body of men not specifically elected for a political purpose, constitutes convincing testimony to the almost universal acceptance of certain underlying political convictions by the American people. They allowed the judges to decide political questions for them, only because the judges were supposed to represent the achieved results of political reason. American political welfare was dependent on political dogma. The dogma was embodied in the Law. The Law in its turn needed to be interpreted by a rule of reason. The rule of reason must emanate from the courts, because judicial decisions are determined by reasoning rather than merely by wilful choice. The courts could enforce their decisions with coercive measures only by the cooperation of the active government. They were disinterested and independent. Inasmuch as the American nation possessed an official political creed which required an authoritative exposition, the courts inevitably assumed the function of providing the regular version. The duty of expounding a political philosophy was never, indeed, expressly granted to them. The exercise of such a grave responsibility was without precedent in the English law or in a public law of any other nation. Yet the American courts assumed it for several generations to the apparent satisfaction of American public opinion. Their decisions upon constitutional cases have been filled with dissertations on political science which are of as much interest to students of politics as they are to possible future litigants. These philosophical jurists were actually possessed of an unique power which might have aroused the envy and admiration of the philosophical dogmatists of all ages—the power of making a real world conform without protest to their own ideas of what a world ought to be. They uttered words based upon a free rational interpretation of other words, and lo! men bowed their heads and submitted. . . .

That kingdom proved to have, like other kingdoms, a large element of human discretion in its composition. Its success was due less to the wisdom of the original formulation of the Word than to the ability with which the Word was adapted by the courts to national and local needs. In consequence of this benevolent administration of the Law, the American people cheerfully accepted its supremacy. Of that there can be no doubt. But even though the fact of acquiescence be fully recognized and even though it be admitted that the submission was based on solid reasons, certain grave questions remain to be asked—questions which concern the effect of their submission upon the American people and American public opinion.

Has our benevolent constitutional monarchy had the same reaction on our people that the national monarchies of Europe have had on theirs? The latter have in the long run not merely conferred upon their citizens the blessings of political stability and protection against foreign aggression, but, as an indirect result of these improved political conditions, the European nations have gradually succeeded in obtaining and in usefully exercising an increasing measure of self-government. Have the American people been prepared by the kingdom of the Law for an analogous increase in popular political responsibility? Or is it just as necessary as ever to subordinate the active expression of the prevailing popular will to tests derived from presumably righteous political dogmas and applied by an aristocracy of lawyers? In short, what is the permanent political value of this kingdom of the Law? Must it continue indefinitely to grind out righteous political conduct for the American people? Or has its function been educational as well as practical? Have the American people submitted to their benevolent monarchy, as well-behaved children submit to a schoolmaster, in the expectation of ultimate emancipation? Or has the increasing political maturity of the pupil availed nothing to make future tutelage less necessary?

The foregoing questions are critical and decisive. They should be considered with care and answered with caution. The current issue between conservatism and progressivism hangs upon the nature of the answers. If the traditional system has not been educational in its reaction on American public opinion, the conservative adherence to it in all its essentials becomes nothing other than obscurantism. But if its reaction has been educational, has not the inevitable result been to make the indefinite perpetuation of some of its specific safeguards less necessary? If the political education of a democracy does not authorize an increasing measure of popular political responsibility, what kind of an education has it been? . . .

The monarchy of the Constitution satisfied the current needs and the contemporary conscience of the American nation. Its government was at once authoritative, national and educational. It instructed the American people during their collective childhood. It trained them during their collective youth. With its assistance the American people have become a nation. They have been habituated to mutual association and joint action. Their union has been consolidated by a frightful Civil War. It has been consecrated by a multitude of sacrifices. It has been symbolized in a succession of national heroes. Established as it is in the nervous system and in the hearts of the American people, its composition is similar to that of the older European nations. . . .

Educational, moreover, as the monarchy of the Constitution has undoubtedly been, it has been in some respects educational in spite of itself. If it had been merely a machine for the grinding out of political righteousness, as it was usually conceived to be by the Fathers, its effect would never have been edifying. The American people were learning quite as much from their own unofficial experiments in democracy as they were from official instruction in the Word. The education which they obtained was the result of an attempt to combine democracy with the rule of a righteous Law. The combination was, as it happened, essentially external. Democracy and a moralistic legalism were both developing, and developing in relation one to the other, but the development was taking place along parallel lines rather than from a common centre. Nevertheless, even under the monarchy of the Constitution, the American people profited by a genuine experience in democracy—enough surely to deprive a more completely democratic polity of its former experimental character. Although the people have never fully exercised their ceremonial power, their supposed actual sovereignty, they have had the illusion of its exercise and their successes have been called the triumph of democracy. They have become more than ever democratic by conviction, and associate their future as a nation with the success of the democratic ideal.

The very means, however, which were adopted to nationalize the monarchy of the Word and make its effect upon public opinion formative, necessarily restricted the scope and value of its educational contribution. . . . In order to protect the monarchy from the aggrandizement of the legislature, it be came necessary to call in the assistance of the courts. The interpretation which the Law received at the hands of the courts, rather than the law itself, constituted the effective vehicle of the rule of reason. What the courts were really interpreting was not merely the written Word, but the ideal of justice, which the written Word was supposed to embody. As long as public opinion was agreed upon the general nature of the ideal of justice, it submitted without protest to the interpretation placed upon that ideal by the courts. But whenever serious differences developed in public opinion in respect to the contents of the ideal of justice, the duty of the courts became much more difficult and its dicta much less educational. Such differences raised an embarrassing question which had theretofore been successfully evaded—the question of a possible conflict between Demos and the traditional monarchy. What would happen in case the ideal of justice cherished by popular opinion began to diverge from that particular formulation of justice which had been worked out by the Fathers, which had been sanctioned in the bills of rights, and which had dominated the long and intricate process of judicial interpretation and amplification?

As a matter of fact a divergence of this kind has been growing. The ideal of individual justice is being supplemented by the ideal of social justice. When our constitutions were written, the traditions of the

English law, the contemporary political philosophy and the economic situation of the American democracy all conspired to embody in them and their interpretation an extremely individualistic conception of justice — a conception which practically confided social welfare to the free expression of individual interests and individual good intentions. Now the tendency is to conceive the social welfare, not as an end which cannot be left to the happy harmonizing of individual interests, but as an end which must be consciously willed by society and efficiently realized. Society, that is, has become a moral ideal, not independent of the individual but supplementary to him, an ideal which must be pursued less by regulating individual excesses than by the active conscious encouragement of socializing tendencies and purposes. . . .

The democracy was subordinated to the rule of reason in order that its behavior might be moralized and rationalized. Its behavior was made comparatively correct by this device, but correct conduct is a poor substitute for positive good-will. In truth, the traditional system was seeking to escape from the conditions and limitations of its own origin. It was afraid to trust the necessary sources of its own power. Democracy does not consist of a devouring popular sovereignty to which all limitations are essentially obnoxious. Many severe limitations are imposed upon it as a condition of its own self expression. But democracy as a living political system does demand the effective recognition of ultimate popular political responsibility. The serious criticism which can be directed against the traditional system is that it did not provide a sound and candid method of making popular political responsibility real and effective. The people are to be made responsible, not by acquiescence in a benevolent monarchy of the Word, but by their own disposition and power to prefer the public good. If democracy is to endure, its own essential good-will is the function which must be fortified; and its good-will can be fortified, not by the abdication but by the exercise of its own proper activity. The traditional system cannot permanently reinforce the function of popular self-government. In effect it asks the popular will to express itself in the act of renouncing certain essential political duties. To comply with the demand would in the long run be suicidal to a sincere democracy. [Herbert Croly, *Progressive Democracy* (Macmillan, 1914): 25–6, 44–5, 131–2, 138–49, 151–2]

23. *Sociological Jurisprudence,* Roscoe Pound (1870–1964)

Pound was born and educated in Lincoln, Nebraska, where his father served as a lawyer and judge. Roscoe had a varied career: after starting out as a botanist, he studied law at Harvard University and

worked for a time as a lawyer. Then, after earning a PhD in botany
from the University of Nebraska, he joined the university's law faculty
and eventually became the dean of the law school. At the University
of Nebraska, Pound was strongly influenced by Edward Ross, his
colleague in the sociology department. After teaching law briefly at
Northwestern University and the University of Chicago, Pound began
his long career at Harvard Law School, serving as its dean from 1916
through 1936. His most creative period in legal reform lasted from
1906 through 1920. Following that period, Pound, like Edward Ross,
became increasingly conservative—even embarrassingly so in the
1930s, when he opposed much of the New Deal, allied himself with
anti-Semitic Harvard alumni, and accepted an honorary degree from
the University of Berlin during the early years of Hitler's rise to
power. Nonetheless, Pound can claim to be the founding spirit of
what came to be called the "realist" movement in American law in
the 1920s.

—1910—

[**Law in Books and Law in Action**] If we look closely, distinctions
between law in the books and law in action, between the rules that pur-
port to govern the relations of man and man and those that in fact govern them, will appear, and it will be found that today also the distinction
between legal theory and judicial administration is often a very real and
a very deep one.

Let us take a few examples. It is a settled dogma of the books that
all doubts are to be resolved in favor of the constitutionality of a
statute—that the courts will not declare it in conflict with the constitution unless clearly and indubitably driven to that conclusion. But it
can not be maintained that such is the actual practice, especially with
respect to social legislation claimed to be in conflict with constitutional guaranties of liberty and property. The mere fact that the Court
of Appeals of New York and the Supreme Court of the United States
differed on such questions as the power to regulate hours of labor on
municipal and public contracts, and the power to regulate the hours
of labor of bakers, the former holding adversely to the one and
upholding the other, while the latter court had already ruled the
opposite on the first question and then reversed the ruling of the New
York court on the second, speaks for itself. Many more instances
might be noted. But it is enough to say that anyone who studies critically the course of decision upon constitutional questions in a majority of our state courts in recent years must agree with Professor

Freund[10] that the courts in practice tend to overturn all legislation which they deem unwise, and must admit the truth of Professor Dodd's statement:

> The courts have now definitely invaded the field of public policy and are quick to declare unconstitutional almost any laws of which they disapprove, particularly in the fields of social and industrial legislation. The statement still repeated by the courts that laws will not be declared unconstitutional unless their repugnance to the constitution is clear beyond a reasonable doubt, seems now to have become a mere courteous and smoothly transmitted platitude.

Another example is to be found in those jurisdictions where the common-law doctrines as to employer's liability still obtain and in those corners of employer's liability in other jurisdictions where recent legislation has left the common law in force. It is notorious that a feeling that employers and great industrial enterprises should bear the cost of the human wear and tear incident to their operations dictates more verdicts in cases of employer's liability than the rules of law laid down in the charges of the courts. Most of the new trials directed by our highest courts of review because the verdicts returned are not sustained by the evidence are in cases of this sort. Here the law in the books is settled and defined. The law administered is very different, and only the charge of the court, rigidly examined on appeal, serves to preserve an appearance of life in the legal theory. . . .

Another attempt at adjusting the letter of the law to the demands of administration in concrete cases, while apparently preserving the law unaltered, is to be seen in our American ritual, for in many jurisdictions it is little else, of written opinions, discussing and deducing from the precedents with great elaboration. As one reads the reports critically the conclusion is forced upon him that this ritual covers a deal of personal government by judges, a deal of "raw equity," or, as the Germans call it, of equitable application of law, and leaves many a soft spot in what is superficially a hard and fast rule, by means of which concrete causes are decided in practice as the good sense or feelings of fair play of the tribunal may dictate. Let one [example] suffice. In the law as to easements it is laid down that a right may be acquired by adverse use, although the known use was not objected to, if it was in fact, adverse. But the same

---

10. Ernst Freund (1864–1932), one of the founding members of the political science faculty at the University of Chicago in 1894, helped establish the university's law school. He was an associate of Jane Addams and fought for many Progressive causes.

courts say properly that a permissive user will give no right. When, however, one turns to the cases themselves and endeavors to fit each case in the scheme, not according to what the court said was the rule, but according to the facts of that case, he soon finds that the apparent rules to a great extent are no rules, and that where to allow the right would work a hardship the courts have discussed the decisions as to permissive user, and where, in the concrete cause, it seemed fair to grant the right they have insisted on the adverse character of the claimant's conduct. And the reason is not far to seek. We have developed so minute a jurisprudence of rules, we have interposed such a cloud of minute deductions between principles and concrete cases, that our case-law has become ultra-mechanical, and is no longer an effective instrument of justice if applied with technical accuracy. In theory our judges are tied down rigidly by hard and fast rules. Discretion is reduced to a strictly defined and narrowly limited minimum. Judicial law-making has produced a wealth of rules that has exhausted the field formerly afforded for the personal sense of justice of the tribunal. Legally, the judge's heart and conscience are eliminated. He is expected to force the case into the four corners of the pigeon-hole the books have provided. In practice, flesh and blood will not bow to such a theory. The face of the law may be saved by an elaborate ritual, but men, and not rules, will administer justice. . . .

Of the defects in our American administration of justice with which fault is found today, the more serious are reducible ultimately to two general propositions: (1) over-individualism in our doctrines and rules, an over-individualist conception of justice, and (2) over-reliance upon the machinery of justice and too much of the mechanical in the administration and application of rules and doctrines. At first sight the coexistence of over-individualism in the rules of law and in the doctrines from which they proceed, with lack of individualization or too little adjustment to individual cases in the application of the rules and doctrines, is a paradox. But in truth the latter is due to exactly the same causes, and is a result of the same attitude toward law and government and of the same frame of mind as the former. The former is an assertion of the individual against his fellows individually. The latter is an assertion of the individual against his fellows collectively. The former expresses the feeling of the self-reliant man that, as a free moral agent, he is to make his own bargains and determine upon his own acts and control his own property, accepting the responsibility that goes with such power, subjecting himself to liability for the consequences of his free choice, but exempt from interference in making his choice. The latter expresses the feeling of the same self-reliant man that neither the state, nor its representative, the magistrate, is competent to judge him better than his own conscience; that he is not to be judged by the discretion of men, but by the inflexible rule of the law. Each proceeds from jealousy of oppression of the individual. The former is due to fear he may be oppressed in the interest or for the protection of others; the latter is due to fear that a magistrate, who has power to adjust rules to concrete cases and discretion in the application of legal doctrines, may misuse that power and abuse that discretion to the injury of some individual. It assumes that oppression by mechanical laws, mechanically executed, is preferable to government by other men exercising their own will and judgment, and that elimination of every personal element and procedure according to hard and fast rules necessarily constitutes justice. Each is a phase, therefore, of the extreme individualism which is one of the chief characteristics of the common law. . . .

When in a period of collectivist thinking and social legislation courts and lawyers assume that the only permissible way of thinking or of law-making is limited and defined by individualism of the old type, when, while men are seeking to promote the ends of society through social control, jurists lay it down that the only method of human discipline is "to leave each man to work out in freedom his own happiness or misery," conflict is inevitable. With jurisprudence once more in the rags of a past century, while kindred sciences have been reclothed, we may be sure that law in the books will often tend to be very different from the law in action. . . .

Let us look the facts of human conduct in the face. Let us look to economics and sociology and philosophy, and cease to assume that jurisprudence is self-sufficient. It is the work of lawyers to make the law in action conform to the law in the books, not by futile thunderings against popular lawlessness, nor eloquent exhortations to obedience of the written law, but by making the law in the books such that the law in action can conform to it, and providing a speedy, cheap and efficient legal mode of applying it. On no other terms can the two be reconciled.

—1909—

[Liberty of Contract] The idea that unlimited freedom of making promises was a natural right came after enforcement of promises when made, had become a matter of course. It began as a doctrine of political economy, as a phase of Adam Smith's[11] doctrine which we commonly

---

11. Adam Smith (1723–1790) was a Scottish philosopher and political economist who, in *Wealth of Nations* (1776), founded classical economics.

call *laisser faire*. It was propounded as a utilitarian principle of politics and legislation by Mill.[12] Spencer[13] deduced it from his formula of justice. In this way it became a chief article in the creed of those who sought to minimize the functions of the state, that the most important of its functions was to enforce by law the obligations created by contract. But we must remember that the task of the English individualists was to abolish a body of antiquated institutions that stood in the way of human progress. Freedom of contract was the best instrument at hand for the purpose. They adopted it as a means, and made it an end. While this evolution of juristic and political thought was in progress, the common law too had become thoroughly individualistic; partly from innate tendency, partly through theological influence, partly through the contests between the courts and the crown in the sixteenth and seventeenth centuries, and partly as a result of the course of thought in the eighteenth and nineteenth centuries. This bit of history may suggest the chief, although not all, of the causes of the phenomenon we are considering.

In my opinion, the causes to which we must attribute the course of American constitutional decisions upon liberty of contract are seven: (1) The currency in juristic thought of an individualist conception of justice, which exaggerates the importance of property and of contract, exaggerates private right at the expense of public right, and is hostile to legislation, taking a minimum of law-making to be the ideal; (2) what I have ventured to call on another occasion a condition of mechanical jurisprudence, a condition of juristic thought and judicial action in which deduction from conceptions has produced a cloud of rules that obscures the principles from which they were drawn, in which conceptions are developed logically at the expense of practical results and in which the artificiality characteristic of legal reasoning is exaggerated; (3) the survival of purely juristic notions of the state and of economics and politics as against the social conceptions of the present; (4) the training of judges and lawyers in eighteenth century philosophy of law and the pretended contempt for philosophy in law that keeps the legal

---

12. John Stuart Mill (1806–1873) was an English philosopher who wrote widely on economics and society; among his many notable books was *Principles of Political Economy* (1848).

13. Herbert Spencer (1820–1903) was an English social philosopher influential in translating evolutionary ideas from biology into "social Darwinism," in which individual economic competition is viewed as the engine of natural selection and social progress. This idea is best illustrated in his books *Social Statics* (1851) and *The Man Versus the State* (1884).

profession in the bonds of the philosophy of the past because it is to be found in law-sheep bindings; (5) the circumstance that natural law is the theory of our bills of rights and the impossibility of applying such a theory except when all men are agreed in their moral and economic views and look to a single authority to fix them; (6) the circumstance that our earlier labor legislation came before the public was prepared for it, so that the courts largely voiced well-meant but unadvised protests of the old order against the new, at a time when the public at large was by no means committed to the new; and (7) by no means least, the sharp line between law and fact in our legal system which requires constitutionality, as a legal question, to be tried by artificial criteria of general application and prevents effective judicial investigation or consideration of the situations of fact behind or bearing upon the statutes.

—1908—

[**Mechanical Jurisprudence**] Scientific law is a reasoned body of principles for the administration of justice, and its antithesis is a system of enforcing magisterial caprice, however honest, and however much disguised under the name of justice or equity or natural law. But this scientific character of law is a means,—a means toward the end of law, which is the administration of justice. Law is forced to take on this character in order to accomplish its end fully, equally, and exactly; and in so far as it fails to perform its function fully, equally, and exactly, it fails in the end for which it exists. Law is scientific in order to eliminate so far as may be the personal equation in judicial administration, to preclude corruption and to limit the dangerous possibilities of magisterial ignorance. Law is not scientific for the sake of science. Being scientific as a means toward an end, it must be judged by the results it achieves, not by the niceties of its internal structure; it must be valued by the extent to which it meets its end, not by the beauty of its logical processes or the strictness with which its rules proceed from the dogmas it takes for its foundation.

Two dangers have to be guarded against in a scientific legal system, one of them in the direction of the effect of its scientific and artificial character upon the public, the other in the direction of its effect upon the courts and the legal profession. With respect to the first danger, it is well to remember that law must not become too scientific for the people to appreciate its workings. Law has the practical function of adjusting every-day relations so as to meet current ideas of fair play. It must not become so completely artificial that the public is led to regard it as wholly arbitrary. No institution can stand upon such a basis today.

Reverence for institutions of the past will not preserve, of itself, an institution that touches every-day life as profoundly as does the law. Legal theory can no more stand as a sacred tradition in the modern world than can political theory. It has been one of the great merits of English law that its votaries have always borne this in mind. . . .

In the other direction, the effect of a scientific legal system upon the courts and upon the legal profession is more subtle and far-reaching. The effect of all system is apt to be petrification of the subject systematized. Perfection of scientific system and exposition tends to cut off individual initiative in the future, to stifle independent consideration of new problems and of new phases of old problems, and to impose the ideas of one generation upon another. This is so in all departments of learning. One of the obstacles to advance in every science is the domination of the ghosts of departed masters. Their sound methods are forgotten, while their unsound conclusions are held for gospel. Legal science is not exempt from this tendency. Legal systems have their periods in which science degenerates, in which system decays into technicality, in which a scientific jurisprudence becomes a mechanical jurisprudence. . . .

I have referred to mechanical jurisprudence as scientific because those who administer it believe it such. But in truth it is not science at all. We no longer hold anything scientific merely because it exhibits a rigid scheme of deductions from *a priori* conceptions. In the philosophy of today, theories are "instruments, not answers to enigmas, in which we can rest." The idea of science as a system of deductions has become obsolete, and the revolution which has taken place in other sciences in this regard must take place and is taking place in jurisprudence also. . . .

Herein is the task of the sociological jurist. Professor [Albion] Small defines the sociological movement as "a frank endeavor to secure for the human factor in experience the central place which belongs to it in our whole scheme of thought and action." The sociological movement in jurisprudence is a movement for pragmatism as a philosophy of law; for the adjustment of principles and doctrines to the human conditions they are to govern rather than to assumed first principles; for putting the human factor in the central place and relegating logic to its true position as an instrument. . . .

The nadir of mechanical jurisprudence is reached when conceptions are used, not as premises from which to reason, but as ultimate solutions. So used, they cease to be conceptions and become empty words. . . .

With legislative law-making in the grip of the imperative theory and its arbitrary results, and judicial decision in the grip of a jurisprudence of conceptions and its equally arbitrary results, whither are we to turn? Judicial law-making cannot serve us. As things are, the cure would be worse than the disease. No court could hold such hearings as those had by legislative committees upon measures for the protection of operatives, described by Mrs. [Florence] Kelley, or that recently had before the Interstate Commerce Commission as to uniform bills of lading. We must soon have a new starting-point that only legislation can afford. That we may put the sociological, the pragmatic theory behind legislation, is demonstrating every day. Legislative reference bureaus, the Comparative Law Bureau, the Conferences of Commissioners on Uniform State Laws, . . . such conferences as the one held recently with respect to the Sherman Anti-trust Law, bar-association discussions of reforms in procedure,—all these are furnishing abundant material for legislation of the best type. . . .

Herein is a noble task for the legal scholars of America. To test the conceptions worked out in the common law by the requirements of the new juristic theory, to lay sure foundations for the ultimate legislative restatement of the law, from which judicial decision shall start afresh,— this is as great an opportunity as has fallen to the jurists of any age. [Roscoe Pound, "Law in Books and Law in Action" (44 *American Law Review*, 1910), 15–6, 19–20, 26–7, 30, 35–6; "Liberty of Contract" (18 *Yale Law Journal*, 1909): 456–8; "Mechanical Jurisprudence" (8 *Columbia Law Review*, 1908): 605–10, 620–2]

24. *Pragmatic Method and the Law,* John Dewey (1859–1952)[14]

Although Dewey is perhaps best known for his writings in philosophy and education, he had an abiding interest in law. To Dewey, law represented an attempt to formalize or "arrest" experience into a set of fixed rules, even as experience and life continuously present new situations and choices. In Ethics *(1908), from which a selection was taken in Chapter 4 of this collection, Dewey stated:*

It is . . . absurd to separate the legal and the ideal aspects of freedom from one another. It is only as men are held liable that they become responsible; even the conscientious man, however much in some respects his

---

14. More biographical information on Dewey prefaces his selection in Chapter 4.

demands upon himself exceed those which would be enforced against him by others, still needs in other respects to have his unconscious partiality and presumption steadied by the requirements of others. . . . It is only as men are exempt from external obstruction that they become aware of possibilities, and are awakened to demand and strive to obtain more positive freedom.[15]

—1924—

If we consider the procedure of the mathematician or of any man of science, as it concretely occurs, instead of considering simply the relations of consistent implication which subsist between the propositions in which his finally approved conclusions are set forth, we find that he, as well as an intelligent farmer or business man or physician, is constantly engaged in making decisions; and that in order to make them wisely he summons before his mental gaze various considerations, and accepts and rejects them with a view to making his decision as rational as possible. The concrete subject with which he deals, the material he investigates, accepts, rejects, employs in reaching and justifying his decision, is different from that of farmer, lawyer, or merchant, but the course of the operation, the form of the procedure, is similar. The scientific man has the advantage of working under much more narrowly and exactly controlled conditions, with the aid of symbols artfully devised to protect his procedure. For that reason it is natural and proper that we should, in our formal treatises, take operations of this type as standards and models, and should treat ordinary 'practical' reasonings leading up to decisions as to what is to be done as only approximations. But every thinker, as an investigator, mathematician, or physicist as well as 'practical man,' thinks in order to determine *his* decisions and conduct—his conduct as a specialized agent working in a carefully delimited field.

It may be replied, of course, that this is an arbitrary notion of logic, and that in reality logic is an affair of the relations and orders of relations which subsist between propositions which constitute the accepted subject-matter of a science; that relations are independent of operations of inquiry and of reaching conclusions or decisions. I shall not stop to try to controvert this position, but shall use it to point [out] the essential difference between it and the position taken in this article. According to the latter, logical systematization with a view to the utmost generality and consistency of propositions is indispensable but is not ultimate. It is an instrumentality, not an end. It is a means of improving, facilitating,

---

15. Dewey and Tufts, *Ethics* (1908), 439.

clarifying the inquiry that leads up to concrete decisions; primarily that particular inquiry which has just been engaged in, but secondarily, and of greater ultimate importance, other inquiries directed at making other decisions in similar fields. And here at least I may fall back for confirmation upon the special theme of law. It is most important that rules of law should form as coherent generalized logical systems as possible. But these logical systematizations of law in any field, whether of crime, contracts or torts, with their reduction of a multitude of decisions to a few general principles that are logically consistent with one another while it may be an end in itself for a particular student, is clearly in last resort subservient to the economical and effective reaching of decisions in particular cases.

It follows that logic is ultimately an empirical and concrete discipline. Men first employ certain ways of investigating, and of collecting, recording and using data in reaching conclusions, in making decisions; they draw inferences and make their checks and tests in various ways. These different ways constitute the empirical raw material of logical theory. The latter thus comes into existence without any conscious thought of logic, just as forms of speech take place without conscious reference to rules of syntax or of rhetorical propriety. But it is gradually learned that some methods which are used work better than others. Some yield conclusions that do not stand the test of further situations; they produce conflicts and confusion; decisions dependent upon them have to be retracted or revised. Other methods are found to yield conclusions which are available in subsequent inquiries as well as confirmed by them. There first occurs a kind of natural selection of the methods which afford the better type of conclusion, better for subsequent usage, just as happens in the development of rules for conducting any art. Afterwards the methods are themselves studied critically. Successful ones are not only selected and collated, but the causes of their effective operation are discovered. Thus logical theory becomes scientific.

The bearing of the conception of logic which is here advanced upon legal thinking and decisions may be brought out by examining the apparent disparity which exists between actual legal development and the strict requirements of logical theory. Justice Holmes has generalized the situation by saying that "the whole outline of the law is the resultant of a conflict at every point between logic and good sense—the one striving to work fiction out to consistent results, the other restraining and at last overcoming that effort when the results become too manifestly unjust." This statement he substantiates by a thorough examination of the development of certain legal notions. Upon its surface, such a statement implies a different view of the nature of logic than that stated. It implies that logic is not the method of good sense, that it has as it were a substance and life of its own which conflicts with the requirements of good decisions with respect to concrete subject-matters. The difference, however, is largely verbal. What Justice Holmes terms logic is formal consistency, consistency of concepts with one another irrespective of the consequences of their application to concrete matters-of-fact. We might state the fact by saying that concepts once developed have a kind of intrinsic inertia on their own account; once developed the law of habit applies to them. It is practically economical to use a concept ready at hand rather than to take time and trouble and effort to change it or to devise a new one. The use of prior ready-made and familiar concepts also gives rise to a sense of stability, of guarantee against sudden and arbitrary changes of the rules which determine the consequences which legally attend acts. It is the nature of any concept, as it is of any habit to change more slowly than do the concrete circumstances with reference to which it is employed. Experience shows that the relative fixity of concepts affords men with a specious sense of protection, of assurance against the troublesome flux of events. Thus Justice Holmes says, "The language of judicial decision is mainly the language of logic. And the logical method and form flatter that longing for certainty and for repose which is in every human mind. But certainty generally is an illusion." From the view of logical method here set forth, however, the undoubted facts which Justice Holmes has in mind do not concern logic but rather certain tendencies of the human creatures who use logic; tendencies which a sound logic will guard against. For they spring from the momentum of habit once forced, and express the effect of habit upon our feelings of ease and stability—feelings which have little to do with the actual facts of the case.

However this is only part of the story. The rest of the story is brought to light in some other passages of Justice Holmes. "The actual life of the law has not been logic: it has been experience. The felt necessities of the times, the prevalent moral and political theories, intuitions of public policy, avowed or unconscious, even the prejudices which judges share with their fellow-men, have had a good deal more to do than the syllogism in determining the rules by which men should be governed." In other words, Justice Holmes is thinking of logic as equivalent with the syllogism, as he is quite entitled to do in accord with the orthodox tradition. From the standpoint of the syllogism as the logical model which was made current by scholasticism there *is* an antithesis between experience and logic, between logic and good sense. For the philosophy embodied in the formal theory of the syllogism asserted that thought or reason has fixed forms of its own, anterior to and independent of concrete subject-matters, and to which the latter have to be adapted whether or no. This defines the negative aspect of this discussion; and it shows by contrast the need of another kind of logic which shall reduce the influence of habit, and shall facilitate the use of good sense regarding matters of social consequence.

In other words, there are different logics in use. One of these, the one which has had greatest historic currency and exercised greatest influence on legal decisions, is that of the syllogism. To this logic the strictures of Justice Holmes apply in full force. For it purports to be a logic of rigid demonstration, not of search and discovery. . . .

It thus implies that for every possible case which may arise, there is a fixed antecedent rule already at hand; that the case in question is either simple and unambiguous, or is resolvable by direct inspection into a collection of simple and indubitable facts, such as, 'Socrates is a man.' It thus tends, when it is accepted, to produce and confirm what Professor Pound has called mechanical jurisprudence; it flatters that longing for certainty of which Justice Holmes speaks; it reinforces those inert factors in human nature which make men hug as long as possible any idea which has once gained lodgment in the mind. In a certain sense it is foolish to criticise the model supplied by the syllogism. The statements made about men and Socrates are obviously true, and the connection between them is undoubted. The trouble is that while the syllogism sets forth the *results* of thinking, it has nothing to do with the *operation* of thinking. . . .

As a matter of fact, men do not begin thinking with premises. They begin with some complicated and confused case, apparently admitting of alternative modes of treatment and solution. Premises only gradually emerge from analysis of the total situation. The problem is not to draw a conclusion from given premises; that can best be done by a piece of inanimate machinery by fingering a keyboard. The problem is to *find* statements of general principle and of particular fact, which are worthy to serve as premises. As a matter of actual fact, we generally begin with some vague anticipation of a conclusion (or at least of alternative conclusions), and then we look around for principles and data which will substantiate it or which will enable us to choose intelligently between rival conclusions. No lawyer ever thought out the case of a client in terms of the syllogism. He begins with a conclusion which he intends to reach, favorable to his client of course, and then analyzes the facts of the situation to find material out of which to construct a favorable statement of facts, to *form* a minor premise. At the same time he goes over recorded cases to find rules of law employed in cases which can be

presented as similar, rules which will substantiate a certain way of looking at and interpreting the facts. And as his acquaintance with rules of
law judged applicable widens, he probably alters perspective and
emphasis in selection of the facts which are to form his evidential data.
And as he learns more of the facts of the case he may modify his selection of rules of law upon which he bases his case.

I do not for a moment set up this procedure as a model of scientific
method; it is too precommitted to the establishment of a particular and
partisan conclusion to serve as such a model. But it does illustrate, in
spite of this deficiency, the particular point which is being made here:
namely, that thinking actually sets out from a more or less confused situation, which is vague and ambiguous with respect to the conclusion it
indicates, and that the formation of both major premise and minor proceed tentatively and correlatively in the course of analysis of this situation and of prior rules. As soon as acceptable premises are given and of
course the judge and jury have eventually to do with their becoming
accepted—and the conclusion is also given. In strict logic, the conclusion does not follow from premises; conclusions and premises are two
ways of stating the same thing. Thinking may be defined either as a
development of premises or development of a conclusion; as far as it is
one operation it is the other.

Courts not only reach decisions; they expound them, and the exposition must state justifying reasons. The mental operations therein
involved are somewhat different from those involved in arriving at a conclusion. The logic of exposition is different from that of search and
inquiry. In the latter, the situation as it exists is more or less doubtful,
indeterminate, and problematic with respect to what it signifies. It
unfolds itself gradually and is susceptible of dramatic surprise; at all
events it has, for the time being, two sides. Exposition implies that a
definitive solution is reached, that the situation is now determinate with
respect to its legal implication. Its purpose is to set forth grounds for the
decision reached so that it will not appear as an arbitrary dictum, and so
that it will indicate a rule for dealing with similar cases in the future. It
is highly probable that the need of justifying to others conclusions
reached and decisions made has been the chief cause of the origin and
development of logical operations in the precise sense; of abstraction,
generalization, regard for consistency of implications. It is quite conceivable that if no one had ever had to account to others for his decisions,
logical operations would never have developed, but men would use
exclusively methods of inarticulate intuition and impression, feeling; so
that only after considerable experience in accounting for their decisions
to others who demanded a reason, or exculpation, and were not satisfied

till they got it, did men begin to give an account to themselves of the process of reaching a conclusion in a justified way. However this may be, it is certain that in judicial decisions the only alternative to arbitrary dicta, accepted by the parties to a controversy only because of the authority or prestige of the judge, is a rational statement which formulates grounds and exposes connecting or logical links.

It is at this point that the chief stimulus and temptation to mechanical logic and abstract use of formal concepts come in. Just because the personal element cannot be wholly excluded, while at the same time the decision must assume as nearly as possible an impersonal, objective, rational form, the temptation is to surrender the vital logic which has actually yielded the conclusion and to substitute for it forms of speech which are rigorous in appearance and which give an illusion of certitude. . . .

This is a legitimate requirement from the standpoint of the interests of the community and of particular individuals. Enormous confusion has resulted, however, from confusion of *theoretical* certainty and practical certainty. There is a wide gap separating the reasonable proposition that judicial decisions should possess the maximum possible regularity in order to enable persons in planning their conduct to foresee the legal import of their acts, and the absurd because impossible proposition that every decision should flow with formal logical necessity from antecedently known premises. To attain the former result there are required general principles of interpreting cases—rules of law—and procedures of pleading and trying cases which do not alter arbitrarily. But principles of interpretation do not signify rules so rigid that they can be stated once for all and then be literally and mechanically adhered to. For the situations to which they are to be applied do not literally repeat one another in all details, and questions of degree of this factor or that have the chief weight in determining which general rule will be employed to judge the situation in question. A large part of what has been asserted concerning the necessity of absolutely uniform and immutable antecedent rules of law is in effect an attempt to evade the really important issue of finding and employing rules of law, substantive and procedural, which will actually secure to the members of the community a reasonable measure of practical certainty of expectation in framing their courses of conduct. The mechanical ease of the court in disposing of cases and not the actual security of agents is the real cause, for example, of making rules of pleading hard and fast. The result introduces an unnecessary element of gamble into the behavior of those seeking settlement of disputes, while it affords to the judges only that factitious ease and simplicity which is supplied by any routine habit of action. It substitutes a mechanical procedure for the need of analytic thought. . . .

Failure to recognize that general legal rules and principles are working hypotheses, needing to be constantly tested by the way in which they work out in application to concrete situations, explains the otherwise paradoxical fact that the slogans of the liberalism of one period often become the bulwarks of reaction in a subsequent era. There was a time in the eighteenth century when the great social need was emancipation of industry and trade from a multitude of restrictions which held over from the feudal estate of Europe. Adapted well enough to the localized and fixed conditions of that earlier age, they became hindrances and annoyances as the effects of methods, use of coal and steam, showed themselves. The movement of emancipation expressed itself in principles of liberty in use of property, and freedom of contract, which were embodied in a mass of legal decisions. But the absolutistic logic of rigid syllogistic forms infected these ideas. It was soon forgotten that they were relative to analysis of existing situations in order to secure orderly methods in behalf of economic social welfare. Thus these principles became in turn so rigid as to be almost as socially obstructive as "immutable" feudal laws had been in their day.

That the remarks which have been made, commonplace as they are in themselves, have a profound practical import may also be seen in the present reaction against the individualistic formulae of an older liberalism. The last thirty years has seen an intermittent tendency in the direction of legislation, and to a less extent of judicial decision, towards what is vaguely known as "social justice," toward formulae of a collectivistic character. Now it is quite possible that the newer rules may be needed and useful at a certain juncture, and yet that they may also become harmful and socially obstructive if they are hardened into absolute and fixed antecedent premises. But if they are conceived as tools to be adapted to the conditions in which they are employed rather than as absolute and intrinsic "principles," attention will go to the facts of social life, and the rules will not be allowed to engross attention and become absolute truths to be maintained intact at all costs. Otherwise we shall in the end merely have substituted one set of formally absolute and immutable syllogistic premises for another set.

If we recur then to our introductory conception that logic is really a theory about empirical phenomena, subject to growth and improvement like any other empirical discipline, we recur to it with an added conviction: namely, that the issue is not a purely speculative one, but implies consequences vastly significant for practise. I should indeed not hesitate to assert that the sanctification of ready-made antecedent universal principles as methods of thinking is the chief obstacle to the kind of thinking which is the indispensable prerequisite of steady, secure and intelligent social reforms in general and social advance by means of law in particular. If this be so infiltration into law of a more experimental and flexible logic is a social as well as an intellectual need. [John Dewey, "Logical Method and the Law" (10 *Cornell Law Quarterly*, 1924): 19–27]

Further Reading

Beard, Charles, *American Government and Politics* (Macmillan, 1928).

Brand, Donald R., *Corporatism and the Rule of Law: A Study of the National Recovery Administration* (Cornell University Press, 1988), Part I.

Cohen, Morris R., and Felix S. Cohen, *Readings in Jurisprudence and Legal Philosophy* (Little, Brown, 1951).

Dewey, John, and James Tufts, *Ethics* (Henry Holt, 1908).

Fine, Sidney, *Laissez-Faire and the General Welfare State* (University of Michigan Press, 1964).

Fisher III, William W., Morton J. Horwitz, and Thomas A. Reed, eds., *American Legal Realism* (Oxford University Press, 1993).

Fried, Barbara H., *The Progressive Assault on Laissez Faire* (Harvard University Press, 2001).

Gillman, Howard, *The Constitution Besieged: The Rise and Demise of Lochner Era Police Powers Jurisprudence* (Duke University Press, 1993).

Horwitz, Morton J., *The Transformation of American Law, 1870–1960: The Crisis of Legal Orthodoxy* (Oxford University Press, 1992).

McCloskey, Robert G., *The American Supreme Court*, ed. Sanford Levinson (University of Chicago Press, 2005).

Orren, Karen, *Belated Feudalism: Labor, the Law, and Liberal Development in the United States* (Cambridge University Press, 1992).

Skowronek, Stephen, *Building a New American State: The Expansion of National Administrative Capacities, 1877–1920* (Cambridge University Press, 1982).

Stevens, Robert, *Law School: Legal Education in America from the 1850s to the 1980s* (University of North Carolina Press, 1983).

White, Morton, *Social Thought in America: The Revolt against Formalism* (Beacon, 1957).

Witt, John Fabian, *The Accidental Republic: Crippled Workingmen, Destitute Widows, and the Remaking of American Law* (Harvard University Press, 2004).

6

The Labor Question

Progressives, who viewed the labor question from a broad perspective, assumed that wage labor would become the standard source of income for most Americans. A good statement of this organizing assumption is found in a recent study of Progressive political economy:

> But once civil society was no longer an assembly of individual proprietors who were equally subject to the anonymous laws of the market—once a certain concentration of wealth and the permanence of a propertyless "wage class" were evident to all interested observers—any expectation of agreement among civil society's constituent elements on the most basic rights and obligations (e.g., of property) became dangerously naïve. Arthur Hadley,[1] the authority on (and director of) railroads from Yale . . . explained the problem in this way: "A republican government is organized on the assumption that all men are free and equal. If the political power is . . . equally distributed while the industrial power is concentrated in the hands of a few, it creates dangers of class struggles and class legislation which menace both our political and our industrial order." . . . It is precisely because they did not try to avoid the issues raised by the "socialistic writers," as Hadley called them, that they were successful in enunciating a new language of political obligation which stressed the active service and progressive functions of capital.[2]

Under this assumption, then, the specific issue of legal recognition for trade unions and the legitimacy of strikes—issues so prominent in New Deal liberalism—were somewhat subordinated by such larger issues as industrial wage labor, immigration, and urbanization. Because Progressives sought to create a consensual model of society, they thought the idea of simply advocating powerful labor interests against powerful capitalist interests was a recipe for social chaos. Because they ardently hoped for assimilation of wage laborers and their families into the larger democratic community, they were primarily interested in investigating, and eliminating, the ideas, institutions,

---

1. Arthur Twining Hadley (1856–1930) studied the economics of the railroad industry at Yale University, where his father was professor of Greek, and in Berlin. When Hadley became president of Yale, he also became a "public moralist" of sorts, speaking and writing on a wide range of public issues.

2. Livingston, *Pragmatism and Political Economy* (1994), 59–60.

and practices that stood in the way of that assimilation. To Progressive moralists, the major barrier was selfishness legitimized by individualism; to Progressive economists, the greatest obstacles were laissez-faire capitalism and the *rentier* values[3] of small-producer capitalism, small shops, and small, under-capitalized farms (the protection of which would sap the dynamism and the economic surplus generated by industrial capitalism); to Progressive social and settlement house workers, the problem was the naïve optimism that social assimilation would occur as the result of exhortation combined with self-righteous acts of charity in times of direst need. They believed that legislative, regulatory, and educational changes were necessary if the problem of permanent wage labor was to be addressed effectively. The clearest institutional expression of consensual and all-embracing goals was the formation in 1894 of the National Civic Federation. The Federation's goal was to construct a kind of progressive corporatism that brought together social scientists, labor leaders, large corporations, and financial institutions.[4]

As the selection from Herbert Croly (later in this chapter) indicates, it was only late in the Progressive period that labor unions, and the legislative response to union demands, became more central in Progressive thinking. John Rogers Commons (1862–1945), Richard Ely's colleague at the University of Wisconsin, was one of the first intellectuals to focus on this shift. Named after a sixteenth-century English Protestant martyr, and educated at Oberlin College, Commons first organized and wrote for the American Institute of Christian Sociology; he then assisted the director of the National Civic Federation. Following his professorial appointment, Commons conceived and drafted many legislative reforms in Wisconsin (ranging from civil service and public utilities to workers' compensation), headed a research bureau for Milwaukee's socialist mayor, and, in 1913–1914, investigated labor unrest for President Wilson's U.S. Commission on Industrial Relations. These experiences and the empirical studies they generated became the basis for Common's most influential book, *Principles of Labor Legislation*. He went on to lead a team of authors to write a definitive four-volume history of American labor.

---

3. *Rentier* values are based on the extra benefits extracted from the economy by virtue of landownership (by definition a local monopoly) and local monopolies in the provisions of goods and services.

4. Weinstein, *The Corporate Ideal* (1968).

25. *A Programme for Labor Reform,* Richard Ely (1854–1943)[5] and Seth Low (1850–1916)

Ely, a great promoter of Progressive causes, wrote for such weekly and monthly journals as Forum, Harper's, Independent, *and* Atlantic Monthly. *He also wrote for more popular audiences: in 1901, he wrote five articles on subjects ranging from tax reform to the steel trust for* Cosmopolitan, *a woman-and-family-oriented monthly with a circulation of more than half a million.* Century Magazine, *from which the following selection is taken, purveyed Progressive values through a monthly selection of biographies, news, and reports. It was also the major source of the surge of interest in, and veneration for, Abraham Lincoln, with scores of articles related to Lincoln and the Civil War. Although the "Programme for Labor Reform" is a report to the Sociological Group by a committee consisting of Ely and Seth Low, it was actually written by Ely. Low (1850–1916) was a remarkable leader: mayor of Brooklyn, America's third largest city, from 1881 to 1885; president of Columbia University, his alma mater, from 1890 to 1901; and then mayor of the newly consolidated New York City, from 1901 to 1903 (he ran on an anticorruption platform). From 1907 until his death in 1916, Low served as chairman of Booker T. Washington's Tuskegee Institute in Alabama.*

—1890—

The labor problem is not a single problem, but a whole group of inter-related problems to which, in popular language the singular noun rightly attributes unity. The labor problem is a part of the great social question of our day, and it concerns us all vitally.

We reach first of all this conclusion: *The labor problem is only a fractional part of the entire problem of industrial society, and the entire problem of industrial society is only one part of the whole social problem, which includes art, religion, literature, and the various other departments of social life.* While, then, its scope is exaggerated by extreme labor reformers, its ramifications are such that it touches all men, and whoever fails to recognize this errs in an opposite direction.

Recent industrial movements show that industrial questions now under discussion affect the merchant, the manufacturer, the farmer,

---

5. More biographical information on Ely prefaces his selection in Chapter 3.

and the professional classes, and in some cases perhaps even more keenly than the class of wage-workers. It is conceivable that a vast network of monopolies, crushing out all independent producers, might give to artisans, mechanics, and unskilled laborers as steady work as they now receive, or even steadier; as high wages as they now receive, or even higher; and might in the exercise of a beneficent paternalism cause strikes to cease. It by no means follows that this consummation would be a desirable one. We are not prepared to say that a society composed of a few plutocrats and a vast mass of even contented day-laborers is in a truly prosperous condition. We would prefer rather a society composed of many grades, with easy transition from any one grade to the next higher, or even the next lower. We arrive then at the second general conclusion: *The labor problem is by no means merely a class problem, and we deprecate as most unfortunate any attempt to treat it as such.*

On the other hand, all social questions touch the labor problem, because the advance of civilization is a matter of vital concern to wage earners, who cannot prosper as members of a diseased organism. The real advance of labor can come only as part of true social progress; but true social progress is, in our day at least, impossible unless even the humblest classes participate to an increasing extent in the benefits of civilization. The most we could grant is this: as the most numerous class, and as the weaker industrial class upon whom burdens are too easily shifted, perhaps the laboring class is on the whole more deeply concerned in the various problems of industrial society than any other element of this society.

It is, then, well to form the habit of looking at society and its movements from the standpoint of the laborers, because their interests are identical with the interests of the whole of society. *Whenever we truly advance the interests of wage-earners we necessarily advance the interests of all society.* We might call this our third general conclusion. This cannot be said without reserve for any other social class, for we see cliques and parties growing rich by the promotion of special interests in legislative halls and elsewhere, while society as a whole may languish. The laboring class is in reality the only class which is not merely a class, and this justifies the use of the now current expression, "The masses against the classes." No one will, it may be hoped, take this as a justification of all measures which are urged upon or in the name of the laboring classes, or suppose that any sanction is hereby given to that claim of industrial preeminence sometimes advanced in their behalf. . . .

Let us, in immediate connection with the foregoing, consider some of the evils of the industrial situation which have a close connection with the labor problem. Only brief comment will be possible, though a book might be written on any one of them.

Child Labor.

First of all must be mentioned child labor as one of the most fruitful sources of evil. Children are removed from home to the dangerous moral atmosphere of the store, shop, and factory at a tender age and their moral natures too often irreparably corrupted. . . .

Normal growth is obstructed, and the very end of life, "the consistent and harmonious expansion of all one's faculties," is defeated.

Childhood should be a period of innocent play and of growing bodily, mental, and moral power. A normal childhood is a source of strength of one's entire life. The mind reverts to it and is refreshed. But in our great cities the children of the working poor are growing up without childhood. They leave infancy only to become little old men and women. They are wronged because not protected at a period when self-protection is an absolute impossibility. . . .

The Labor of Women in Industrial Establishments.

This, like child labor, is rapidly on the increase in the United States. It is not always an evil, but it is too often a most serious one, and it is desirable to restrict it. The wives and children of the laboring men become the unnatural competitors, and it has happened in Massachusetts and New Jersey, as well as in England, that the father has remained at home to care for the house and perform those duties which nature has assigned to woman, while wife and children are at work in the mill. Women become too often demoralized, and in mines so notoriously so that their employment underground has been entirely prohibited in England. Children, without a mother's care grow up wild and undisciplined, an easy prey to the worst agitators and other bad men! The question involved in the labor of women and children is no less than the preservation of the American home, the only sure foundation on which our institutions can rest. . . .

The Dwellings of the Urban Laboring Classes.

Men, women, and children crowded together in unsanitary condition, and disease is accompanied by a fearful death-rate. The conditions of a wholesome family life are almost entirely wanting, and virtue is gone and character is destroyed before their value can by any possibility be realized. The slums of cities are breathing-holes of hell, and the only way to reform them is to sweep them from the face of the earth. . . .

Sunday Work.

This is a rapidly growing evil in all our cities, against which working-men all over the length and breadth of the land are crying out, and their complaint is becoming bitter because their cry passes unheeded. Wherever laboring men meet in conventions this complaint is very apt to be heard, and labor papers agitate the matter perpetually. . . .

Night Work.

This has become quite common in order to utilize the expensive plant of the modern manufacturing establishment. It is demoralizing for all, men, women, and children, and for the two latter classes ought never to be permitted. It is an evil to be kept within as narrow bounds as possible for all.

Overwork.

It requires a perpetual struggle to keep the length of the labor day within the bounds required by physiology and hygiene, and often the struggle to do so is unsuccessful. No nation in which modern industry prevails has been exempt from the evils of overwork. Working days of fifteen, sixteen, and seventeen hours have not been infrequent, and cases are occasionally reported of men working for more than twenty-four hours in succession. . . .

Excessive Mortality of Working People, especially of Children.

The influence of occupation and economic condition upon length of life has never been sufficiently investigated, but all investigations which have ever been conducted point with unmistakable clearness in one direction. There is no popular impression more entirely groundless than that the poor are blessed with good health. . . .

REMEDIES

The evils described will suggest many of the remedies required for the diseased social body, but these remedies must be enumerated and described in the fewest possible words. Other evils than those mentioned will also be brought forward incidentally in the treatment of remedies.

Optimism Perhaps one of the first things to be done is to vanquish and utterly drive from among us an ignoble but too common optimism, which blinds men to actual conditions, deadens conscience, and puts a stop to useful activity. This popular optimism of the day would have us believe that all things are as they should be, and bids us eat, drink, and be merry while our fellow-men are enduring such evils. This unworthy optimism is a lie, and surely those who keep it going are doing the devil's service. From the rise of the first attempts to bring God's will to pass in this world until now it has stood athwart the path of progress. Weak and imperfect as man is, it would be strange indeed if in this one department of social life which we are considering—the industrial field—he had attained perfection, while art, religion, the family, literature, and politics are sadly faulty and defective.

Sin, misery, and injustice everywhere abound, and all who try to be guided by ethical and Christian principles must strive uninterruptedly with all their resources to remove or mitigate these. While this ignoble optimism is rejected, we find as little occasion for pessimism. Progress has been made by those who in the past have suffered and toiled for humanity, and the field for reform was never more promising than today. . . .

The Church. To establish a legitimate authority over the minds and wills of men, the Church must show the Christian faith and love of early Christianity—light for all and love for all from the ministers of the gospel will alone reestablish that authority which makes the Church what it should be, a healthy life-giving member of civilization.

She is too modest in the territory which she claims for herself, and practically too much inclined to admit that there are secular concerns and secular days with which religion is not vitally concerned. The spirit of caste which separates man from man and produces mutual hatred is a chief cause of troubles, and against this headway must be made. But if the Church is to exercise control over social life, ministers must understand this social life far better than they do, and this requires instruction from the best minds of our time. Social science should be pursued in every seminary for the training of ministers of religion.

The Family. Perhaps a reform, purification, and elevation of the family ought to be placed first among remedies for labor problems—certainly it is among the first; and how far-reaching and diverse are the efforts needed for this purpose, what has already been said will indicate. The reforms which the family institution needs must be brought about partly by individual effort, partly through the effort of voluntary associations like the Divorce Reform League, partly through the Church, and partly through legislation and the action of government. One cause of labor troubles is imprudent and hasty marriages, also marriages at too early an age, resulting in feeble offspring, poorly cared for. It is the duty of all public teachers to impress upon the minds of the young the gravity of the duties which marriage brings, and to enforce in every way the responsibilities of parenthood. Among large classes of the community it is not realized that it is a grievous sin to bring children into the world without a prospect of means to bring them up properly.

Improved Educational Facilities. Improved educational facilities are greatly needed, but our schools have not kept pace with the demands on them. A recent writer observes that American common schools were the best in the world thirty or forty years ago, — a doubtful statement, — but that now other countries, like Germany, Switzerland, and England, are far ahead of us. The last part of the statement is true. While in the self-complacency of optimism the American eagle has been deafening us with his screams, other countries have been slowly but quietly improving their schools, and we have stood still or made but slight advance. . . .

Compulsory education laws should everywhere be passed and enforced as in other civilized countries. Education is a right of a child, — the right to existence carrying with it the right to an opportunity for an unfolding of its powers, — and if parents fail to do their duty it only remains for the state to step in and protect the child. This is a more sacred duty even than the protection of property, for property is but a means to an end; namely, the welfare of man. It is not an interference with the rights of the parent, but a protection of the rights of the child. Compulsory education should continue in ordinary schools until the age of fourteen. . . .

Dwellings of the Poor. Stricter sanitary laws are required, and a better organization of the sanitary administration of cities. Houses unfit for habitation should be torn down, and small parks provided to give breathing-places for the crowded sections. The beginning made in New York City deserves commendation. While not prepared to recommend at present the construction of houses by the municipality, we regard English experiments in this direction as worthy of study. Private philanthropy should concern itself more than heretofore with the dwellings of the poor and strive to make them fit for human beings. . . .

Factory Laws. These have produced excellent effects wherever they have been honestly conceived, and honestly administered. With us they have too often been a mere sham and farce. Unfortunately in this matter we have lagged behind the rest of the civilized world. We recommend an adequate system of factory inspection by men of character—not political demagogues—and by men who have been trained for such work: further, heavier fines and even imprisonment for a violation of factory laws. These laws should include protection against dangerous machinery, sufficient fire-escapes and satisfactory sanitary arrangement. . . .

It is curious that never in the world's history have shorter hours been introduced without prophecies of terrible evils and that never once in the world's history have these prophecies been fulfilled. If we arrange in a line the names of the countries, placing them in order according to the number of hours worked per week, we shall find that the country with shortest hours is most dreaded in international competition, and as we go down the line we shall find longer hours mean increasing weakness in international competition, and that with few, if any, exceptions, countries with long hours and poorly paid work always seek protection against countries with few hours and highly paid work. Factory laws do not prevent competition or weaken it, but simply raise its moral level in the manner described by Prof. Henry C. Adams[6] in his monograph "Relation of the State to Industrial Action." . . .

Labor Organizations. Labor organizations ought to be carefully studied and their nature understood. They must exist, and to harass them by injustice, as is being done too often by our courts under revival of obsolete laws and constructions, will inevitably lead to their degradation. A frank recognition of their necessity, an encouragement of all that is good in them, and repression of the evil, ought to be our aim. In the labor movement we have a stream which can be guided, but which cannot be dammed up with impunity.

Public Property. There is a call in every city, every State, and in the nation for public property defense leagues. It is by protecting the property of the public, that is, of the masses, that we shall secure general respect for the institution of property. The work of public property defense leagues would be, among other things, to guard public domain, public parks, and to secure for the public the full value of public rights, like the right to use

---

6. A selection from Henry Carter Adams and his biography are found in Chapter 5.

streets by horse and electric cars, elevated roads, etc. The property of the public should be paid for and protected like property of individuals. . . .

Savings Banks. These occupy an important position in any programme for reform. Without thrift the masses can never prosper, and this must be cultivated by savings banks of undoubted security. Private banks must be rendered secure, and, where practicable, state and municipal savings banks started. It would be well to have the debt of a city like New York held in small sums by the masses. This would also give them a "stake" in the city and produce excellent political effects. . . .

Other Remedies. Other remedies can only be mentioned. Amusement is of an importance increasingly recognized. Playgrounds for children come under this head, and these should be provided by the public when private initiative is wanting. This would prevent crime, and thereby lessen taxation. Every teacher of college boys knows that if a legitimate opportunity for the vent of animal spirits is not provided mischief will come. City boys have, however, no opportunities for innocent play, and mischief too often degenerates into bad habits, intemperance, crime.

Public libraries, like the Enoch Pratt library, which has done so much for Baltimore, ought to become more numerous.

A reform of taxation has already been alluded to. Present State and local taxes are, according to unanimous testimony, unjustly distributed, bearing most heavily on the poor and on people in ordinary circumstances, those who are barely well-to-do. Besides, they obstruct industry and diminish opportunities for employment.

A further development of labor bureaus may be mentioned, these to be managed by trained experts, and not by demagogues used as baits to catch the labor vote.

Arbitration and conciliation have accomplished great things in some places and ought to become more general. It would be proper to make these methods of settling controversies compulsory for corporations. It is entirely a matter of expediency.

We are not prepared to indorse compulsory State insurance like that which obtains in Germany, but we recommend the subject of insurance against accident, sickness, old age, and incapacity to general consideration, in hope that some plan may be devised for accomplishing so beneficent a purpose by ways more in consonance with American ideas. A development of fraternal beneficiary societies and of insurance features of labor organizations, with examination of accounts by insurance departments or by a competent registrar of friendly societies, is certainly desirable.

Profit-sharing, when introduced by upright and prosperous employers, unites their interests with those of their employees most advantageously. Still better is it when laborers like the Minneapolis coopers themselves become capitalists and self-employers by placing in a common fund their savings and managing their own business. This always promotes thrift and temperance, and shows its highest success in the making of men. The prudent encouragement of cooperation deserves commendation.

Our ideal is a social state, not of equality, but of equal opportunities, giving to each the means for the development, complete and harmonious, of all his faculties. Not the self-made man—that is, the self-made millionaire—can ever be a model for the masses, but the contented and really prosperous artisan or mechanic, gradually getting ahead in the world, enjoying life, developing all his powers and living worthily with his family, partaking according to their capacities of the blessings of civilization. [Richard Ely, "A Program for Labor Reform," *Century Magazine*, vol. 39, no. 6 (April 1890): 938–9, 941–4, 946–51]

26. *Economic Surplus and the Rights of Labor,* Simon N. Patten (1852–1922)[7]

Patten's analysis of wages, profits, and rents provided the basis for Charles Beard's examination of the sources of political conflicts in America (which began with the battle between Antifederalists and Federalists over the adoption of the Constitution and continued up to the party conflicts of his day). Patten's basic argument was simple: the major battle is not between working people and capitalists, but between the productivity and profits of the industrial economy and the somewhat parasitic benefits from rents—that is, unearned income from rising land values and market monopolies. McKinley preached the same sermon against Bryan:[8] the interests of workers lie in a thriving industrial capitalism producing economic surplus, not in a class alliance with marginal farmers, main

---

7. More biographical information on Patten prefaces his selection in Chapter 3.

8. In the decisive presidential election of 1896, William McKinley (1843–1901) ran as the Republican candidate against William Jennings Bryan (1860–1925), the Democratic candidate. McKinley ran on a platform supporting the gold standard to encourage foreign capital investment in American industry. Bryan advocated monetary inflation as a means of helping small producers and indebted landholders. Northern industrial labor largely supported McKinley, ushering in a long period of Republican Party dominance in national politics.

street shop owners, and southern rentier interests against capitalists. The
deeper conflict is between the dynamic systems of national industry—
including mechanized agriculture—and the relatively stagnant systems of
local wealth distribution. Croly's writings on labor in his Promise of
American Life *are premised on this same argument. In the selection here,*
Patten outlines the highest expectations for the working man to be derived
from the surplus wealth creation of the industrial economy.

—1902—

In a complex nation like the American, there is no rational principle
uniting the various classes, sections, and races. Each class has its own
needs, each section has its own peculiarities evoking particular desires,
and each race has its own heredity. No class becomes large enough to
dominate; no section is so important that the others must yield; nor is
any race so superior that it can impose its heredity and tradition on the
nation. There is, therefore, no rational source of unity. Each state or
group of similar states has its own environment and develops desires
that fit its situation; and the rational code of each region conforming to
these conditions can have little force beyond its boundaries. But common to all are the new impulses that prosperity brings, and from them
will come the forces creating national unity. . . .

In each locality and class a group of desires in harmony with the local
environment must displace or modify the old desires upon which the
existing tradition is based. There will then develop a new moral code,
local in character, and yet general enough to induce large bodies of men
to accept it. A rational procedure based on the desires can thus reconstruct race traditions, and unite men into groups with a basis in the present environment. Beyond this, rationalism cannot go. But it may be
supplemented by impulses due to the surplus energy that prosperity creates; and these impulses, going out in the same direction, form ideals
and superimpose on the local codes rights that all classes will accept.
The local, class, and sectional forces making for unity are moral; the general forces are impulses and ideals formulated as rights. It is not, therefore, from a theory of distribution that a solution of present difficulties
will come, but from a better formulation of the moral code and from a
clearer perception of the common rights that new impulses and ideals
evoke. Economic analysis will show the causes of prosperity; but prosperity must cause surplus energy to go out in natural channels before useful
checks to action and pleasurable modes of activity become apparent.

There are many indications of progress in both these directions. In each
section and class a new morality is building safeguards against local, class,
and party evils. New rights are also gaining recognition, even if they have

not been formulated and consciously accepted. We should look for these, not where strife and party conflict force unsolved problems on the attention of the public, but rather upon those occasions and moments when great prosperity induces men and classes to lay aside the armor of struggle and to be natural because they are successful. A capitalist is rational and pugnacious in conflict, but generous and impulsive in giving. A corporation is reactionary in adversity, but sets better standards when success is assured. A party is made moral and rational by defeat; it represents the national impulse only in moments of victory. The ideals of laborers are not shown in a strike, but at times when they are organizing for mutual advantage. The progressive element of city life comes to the front, not in struggle with corruption, but in the many voluntary associations that men enter from a love of their locality. Each new organization represents some incipient ideal which, when clearly perceived, becomes a right that all enjoy. Economic rights are born of adjustment, not of struggle. Being the emotions of success, they are first felt by men with surplus energy and then imposed on society. The income such rights transfer comes directly from the social surplus and so makes no national deficit.

The rights upon which political freedom depends have already been worked out. They were obtained by picturing a primitive society where men were so isolated that their relations were simple and plain. The problem of economic freedom is to find a modern equivalent for the rights that in earlier times went with land. The workman of today should have all that the landowner of the past enjoyed. Freedom consists not merely of political rights, but is dependent upon the possession of economic rights, freely recognized and universally granted to each man by his fellow citizens. These economic rights measure freedom in proportion as there is a mutual agreement concerning their desirability, and as complete adjustment makes their realization possible. Only those rights that American conditions permit and the impulses of unimpeded activity may attain can be properly considered ideal. . . .

1. PUBLIC OR MARKET RIGHTS

The right to an open market. The right to publicity.
The right to security. The right to cooperate.

The essential point is that the workman, instead of watching his product slowly going through its many changes and finally claim it, sells it in the general market and buys from it whatever he needs. The market thus stands for all the unseen change taking place between the day when the laborer does his work and the day when his final reward appears. . . .

When each workman passes to other workmen the product of his labor, the openness of the market can be insured only by the right of

publicity. He must be able to watch the circuit through which his product passes from the time it leaves him until it returns in the form of
goods fit for use. Each workman must assert this right to maintain his
economic freedom. Transactions hidden from the public view disturb
the relations between the outflow of energy and the return of goods.
Those who are exempted from inspection extract an unearned share
from the gross product of industry, leaving the real workers to struggle
as best they may for the diminished remainder. Unseen claimants are
preferred creditors and get their shares paid first.

Security is another right belonging to isolated producers which must
be fully preserved in modern industry. The product of a man's industry
must be left in his possession, and all his industrial relations must be
free from arbitrary changes. A bad monetary standard is no less harmful
than an unjust system of taxation. Speculation and other arbitrary
changes in prices also violate the right of security by forcing men to sell
at low prices and to buy back the final product at high rates. Security,
moreover, is not merely a question of property rights. It also relates to
utilities and activities. The consumer has a right to stable prices and the
workman to a steady position. An arbitrary discharge of workmen dis-
turbs industrial processes and should be carefully guarded against.

Industrial efficiency results from the formation of productive groups
whose members work for common ends but in different ways. This division of labor, though due to objective conditions, cannot be made effective unless psychic changes in men permit them to work and live in
harmony. Group activity, a feeling of unity, and a community of interests add quite as much to the efficiency of labor as do favorable conditions. Cooperation is not an objective relation, but a cohesive instinct
which will not be formed without some flow of income raising the condition of the group above the bare minimum of existence. A group with
steadily lowering wages will not hold together. Social interests are created by upward movements in the standards of living, through which
greater cohesion and more power in struggle are obtained. The right to
cooperate is a right to increased income. . . .

2. SOCIAL RIGHTS

The right to a home. The right to develop. The right to
wholesome standards. The right to homogeneity of population.
The right to decision by public opinion.

Marriage is a permanent cooperation between the sexes under such
conditions that its purity can be maintained, and children raised that
will be a credit to parents and the community; and it involves everything

needed to secure these ends. There should be no necessity of living in a social environment where either party is tempted to break marital vows, or where the lack of income to support a family prevents pure social relations. . . .

Education has become an essential feature of state activity. Each generation should reach a closer adjustment to its environment and be able to secure better conditions from it than its predecessors enjoyed. This means that sons should be better prepared for life, and their education should be extended through a longer period. . . .

An opportunity to develop depends on the social surroundings of a people as much as it does on the educational advantages. If a man must work and keep his family in contact with the degrading influences found in cities, it is impossible for him or them to maintain their moral purity. Wholesome social standards are a part of the conditions demanded for the steady improvement of each person and family. It is not enough that moral principles and elevating ideals be taught in the schools. These can have but little permanent influence unless embodied in practical rules of conduct which individuals observe throughout life. . . .

It is . . . homogeneity of population, not homogeneity of opinion, that is demanded. Population is homogeneous when intermarriage takes place and common instincts, habits, and impulses develop. Opinions are homogeneous when the premises of reasoning are the same, and this involves firmer social bonds and identical environing conditions. The homogeneity of opinion is demanded only in the case of public decisions. The minority must cheerfully submit to the majority, and accept for the time a public decision reached through calm discussion. The decisions of a homogeneous population will represent the general welfare. . . .

3. RIGHTS OF LEISURE

The right to comfort. The right to leisure. The right to recreation. The right to cleanliness. The right to scenery.

In modern nations the productive power is more than sufficient to produce the minimum of existence. There is a social surplus above the costs of production in which every worker has a right to share. All men cannot be made wealthy, but they can be made comfortable by some of the social surplus going to each of them. . . .

The right to leisure is a corollary to the right to comfort. No matter what income a person receives, he cannot be comfortable without some time for enjoyment. Leisure means more than time to eat and sleep.

The full revival of mental and physical powers demands a period of rest in which the loss of surplus energy can be restored. . . .

The right to recreation may be regarded as an outcome of the narrow division of labor demanded by production on a large scale; for then work is a constant repetition of single acts, tiring some parts of the body but leaving other parts without sufficient exercise. The normal man must have all the parts of his body developed and all his mental powers kept active. Recreation is the only process by which this is accomplished. . . .

Clear water, pure air, and clean streets are matters of public interest, and for these ends the social surplus should be freely used. Public control should be extended to everything that lowers the vitality of the working population. . . .

Men should provide for their visual environment with the same care they exert in providing for other material conditions. Not only must natural scenery be preserved and restored, but the demands of city life for corresponding advantages in its architecture, museums, and parks must be met. The eye should never be needlessly wearied nor its sensitiveness to harmonious relations destroyed. Bad streets, incongruous buildings, and glaring advertisements depress men, reduce their productive power, and check the growth of social feelings.

4. EXCEPTIONAL RIGHTS

The right to relief. The right of women to income.

The orderly development of higher wants, tastes, and standards is delayed or prevented by any disturbing fear that the forethought and energy providing for them will not attain the desired end. Society alone can remove this dread by giving full protection against the evils of the industrial world. . . . In such cases social evils should be met by social action. Make the individual responsible for the results of his own acts, but do not let him suffer from what he could not avoid. A system of relief is an essential to industrial freedom;— economic activity will not reach its maximum until it is so effective that the energy of individuals can be applied to the satisfaction of their own wants. . . .

There is another special right growing out of the peculiar position of women. Certain restrictions to woman's activities have become general, partly the result of her position as a mother, and partly as an outcome of social conventions which have grown up in advanced nations. It is not necessary to determine whether woman's evils are physical or social. If physical, there is a natural ground for giving woman a preference; if social, this preference should continue until society is reorganized on some other plan. . . . In some occupations women have an income adequate for their support. This, however, cannot become the general rule so long as the present family arrangements and social conventions continue. Grave evils must continue until society gives to women workers an income large enough to insure their physical and moral well-being. The operation of economic forces may do this for men, but it must fail in the case of women so long as they suffer from physical and social disabilities. The social surplus should therefore be freely used for women. No one has a right to bring a girl into the world without providing for her support, and this support should have a first claim on every estate. If women are kept from industry for family reasons, the family should provide an income for them. Where private means of support fail, preference should be given them in industries for which they are especially fitted. No society is safe, nor can it be moral and progressive, until women are fully protected and have independent incomes. [Simon Patten, *The Theory of Prosperity* (Macmillan, 1902), 212–21, 223–9]

27. *Ethical Gains through Labor Legislation,* Florence Kelley (1859–1932)[9]

Kelley was best known as the first Executive Secretary of the National Consumers League, a prominent Progressive reform organization founded in 1899 by women (who, like Kelley, were residents of Hull House) to strengthen their campaign for better working conditions. A native of Philadelphia with strong Quaker roots, Kelley attended Cornell University. She then went to Germany and Switzerland for further study before earning a law degree from Northwestern University. Kelley served as associate editor of Charities *and was continuously active in political movements focused on women's labor and child-labor issues. The book from which this selection is taken grew out of her experiences as a special agent for the Illinois Bureau of Labor Statistics investigating the tenements of Chicago (1892), as Chief Inspector of Factories for the state (1893–97), and as agent in charge of investigating large city slums for the Chicago division of the U.S. Department of Labor—all jobs created by the implementation of Progressive reform ideas in the new bureaucratic structures of the state and national governments.*

---

9. More biographical information on Kelley prefaces her selection in Chapter 8.

—1905—

THE CHILD, THE STATE, AND THE NATION

It has been shown that children are working in their homes, in the streets, in commerce, and in manufacture; and it appears that there are divers economic and social causes for their work.

Chief among these causes of child labor is the greed of parents, due largely but not exclusively to poverty. . . .

A second cause of child-labor is the greed of employers for cheap labor, enhanced by every improvement in machinery of the kind that makes the work of children available; and enhanced, also, by the very cheapness of the children to such an extent as to delay the introduction of new machinery if its installation is costly. This greed is exhibited in its most odious form in the glass industry, the textile industry, and the sweating-system. It knows no restraints except those of effective legislation enforced by enlightened public opinion, as is shown by the action of those Northern cotton mill men who obey the laws of Massachusetts and New York in their mills in those states, but in Georgia fall to the level of their local competitors, employing children ten years old and less, throughout eleven hours a day.

A third cause of child labor is the greed of the community in desiring to keep down the cost of maintenance of its dependent class. This greed disguises itself under the form of solicitude for the moral welfare of the children. Just as the managers of the worst so-called reformatories insist that children must work under the contract system, "because they must be kept busy to keep them from being bad," so this solicitude for child- ish morals insists that "children must not be habituated to dependence," quite forgetting that dependence is the quality bestowed upon child- hood as its distinguishing characteristic. . . .

THE RIGHT TO LEISURE

America having produced no great philanthropic leader devoted to securing leisure for the young and defenseless workers, no Lord Shaftes- bury,[10] the task of establishing their right went by default to the trade

---

10. Anthony Ashley Cooper (1801–1885), the seventh Earl of Shaftsbury, was responsible for factory and coal mine safety legislation in the English Parlia- ment. His philanthropic interests included the establishment of "ragged schools" in metropolitan slums, the Young Men's Christian Association, work- ingmen's institutes, and foreign missions.

unions, to whom is due the credit for all child labor legislation prior to the year 1889. Now, however, the effort has become national in its scope, enlisting the most diverse advocates. Mr. Grover Cleveland and other members of the National Child Labor Committee, and the General Federation of Women's Clubs, in striving to stop the work of children at night in manufacture and commerce, are as truly enlisted in behalf of the right to leisure as are the miners in Colorado, the butchers in Chicago, and the garment workers in New York. The National Educational Association, working to prolong the period of compulsory attendance at school, and the National Congress of Mothers, with its standing committee on child labor, are pledged to the same endeavor. To educate the purchasing public to act in considerate recognition of the right of the clerks to leisure is one of the reasons for being of the Consumers' League. However different the methods of these diverse organizations, their goal is the same,—the establishment of reasonable daily leisure in the lives of working people.

The Supreme Court of the United States has made plain the way by sustaining the constitutionality of statutes establishing the working day of eight hours for persons in the employ of the federal government, in the employ of states or municipalities under contract, and in the employ of corporations where the nature of the occupation may be injurious to health.

The establishment of universal leisure is increasingly recognized as a social aim, an effort to be participated in by all those who care for the social welfare, and as a national effort, since, under the pressure of competition, the conditions prevailing in any industry must be as nearly uniform as possible, and one part of the country cannot long maintain itself far in advance of a different part having identical industries, a truth which finds conspicuous illustration in the experience of New England suffering under the pressure of competition of the textile mills of Georgia. . . .

Assured daily leisure is an essential element of healthy living. Without it childhood is blighted, perverted, deformed; manhood becomes ignoble and unworthy of citizenship in the Republic. Self-help and self-education among the wage-earners are as dependent upon daily leisure as upon daily work. Excessive fatigue precludes the possibility of well conducted meetings of classes, lodges, cooperative societies and all other forms of organized effort for self-improvement. . . .

Shortening the hours of labor gives to working people a wider range of selection in the location of their homes, thus benefiting wives and children as well as the operatives themselves.

Daily assured leisure serves a purpose of the highest social value by enabling the wage-earner to husband that resource of nervous energy which is required to continue active working-life after the passing of youth. . . .

PURCHASERS AND COURTS

Trade Unions and the Union Label. — The decision of the Court of Appeals in re Jacobs[11] virtually turned over to the wage-earners the task of providing, through the machinery of their organizations, for the protection of themselves and the purchasers against the evils of the sweating system. For twenty years the unions have faithfully striven to perform a task which it was, from the beginning, impossible that they should achieve. Just as they long before introduced child-labor legislation and factory inspection, which have come to be recognized as benefactions to the whole people; so they now invented that method of dealing with the sweated trades, by offering the label as a guaranty of conditions approved by the workers which is accepted as the best available under the circumstances, and in view of the conditions imposed by the decision of the Court of Appeals in re Jacobs. It is, of course, out of their power ever to do, with palliatives, what a sweeping prohibition could have done long since.

The public, however, cannot afford to allow the courts to relegate to the labor organizations the duty of protecting the public health against the reckless willingness of manufacturers to take risks. For, if the union is not strong enough to dominate the trade (and no union of garment workers has ever been strong enough to do this), the public must take the consequences in disease and death sent out from the tenement sewing rooms. Or, if a union were not only insufficiently strong but imperfectly honest as well, the public would pay the penalty for every label dishonestly sold to contractors for use in places which fell below the accepted standard of wholesome and clean conditions.

Or, let us suppose that a portion of the public may be honestly opposed on principle to the maintenance of trade unions; and unwilling, therefore, to purchase goods guaranteed by the union label. Such abstainers, if left without other means of discrimination in favor of goods made under

---

11. *In re Jacobs* (1885) held that a New York state law restricting the manufacture of cigars in tenement housing deprived cigar makers of liberty and property. This case forced tenement-based clothiers' unions to sponsor programs guaranteeing that products with the union label were made under sanitary conditions and with high standards of working conditions and hours.

wholesome conditions, are in danger, not only of incurring disease and death, but of disseminating them throughout the community.

Finally, a large part of the membership of the unions in the garment trades consists of immigrants so recently arrived from Eastern Europe as to have no adequate standards of wholesome conditions for home and workshop, of persons wholly unprepared to defend their own health, much more that of the general public. Clearly the unions, however valuable to their members and to the community in other relations, cannot, in the nature of things, be a sufficient guardian of the health and safety of all the purchasing public. . . .

Thus we have, after twenty years of effort, two ineffectual methods of dealing with tenement manufacture, pursued side by side. The state, by statute, legalizes the manufacture in the tenements of thirty-four articles, and proceeds by a cumbersome threefold inspection (by the State Factory Inspectors, the Board of Health Inspectors and the Tenement House Department), to minimize the danger to the public health, including that of the workers themselves. But, as has been pointed out, the public health is not really safeguarded. The people are merely lulled into a false sense of security.

The unions, meanwhile, have spent untold thousands of dollars in their effort to induce the purchasing public to avoid the dangers attending sweated goods, by the individual method of discrimination against tenement made products and in favor of goods guaranteed by the union label.

Ethical Loss through Lack of Legislation. — The ethical loss by reason of this decision of the Court of Appeals of New York, quite apart from the loss of money in advertising by the unions and in futile, hopeless inspection on the part of the state, is quite beyond the possibility of calculation.

From the day when this decision became effective, the interests of the purchasing public and of the tenement dwellers have been practically identical, and both have been sacrificed to the convenience and the profit of the manufacturers.

For twenty years the state of New York has proclaimed through its highest court that it cannot protect the homes of its industrially weakest citizens from invasion by the materials of their industry. These materials are owned by rich and powerful employers, strongly organized locally and nationally, and are foisted upon the meager dwellings of the poor solely for the purpose of saving to the employers the cost of heat, light, cleaning and, far more important, rent of workrooms. For the convenience of the powerful, the weakest industrial factors in the community, the widows burdened with young children, the daughters kept at home by bedridden parents, have been invaded by industry and by inspectors. This forcing of industry into the tenements has fostered the belief that work *must* be done by all who live there, particularly if they are poor and sick. Thus devotion to the needle and the pastepot has become a sort of touchstone measuring the "worthiness" or the "helpableness" of the women who have dependent members of the family. [Florence Kelley, *Some Ethical Gains through Legislation* (Macmillan, 1905), 58, 61, 105–9, 240–2, 244–6]

28. *Labor Unions,* Herbert Croly (1869–1930)[12]

Croly's view of labor unions changed between the publication of The Promise of American Life *in 1909 and the publication of* Progressive Democracy *five years later. In* Promise, *Croly proposed that certain legal privileges and protections be granted to trade unions in exchange for responsible behavior oriented toward the larger public good. Under these conditions, the trade union member could expect "not equal rights, but special opportunities." Conversely, Croly declared "the non-union laborer" to be "a species of industrial derelict" who "does not deserve any special protection" (386–7). By 1914, Croly thought that trade unions had to exert their particular interests more forcefully and on their own terms to counter the power of private business corporations. This "conflict model" of labor relations was more in accord with the emerging views of the Democratic Party; it was also an acknowledgment that reform might be more effective if it resulted from conflicts between interest groups instead of a deliberate campaign based on social consensus and national public opinion. In the end, however, Croly remained the good Progressive by hoping that this conflict would yield measures of union self-government conducive to a consensus favoring both scientific management and technological innovation in industry.*

—1914—

If the organization of political democracy for educational purposes is of so much importance, the educational organization of democracy in its economic aspect is certainly of no less importance. The creation of an industrial organization which will serve to make individual workers enlightened, competent and loyal citizens of an industrial

12. More biographical information on Croly prefaces his selections in Chapters 1, 2, and 5.

commonwealth, is most assuredly a task just as essential as the creation
of a loyal and enlightened body of voters. I do not believe, as do many
social democrats, that a more democratic industrial organization will
bring with it necessarily a more enlightened democratic political organization. But neither do I believe that the creation of an industrial democratic citizenship will take care of itself, provided we can obtain a
more satisfactory democratic political organization. Effective measures
of an essentially non-political character must be taken for the creation
of an industrial democratic citizenship. . . .

The truth is that the wage-system in its existing form creates a class of
essential economic dependents. Even if they attain some measure of
emancipation as small property owners, they remain dependent as
wage-earners. Their economic situation is determined in part by forces
over which they as individuals can exercise but little control, and in part
by the good or ill will and the good or bad management of their employers. Their employer is literally their master. He supplies the opportunity
of work, determines its conditions to a large extent, and is responsible
for its success or failure. They are often free to change their employer,
but a new employer is only a new master. In a multitude of individual
cases the autocratic control is benevolently exercised. Fidelity and competence are rewarded, and the deserving wage-earner comes to occupy
a privileged position as compared to his fellow-workers. But he has no
assurance of any such reward. The number of people who graduate
from the wage-earning class without the assistance of some kind of
favoritism, is small compared to the total number of wage-earners. By
the very necessities of the case the vast majority of wage-earners are con-
demned to a Hobson's choice[13] among masters.

Ordinary progressive special legislation is intended to improve the
operation of the system without touching its essential defect. But if
plans of social insurance and minimum-wage boards have any tendency
to undermine the independence of the wage-earner, that tendency
results from the system itself, not from the attempts to improve it. The
social legislative program cannot give real independence to people
whose relation to their employers is one of dependence. In undertaking
such a program the state is merely assuming a responsibility towards
wage-earners whose fulfilment is necessary to social conservation. This

---

13. Named for a keeper of horses in a livery stable in Cambridge, England.
Thomas Hobson (c. 1544–1631) let his customers choose any horse in the stable so long as it was nearest the door—a proposition similar to Henry Ford's
offer to sell his customers a 1914 Model-T in any color, so long as it was black.

responsibility should already have been assumed by employers capable of recognizing the righteous claims which their employees had upon them as the result of the employment. But no matter who assumes the responsibility, the relation of dependence remains; and the wage-earner has to choose between two grim alternatives as a means of possible emancipation. He may seek independence either by becoming a favored worker or by becoming himself a property owner. The first of these alternatives is denied by the very necessities of the case to the vast majority of wage-earners. The second costs more in human satisfaction than it is worth as a discipline of independence. Both of them divide the interest of the individual worker from that of the mass of his fellow workers.

The creation of industrial citizens out of wage-earners, if it is to be brought about at all, will demand the adoption of different methods. The wage-system itself will have to be transformed in the interest of an industrial self-governing democracy. Progressives must come to recognize two fundamental facts. Modern civilization in dealing with the class of wage-earners is dealing with an ultimate economic condition, the undesirable aspects of which cannot be evaded by promoting one wage-earner out of every thousand into a semi-capitalist or a semi-employer. If wage-earners are to become free men, the condition of freedom must somehow be introduced in the wage-system itself. The wage-earner must have the same opportunity of being consulted about the nature and circumstances of his employment that the voter has about the organization and policy of the government. The work of getting this opportunity for the wage-earner is the most important single task of modern democratic social organization. . . .

The emancipation of the wage-earner demands that the same legal security and dignity and the same comparative control over his own destiny shall be attached to his position as to that of the property owner. As soon as such legal security is granted, the good worker will no longer be offered a strong inducement to separate himself from his fellows by becoming a property owner. His work will be his fortune, and will depend for its productivity upon effective cooperation. The wage-earner whose greatest stimulus to work is assumed to be the ultimate chance of becoming a property owner, may be a hard worker, but he will rarely be a good worker or a desirable citizen in an industrial democracy. As a worker his eye will be fixed rather on the goal than on the job. As a property owner he will be afraid of being unable to keep his property. In both aspects his motives will be interested and self-involved rather than disinterested and social.

Hitherto, however, neither the conscience nor the intelligence of modern industrial society has recognized the impolicy and the injustice of asking workers to seek economic independence by taking their eye off their work, by impoverishing their own lives and by practically deserting their associates. The wage-earners have been obliged to seek on their own hook an inferior kind of emancipation by means of an inferior kind of associated action. They have borne witness to the necessary fellowship of workers by organizing trades-unions; and these trade associations have had to make the economic emancipation of the individual depend on the emancipation of the whole class. The individual wage-earner has been compelled to forego whatever chance he has of obtaining a better position for himself by agreeing to accept nothing which is not shared with his fellows. The fight for associated independence requires of the individual worker great sacrifices, of which the greatest sacrifice of all is an obligation to take his eye off his work. Society is responsible for this sacrifice by refusing to him the security and dignity appertaining to his calling.

The attitude of the employing class has forced trades-unions to become for the most part fighting organizations. Workers have been obliged to fight primarily for an increased share of the necessaries of life and for the recognition of their unions. In the case of certain skilled trades they have compelled their employers to recognize the unions, to pay a comparatively liberal rate of wages and to submit to conditions in the conduct of the business which tended to restrict the output. They have not used the power which they have obtained in the interest of industrial productivity; but why should they do so? Both the economic and the legal systems with which they are dealing force them to seek primarily their own class interests, and refuse to grant to them as workers an appropriate dignity and security. They naturally take their social ethics from their opponents and regard their work as a kind of property, which has to be saved for the benefit of a private interest rather than expended in the public interest. They have their eye fastened not on the work, but upon the goal. . . .

It was a distinct gain when syndicalism[14] demanded of the old craft unionism that it cease to be a parasite upon a perverted economic system, and that it should fight and plan for the creation of a new system,

---

14. "Syndicalism" was the name given to labor movements that encouraged industry-wide organization of workers instead of unions organized by craft or company. In its most radical form—a form that resembled outright anarchy— syndicalism urged workers to ignore the laws of the state and appropriate all industries for themselves.

based upon the dignity, the responsibility and the moral value of human work. The fact that the advocates of the new system propose to establish it by methods which might be fatal to civilization must not be allowed to obscure the essential nobleness and humanity of their underlying purpose. They are proposing to secure to the laborers of all kinds the opportunity and responsibility of operating the business mechanism of modern life; and in so far as they succeed, work will cease to be convertible merely into property, and the worker will gain every inducement to keep his eye upon his work. The attempt to establish such a system may fail, but assuredly it is a profoundly practicable system, born of the will to enhance the essential human values involved in the process of economic civilization. . . .

The process of industrial education, like the process of political education, does not, however, consist primarily in going to school. It consists primarily in active effort on behalf of an increasing measure of self-government; and the only form which such active effort can take is that of fighting for its attainment. The independence of the wage-earners as a class would not amount to much, in case it was handed down to them by the state or by employers' associations. They must earn it in the same way that every modern nation has earned or protected its independence — that is, by warfare appropriate for the purpose. Their "Constitution of Freedom" must be gradually extorted from their employers by a series of conflicts in which the ground is skilfully chosen and permanent defeat is never admitted. In that way only can the wage-earning class win effective power, the devotion of its own members and the respect of its opponents. It requires for the purpose of this warfare a much more general and intense feeling of class consciousness and responsibility than it has at present, and a much more tenacious and enlightened class policy. Practically all of the wage-earners as a group should be unionized as the result of this warfare; and they should be unionized because of the substantial benefits which the unions were able to confer on their members.

This warfare, in so far as it was successfully conducted, would be educational in several different ways. The wage earners would become actually less dependent on their employers and would have earned their independence. Their independence would be bound to assume a definite legal form. They would obtain as the result of collective bargaining effective control over some of the conditions under which they worked. Their observation of the working of these agreements would give to them an increasing knowledge of the business and of the problems and difficulties of its management. Finally, their sense of fellowship with their classmates would be very much enhanced. They would learn the necessity of standing together, and of not allowing any differences in grades of employment to divide them one from another. All this would still be very far from a really democratic industrial system; but in so far as it was represented in definite agreements, it would assume the form of an industrial constitutionalism. The unions would gradually appropriate the function of criticising and vetoing any action of the management of the business which vitally affected the welfare of employees either individually or as a whole. . . .

However liberating and enlightening the education would be which democratic citizens might derive from the actual exercise of political responsibilities, they would derive very much more from the exercise of industrial or business responsibility. The phrase "industrial education" usually means the prevailing system of technical instruction; and the importance of the best methods in a complete system of industrial education can scarcely be exaggerated; but behind any sound technical instruction there must be taking place a process of educating workers to get and keep a fruitful moral and mental attitude towards their work. To industrial education of this kind the installation first of constitutional and then of democratic government in industry is indispensable. As soon as a business becomes in certain respects the business of all the participating workers, the latter will undergo a change of attitude towards their work. The dignity and the serviceability of their calling and of their occupation will be recognized in the economic organization. Presumably they are being rewarded, not perhaps according to the value or cost of the work (if that were possible), but at least with as much liberality as the productivity of the business will permit. The further improvement of their position does not depend upon their acquisition of property. It depends upon the increasing productivity of the industry; and increasing production will depend upon the increasing excellence of individual work, upon the equally meritorious work of the cooperators, upon skilful and economical management, and, finally, upon the general increase in industrial and social efficiency. Thus the wage-earners will have won a kind of independence, in which devotion to work will individualize their lives without dividing them from their fellow-workers. The democracy will derive its education, both morally and socially, from the liberalizing, leavening and humanizing effect of its working activity and of the resulting responsibilities and discipline.

Those who believe in the strengthening of the unions as a necessary step in the direction of industrial democracy, and who also believe in the regeneration of industry by the application of scientific methods, are apparently confronted by a disastrous contradiction. The alliance between business and science, from which business may be expected to derive some of the fearless, critical, candid and disinterested scientific spirit, and a technical efficiency which is indispensable to a generally higher standard of living, has incurred the enmity of the practical living agency of a future industrial democracy. . . .

In asserting that industrial democracy may reconcile the workers to the discipline required by industrial efficiency, I am not merely allowing the wish to be father to the thought. The adjustment between the two will not be automatic and general. But it will take place in certain instances as the result either of enlightened planning by employers or enlightened leadership among the workers; and wherever it takes place, it should quickly and decisively prove its superiority. The mutual dependence between democracy in business and science in business will be established in practice. Scientific management can never reach its highest efficiency in a community of apprehensive and self-regarding dependent wage-earners. It requires for its better operation alert, intelligent and interested workers and cordial and insistent cooperation among them. The morale of the scientifically managed shops, which are also self-governing communities, will be superior to that of the business autocracies, just as the morale of an army of patriots, who are fighting on behalf of a genuinely national cause, is superior to that of an army of merely mercenary or drafted soldiers. The severer the discipline which men are required to undergo, the more they need the inspiration of a disinterested personal motive and complete acquiescence in the purpose for the benefit of which the discipline has been contrived. Scientific management will need the self-governing workshop quite as much as industrial democracy will need the application of scientific methods to business. . . .

Democracy can never permit science to determine its fundamental purpose, because the integrity of that purpose depends finally upon a consecration of the will, but at the same time democracy on its spiritual side would be impoverished and fruitless without science. The fulfilment of democratic purposes depends upon the existence of relatively authentic knowledge, the authority of which a free man may accept without any compromise of his freedom. The acceptance of such authority becomes a binding and cohesive influence. Its representatives can within limits serve the purposes of a democratic community without the friction or the irrelevance of an election. Yet just because science is coming to exercise so much authority and be capable of such considerable achievements, a completer measure of industrial and political democracy becomes not merely natural, but necessary. The enormous powers for good and evil which science is bringing into existence cannot be intrusted to the goodwill of any one class of rulers in

the community. The community as a whole will not derive full benefit
from scientific achievements unless the increased power is widely distributed and until all of the members share in its responsibilities and
opportunities. All along the line science is going to demand of faithful
and enlightened men an amount of self-subordination which would be
intolerable and tyrannical in any but a self-governing community. [Her-
bert Croly, *Progressive Democracy* (Macmillan, 1914), 379, 382–7,
389–92, 395–6, 401, 403–5]

Further Reading

Commons, John R., and John B. Andrews, *Principles of Labor Legislation*
(Harper & Brothers, 1916).
Glickman, Lawrence B., *A Living Wage: American Workers and the Making of
Consumer Society* (Cornell University Press, 1997).
Gutman, Herbert, "Protestantism and the American Labor Movement," chap-
ter 2 in *Work, Culture, and Society in Industrializing America* (Knopf, 1976).
Livingston, James, *Pragmatism and the Political Economy of Cultural Revolu-
tion, 1850–1940* (University of North Carolina Press, 1994).
Orren, Karen, *Belated Feudalism: Labor, the Law, and Liberal Development in
the United States* (Cambridge University Press, 1991).
Salvatore, Nicholas, *Eugene V. Debs: Citizen and Socialist* (University of Illinois Press, 1982).
Tomlins, Christopher L., *The State and the Unions: Labor Relations, Law, and
the Organized Labor Movement in America, 1880–1960* (Cambridge University Press, 1985).
Weinstein, James, *The Corporate Ideal and the Liberal State: 1900–1919* (Beacon Press, 1968).
Witt, John Fabian, *The Accidental Republic: Crippled Workingmen, Destitute
Widows, and the Remaking of American Law* (Harvard University Press,
2004).

7

The Social Gospel and Social Christianity

As seen in earlier selections, a religious sensibility pervaded Progressive social and political thought. This religiosity was not so much philosophical as it was nationalist and rhetorical. In the Progressives' ethical writings, Christ of the Gospels was held up as the ethical ideal. In the Progressives' historical and evolutionary writings, this reliance on biblical imagery was extended to include the Hebraic tradition of kingdom theology and its messianic hopes. In these writings, which also incorporated the traditional Puritan covenantal political theology, national and millennial themes came to the fore, simultaneously evoking Lincoln's renewal of the American covenant and the Progressive passion for social justice.[1]

The equation of America's promise with the achievement of the millennial promise of Christianity was a hallmark of much Progressive thought, especially among liberal evangelical Protestants who worked to shape a "modernist" theology shorn of the creedal elements that divided American Protestantism. George Herron, one of America's foremost Social Gospel ministers, declared that "Jesus Christ offers sociology the only scientific ground of discovering all the facts and forces of life. That ground is his revelation of universal unity. . . . Sociology and theology will ultimately be one science."[2] A meeting of Wisconsin Congregationalists in 1895 proclaimed "the right of sociology to demand that theology be ethicized" and said that "the best book for social guidance is the New Testament; the best commentaries are the works of scientific sociology."[3]

As sociology seemed interchangeable with theology, so, too, did Progressivism seem to become increasingly "secular," especially as the social sciences became more professional and institutionalized. This particular secularization thesis, however, should not be accepted uncritically.[4] It

---

1. Bercovitch, *Puritan Origins* (1977); Tuveson, *Redeemer Nation* (1968).

2. Quoted in Eisenach, *Lost Promise* (1994), 102 n42. In fact, theological education in major university divinity schools, led by Shailer Mathews at the University of Chicago (see his biography and selection in Chapter 10), almost seamlessly integrated social economy, sociology, and social work into their curricula.

3. Quoted in Thelen, *The New Citizenship* (1972), 108–9.

4. Sommerville, "Tacit Rules for Using the Term 'Secularization'" (2000).

might even be interpreted the other way: as the social sciences became increasingly ethical and moral, they became infused with liberal evangelical Protestant sensibilities. One close student of American Protestantism put it this way:

> A key paradox of [American] liberal Protestantism—one that must be a cornerstone of any history of liberal Protestantism—is that its goal has always been, in part, to sanctify the secular, to bring forth out of the natural and human worlds the divine potential contained within them. Secularization can be seen, in some of its forms, as a sign of success for liberal Protestantism, not a marker of defeat.[5]

No one better symbolized this goal than W.D.P. Bliss, whose name has appeared frequently in this collection as a founder of Christian socialism and publicist for the reform causes that first attracted so many Progressive intellectuals. His *New Encyclopedia of Social Reform* (1908) was a massive compendium of the progress of the spirit of Christianity into secular and material life. Through its many graphs and tables of social statistics, its comprehensive lists of reform organizations, causes, and publications, its biographies of prominent reform leaders, and (most significantly) its analysis linking religion and society, church and state, and ethics and economics, it charted this progress and measured its comparative advances in America and the nations of Europe. The *Encyclopedia* includes separate biographical entries of thirteen of the authors in this collection, with entries by, and quotations from, the writings of many more. In ways that will become clearer in Chapter 10, Bliss created a sort of repository for the ideas that helped create an international Progressive and Social Democratic united front.

29. *The Christian State,* Samuel Zane Batten (1859–1925)

Born in New Jersey, Batten received his university education at Bucknell College in Pennsylvania and his theological training at Crozer Seminary. (Crozer, another Pennsylvanian school, was the same seminary that Martin Luther King Jr. would attend from 1948 to 1951.) With Walter Rauschenbusch, whose writing appears later in this chapter, Batten was an active member of the Brotherhood of the Kingdom, one of the first Social Gospel organizations. Batten was a

---

5. Fox, "Experience and Explanation," in Stout and Hart, *New Directions* (1997), 400; and see Fox, "The Culture of Liberal Protestant Progressivism" (1993).

pastor in Northern Baptist Churches, first in the east and then in the midwest. Later, he became a professor of social science at Des Moines (Drake) College in Iowa and chairman of the Social Service Commission of the Northern Baptist Convention, and he was active in the Federal Council of Churches, an alliance of Protestant evangelical churches that shared a similar commitment to social reform. Batten was a prolific author. His most notable books were The New Citizenship *(1898),* The Christian State *(1909), and* The Social Tasks of Christianity *(1911).*

—1898—

Individual effort may do much for the improvement of other individuals; but individual effort to be highly successful must be supported by the social order: it must work through the social order. The state is in the best sense the medium through which personal power is conveyed to all and is made effective for all. The state is the only organ or medium great enough to express these varied powers of men, the only medium through which men can most effectually co-operate in the attainment of social perfection. Political visionaries have drawn beautiful pictures of the blessedness and freedom of man in what they are pleased to call a state of nature. But no such men have been found; such men are not perfect men in the full meaning of the term. . . .

Since this is so, every citizen should be a politician in the larger and better sense of the word. This means that every member of the state should be concerned in all that makes for the welfare of the state. . . .

Whether all men are willing to accept the responsibilities of citizenship is one question; the fact remains that in many nations today they are charged with these responsibilities, and cannot evade or escape them without being recreant to high trusts. A great and significant movement is going on in the world today, a movement fraught with immeasurable woe or immeasurable blessing to countless numbers of our race. The great nations of the world are launching forth full on the tide of popular government. Slowly the scepter of authority has passed from the monarch to the few, and from the few to the many. Today, in half-a-dozen leading nations, the people are practically supreme, and more or less determine the laws and manage the government. This means that all the people are summoned to participate in the responsibilities of the social welfare. At a great price humanity has gained this privilege. The past three centuries have witnessed a great change; the transit and transfer of power first from the monarch to the aristocracy; then from the aristocracy to the people. . . . In a popular government the responsibility of the state is laid upon the minds and consciences of the people. They must face all the problems of the state; they must consider the social welfare; they must frame legislation, they must form the nation's conscience; in a word, every citizen is called to bear the burden and heat of the struggle for life and progress in the state. . . .

The Christian citizen will do all in his power to secure the enactment of good laws, and to bring in a better social order. One great purpose of all law is to declare what is socially right and wrong. What law allows as a rule the conscience of man approves, and what law condemns the conscience of the people does not commend. One great function of law is to be the standard of social judgment and conduct. The legislation of a nation is at once the expression of the nation's life and the determiner of the nation's morality. . . . Right and wrong, it cannot be too strongly emphasized, are not the creations of the ballot-box; justice and injustice are not the will of the majority. To read that law whose dwelling-place is none other than the bosom of the living God is the business of the human law maker. The real law maker endeavors to express and realize in human legislation the moral distinctions which are wrought into the very fabric of the universe. The only argument adducible in favor of any law is its fairness, its justice, its righteousness; the mere question of expediency and popularity does not enter. Only by the honest votes of good men can moral considerations obtain sway in political affairs. As a believer in God and in his kingdom the Christian citizen must endeavor to enact and execute laws which shall be the transcript of the writing on the adamant tables. A law that is simply the will of the majority speaks with no deep tone of authority and commands little reverence. But law becomes majestic, when it is regarded not as a mere conventional arrangement adopted by a majority vote, but as an expression of the will and righteousness of God. The believer in God must do what lies in his power to secure the dominance of moral principles in civil affairs; he must seek to establish, and maintain in human relations the justice of God; the life and law of that kingdom which is over all are to color all his thoughts, determine every duty, and be supreme in every part of life.

—1909—

Democracy will not fulfil its task till it has taught men the full meaning of liberty and has trained them in the art of living together. It is the recognition of the fact that all men are brothers, with common interests, common rights, and common duties. Liberty, on its negative side, means deliverance from arbitrary and external rule. Liberty in its positive aspect means the voluntary submission to law, with voluntary self-sacrifice for the common good. It is just here that we discover a danger that is as real in a democracy as in an autocracy. In a monarchy the world has often beheld the spectacle of one man making himself supreme and compelling the service and obedience of his fellows. And in a democracy we may behold the same spectacle under other forms, in the free and independent citizen who makes his own interests and preferences supreme. That man who in the democratic State regards the machinery of government as the agent of his own interests and desires, differs in no essential respect from the autocrat who imposes his will upon his fellows. Liberty that means self-assertion and self-seeking is death; liberty that means self-sacrifice and social service is life. We never shall have a real liberty or a true democracy till this principle is recognized and honored. . . .

We have discovered that not everything has been done that needs to be done. There are whole classes of rights which are not yet defined and secured. The citizen possesses the ballot, but he is not content. He lives under a written constitution, but his rights are not all therein defined. He possesses the political franchise, but the golden age has not yet dawned. He is a free citizen, and yet he feels himself defrauded of some of his dearest rights. In a word, man has gained religious and political democracy, but he has come to see that the democratic task is not finished till he has gained industrial and social democracy. Perhaps we can best describe this new task before democracy by applying some of the democratic principles to man's social and industrial life. . . .

Two things . . . have contributed to bring about this separation of the people from their government. The first is the system of representative government which removes it as far as possible from the people themselves. And the second is the American party system which provides the very means for designing men to use the government for their own ends. And thus we are brought face to face with another unfinished task of democracy, and one of the most difficult of all. That democracy may be in fact as in name it is necessary that there be a direct participation of the people in the affairs of government. It is not necessary to discuss all of the measures that may contribute to this end; but two are worthy of a full trial.

The first is what may be called direct legislation by the people. The power to enact laws may be exercised by the people directly or through their chosen representatives. The latter method is the one that prevails generally in democratic lands. Under this system there is often a complete divergence between the will of the people and the action of their representatives, and hence the legislation does not represent the consent of the governed. To remedy these evils and to give the people a direct voice in the affairs of government is the one object of the system known as the initiative and referendum. . . .

The second measure that must be adopted in some form if democracy is to be more than a name, is that of direct popular nomination of candidates. Through the system of party government with delegated conventions it has come about that the people have no direct voice in the nomination of candidates and the making of platforms. Because of all this the average citizen now takes little interest in political matters. Thus the control of the party machine, and consequently the direction of the affairs of government, have fallen into the hands of the few active and interested men who are able to manipulate the party machinery and dictate the government's policy. To obviate this, and to give the people a direct voice in the selection of candidates some such method as the direct primary has been devised. . . .

Thus far democracy in its spirit and method has been largely negative and individualistic. It has emphasized individualism and has overlooked solidarity. It has been suspicious of government, and has been resentful of social control. It has cleared the ground but it has not built the temple. It has outlined the new society, but it has not created the society itself. To complete its task, to fulfil its mission, democracy must become positive and constructive. It must learn the meaning of government and must teach men how to use it for the whole welfare of all. It must create a human society in which the person shall be accorded all of his rights, and must insure a liberty that means the highest solidarity. In a word, it must complete itself in fraternity, which is the democracy of all life. . . .

In view of what was said . . . it is evident that the democratic principle must be extended and applied in what may be called the social and industrial realms of life. It is impossible here to enter upon the discussion of this task in all its breadth of meaning, but it is one of the most insistent and difficult of modern times. The fate of democracy itself as a religious principle and a political doctrine is at stake here; for in the long run we must either abandon the democratic faith in political affairs or we must realize it in all life. We cannot permanently maintain a civic State based on democratic principles while living in an industrial society that is oligarchic both in form and spirit. "No man," said Abraham Lincoln, "is good enough to rule his fellows." If this saying is true at all, it is as true in economic and industrial affairs as it is in ecclesiastical and political relations. [Samuel Zane Batten, *The New Citizenship: Christian Character in Its Biblical Ideals, Sources, and Relations* (Union Press, 1898), 241, 246, 248–9, 253–5; *The Christian State: The State, Democracy, and Christianity* (Griffith and Rowland Press, 1909), 221–3, 240–4, 248]

30. *The Christian Society*, George D. Herron (1862–1925)

*In the 1890s, under the leadership of its president, George Gates,
Grinnell College in Iowa became a center of the Social Gospel. Thanks
to the generosity of Mrs. E. D. Rand, a department of Applied
Christianity was established, along with a weekly magazine,* The
Kingdom, *and a series of national conferences called the School of the
Kingdom conferences. The best summary of the theology represented at
Grinnell College was given by Gates:*

> The Kingdom of heaven and the Kingdom of God does not refer to a life
> beyond the grave; the kingdom of God does not mean the Church or any
> other institution; such an identification of the kingdom with the Church
> either concrete or invisible being "one of the most dangerous of here-
> sies"; the Kingdom of God [means] a society upon this earth in which all
> human affairs exhibit the nature and spirit of God.[6]

*George Herron graduated from Ripon College in Wisconsin and went on
to become a notable Congregational minister in Minnesota and Iowa,
preaching and writing the Social Gospel message. In 1893 he was
appointed to head the Applied Christianity department at Grinnell
College. Alas, Professor Herron, already married, began a love affair with
Carrie Rand, daughter of the benefactress, and was forced to leave
Grinnell in disgrace, taking Gates down with him. During a
companionate marriage to Carrie Rand, Herron resumed his writing and
launched a national speaking career, lecturing most frequently at
colleges and universities. Herron campaigned for Eugene Debs[7] in 1900
and gave one of the nominating speeches for Debs at the Socialist Party
Convention in 1904. These socialist affiliations did not prevent Herron
from delivering the commencement address at the University of Nebraska
in 1902. Together with his wife, Herron founded the Rand School of
Social Science, a center of socialist thought and teaching, in New York
City in 1905.*

    *As a curious footnote, Herron's successor at Grinnell College was a
Jew, Edward Steiner, who immigrated to America with a PhD from the
University of Heidelberg. After receiving a divinity degree from Oberlin
Seminary, Steiner fit easily into Grinnell's brand of Social Gospel
theology.*

---

6. Quoted in Dombrowski, *Early Days of Christian Socialism* (1936), 112–3.

7. Eugene Victor Debs (1855–1926), a labor organizer, was a Socialist presidential candidate five times between 1900 and 1920. He appealed to older
native populists as well as newer, politically radical immigrants.

I have the conviction that when Christ comes fully to His own in the
church, He will also come to His own in the synagogue. . . . When He
emerges from the tangle of Greek philosophy, Roman legalism and
Byzantine traditionalism—when "in deed and in truth" He becomes the
Gentile's Messiah, He will also become the Messiah of the Jew.[8]

Steiner gained recognition as the author of many books on immigration.
By calling on his readers to respect their separate religious traditions and
practices, Steiner hoped to prepare them for their inclusion into the
American nation as one people dedicated to universal principles of
justice. In this regard, Steiner reflected the views of such Jewish writers as
Mary Antin and Israel Zangwill. These writers, along with Steiner, were
published in Outlook, edited by Lyman Abbott; Abbott was another
Congregational minister and close associate of Theodore Roosevelt.

—1894—

Sociology cannot be dissociated from theology. Sociology and theology
will ultimately be one science. Society depends upon theology. Men will
be what they think God is. We need a Christian theology that we may
have a Christian society. We cannot have a Christian society without a
faith in Christ as a revelation of the character of God. If Christ is simply
a divine accident, if his character is a concession to human weakness, if
his revelation of God is only partial, if the right that is in God is more or
less than the right that is in Christ, or if it differs in quality from the right
that inheres in the nature of man, then neither sociology nor theology
have more than a speculative foundation on which to build; neither can
become a science. Unless all there is of God was revealed in Christ,
unless the revelation be eternal as well as historical, we worship a God
who is yet unknown, and we know not whither our steps are tending.
Theology must begin with Christ. It must cease to fear and learn to trust
the revelation of God which Christ has made. It must tolerate no doctrines which look dark in the light of the revelation of the Father in the
Son of Man. It is a fatal infidelity for the Christian to separate the justice
of God from the love of Christ in his thinking; for the result can be nothing else than the separation of religion from life. He that sees the Son
sees the Father: sees what the character of the Father is: sees what his attitude toward man is: sees what God is like, and how he thinks and feels
and acts toward man. All the fullness of God's life was in Christ. All that
makes up the character of the Father was in the Son. Their unity, their

8. Steiner, *The Immigrant Tide* (1909), 273–4.

harmony, their co-working, was perfect. The mind of Christ was the
mind of God. He thought God's thoughts, felt God's feelings, did God's
works; and all he said and did, all he taught and suffered, witnesses that
there are no contradictions in the character of God. Christ upon the
cross is what God eternally is. Christ proved the justice of God in the for-
giveness of our sins. He revealed the moral majesty of God when he
washed the disciples' feet. He manifested the sovereignty of God in sub-
mitting to the crucifixion. He expressed the love of God in his wrath at
the covetousness and hypocrisy of the Pharisees and Sadducees. He
showed that the justice and mercy of God are one and the same thing;
that justice is love at work, and punishment for sin is mercy in action.
The fullness of the revelation of the Father in the Son was made in the
words of the beloved apostle: God is love. Our theological dogmas must
bear the light and be stated in the terms of this revelation. When theology begins to learn its knowledge of God from Jesus, it will be saved for
moral uses; it will be changed from the metaphysical to the sociological.

A Christian sociology will save the great doctrines of theology from
being lost in the abstractions of the schools by translating them into the
actual experiences of man. It will answer the question as to what the
atonement historically was by showing what the atonement eternally
and socially is; by projecting the idea of the atonement into the future
through the creation of redemptive social phenomena by disclosing and
teaching the principle of sacrifice as the vital force of history and
progress, of personality and fellowship. Sociology is a science of sacrifice; of redemption; of atonement. The realization of society is the realization of the atonement through the fulfillment of the incarnation.
Society is sacrifice. It is the manifestation of the eternal sacrifice of God,
as it was unveiled on the cross, in human relations. Sociology will interpret the fact of propitiation by educating a societary conscience that will
compel every rational man to engage in bearing away the sin of the
world. A Christian sociology will save the doctrine of inspiration by
showing that its real peril has been in its being dogmatized and
defended as a past fact while rejected as a present fact and condition of
life. *The real problem of inspiration is not as to the manner in which holy
men of old were inspired, but whether there are now holy men willing to
be inspired and consumed in the service of truth and justice.* Inspiration
is always the passion for righteousness in human relations, and the passion for social righteousness is always inspiration. Inspiration is the final
and natural moral atmosphere. One thing that Jesus could not and
would not tolerate, because it is the very spirit of false prophecy, was
the condition of being uninspired. Inspiration will finally organize the
economic justice which law has no power to utter; which custom is

impotent to procure. The Patmos vision of John is the fulfillment of Christianity in the world, through sacrificial processes, in a history whose nations shall be governed through the immediate inspiration of God.

Progress is Christian. It is the evolution and fruit of sacrifice. The formative movements of history have been sacrificial and redemptive. The ages witness that the justice procured through love, that the right-eousness manifested in sacrifice, is not the enemy of man, the foe of civ-ilization, as Satan and the old political economists would have us think, but the progress of man and the ground of civilization. Covetousness and falsehood have never been profitable or wise, but are now and ever have been the waste of the earth and the woe of life. Prosperity has not come through obedience to selfish principles, but in spite of them. Lies and despotisms, intrigues and expediences, self-will and social caste, luxury and pride, never have ruled the world, and never can. Behind the shadows which our moral unbelief has cast upon the glory of his providence, in spite of the self-will which has been the tyrant and deceiver of man, God has been working out the vital progress of the world. The kingdoms and the power and the glory are God's and not the devil's. *This is a redeemed and not a lost world. . . .*

Social order is Christian. The incarnation of the Son of man is the revelation of the social order in which God created and is perfecting the world. Society is the fellowship of the sacrifice of Christ in human rela-tions. The growth of the social organism is the increase of eternal life in human motives and products, making each unrecorded thought and forgotten deed an undying note in the harmony of man with God and nature which has been the song of prophecy and the surprise of science. Society is the fulfillment of nature in man, and the indwelling of God with man, through the obedience of man to the law of life enunciated by Jesus in his new commandment to love one another sacrificially and redemptively, as he loved us. The birth of the social consciousness, with which the world is now in travail, is the conversion of social institutions from the protective to the redemptive basis; from the Roman to the Christian conception of society. The discovery of men that they may advance together in the fulfillment of righteousness, that they may act as one person in bearing away the sin of the world, is the awakening of society to its self-consciousness in the light of the universal unity which was the vision of Jesus. . . .

A Christian sociology will no doubt have to defend itself against the theologian and the scientist; against custodial religion and social ego-ism; against pietist and secularist. Theology does not yet believe that God is Christian, and science does not yet see that nature is Christian.

Such a faith is unknown to institutional religiousness, and can mean nothing but the complete overthrow of all social despotisms. Such a vision is an offense to pietism, and hateful to secularism. Between the unbelief of organized religion in the Christianity of God, and the unbelief of organized selfishness in the Christianity of nature, Christ is likely to come to a new crucifixion. In this crucifixion the sociology that follows Christ will have to share. But its resurrection will be a Messianic age, educated in the science of redemption to bear away the sins of society and bring in the thousand years of peace. . . .

The Christian constitution of society is not a church. The gathering of the peoples under the dominion of a religious institution has never been the idea of God. The purest institutional rule of the world would yet be other than a Christian rule. An institution of religion is not a constitution of society. It is at best but a medium through which the Spirit of God may pour upon society the anointing of Christ, and constitute it in the likeness of Christ. Society is not an institution, but a life. Institutions are a means to the divine social end. They are but the scaffolding of the living social temple, and shall be taken down when their work is done. . . .

The church is a means to an end, and that end is the kingdom of God, which is the just social order. Like the family and the state, it is one of the triune modes of the kingdom of God. It was not sent to build itself up out of the world, but to build the world up out of itself. The idea of God is not to gather humanity into a church, and make that church the embodiment of his moral dominion over men, but to make the church the incarnation of the passion of Jesus, and send it to be lost in the life of the redeemed and perfected humanity. There is no temple in that city of God, no religious institution in that universal social order, which was the vision of the beloved apostle and seer; the fellowship of the people with God was the social order of the new earth. The work of the church is the regeneration of human society; but it is not itself that society. The mission of the church is the establishment of the Christian constitution of society; but it is not itself that constitution. The conception of the church as the supreme end in itself, as being an ark of safety instead of an organ of sacrifice, has gradually converted Christendom into an organized misrepresentation of Christ. The Christian persons, the sacrificial and redemptive lives, are more in this age than any other; they are a great multitude whom no man can number; but they are not a part of the actual church organism. They are in the church but not of it. The collective attitude of the church toward God and his world, notwithstanding the many who are waiting to be led to the Calvary of a

social redemption, is precisely the attitude of the Pharisees and Sadducees that wrought the destruction of the Jewish church and nation in
the day of its visitation. As truly as Jesus would have gathered Israel into
the fellowship of his sacrifice, and made it a nation of redeemers, so he
would now gather the church into the fellowship of his sacrifice, and
send it to be crucified for the social redemption of the world. He would
save the church from the leaven of the Pharisees and Sadducees; from
its unfaith in God and the people; from its mistaking respectability for
virtue; from its substitution of opinion for faith. The church is called to
be the Christ of God to society. And it may be that only a very small
remnant will hear and obey this call. . . .

The world has never been institutionally governed. The government of
the peoples has not yet appeared, yet history witnesses that inspirations
and not institutions have actually ruled the world. The great epochal
and formative movements have been the marshalling of human forces
under the command of great impulsions to righteousness. Progress has
been the increasing apprehension of unseen spiritual forces; the closing
together of God and the people in the communion and power of the
Holy Ghost. The bonds of this divine social order are unseen, and yet
in the crisis of history their strength is made manifest in the security
with which the world meets the shocks of terrible and resistless judgments. History is the progressive disclosure of the presence and fellowship of that just society which is the city of God coming down out of
heaven. And the progress of man toward the fulfillment of his social destiny in Christ has never been institutional, but inspirational, sacrificial,
and free. Society is not rule and letter, institution and organization, but
spirit and life; and they must be born of the Spirit who would enter the
social order of the communion of the Spirit, and see the kingdom of
God. The social ideals which institutions have crucified are the unseen
thrones of the divine government of the world, the increase and peace
of which shall have no end. Not God *and* the people, which the Italian
Revolution inscribed upon its banner, but God *in* the people, is the
power that is overcoming the tyrannies and slaveries, the falsehoods and
hypocrisies, of the world. The Christian constitution of society is the
incarnation of the Son of God. The coming social order is Immanuel,
God with us. . . .

The gospel of Jesus to the poor was the democracy of the people. Pure
democracy and pure theocracy are one. Democracy is the communion
of the people in the social order of the Holy Ghost; and theocracy is the
government of the people by the immediate inspiration of God. The

democracy of the people has not yet been manifested; but our social troubles are preparing the way for its realization; and when it appears in social justice, it will be the incarnation of him who first preached the gospel of democracy to the people.

Our industrial society has had brought down to it all the conflicting and the uniting elements of past stages of society. The forces at war in modern society are not new, but old. The principles that fight for supremacy in our industrial society are the same that fought in the subjection of provinces to oriental monarchs; in the long strifes between the popes and the nations; in peasant wars and insurrections; in the Puritan, French, and American revolutions of the people against the divine right of kings. The principle of absolutism, and the principle of democracy which we have long thought triumphant, are here in the social problem, drawing up their longest and strongest and most fearful lines of battle at our doors. The doctrine of the divine right of the king to rule the people, of the divine right of the pope to have upon his shoulder the government of all peoples, has been translated into the doctrine of the divine right of property to govern the social well-being of the people for its own gain. The people may not be able to define what they know, but they know that they are serving and toiling with hands and brains for masters who are absolutely irresponsible for their welfare, and absolutely authoritative in the government of economic production and distribution, of employment and unemployment. The social question is simply the field upon which the forces of democracy and absolutism are deliberately and knowingly preparing for their greatest conflict. Whether the conflict be moral or military depends upon whether the church receives or rejects the social incarnation and redemption of the Christ who preached the gospel that has been responsible for all the revolutions, however much their violence misrepresents him, since he gave to men the vision and motive of the kingdom of heaven upon the earth.

The social problem is the problem of democracy against absolutism; of the people against irresponsible masters; of freedom against the institutional dominion that would subject the living present to the dead past. It is not a problem of wealth and wages merely, but of the right to work; the right to do one's duty; the right to sacrifice; the right to live as becomes a son of God; the right to be free. People will starve and die; they will live in dug-outs and tenements and miners' huts; *but they will be free.* And the freedom wherewith the kingdom of God shall make them free is the freedom of the Son of God.

We sometimes hear it said that young men and women of today have no incentive to heroic action, such as inspired the heroism of the great epochal days that have made men free in the past. But I say to you that there were no opportunities in the constructions and reformations of the past that opened such doors of service and sacrifice, of moral glory and pure courage, as now open to you in the coming of that social redemption of the world, which is but the uprising of the sons of God in the preparation of the way for the coming of his kingdom.

The old passion for freedom comes to us vaster and regenerated; it comes to us with universal and heavenly meaning. It is not now freedom for Switzerland, freedom for France, freedom for Puritan England, freedom for America, that inspires the world with a quickened life, but the freedom of man. With the vision of the universal democracy of the sons of God, Jesus has forever lighted all the heavens of political freedom and religious truth; of social justice and human destiny. The collective obedience of a thousand men to that vision would be the creation of a new world; a world in which all absolutisms, be they social or political, industrial or theological, would be overcome.

The opinion of priest and theologian, of industrial master and party manager, that the people cannot be trusted, is a denial of the good news of the kingdom of God, which was the gospel of Jesus to the poor. Unbelief in the divine sonship of man is the ground of the practical atheism toward God, the separation of religion from life, for which theology is responsible. The political leaders and the clergy are almost unconscious of the collective moral faith of the people because they do not know God as Immanuel, which knowledge is the gospel of the kingdom of God, and the ground of all democracy; of all faith and freedom. It was the faith of Moses and Jesus, of Milton[9] and Mulford,[10] of Mazzini[11] and Lincoln, that the people are abler than any institution to organically express the will of God in a communion of justice. The

---

9. John Milton (1608–1674) was an English poet and propagandist for Cromwell and the Commonwealth established following the victory of the Puritans in the English Civil War. He was the author of *Paradise Lost* (1667), arguably the most famous poem in the English language.

10. Probably a reference to Prentice Mulford (1834–1891), a pioneer of American New Thought and a secular prophet. He was famous for the books on mental and spiritual laws he published as *The White Cross Library*. Something of a recluse, he spent many years living and writing in the swamps of Passaic, New Jersey.

11. Giuseppe Mazzini (1805–1872) was an Italian liberal-nationalist and a prophet of the unification of Italy (Risorgimento) as a republic. He associated with many reformers during his many years of exile in London.

living faith of the living people in the living God is defeated and inarticulate because they have no organ through which they can express their faith.

But there draws near the kingdom of God which shall organize the faith of the people in a democracy of justice, in a social order of the Holy Ghost. And our call to repentance toward God as Immanuel, and to faith in the people as sons of God, is the good news of the coming of God's kingdom among men, which was the gospel of Jesus to the poor. [George D. Herron, *The Christian Society* (Fleming H. Revell, 1894), 32–7, 40–1, 46–7, 55, 61–3, 68–9, 90–5]

31. *Christianity and the Social Crisis,* Walter Rauschenbusch (1861–1918)

Born in upstate New York to a family with a strong German-Baptist heritage, Rauschenbusch attended the same German college preparatory school his father had, then returned to America to earn his BA at the University of Rochester. He received his theological training at Rochester Seminary (where his father was a professor) while also serving as minister in a local German Baptist church. Rauschenbusch began his career in New York City as pastor of the Second German Baptist church, located on the edge of the Hell's Kitchen[12] area. In response to his experiences there, he became an ardent fighter for wage equality and the redistribution of wealth. His commitment to social reform led him to support Henry George's 1886 mayoral campaign and, in 1892, to establish the Brotherhood of the Kingdom, an early Social Gospel organization of which Samuel Zane Batten was also a member. Rauschenbusch published several books, the most influential of which are Christianity and the Social Crisis *(1907) and* God and the People: Prayers for the Social Awakening *(1910).*

—1914—

The sadness of the failure hitherto is turned into brightest hopefulness if we note that all the causes which have hitherto neutralized the social efficiency of Christianity have strangely disappeared or weakened in modern life. Christianity has shed them as an insect sheds its old casing

---

12. In the post-Civil War period, Hell's Kitchen, an area of railroad yards, slaughterhouses, bars, and tenements on New York City's West Side, was a center of crime, corruption, and gang warfare.

in passing through its metamorphosis, and with the disappearance of each of these causes, Christianity has become fitter to take up its regenerative work. Let us run over the causes of failure . . . and note how they have weakened or vanished.

In the Roman Empire . . . social agitation would have been suppressed promptly. Today it still encounters the moral resentment of the classes whose interests are endangered by a moral campaign and, if necessary, these interests are able to use the political machinery to suppress agitation. But in the freer countries of Western civilization the dissemination of moral ideas is almost untrammelled. The prophet's message still brings the prophet's odium; but a man will have to go far if he wants to be stoned or put in the stocks.

Primitive Christianity did not work for social changes which required a long outlook, because it expected the immediate return of Christ. That the return of Christ will end the present world is still part of general Christian teaching; but the actual lapse of nineteen centuries has proved so plainly that we have to reckon with long reaches of time, that this expectation deters very few from taking a long look ahead in all practical affairs. There are, indeed, a number of Christian bodies and a great number of individuals who have systematized the apocalyptic ideas of later Judaism and early Christianity and have made them fundamental in their religious thought. They are placing themselves artificially in the attitude of mind which primitive Christianity took naturally. They are among the most devout and earnest people. By their devotional and missionary literature they exert a wide influence. They share with splendid vigor in evangelistic work, because evangelism saves individuals for the coming of the Lord, and in foreign missionary work, because it is an express condition that the Lord will not return "until the gospel has been preached to all nations." They take a lively interest in the destructive tendencies of modern life, because these are "signs of the times" which herald the end; but they do not feel called to counteract them. Such an effort would be predestined to failure, because the present world is doomed to rush through increasing corruption to moral bankruptcy, and Christ alone by his coming can save it. Historical pessimism is generally woven into the texture of this pattern of thought, and it is this pessimistic interpretation of history, more than the somewhat academic expectation of the immediate return of Christ, which neutralizes the interest of this school of thought in comprehensive moral reformation. . . . But outside of this sphere of thought the hope of the immediate millennium, which was once so influential is no longer a factor to deter Christians from their wider mission to society.

The primitive attitude of fear and distrust toward the State has passed away. We do not regard the existing civilization and its governments as hostile to Christianity. The ancient feeling that demon powers inspire the State has vanished with the belief in demons. Some today regard the State as the organization of secular life, which, though in a sphere apart from religion, is good and useful in its way. Others take the more religious view of it, that it is one of the divinely constituted factors to train the race for the kingdom of God, of equal dignity with the family and the Church. Under either conception it is possible to cooperate with it and turn the regenerative moral power of religion into the channels of organized civil life.

The other-worldliness of Christian desire is strangely diminished. We all believe in immortality, but we are not weary of this world. The longing to die and go to heaven is not regarded as a test of spiritual life as it used to be, even within the memory of many of us. To us salvation means victory over sin rather than escape from hell. This change of attitude dignifies the present life. It is not, then, too paltry for earnest effort. The hope of personal salvation after death no longer monopolizes the Christian hope. There is now room beside it for the social hope.

The ascetic and monastic ideal, which dominated Christian life for a thousand years and more, has disappeared almost completely. If the saints that lie buried under the stone floor of some ancient European church could rise and listen to a modern sermon, they would find their gospel turned upside down. Instead of praise of virginity, they would hear eulogies of family life. Instead of the call to poverty, they would hear the praise of Christianity because it makes men and nations prosperous and wealthy. Instead of exhortations to wear their flesh thin with fasting and vigil, they would be invited to membership in the Y.M.C.A., with gymnasium and bath to keep their flesh in a glow of health. If the old gospel of individualism should hereafter change into the gospel of socialism, the change would not be half as great as that involved in the surrender of the ascetic ideal of the Christian life. Some ascetic practices still linger in the observance of Lent. The ascetic notion occasionally crops up that men are best turned to God by affliction, and that revivals follow on hard times. The distrust of the intellectual and artistic and political life in English evangelicalism and German pietism, the retirement of the Christian within the untroubled realm of family and business life is a diluted Protestant form of the ascetic flight from the world. The Roman Church, by force of its strong mediæval traditions, still exalts the monastic life as the crown of religious living; but its mediæval saints would think their Church was dead if they saw the scarcity of monks in America. The current of modern religion does not run away from the world, but toward it. . . .

Ceremonialism, which early clogged the ethical vigor of Christianity, was broken in the Reformation and is slowly dying out. The Greek and Roman Catholicism are faithful to it by virtue of their conservatism, but even there it is no longer a creative force. There are ritualistic drifts in a few Protestant bodies, but they are not part of modern life, but romantic reactions toward the past. The present tendency to a more ornate and liturgical worship in the radical Protestant denominations of America is æsthetic and not sacramental in motive. It is proof that sacramentalism is so dead that Protestant churches no longer need to fear the forms that might revive it. The priest is dying. The prophet can prepare to enter his heritage, provided the prophet himself is still alive with his ancient message of an ethical and social service of God.

It is a commonplace that Christianity has grown less dogmatic. There is probably just as much earnest conviction, but it is modified by greater respect for the conviction of others and by a deeper interest in right living. Men and churches fellowship freely with little regard to doctrinal uniformity. One of the chief anti-social forces has therewith disappeared from Christianity, and the subsidence of the speculative interest has to that extent left Christianity free to devote its thought to ethical and social problems.

Christianity in the past was almost wholly churchly. The organized Church absorbed the devotion, the ability, and the wealth of its members. To some degree that is still true. The churches need time and money and must strive to get their share. For very many men and women the best service they can render to the kingdom of God is really through the local church and its activities. . . . The wiser leaders of Christianity [however] do not desire to monopolize the services of Christian men for the churches, but rejoice in seeing the power of religion flow out in the service of justice and mercy. Religion is less an institution and more a diffused force than ever before. The brazen vessel of the Church was fatally cracked and broken by the Reformation, and its contents have ever since been leaking away into secular life. The State, the schools, the charitable organizations, are now doing what the Church used to do. The Roman Church continues its traditions of churchly authority and exclusiveness. Some Protestant bodies try with more or less success to imitate her rôle, but Protestantism cannot compete with the Roman Catholic Church in churchliness. In spite of itself, Protestantism has lost its ecclesiastical character and authority. But at the same time Protestant Christianity has gained amazingly in its spiritual effectiveness on society. The Protestant nations have leaped forward in wealth, education, and political preponderance. The unfettering of intellectual and economic ability under the influence of this diffused force of Christianity is an historical miracle. Protestantism has even protestantized the Roman Catholic Church. The Roman Church crumbles away before it in our country and can only save its adherents by quarantining its children in parochial schools and its men and women in separate social and benevolent societies. The churches are profoundly needed as generators of the religious spirit; but they are no longer the sole sphere of action for the religious spirit. They exist to create the force which builds the kingdom of God on earth, the better humanity. By becoming less churchly Christianity has, in fact, become fitter to regenerate the common life.

Modern Christianity everywhere tends toward the separation of Church and State. But when the Church is no longer dependent on the State for its appointments and its income and the execution of its will, it is by that much freer to champion the better order against the chief embodiment of the present order. We shall see later that even when Church and State are separated, the Church may still be in bondage to the powers of the world. It can still be used as a spiritual posse to read the Riot Act to the rebellious minds of men. But as the formal control of the Church by the State slackens, and the clerical interests are withdrawn from politics, the Church is freer to act as the tribune of the people, and the State is more open to the moral and humanizing influence of Christianity. At the same time the political emancipation and increasing democracy of the people is bound to draw the larger social and political problems within the interests of the masses, and there is sure to be a silent extension of the religious interest and motive to social and political duties.

In the past the Church was dominated by the clergy and it was monarchical in its organization. The Reformation brought a slow turn on both points. The power of the hierarchy was broken; the laity began to rise to increased participation in church life. That in itself insured an increasing influence of Christianity on secular life. At the same time the Protestant bodies, in varying degrees, reverted toward democracy in organization. Those Protestant bodies which constitute the bulk of Protestantism in America and of the free churches in England all have the essence of church democracy. Even the churches with episcopal government are affected by the spirit of democratic self-government. The Roman Church in America itself has not escaped this influence. All this lays the churches open to democratic sympathies, provided they are not merely organizations of the possessing classes.

The intellectual prerequisites for social reconstruction were lacking formerly. They are now at hand. Travel and history are breaking the spell of existing conditions and are telling even the common man that social relations are plastic and variable. We have the new sciences of political economy and sociology to guide us. It is true, political economy in the past has misled us often, but it too is leaving its sinful laissez faire ways and preparing to serve the Lord and human brotherhood. All the biblical sciences are now using the historical method and striving to put us in the position of the original readers of each biblical book. But as the Bible becomes more lifelike, it becomes more social. We used to see the sacred landscape through allegorical interpretation as through a piece of yellow bottle-glass. It was very golden and wonderful, but very much apart from our everyday modern life. The Bible hereafter will be "the people's book" in a new sense. For the first time in religious history we have the possibility of so directing religious energy by scientific knowledge that a comprehensive and continuous reconstruction of social life in the name of God is within the bounds of human possibility.

To a religious man the contemplation of the larger movements of history brings a profound sense of God's presence and overruling power. "Behind the dim unknown standeth God within the shadow, keeping watch above his own." Christ is immanent in humanity and is slowly disciplining the nations and lifting them to share in his spirit. By great processes of self-purification the alien infusions in Christianity have been eliminated, and Christianity itself is being converted to Christ.

But all these larger movements, by which the essential genius of Christianity is being set free, have also equipped it for a conscious regenerating influence on the common life of the race. It is now fitter for its social mission than ever before. . . .

THE PRESENT CRISIS

That fundamental democracy of social intercourse, which is one of the richest endowments of our American life, is slipping from us. Actual inequality endangers the sense of equality. The rich man and the poor man can meet on a level if they are old friends, or if they are men of exceptional moral qualities, or if they meet under unusual circumstances that reduce all things to their primitive human elements. But as a general thing they will live different lives, and the sense of unlikeness will affect all their dealings. With women the spirit of social caste seems to be even more fatally easy than with men. It may be denied that the poor in our country are getting poorer, but it cannot well be denied that the rich are getting richer. The extremes of wealth and poverty are much farther apart than formerly, and thus the poor are at least relatively poorer. There is a rich class and a poor class, whose manner of life is wedged farther and farther apart, and whose boundary lines are becoming ever more distinct. The difference in housing, eating, dressing, and speaking would be a sufficient barrier. The dominant position of the one class in industry and the dependence of the other is even more decisive. The owners or managers of industry are rich or highly paid; they have technical knowledge, the will to command, the habits of mind bred by the exercise of authority; they say "Go," and men go; they say "Do this," and an army of men obeys. On the other side is the mass who take orders, who are employed or dismissed at a word, who use their muscles almost automatically, and who have no voice in the conduct of their own shop. These are two distinct classes, and no rhetoric can make them equal. Moreover, such a condition is inseparable from the capitalistic organization of industry. As capitalism grows, it must create a proletariat to correspond. Just as militarism is based on military obedience, so capitalism is based on economic dependence. . . .

In the past the sympathy between the richer and the poorer members of American society has still run strong. Many rich men and women were once poor and have not forgotten their early struggles and the simple homes of their childhood. As wealth becomes hereditary, there will be more who have never known any life except that of luxury, and have never had any associates except the children of the rich or their servants. Formerly the wealthiest man in a village or town still lived in the sight of all as a member of the community. As the chasm widens, the rich withdraw to their own section of the city; they naturally use means to screen themselves from the intrusive stare of the public which concentrates its gaze on them; they live in a world apart, and the mass of the people have distorted ideas about them and little human sympathy for them. There are indications enough how far apart we already are. We have a new literature of exploration. Darkest Africa and the polar regions are becoming familiar; but we now have intrepid men and women who plunge for a time into the life of the lower classes and return to write books about this unknown race that lives in the next block. It is amazing to note how intelligent men and women of the upper classes bungle in their judgment on the virtues and the vices of the working people, and *vice versa*. Socialism is coming to be the very life-breath of the intelligent working-class, but if all the members of all the social and literary clubs of a city were examined on socialism, probably two-thirds would fail to pass. Many are still content to treat one of the great elemental movements of human history as the artificial and transitory misbehavior of a few agitators and their dupes. The inability of both capital and labor to understand the point of view of the other side has been one chief cause of trouble, and almost every honest effort to get both sides together on a basis of equality has acted like a revelation. But that proves how far they have been apart.

Individual sympathy and understanding has been our chief reliance in the past for overcoming the differences between the social classes. The feelings and principles implanted by Christianity have been a powerful aid in that direction. But if this sympathy diminishes by the widening of the social chasm, what hope have we? It is true that we have an increasing number who, by study and by personal contact in settlement work and otherwise, are trying to increase that sympathetic intelligence. But it is a question if this conscious effort of individuals is enough to offset the unconscious alienation created by the dominant facts of life which are wedging entire classes apart. . . .

If we allow deep and permanent inequality to grow up in our country, it is as sure as gravitation that not only the old democracy and frankness of manners will go, but even the theory of human equality, which has been part of our spiritual atmosphere through Christianity, will be denied. It is already widely challenged.

Any shifting of the economic equilibrium from one class to another is sure to be followed by a shifting of the political equilibrium. If a class arrives at economic wealth, it will gain political influence and some form of representation. . . . A class which is economically strong will have the necessary influence to secure and enforce laws which protect its economic interests. In turn, a class which controls legislation will shape it for its own enrichment. Politics is embroidered with patriotic sentiment and phrases, but at bottom, consciously or unconsciously, the economic interests dominate it always. If therefore we have a class which owns a large part of the national wealth and controls nearly all the mobile part of it, it is idle to suppose that this class will not see to it that the vast power exerted by the machinery of government serves its interests. And if we have another class which is economically dependent and helpless, it is idle to suppose that it will be allowed an equal voice in swaying political power. In short, we cannot join economic inequality and political equality. As Oliver Cromwell wrote to Parliament, "If there be anyone that makes many poor to make a few rich, that suits not a Commonwealth." The words of Lincoln find a new application here, that the republic cannot be half slave and half free.

The power of capitalism over the machinery of our government, and its corroding influence on the morality of our public servants, has been revealed within recent years to such an extent that it is almost superfluous to speak of it. If anyone had foretold ten years ago the facts which are now understood by all, he would have been denounced as an incurable pessimist. Our cities have surrendered nearly all the functions that bring an income, keeping only those that demand expenditure, and they are now so dominated by the public service corporations that it takes a furious spasm of public anger, as in Philadelphia, or a long-drawn battle, as in Chicago, to drive the robbers from their intrench-ments in the very citadel of government; and after the victory is won there is absolutely no guarantee that it will be permanent. There is probably not one of our states which is not more or less controlled by its chief railways. How far our national government is constantly warped in its action, the man at a distance can hardly tell, but the public confi-dence in Congress is deeply undermined. Even the successful action against the meat-packers and against railway rebates only demonstrated what overwhelming popular pressure is necessary to compel the govern-ment to act against these great interests.

The interference of President Roosevelt in the great coal strike was hailed as a demonstration that the people are still supreme. In fact, it rather demonstrated that the supremacy of the people is almost gone. The country was on the verge of a vast public calamity. A sudden cold snap would have sent Death through our Eastern cities, not with his old-fashioned scythe, but with a modern reaper. The President merely undertook to advise and persuade, and was met with an almost insolent rejoinder. Mr. Jacob A. Riis,[13] in his book "Theodore Roosevelt, the Cit-izen," says that the President, when he concluded to interfere, set his face grimly and said: "Yes, I will do it. I suppose that ends me; but it is right, and I will do it." The Governor of Massachusetts afterward sent him "the thanks of every man, woman, and child in the country." The President replied: "Yes, we have put it through. But heavens and earth! It has been a struggle." Mr. Riis says, "It was the nearest I ever knew him to come to showing the strain he had been under." Now what sinister and ghostly power was this with which the President of our nation had wrestled on behalf of the people, and which was able to loosen even his joints with fear? Whose interests were so inviolable that they took prece-dence of the safety of the people, so that a common-sense action by the most august officer of the nation was likely to bring political destruc-tion upon him? To what extent is a power so threatening able to turn the government aside from its functions by silent pressure, so that its

---

13. Jacob Riis (1849–1914) was a Danish-born American journalist. Riis' book, *How the Other Half Lives* (1890), which was illustrated with his own photo-graphs, documented life in the slums of New York City. The book brought him to the attention of Theodore Roosevelt, who was then serving as the city's Police Commissioner.

fundamental purpose of public service is constantly frustrated? Have we a dual sovereignty, so that our public officers are in doubt whom to obey? . . .

Nations do not die by wealth, but by injustice. The forward impetus comes through some great historical opportunity which stimulates the production of wealth, breaks up the caked and rigid order of the past, sets free the energies of new classes, calls creative leaders to the front, quickens the intellectual life, intensifies the sense of duty and the ideal devotion to the common weal, and awakens in the strong individuals the large ambition of patriotic service. Progress slackens when a single class appropriates the social results of the common labor, fortifies its evil rights by unfair laws, throttles the masses by political centralization and suppression, and consumes in luxury what it has taken in covetousness. Then there is a gradual loss of productive energy, an increasing bitterness and distrust, a waning sense of duty and devotion to country, a paralysis of the moral springs of noble action. Men no longer love the Commonwealth, because it does not stand for the common wealth. Force has to supply the cohesive power which love fails to furnish. Exploitation creates poverty, and poverty is followed by physical degeneration. Education, art, wealth, and culture may continue to advance and may even ripen to their mellowest perfection when the worm of death is already at the heart of the nation. Internal convulsions or external catastrophes will finally reveal the state of decay. . . .

THE CHURCH AND THE SOCIAL MOVEMENT

This is the stake of the churches in modern poverty. They are buried at times under a stream of human wreckage. They are turned aside constantly from their more spiritual functions to "serve tables." They have a right, therefore, to inquire who is unloading this burden of poverty and suffering upon them by underpaying, exhausting, and maiming the people. The good Samaritan did not go after the robbers with a shotgun, but looked after the wounded and helpless man by the wayside. But if hundreds of good Samaritans travelling the same road should find thousands of bruised men groaning to them, they would not be such very good Samaritans if they did not organize a vigilance committee to stop the manufacturing of wounded men. If they did not, presumably the asses who had to lug the wounded to the tavern would have the wisdom to inquire into the causes of their extra work. . . .

There is an old maxim current among religious workers that times of national disaster are followed by a revival of religion, for trouble drives men to God. It is true that in the lower stages of religion, famine, pestilence, and earthquake drove men to their temples and churches to plead with their angry gods. The priests of the temples would be likely to regard that as a hopeful revival of religion; we should call it a superstitious panic. It is true also that every deep emotion of joy or sorrow acts like the earthquake at Philippi: it opens the gates of the soul in the darkness, and then great things may happen. Both the birth and the death of a child may turn the parents to nobler thoughtfulness. But longcontinued economic helplessness of entire classes acts differently. That bears the soul down with a numbing sense of injustice and despair. Israel in Egypt "hearkened not unto Moses for anguish of spirit and for cruel bondage." The industrial depression of the 90's was followed by moral disintegration and religious lethargy. It took the churches longer than commerce to recover from that paralysis of hopelessness. The maxim quoted is a relic of the ascetic view of life, which assumed that a man was closest to holiness when he was most emaciated and stripped of the joys of life. . . .

As soon as the competitive philosophy of life encounters an opposing philosophy in socialism, it is angrily insistent on its own righteousness. The same is the case when any attempt is made to urge the Christian law of life as obligatory for business as well as private life. "Don't mix business and religion." "Business is business." These common maxims express the consciousness that there is a radical divergence between the two domains of life, and that the Christian rules of conduct would forbid many common transactions of business and make success in it impossible. Thus life is cut into two halves, each governed by a law opposed to that of the other, and the law of Christ is denied even the opportunity to gain control of business. When a man lives a respectable and religious life in one part of the city and a life of vice in another part, he is said to live a double life. That is the heart-breaking condition forced upon Christian business men by the antagonism of Christianity and competitive commerce. They have to try to do what Christ declares impossible: to serve God and mammon. It is no wonder that many try to maintain their faith in their own integrity of character by denying that business life is antagonistic to Christianity at all. But the rest of the community judge differently. The moral sincerity of the most prominent members of the churches is impugned by the public, which has little sympathy with the tragic situation in which Christian business men find themselves. This deeply affects the moral prestige of the churches in the community. They are forced into the defensive instead of challenging the community to a higher standard of morals.

When two moral principles are thus forced into practical antagonism in daily life, the question is which will be the stronger. If the Church cannot Christianize commerce, commerce will commercialize the Church. When the churches buy and sell, they follow the usual methods and often drive hard bargains. When they hire and dismiss their employees, they are coming more and more to use the methods of the labor market. In the teaching of the Church those elements of the ethics of Jesus which are in antagonism to commercial life are toned down or unconsciously dropped out of sight. The Sermon on the Mount, in which Jesus clearly defines the points of difference between his ethics and the current morality, is always praised reverently, but rarely taken seriously. Its edge is either blunted by an alleviating exegesis, or it is asserted that it is intended for the millennium and not for the present social life. When the religious teachings of Tolstoi[14] first became known in the 80's, they gave many of us a shock of surprise by asserting with the voice of faith that these were the obligatory and feasible laws of Christian conduct. Thus the principles of commerce affect the moral practice of the Church and silence its moral teachings in so far as they are antagonistic to business morality. . . .

If the Church cannot bring business under Christ's law of solidarity and service, it will find his law not merely neglected in practice, but flouted in theory. With many the Darwinian theory has proved a welcome justification of things as they are. It is right and fitting that thousands should perish to evolve the higher type of the modern business man. Those who are manifestly surviving in the present struggle for existence can console themselves with the thought that they are the fittest, and there is no contradicting the laws of the universe. Thus an atomistic philosophy crowds out the Christian faith in solidarity. The law of the cross is superseded by the law of tooth and nail. It is not even ideal and desirable "to seek and to save the lost," because it keeps the weak and unfit alive. The philosophy of Nietzsche,[15] which is deeply affecting the ethical thought of the modern world, scouts the Christian virtues as the qualities of slaves. It glorifies the strong man's self-assertion which treads

----

14. Count Leo Nikolayevich Tolstoy (1828–1910) was a Russian novelist and moral philosopher whose teachings on Christian humility and pacifism greatly influenced American Progressive thinking. His novels *War and Peace* (1864–1869) and *Anna Karenina* (1873–1876) are regarded as his literary masterpieces.

15. Friedrich Nietzsche (1844–1900) was a German existentialist philosopher who called for heroic-redemptive men—popularly known as "supermen"—to save Europe from the nihilism he thought was built into the Judeo-Christian tradition. Contrast Rauschenbusch's treatment of Nietzsche to Walter Lippmann's in Chapter 9.

under foot whatever hinders him from living out his life to the full. The philosophy regnant in any age is always the direct outgrowth of the sum total of life in that age. . . .

It cannot well be denied that there is an increasing alienation between the working class and the churches. That alienation is most complete wherever our industrial development has advanced farthest and has created a distinct class of wage-workers. Several causes have contributed. Many have dropped away because they cannot afford to take their share in the expensive maintenance of a church in a large city. Others because the tone, the spirit, the point of view in the churches, is that of another social class. The commercial and professional classes dominate the spiritual atmosphere in the large city churches. As the workingmen grow more class-conscious, they come to regard the business men as their antagonists and the possessing classes as exploiters who live on their labor, and they resent it when persons belonging to these classes address them with the tone of moral superiority. When ministers handle the labor question, they often seem to the working class partial against them even when the ministers think they are most impartial. Foreign workingmen bring with them the long-standing distrust for the clergy and the Church as tools of oppression which they have learned abroad, and they perpetuate that attitude here. The churches of America suffer for the sins of the churches abroad. The "scientific socialism" imported from older countries through its literature and its advocates is saturated with materialistic philosophy and is apt to create dislike and antagonism for the ideas and institutions of religion.

Thus in spite of the favorable equipment of the Church in America there is imminent danger that the working people will pass from indifference to hostility, from religious enthusiasm to anti-religious bitterness. That would be one of the most unspeakable calamities that could come upon the Church. If we would only take warning by the fate of the churches in Europe, we might avert the desolation that threatens us. We may well be glad that in nearly every city there are a few ministers who are known as the outspoken friends of labor. Their fellow-ministers may regard them as radicals, lacking in balance, and very likely they are; but in the present situation they are among the most valuable servants of the Church. The workingmen see that there is at least a minority in the Church that champions their cause, and that fact helps to keep their judgment in hopeful suspense about the Church at large. Men who are just as one-sided in favor of capitalism pass as sane and conservative men. If the capitalist class have their court-chaplains, it is only fair that the army of labor should have its army-chaplains who administer the consolations of religion to militant labor.

Thus the Church has a tremendous stake in the social crisis. It may try to maintain an attitude of neutrality, but neither side will permit it. If it is quiescent, it thereby throws its influence on the side of things as they are, and the class which aspires to a fitter place in the organization of society will feel the great spiritual force of the Church as a dead weight against it. If it loses the loyalty and trust of the working class, it loses the very class in which it originated, to which its founders belonged, and which has lifted it to power. If it becomes a religion of the upper classes, it condemns itself to a slow and comfortable death. Protestantism from the outset entered into an intimate alliance with the intelligence and wealth of the city population. As the cities grew in importance since the Reformation, as commerce overshadowed agriculture, and as the business class crowded the feudal aristocracy out of its leading position since the French Revolution, Protestantism throve with the class which had espoused it. It lifted its class, and its class lifted it. On the other hand, the Anabaptist movement in Germany, which propagated within the lower classes, was crushed with the class that bore its banner. If the present class struggle of the wage-workers is successful, and they become the dominant class of the future, any religious ideas and institutions which they now embrace in the heat of their struggle will rise to power with them, and any institution on which they turn their back is likely to find itself in the cold. . . .

The social crisis offers a great opportunity for the infusion of new life and power into the religious thought of the Church. It also offers the chance for progress in its life. When the broader social outlook widens the purpose of a Christian man beyond the increase of his church, he lifts up his eyes and sees that there are others who are at work for humanity besides his denomination. Common work for social welfare is the best common ground for the various religious bodies and the best training school for practical Christian unity. The strong movement for Christian union in our country has been largely prompted by the realization of social needs, and is led by men who have felt the attraction of the kingdom of God as something greater than any denomination and as the common object of all. Thus the divisions which were caused in the past by differences in dogma and church polity may perhaps be healed by unity of interest in social salvation. . . .

This is the stake of the Church in the social crisis. If society continues to disintegrate and decay, the Church will be carried down with it. If the Church can rally such moral forces that injustice will be overcome and fresh red blood will course in a sounder social organism, it will itself rise to higher liberty and life. Doing the will of God it will have new visions of God. With a new message will come a new authority. If the salt lose its saltness, it will be trodden under foot. If the Church fulfils its prophetic functions, it may bear the prophet's reproach for a time, but it will have the prophet's vindication thereafter. . . .

WHAT TO DO

There are two great entities in human life,—the human soul and the human race,—and religion is to save both. The soul is to seek righteousness and eternal life; the race is to seek righteousness and the kingdom of God. The social preacher is apt to overlook the one. But the evangelical preacher has long overlooked the other. It is due to that protracted neglect that we are now deluged by the social problem in its present acute form. . . .

It seems likely that even after this present inequality of emphasis is balanced, some preachers will put more stress on the social aspects of religion. In that case we must apply Paul's large and tolerant principle, "There are diversities of gifts, but the same Spirit." Some by nature and training have the gift of dealing with individuals and the loving insight into personal needs; others have the passionate interest in the larger life and its laws. The Church needs evangelists and pastors, but it needs prophets too.

If a minister uses the great teaching powers of the pulpit sanely and wisely to open the minds of the people to the moral importance of the social questions, he may be of the utmost usefulness in the present crisis. Intelligent men who live in the midst of social problems do not yet know that there is a social problem, just as one may pass among the noises and sights of a city street without noticing them. If the minister can simply induce his more intelligent hearers to focus what is in their very field of vision, thereafter they can not help seeing it, and information will begin to collect automatically in their minds. The Church itself has riveted the attention of the people on other aspects of life hitherto and thereby has diverted their attention from the social problems. It ought to make up for this.

A minister mingling with both classes can act as an interpreter to both. He can soften the increasing class hatred of the working class. He can infuse the spirit of moral enthusiasm into the economic struggle of the dispossessed and lift it to something more than a "stomach question." On the other hand, among the well-to-do, he can strengthen the consciousness that the working people have a real grievance and so increase the disposition to make concessions in practical cases and check the inclination to resort to force for the suppression of discontent.

If the ministry would awaken among the wealthy a sense of social compunction and moral uneasiness, that alone might save our nation from a revolutionary explosion. It would be of the utmost importance to us all if the inevitable readjustment could be secured by a continuous succession of sensible demands on the one side and willing concessions on the other. We can see now that a little more wisdom and justice on both sides might have found a peaceable solution for the great social problem of slavery. Instead of that the country was plunged into the Civil War with its fearful cost in blood and wealth. We have been cursed for a generation with the legacy of sectional hatred, and the question of the status of the black race has not been solved even at such cost. If Pharaoh again hardens his heart, he will again have to weep for his first-born and be whelmed in the Red Sea. It is a question if we can rally enough moral insight and good-will to create a peaceable solution, or if the Bourbon spirit is to plunge our nation into a long-continued state of dissolution and anarchy which the mind shrinks from contemplating. The influence of the Christian ministry, if exercised in the spirit of Christian democracy, might be one of the most powerful solvents and the decisive influence for peace. [Walter Rauschenbusch, *Christianity and the Social Crisis* (Macmillan, 1914), 201–10, 249–56, 284, 305, 307, 313–6, 329–31, 340–2, 367–9]

32. *The Federal Council of Churches Social Program*

The Federal Council of Churches was organized in 1908 by more than thirty Protestant denominations. One of its founding purposes was "to secure a larger combined influence for the churches of Christ in all matters affecting the moral and social condition of the people, so as to promote the application of the law of Christ in every relation of human life."[16] The selection below was the first product of that purpose. A modified version of this program was adopted four years later and remained effective until 1932.

—1908—

Many things indicate that the churches are beginning to realize their obligations to society and are seriously seeking to lead the social faith. The Federal Council of the Churches of Christ in America, representing

---

16. White and Hopkins, *The Social Gospel*, 200.

thirty-five religious bodies and about twenty million members, has created a Social Service Commission charged with the duty "to study social condition, to afford by its action and utterance an expression of the purpose of the churches of Christ in the United States, to recognize the import of present social movements and industrial conditions, and to cooperate in all practicable ways to promote in the churches the development of the spirit and practice of social service." This commission has issued a statement outlining some of the things for which the churches should stand. This platform and program has been accepted and ratified by a number of religious bodies in the country, as the Northern Baptist Convention, the Presbyterian Assembly, the Methodist Federation for Social Service and the Congregational Council.

THE CHURCH AND MODERN INDUSTRY

For equal rights and complete justice for all men in all stations of life.

For the right of all men to the opportunity of self-maintenance, a right ever to be wisely and strongly safeguarded against encroachments of every kind.

For the right of the workers to some protection against the hardships often resulting from the swift crises of industrial change.

For the principle of conciliation and arbitration in industrial dissensions.

For the protection of the worker from dangerous machinery, occupational disease, injuries and mortality.

For the abolition of child labour.

For such regulation of the conditions of toil for women as shall safeguard the physical and moral health of the community.

For the gradual and reasonable reduction of the hours of labour to the lowest practicable point, and for that degree of leisure for all which is a condition of the highest human life.

For the release from employment one day in seven.

For the suppression of the "sweating system."

For a living wage as a minimum in every industry and for the highest wage that each industry affords.

For the most equitable division of the products of industry that can ultimately be devised.

For suitable provision for the old age of workers and for those incapacitated by injury.

For the abatement of poverty .

In addition the Social Service Commission of the Northern Baptist Convention issues a program for the Family and the Civic Community.

THE CHURCH AND THE FAMILY

For home training for social living.

For the single standard of purity.

For the teaching of sex hygiene.

For uniform divorce legislation and for stricter regulations of matrimony.

For sanitary homes and tenements and systematic inspection.

For the abolition of overcrowding and the guarantee of sufficient room for health and decency.

For the preservation of the home against industrial invasion.

THE CHURCH AND THE COMMUNITY

For the suppression of vile shows, unclean literature and unfit posters.

For the abolition of the liquor traffic, opium, cocaine and other habit-forming drugs.

For the suppression of the red light district, the white slave traffic and sex diseases.

For the suppression of gambling in all its forms.

For the cleansing and prevention of city slums.

For the administration of justice with a saving purpose.

For playgrounds and city parks accessible to the people.

For more rational and moral forms of amusement.

For an investigation of civic conditions and for a civic plan.

For civil service methods in all civic offices.

For the active participation of men of good will in civic affairs.

[In Samuel Zane Batten, *The Social Task of Christianity: A Summons to the New Crusade* (Fleming H. Revell, 1911), 229–30]

Further Reading

Bercovitch, Sacvan, *The Puritan Origins of the American Self* (Yale University Press, 1977).

Bliss, William Dwight Porter, ed., *New Encyclopedia of Social Reform* (Funk and Wagnalls, 1908).

Bloom, Harold, *The American Religion: The Emergence of a Post-Christian Nation* (Simon and Schuster, 1992).

Boyer, Paul, *Urban Masses and Moral Order in America, 1820–1920* (Harvard University Press, 1978).

Crunden, Robert M., *Ministers of Reform: The Progressives' Achievement in American Civilization, 1889–1920* (University of Illinois Press, 1984).

Curtis, Susan, *A Consuming Faith: The Social Gospel and American Culture* (Johns Hopkins University Press, 1991).

Dombrowski, James, *The Early Days of Christian Socialism in America* (Octagon, 1966/1936).

Eisenach, Eldon J., "Bookends: Seven Stories Excised from *The Lost Promise of Progressivism*," in *Studies in American Political Development*, vol. 10 (Spring 1996): 168–83.

———. *The Lost Promise of Progressivism* (University Press of Kansas, 1994).

Fox, Richard Wightman, "Experience and Explanation in American Religious History," in Harry S. Stout and P. G. Hart, eds., *New Directions in American Religious History* (Oxford University Press, 1997).

———. "The Culture of Liberal Protestant Progressivism, 1875–1925," *Journal of Interdisciplinary History* 23 (Winter 1993): 639–60.

Greek, Cecil E., *The Religious Roots of American Sociology* (Garland, 1992).

Handy, Robert T., *A Christian America: Protestant Hopes and Historical Realities* (Oxford University Press, 1984).

Hopkins, Charles H., *The Rise of the Social Gospel in American Protestantism, 1865–1915* (Yale University Press, 1940).

Hutchison, William R., *The Modernist Impulse in American Protestantism* (Duke University Press, 1992).

Minus, Paul M., *Walter Rauschenbusch: American Reformer* (Macmillan, 1988).

Somerville, C. John, "Secular Society/Religious Population: Our Tacit Rules for Using the Term 'Secularization,'" *Journal for the Scientific Study of Religion*, vol. 37, no. 2 (2000): 249–53.

Steiner, Edward A., *The Immigrant Tide: Its Ebb and Flow* (New York: Fleming H. Revel, 1909).

Thelen, David Paul, *The New Citizenship: The Origins of Progressivism in Wisconsin, 1885–1900* (University of Missouri Press, 1972).

Tuveson, Ernest, *Redeemer Nation: The Idea of America's Millennial Role* (University of Chicago Press, 1968).

White, Ronald C., and C. Howard Hopkins, *The Social Gospel: Religion and Reform in Changing America* (Temple University Press, 1976).

8

Women and Families in the New Society

This collection has already noted the prominence of women—as journalists, authors, institution founders, and reform activists—in the Progressive movement. One might even go so far as to say that "women," along with "labor" came to symbolize the core ideals of Progressivism. Like Charlotte Perkins Gilman, Walter Lippmann considered women and laborers to be the "two greatest forces for human emancipation," as he said in *Drift and Mastery* (1914). Both emancipating movements are the product of a surplus economy: "In the midst of plenty, the imagination becomes ambitious, rebellion against misery is at last justified, and dreams have a basis in fact."[1] In representing consumption, women exemplified what Simon Patten (whose writings appear in Chapters 3 and 6) had termed the "pleasure" economy and the emerging culture of positive freedom and cooperation. And, in representing the household, women stood for the ideal of consensual "administration" as opposed to antagonistic "politics." The social evolutionary framework that underlay the new social sciences might even be termed "feminine" in these respects: women's full participation in the larger society—like labor's—would be proof that a higher moral plane had been reached. The mutually supportive writings of Simon Patten and Charlotte Perkins Gilman best express this relationship. More generally, within this evolutionary framework the concepts of "consummation" and "fulfillment" were used to denote a genuine "marriage" between thought and feeling, man and woman, head and heart, market and family, self-interest and social interest, capitalist competition and cooperation. These new unities all required the emancipation of women and the reform of the family.

The flood of women pouring into colleges and universities during the 1880s, primarily in the midwest, had its own special effects on the young Progressive academics joining the schools' faculties. The University of Michigan began admitting women in 1860. Two notable social scientists represented in this collection, Henry Carter Adams and Charles Horton Cooley, married undergraduate psychology students of their colleague, John Dewey (Dewey himself married one of his former students, Alice Chipman). These academics, and other

---

1. Lippmann, *Drift and Mastery* (1914/1961), 141, 142.

Progressives like them, wanted their marriages to represent a relationship of moral equals and their families to exemplify a new democratic ethic.

One of the more celebratory writings on the college-educated woman as harbinger of Progressive reform is found in a book jointly authored by Scott and Nellie Nearing,[2] *Women and Social Progress* (1912). Incorporating ideas from Lester Ward,[3] Charlotte Perkins Gilman, and others, it calls for the old restraints of marriage and family to be replaced with new careers for women and the opportunity for educated women to be a vanguard in the fight for moral progress:

> Physically robust from the splendid course in physical training, and the invigorating games of college life; trained to think accurately and clearly; learned in method of study and presentation; effective through the power of cooperation; and thoroughly alive to the desirability of making time and life count, these college girls furnish the most optimistic argument for the future of women. The college girl with her atmosphere of efficiency and capability has penetrated every group of women who have the time and intelligence to think. Whether college educated or not, the women in America are taking their cue from the college graduate. They see in her the prototype of what they might have been, and they take from her successes new inspiration for their efforts. The college girl is the

---

2. Scott Nearing (1883–1983) started out as a Social Gospel minister. He then studied political economy under Simon Patten at the Wharton School before accepting a position at the University of Pennsylvania. Nearing was fired from Penn after he attacked, in print, some Philadelphia businessmen who were underwriting Billy Sunday's religious revival in that city. Patten and his colleague Edmund J. James then hired Nearing to edit *Annuals of the American Academy of Political and Social Science*. Unfortunately, the incident in Philadelphia only marked the beginning of Nearing's troubles. Publication of his vehemently antiwar pamphlet *The Great Madness: A Victory for American Plutocracy* (1918) led to his dismissal from a college teaching position in Ohio; he was also indicted under the U.S. Espionage Act. In the late 1920s, Nearing joined the Communist Party and, after leaving Nellie, his wife, joined Helen Knothe, a rich heiress. Nearing and Knothe led a series of back-to-earth movements on farms in New England and together wrote *Living the Good Life: How to Live Sanely and Simply in a Troubled World* in 1954. Nearing became a hero to the American left in the McCarthy period and to the counterculture in the 1960s and 1970s.

3. Lester Ward (1841–1913) was an early American sociologist who translated social Darwinism into an evolutionary theory of the progressive socialization of the human struggle with nature—turning Herbert Spencer on his head.

type of the future for women. But what shall she do? She can do anything she pleases.[4]

These "new women" did, in fact, do many new things. Herbert Croly's mother, Jane Cunningham Croly, was one of America's first female professional journalists and magazine editors, and the founder of the Women's Club movement in America; she eventually wrote the Club's history.[5] Not only did Charles Beard's wife, Mary, co-author a history series with her husband, she also did much of the research for, and writing of, the books published under his name. She published her own book, *Women's Work in Municipalities*, in 1915. John Dewey's wife, Alice, was instrumental in the formation and administration of the Laboratory School at the University of Chicago.

The first three decades of the twentieth century witnessed remarkable progress in the status and roles of women. In 1912, President Taft, in response to a massive campaign by women's organizations, signed into law the creation of the Children's Bureau, run and largely staffed by women associated with Hull House. Changes in divorce and property law, access to education and the professions, and even the portrayal of women in popular literature and the rise of women's magazines in the mass media were all evidences of this change.

The Great Depression and the hegemonic electoral victories of the Democratic Party in the 1930s and 1940s signaled the waning of this progress. Newly empowered religious and ethnic cultures, industrial unions, and the southern Democrats' rise to power in the national government left much less room for this side of national Progressive reform. To be sure, many of the women's organizations formed during the Progressive period remained strong. But by the 1950s, far fewer women were entering business and the professions than in the 1910s and 1920s, depriving an entire generation of women of strong leaders and advocates. With these developments, the ideal of the family retreated for a time into more traditional bounds.

———

4. Nearing and Nearing, *Women and Social Progress* (1912), 236. This triumphalism had a strong regional bias. In the north Atlantic states, for example, the ration of men to women attending college was more than 7 to 1; in the north-central states, less than 2 to 1; and in the west 3 to 2.

5. See *Leach, True Love and Perfect Union* (1980) on Jane Croly and mid-nineteenth century feminist thought.

33. *Women in Evolutionary Economics,* Charlotte Perkins Gilman (1860–1935)

*Because of the rise of women's studies and feminist scholarship in the American university, Charlotte Perkins Gilman's name is now well known. Achieving fame and success in her own day, however, was much more difficult. Born in Connecticut to Frederick Beecher and Mary Westcott Perkins, she had a distinguished lineage: she was related to Lyman Beecher, Henry Ward Beecher, Harriet Beecher Stowe, and Edward Everett Hale. With no formal education beyond grade school, later divorced and abandoned, Charlotte Perkins Gilman was forced to support herself and her children through her writing, lecturing, and editorships. Active in labor and woman's movements, she began her career as a Bellamy Nationalist and a writer for W.D.P. Bliss' *American Fabian, *a Christian socialist publication. Her most famous literary product, now revived and often performed, is the play* Yellow Wallpaper* (1899). Most of her works were republished, first in the 1970s, and then in the 1990s. Given her personal independence and her views on family and marriage, she was a controversial figure even among reformers. Albion Small, for example, both published her views and vigorously attacked them in the* American Journal of Sociology. Simon Patten just as strenuously defended them. This combination of tolerance and controversy within the reform community speaks to the strength of the other ties—regional, religious, ethnic, and educational—that bound them.*

—1898—

PROEM

In dark and early ages, through the primal forests faring,
Ere the soul came shining into prehistoric night,
Twofold man was equal; they were comrades dear and daring,
Living wild and free together in unreasoning delight.

Ere the soul was born and consciousness came slowly,
Ere the soul was born, to man and woman, too,
Ere he found the Tree of Knowledge, that awful tree and holy,
Ere he knew he felt, and knew he knew.

Then said he to Pain, "I am wise now, and I know you!

No more will I suffer while power and wisdom last!"
Then said he to Pleasure, "I am strong, and I will show you
That the will of man can seize you,—aye, and hold you fast!"

Food he ate for pleasure, and wine he drank for gladness.
And woman? Ah, the woman! the crown of all delight!
His now,—he knew it! He was strong to madness
In that early dawning after prehistoric night.

His,—his forever! That glory sweet and tender!
Ah, but he would love her! And she should love but him!
He would work and struggle for her, he would shelter and
  defend her,—
She should never leave him, never, till their eyes in death were
  dim.

Close, close he bound her, that she should leave him never;
Weak still he kept her, lest she be strong to flee;
And the fainting flame of passion he kept alive forever
With all the arts and forces of earth and sky and sea.

And, ah, the long journey! The slow and awful ages
They have labored up together, blind and crippled, all astray!
Through what a mighty volume, with a million shameful
  pages,
From the freedom of the forests to the prisons of today!

Food he ate for pleasure, and it slew him with diseases!
Wine he drank for gladness, and it led the way to crime!
And woman? He will hold her,—he will have her when he
  pleases,—
And he never once hath seen her since the pre-historic time!

Gone the friend and comrade of the day when life was
  younger,
She who rests and comforts, she who helps and saves.
Still he seeks her vainly, with a never-dying hunger;
Alone beneath his tyrants, alone above his slaves!

Toiler, bent and weary with the load of thine own making!
Thou who art sad and lonely, though lonely all in vain!
Who hast sought to conquer Pleasure and have her for the
*   taking,*
And found that Pleasure only was another name for Pain—

Nature hath reclaimed thee, forgiving dispossession!
God hath not forgotten, though man doth still forget!
The woman-soul is rising, in spite of thy transgression—
Loose her now, and trust her! She will love thee yet!
Love thee? She will love thee as only freedom knoweth!
Love thee? She will love thee while Love itself doth live!
Fear not the heart of woman! No bitterness it showeth!
The ages of her sorrow have but taught her to forgive!

A condition so long established, so widespread, so permanent as the sexuo-economic relation in the human species could not have been introduced and maintained in the course of social evolution without natural causes and uses. No wildest perversion of individual will could permanently maintain a condition wholly injurious to society. Church and State and social forms move and change with our growth, and we cannot hinder them long after the time has come for further progress. Once it was of advantage to society that the sexuo-economic relation should be established. Now that it is no longer of advantage to society, the "woman's movement" has set in; and the relation is changing under our eyes from year to year, from day to day, in spite of our traditional opposition. The change considered in these pages is not one merely to be prophesied and recommended: it is already taking place under the forces of social evolution; and only needs to be made clear to our conscious thought, that we may withdraw the futile but irritating resistance of our misguided will. . . .

The period of women's economic dependence is drawing to a close, because its racial usefulness is wearing out. We have already reached a stage of human relation where we feel the strength of social duty pull against the sex-ties that have been for so long the only ties that we have recognized. The common consciousness of humanity, the sense of social need and social duty, is making itself felt in both men and women. The time has come when we are open to deeper and wider impulses than the sex-instinct; the social instincts are strong enough to come into full use at last. This is shown by the twin struggle that convulses the world today, — in sex and economics, — the "woman's movement" and the "labor movement.". . .

The woman's movement rests not alone on her larger personality, with its tingling sense of revolt against injustice, but on the wide, deep sympathy of women for one another. It is a concerted movement, based on the recognition of a common evil and seeking a common good. So with the labor movement. It is not alone that the individual laborer is a better educated, more highly developed man than the stolid peasant of earlier days, but also that with this keener personal consciousness has come the wider social consciousness, without which no class can better its conditions. The traits incident to our sexuo-economic relation have developed till they forbid the continuance of that relation. In the economic world, excessive masculinity, in its fierce competition and primitive individualism; and excessive femininity, in its inordinate consumption and hindering conservatism; have reached a stage where they work more evil than good. . . .

The development of democracy has brought to us the fullest individualization that the world has ever seen. Although politically expressed by men alone, the character it has produced is inherited by their daughters. The Federal Democracy in its organic union, reacting upon individuals, has so strengthened, freed, emboldened, the human soul in America that we have thrown off slavery, and with the same impulse have set in motion the long struggle toward securing woman's fuller equality before the law.

This struggle has been carried on unflaggingly for fifty years, and fast nears its victorious end. It is not only in the four States where full suffrage is exercised by both sexes, nor in the twenty-four where partial suffrage is given to women, that we are to count progress; but in the changes legal and social, mental and physical, which mark the advance of the mother of the world toward her full place. . . . The false sentimentality, the false delicacy, the false modesty, the utter falseness of elaborate compliment and servile gallantry which went with the other falsehoods, — all these are disappearing. Women are growing honester, braver, stronger, more healthful and skilful and able and free, more human in all ways.

A truer spirit is the increasing desire of young girls to be independent, to have a career of their own, at least for a while, and the growing objection of countless wives to the pitiful asking for money, to the beggary of their position. More and more do fathers give their daughters, and husbands their wives, a definite allowance, — a separate bank account,—something which they can play is all their own. The spirit of personal independence in the women of today is sure proof that a change has come. . . .

With the larger socialization of the woman of today, the fitness for and accompanying desire for wider combinations, more general interest, more organized methods of work for larger ends, she feels more and more heavily the intensely personal limits of the more primitive home duties, interests, methods. And this pain and strain must increase with the advance of women until the new functional power makes to itself organic expression, and the belated home industries are elevated and organized, like the other necessary labors of modern life.

The woman's club movement is one of the most important sociologic phenomena of the century,—indeed, of all centuries,—marking as it does the first timid steps toward social organization of these, so long unsocialized members of our race. Social life is absolutely conditioned upon organization. . . . [I]t is plain, therefore, that while women had no part in these organizations they had no part in social life. Their main relation to society was an individual one; an animal one, a sexual one. . . . Women have made the people who made the world, and will always continue so to do. But they have heretofore had a most insignificant part in the world their sons have made. . . .

To labor together, together to raise funds for a common end, for a new building or a new minister, for local charities or for foreign missions,—but to labor together, and for other needs than those of the family relation,—this has always met glad response from the struggling human soul in woman. When it became possible to work together for other than religious ends,—when large social service was made possible to women, as in our sanitary commission during the last war,—women everywhere rose to meet the need. The rise and spread of that greatest of women's organizations, the Woman's Christian Temperance Union, has shown anew how ready is the heart of woman to answer the demands of other than personal relations.

And now the whole country is budding into women's clubs. The clubs are uniting and federating by towns, States, nations: there are even world organizations. The sense of human unity is growing daily among women. Not to see it is impossible. Not to watch with pleasure and admiration this new growth in social life, this sudden and enormous re-enforcement of our best forces from the very springs of life, only shows how blind we are to true human advantage, how besotted in our fondness for sex-distinction in excess. . . .

Nothing in the exquisite pathos of woman's long subjection goes deeper to the heart than the degradation of motherhood by the very conditions we supposed were essential to it. To see the mother's heart and mind longing to go with the child, to help it all the way, and yet to see it year by year pass farther from her, learn things she never was allowed to know, do things she never was allowed to do, go out into "the world"—their world, not hers—alone, and

"To bear, to nurse, to rear, to love, and then to lose!"

this not by the natural separation of growth and personal divergence, but by the unnatural separation of falsely divided classes,—rudimentary women and more highly developed men. It is the fissure that opens before the boy is ten years old, and it widens with each year.

A mother economically free, a world-servant instead of a house-servant; a mother knowing the world and living in it,—can be to her children far more than has ever been possible before. Motherhood in the world will make that world a different place for her child. . . .

The changes in our conception and expression of home life, so rapidly and steadily going on about us, involve many far-reaching effects, all helpful to human advancement. Not the least of these is the improvement in our machinery of social intercourse. . . .

This necessity of civilization was unknown in those primitive ages when family intercourse was sufficient for all, and when any further contact between individuals meant war. Trade and its travel, the specialization of labor and the distribution of its products, with their ensuing development, have produced a wider, freer, and more frequent movement and interchange among the innumerable individuals whose interaction makes society. Only recently, and as yet but partially, have women as individuals come to their share of this fluent social intercourse which is the essential condition of civilization. It is not merely a pleasure or an indulgence: it is the human necessity.

For women as individuals to meet men and other women as individuals, with no regard whatever to the family relation, is a growing demand of our time. As a social necessity, it is perforce being met in some fashion; but its right development is greatly impeded by the clinging folds of domestic and social customs derived from the sexuo-economic relation. The demand for a wider and freer social intercourse between the sexes rests, primarily, on the needs of their respective natures, but is developed in modern life to a far subtler and higher range of emotion than existed in the primitive state, where they had but one need and but one way of meeting it; and this demand, too, calls for a better arrangement of our machinery of living. . . .

What the human race requires is permanent provision for the needs of individuals, disconnected from the sex-relation. Our assumption that only married people and their immediate relatives have any right to live in comfort and health is erroneous. Every human being needs a home,—bachelor, husband, or widower, girl, wife, or widow, young or old. They need it from the cradle to the grave, and without regard to sex-connections. We should so build and arrange for the shelter and comfort of humanity as not to interfere with marriage, and yet not to make that comfort dependent upon marriage. With the industries of home life managed professionally, with rooms and suites of rooms and houses obtainable by any person or persons desiring them, we could live singly without losing home comfort and general companionship, we could meet bereavement without being robbed of the common conveniences of living as well as of the heart's love, and we could marry in ease and freedom without involving any change in the economic base of either party concerned.

Married people will always prefer a home together, and can have it; but groups of women or groups of men can also have a home together if they like, or contiguous rooms. And individuals even could have a house to themselves, without having, also, the business of a home upon their shoulders. . . .

In reality, we may hope that the most valuable effect of this change in the basis of living will be the cleansing of love and marriage from this base admixture of pecuniary interest and creature comfort, and that men and women, eternally drawn together by the deepest force in nature, will be able at last to meet on a plane of pure and perfect love. We shame our own ideals, our deepest instincts, our highest knowledge, by this gross assumption that the noblest race on earth will not mate, or, at least, not mate monogamously, unless bought and bribed through the common animal necessities of food and shelter, and chained by law and custom. . . .

When our sex-relation is made pure and orderly by the economic independence of women, when sex-attraction is no longer a consuming fever, forever convulsing the social surface, under all its bars and chains, we shall not be content to sit down forever with half a dozen blood relations for our whole social arena. We shall need each other more, not less, and shall recognize that social need of one another as the highest faculty of this the highest race on earth.

The force which draws friends together is a higher one than that which draws the sexes together,—higher in the sense of belonging to a later race-development. "Passing the love of women" is no unmeaning phrase. Children need one another: young people need one another. Middle-aged people need one another: old people need one another. We all need one another, much and often. Just as every human creature needs a place to be alone in, a sacred, private "home" of his own, so all human creatures need a place to be together in, from the two who can show each other their souls uninterruptedly, to the largest throng that can throb and stir in unison. . . .

The economic independence of woman will change all these conditions as naturally and inevitably as her dependence has introduced them. In her specialization in industry, she will develope more personality and less sexuality; and this will lower the pressure on this one relation in both women and men. And, in our social intercourse, the new character and new method of living will allow of broad and beautiful developments in human association. As the private home becomes a private home indeed, and no longer the woman's social and industrial horizon; as the workshops of the world—woman's sphere as well as man's—become homelike and beautiful under her influence; and as men and women move freely together in the exercise of common racial functions,—we shall have new channels for the flow of human life. . . .

—1911—

The child should receive in the family, full preparation for his relation to the world at large. His whole life must be spent in the world, serving it well or ill; and youth is the time to learn how. But the androcentric home cannot teach him. We live today in a democracy—the man-made family is a despotism. It may be a weak one; the despot may be dethroned and overmastered by his little harem of one; but in that case she becomes the despot—that is all. The male is esteemed "the head of the family"; it belongs to him; he maintains it; and the rest of the world is a wide hunting ground and battlefield wherein he competes with other males as of old.

The girl-child, peering out, sees this forbidden field as belonging wholly to menkind; and her relation to it is to secure one for herself— not only that she may love, but that she may live. He will feed, clothe and adorn her—she will serve him; from the subjection of the daughter to that of the wife she steps; from one home to the other, and never enters the world at all—man's world. The boy, on the other hand, considers the home as a place of women, an inferior place, and longs to grow up and leave it for the real world. He is quite right. The error is that this great social instinct, calling for full social exercise, exchange, service, is considered masculine, whereas it is human, and belongs to boy and girl alike. . . .

In [the father's] dominance over servile women and helpless children, free rein was given to the growth of pride and the exercise of irresponsible tyranny. To these feelings, developed without check for thousands of years, and to the mental habits resultant, it is easy to trace much of the bias of our early ethical concepts.

Perhaps it is worth while to repeat here that the effort of this book is by no means to attribute a wholly evil influence to men, and a wholly good one to women; it is not even claimed that a purely feminine culture would have advanced the world more successfully. It does claim that the influence of the two together is better than that of either one alone; and in special to point out what special kind of injury is due to the exclusive influence of one sex heretofore. . . .

Democratic government is no longer an exercise of arbitrary authority from those above, but is an organization for public service of the people themselves—or will be when it is really attained. In this change government ceases to be compulsion, and becomes agreement; law ceases to be authority and becomes co-ordination. . . .

It is the old masculine spirit of government as authority which is so slow in adopting itself to the democratic idea of government as service. That it should be a representative government they grasp, but representative of what? Of the common will, they say; the will of the majority— never thinking that it is the common good, the common welfare, that government should represent.

It is the inextricable masculininty [sic] in our idea of government which so revolts at the idea of women as voters. "To govern:" that means to boss, to control, to have authority, and that only, to most minds. They cannot bear to think of the women as having control over even their own affairs; to control is masculine, they assume. Seeing only self-interest as a natural impulse, and the ruling powers of the state as a sort of umpire, an authority to preserve the rules of the game while men fight it out forever; they see in a democracy merely a wider range of self-interest, and a wider, freer field to fight in. . . .

As human beings both male and female stand alike useful and honorable, and should in our governments be alike used and honored; but as creatures of sex, the female is fitter than the male for administration of constructive social interests. The change in governmental processes which marks our times is a change in principle. Two great movements convulse the world today, the woman's movement and the labor movement. Each regards the other as of less moment than itself. Both are parts of the same world-process. . . .

In this change of systems a government which consisted only of prohibition and commands; of tax collecting and making war; is rapidly giving way to a system which intelligently manages our common interests, which is a growing and improving method of universal service.

Here the socialist is perfectly right in his vision of the economic welfare to be assured by the socialization of industry, though that is but part of the new development; and the individualist who opposes socialism, crying loudly for the advantage of "free competition" is but voicing the spirit of the predaceous male.

So with the opposers of the suffrage of women. They represent, whether men or women, the male view-point. They see the women only as a female, utterly absorbed in feminine functions, belittled and ignored as her long tutelage has made her; and they see the man as he sees himself, the sole master of human affairs for as long as we have historic record.

This, fortunately, is not long. We can now see back of the period of his supremacy, and are beginning to see beyond it. We are well under way already in a higher stage of social development, conscious, well-organized, wisely managed, in which the laws shall be simple and founded on constructive principles instead of being a set of ring-regulations within which people may fight as they will; and in which the government shall be recognized in its full use; not only the sternly dominant father, and the wisely serviceable mother, but the real union of all people to sanely and economically manage their affairs. . . .

What do we find, here in America, in the field of "politics?"

We find first a party system which is the technical arrangement to carry on a fight. It is perfectly conceivable that a flourishing democratic government be carried on *without any parties at all*; public functionaries being elected on their merits, and each proposed measure judged on its merits; though this sounds impossible to the androcentric mind.

"There has never been a democracy without factions and parties!" is protested.

There has never been a democracy, so far, — only an androcracy.

A group composed of males alone naturally divides, opposes, fights; even a male church, under the most rigid rule, has its secret undercurrents of antagonism.

"It is the human heart!" is again protested. No, not essentially the human heart, but the male heart. This is so well recognized by men in general, that, to their minds, in this mingled field of politics and warfare, women have no place. . . .

In other words men have made a human institution into an ultra-masculine performance; and, quite rightly, feel that women could not take part in politics *as men do*. That it is not necessary to fulfill this human custom in so masculine a way does not occur to them. Few men can overlook the limitations of their sex and see the truth; that this business of taking care of our common affairs is not only equally open to women and men, but that women are distinctly needed in it. . . .

We can make no safe assumption as to what, if any, distinction there will be in the free human work of men and women, until we have seen generation after generation grow up under absolutely equal conditions. In all our games and sports and minor social customs, such changes will occur as must needs follow upon the rising dignity allotted to the woman's temperament, the woman's point of view; not in the least denying to men the fullest exercise of their special powers and preferences; but classifying these newly, as not human—merely male. . . .

The effect of the change upon Ethics and Religion is deep and wide. With the entrance of women upon full human life, a new principle comes into prominence; the principle of loving service. That this is the governing principle of Christianity is believed by many; but an androcentric interpretation has quite overlooked it; and made, as we have shown, the essential dogma of their faith the desire of an enternal [sic] reward and the combat with an eternal enemy.

The feminine attitude in life is wholly different. As a female she has merely to be herself and passively attract; neither to compete nor to pursue; as a mother her whole process is one of growth; first the development of the live child within her, and the wonderful nourishment from her own body; and then all the later cultivation to make the child grow; all the watching, teaching, guarding, feeding. In none of this is there either desire, combat, or self-expression. The feminine attitude, as expressed in religion, makes of it a patient practical fulfillment of law; a process of large sure improvements; a limitless comforting love and care.

This full assurance of love and of power; this endless cheerful service; the broad provision for all people; rather than the competitive selection of a few "victors;" is the natural presentation of religious truth from the woman's viewpoint. Her governing principle being growth and not combat; her main tendency being to give and not to get; she more easily and naturally lives and teaches these religious principles. It is for this reason that the broader, gentler teaching of the Unitarian and Universalist sects have appealed so especially to women, and that so many women preach in their churches.

This principle of growth, as applied and used in general human life, will work to far other ends than those now so painfully visible.

In education, for instance, with neither reward nor punishment as spur or bait; with no competition to rouse effort and animosity, but rather with the feeling of a gardener towards his plants; the teacher will

teach and the children learn, in mutual ease and happiness. The law of
passive attraction applies here, leading to such ingenuity in presentation
as shall arouse the child's interest; and, in the true spirit of promoting
growth, each child will have his best and fullest training, without regard
to who is "ahead" of him, or her, or who "behind." . . .

With all women full human beings, trained and useful in some form
of work, the class of busy idlers who run about forever "entertaining"
and being "entertained" will disappear as utterly as will the prostitute.
No woman with real work to do could have the time for such petty
amusements; or enjoy them if she did have time. No woman with real
work to do, work she loved and was well fitted for, work honored and
well-paid, would take up the Unnatural Trade. Genuine relaxation and
recreation, all manner of healthful sports and pastimes, beloved of both
sexes today, will remain of course; but the set structure of "social functions"—so laughably misnamed—will disappear with the "society
women" who make it possible. Once active members of real Society, no
woman could go back to "society," any more than a roughrider could
return to a hobbyhorse.

New development in dress, wise, comfortable, beautiful, may be confidently expected, as woman becomes more human. No fully human
creature could hold up its head under the absurdities our women wear
today—and have worn for dreary centuries.

So on through all the aspects of life we may look for changes, rapid
and far-reaching; but natural and all for good. The improvement is not
due to any inherent moral superiority of women; nor to any moral infe-
riority of men; men at present, as more human, are ahead of women in
all distinctly human ways; yet their maleness, as we have shown repeat-
edly, warps and disfigures their humanness. The woman, being by
nature the race-type, and her feminine functions being far more akin to
human functions than are those essential to the male, will bring into
human life a more normal influence. . . .

The normal woman is a strong creature, loving and serviceable. The
kind of woman men are afraid to entrust with political power, selfish,
idle, over-sexed, or ignorant and narrow-minded, is not normal, but is
the creature of conditions men have made. We need have no fear of her,
for she will disappear with the conditions which created her. [Charlotte
Perkins Gilman, *Women and Economics: A Study of the Economic Relation between Men and Women as a Factor in Social Evolution* (Small,
Maynard & Company, 1898), xxxvi–xxxviii, 122, 137–40, 147–9, 152,
156, 164–6, 268–9, 295–6, 298–9, 300–1, 304–5, 312–3, and *The Man-
Made World, or Our Androcentric Culture* (Charlton Company, 1911),
40–1, 132, 185, 187–8, 190–2, 221–3, 250–7]

34. *The Democratic Household,* Jane Addams (1860–1935)[6]

The female residents at Hull House were only the most visible sign that, by the end of the nineteenth century, women were active in public life at all levels—infant mortality, child labor, housing and sanitary conditions, workers' compensation, and consumer safety were just a few of the issues they hoped to address through public policy. The link connecting these issues was the family and its civic importance as a formative agent in creating a more democratic society. Indeed, in a poem celebrating Jane Addams, biological, civic, and even redemptive "motherhood" are combined:

> Mother of races fusing into one,
> And keeping open house with presence sweet
> In that loud city where the nations meet
> Around thy ample hearth when day is done,
> When I behold the wild tribes thou hast won
> And see thee wooing from the witching street
> By thy own saintly face the erring feet,
> I know Love still has power beneath the sun.[7]

Democracy and Social Ethics, *from which the following selection is taken, was originally a series of twelve lectures delivered at colleges and through university extension courses. The book, addressed to charitable, industrial, educational, and political reform as well as to the family and household, was published continuously from 1902 through 1923. It was Addams' second-most popular book after her autobiography,* Twenty Years at Hull House, *which had twenty-three printings between 1910 and 1949.*

—1902—

[**The College Woman**] Our democracy is making inroads upon the family, the oldest of human institutions, and a claim is being advanced which in a certain sense is larger than the family claim. The claim of the state in time of war has long been recognized, so that in its name the family has given up sons and husbands and even the

---

6. More biographical information on Addams prefaces her selections in Chapters 1 and 4.

7. Quoted in Davis, *American Heroine* (1973), 205.

fathers of little children. If we can once see the claims of society in
any such light, if its misery and need can be made clear and urged as
an explicit claim, as the state urges its claims in the time of danger,
then for the first time the daughter who desires to minister to that
need will be recognized as acting conscientiously. This recognition
may easily come first through the emotions, and may be admitted as
a response to pity and mercy long before it is formulated and perceived by the intellect.

The family as well as the state we are all called upon to maintain
as the highest institutions which the race has evolved for its safeguard
and protection. But merely to preserve these institutions is not
enough. There come periods of reconstruction, during which the
task is laid upon a passing generation, to enlarge the function and
carry forward the ideal of a long-established institution. There is no
doubt that many women, consciously and unconsciously, are struggling with this task. The family, like every other element of human
life, is susceptible of progress, and from epoch to epoch its tendencies and aspirations are enlarged, although its duties can never be
abrogated and its obligations can never be cancelled. It is impossible
to bring about the higher development by any self-assertion or breaking away of the individual will. The new growth in the plant swelling
against the sheath, which at the same time imprisons and protects it,
must still be the truest type of progress. The family in its entirety must
be carried out into the larger life. Its various members together must
recognize and acknowledge the validity of the social obligation.
When this does not occur we have a most flagrant example of the ill-
adjustment and misery arising when an ethical code is applied too
rigorously and too conscientiously to conditions which are no longer
the same as when the code was instituted, and for which it was never
designed. We have all seen parental control and the family claim
assert their authority in fields of effort which belong to the adult judgment of the child and pertain to activity quite outside the family life.
Probably the distinctively family tragedy of which we all catch
glimpses now and then, is the assertion of this authority through all
the entanglements of wounded affection and misunderstanding. We
see parents and children acting from conscientious motives and with
the tenderest affection, yet bringing about a misery which can
scarcely be hidden. . . .

It is always difficult for the family to regard the daughter otherwise
than as a family possession. From her babyhood she has been the charm
and grace of the household, and it is hard to think of her as an integral
part of the social order, hard to believe that she has duties outside of the

family, to the state and to society in the larger sense. This assumption that the daughter is solely an inspiration and refinement to the family itself and its own immediate circle, that her delicacy and polish are but outward symbols of her father's protection and prosperity, worked very smoothly for the most part so long as her education was in line with it. When there was absolutely no recognition of the entity of woman's life beyond the family, when the outside claims upon her were still wholly unrecognized, the situation was simple, and the finishing school harmoniously and elegantly answered all requirements. She was fitted to grace the fireside and to add lustre to that social circle which her parents selected for her. But this family assumption has been notably broken into, and educational ideas no longer fit it. Modern education recognizes woman quite apart from family or society claims, and gives her the training which for many years has been deemed successful for highly developing a man's individuality and freeing his powers for independent action. . . . The ideal for the education of woman has changed under the pressure of a new claim. The family has responded to the extent of granting the education, but they are jealous of the new claim and assert the family claim as over against it.

The modern woman finds herself educated to recognize a stress of social obligation which her family did not in the least anticipate when they sent her to college. She finds herself, in addition, under an impulse to act her part as a citizen of the world. She accepts her family inheritance with loyalty and affection, but she has entered into a wider inheritance as well, which, for lack of a better phrase, we call the social claim. This claim has been recognized for four years in her training, but after her return from college the family claim is again exclusively and strenuously asserted. . . .

If the college woman is not thus quietly reabsorbed, she is even reproached for her discontent. She is told to be devoted to her family, inspiring and responsive to her social circle, and to give the rest of her time to further self-improvement and enjoyment. She expects to do this, and responds to these claims to the best of her ability, even heroically sometimes. But where is the larger life of which she has dreamed so long? That life which surrounds and completes the individual and family life? She has been taught that it is her duty to share this life, and her highest privilege to extend it. . . . The social claim is a demand upon the emotions as well as upon the intellect, and in ignoring it she represses not only her convictions but lowers her springs of vitality. . . .

It is quite true that the family often resents her first attempts to be part of a life quite outside their own, because the college woman frequently makes these first attempts most awkwardly; her faculties have not been trained in the line of action. She lacks the ability to apply her knowledge and theories to life itself and to its complicated situations. This is largely the fault of her training and of the one-sidedness of educational methods. The colleges have long been full of the best ethical teaching, insisting that the good of the whole must ultimately be the measure of effort, and that the individual can only secure his own rights as he labors to secure those of others. But while the teaching has included an ever-broadening range of obligation and has insisted upon the recognition of the claims of human brotherhood, the training has been singularly individualistic; it has fostered ambitions for personal distinction, and has trained the faculties almost exclusively in the direction of intellectual accumulation. Doubtless, woman's education is at fault, in that it has failed to recognize certain needs, and has failed to cultivate and guide the larger desires of which all generous young hearts are full.

During the most formative years of life, it gives the young girl no contact with the feebleness of childhood, the pathos of suffering, or the needs of old age. It gathers together crude youth in contact only with each other and with mature men and women who are there for the purpose of their mental direction. The tenderest promptings are bidden to bide their time. This could only be justifiable if a definite outlet were provided when they leave college. Doubtless the need does not differ widely in men and women, but women not absorbed in professional or business life, in the years immediately following college, are baldly brought face to face with the deficiencies of their training. Apparently every obstacle is removed, and the college woman is at last free to begin the active life, for which, during so many years, she has been preparing. But during this so-called preparation, her faculties have been trained solely for accumulation, and she has learned to utterly distrust the finer impulses of her nature, which would naturally have connected her with human interests outside of her family and her own immediate social circle. . . .

[The Servant Woman] As industrial conditions have changed, the household has simplified, from the mediæval affair of journeymen, apprentices, and maidens who spun and brewed to the family proper; to those who love each other and live together in ties of affection and consanguinity. Were this process complete, we should have no problem of household employment. But, even in households comparatively humble, there is still one alien, one who is neither loved nor loving.

The modern family has dropped the man who made its shoes, the woman who spun its clothes, and, to a large extent, the woman who washes them, but it stoutly refuses to drop the woman who cooks its food and ministers directly to its individual comfort; it strangely insists that to do that would be to destroy the family life itself. The cook is uncomfortable, the family is uncomfortable; but it will not drop her as all her fellow-workers have been dropped, although the cook herself insists upon it. So far has this insistence gone that every possible concession is made to retain her. . . .

If it were not for the undemocratic ethics used by the employers of domestics, much work now performed in the household would be done outside, as is true of many products formerly manufactured in the feudal household. The worker in all other trades has complete control of his own time after the performance of definitely limited services, his wages are paid altogether in money which he may spend in the maintenance of a separate home life, and he has full opportunity to organize with the other workers in his trade.

The domestic employee is retained in the household largely because her "mistress" fatuously believes that she is thus maintaining the sanctity of family life.

The household employee has no regular opportunity for meeting other workers of her trade, and of attaining with them the dignity of a corporate body. The industrial isolation of the household employee results, as isolation in a trade must always result, in a lack of progress in the methods and products of that trade, and a lack of aspiration and education in the workman. Whether we recognize this isolation as a cause or not, we are all ready to acknowledge that household labor has been in some way belated; that the improvements there have not kept up with the improvement in other occupations. . . .

The household employee, in addition to her industrial isolation, is also isolated socially. It is well to remember that the household employees for the better quarters of the city and suburbs are largely drawn from the poorer quarters, which are nothing if not gregarious. The girl is born and reared in a tenement house full of children. She goes to school with them, and there she learns to march, to read, and write in companionship with forty others. When she is old enough to go to parties, those she attends are usually held in a public hall and are crowded with dancers. If she works in a factory, she walks home with many other girls, in much the same spirit as she formerly walked to school with them. She mingles with the young men she knows, in frank, economic, and social equality. Until she marries she remains at home with no special break or change in her family and social life. If she is employed in a household, this is not true. Suddenly all the conditions of her life are altered. This change may be wholesome for her, but it is not easy, and thought of the savings-bank does not cheer one much, when one is twenty. She is isolated from the people with whom she has been reared, with whom she has gone to school, and among whom she expects to live when she marries. . . .

Curiously enough the same devotion to family life and quick response to its claims, on the part of the employer, operates against the girl employed in household labor, and still further contributes to her isolation.

The employer of household labor, in her zeal to preserve her own family life intact and free from intrusion, acts inconsistently and grants to her cook, for instance, but once or twice a week, such opportunity for untrammeled association with her relatives as the employer's family claims constantly. This in itself is undemocratic, in that it makes a distinction between the value of family life for one set of people as over against another; or, rather, claims that one set of people are of so much less importance than another, that a valuable side of life pertaining to them should be sacrificed for the other.

This cannot be defended theoretically, and no doubt much of the talk among the employers of household labor, that their employees are carefully shielded and cared for, and that it is so much better for a girl's health and morals to work in a household than to work in a factory, comes from a certain uneasiness of conscience, and from a desire to make up by individual scruple what would be done much more freely and naturally by public opinion if it had an untrammeled chance to assert itself. One person, or a number of isolated persons, however conscientious, cannot perform this office of public opinion. Certain hospitals in London have contributed statistics showing that seventy-eight per cent of illegitimate children born there are the children of girls working in households. These girls are certainly not less virtuous than factory girls, for they come from the same families and have had the same training, but the girls who remain at home and work in factories meet their lovers naturally and easily, their fathers and brothers know the men, and unconsciously exercise a certain supervision and a certain direction in their choice of companionship. The household employees living in another part of the city, away from their natural family and social ties, depend upon chance for the lovers whom they meet. The lover may be the young man who delivers for the butcher or grocer, or the solitary friend, who follows the girl from her own part of town and pursues unfairly the advantage which her social loneliness and isolation afford him. There is no available public opinion nor any standard of convention which the girl can apply to her own situation.

It would be easy to point out many inconveniences arising from the fact that the old economic forms are retained when moral conditions which befitted them have entirely disappeared, but until employers of domestic labor become conscious of their narrow code of ethics, and make a distinct effort to break through the status of mistress and servant, because it shocks their moral sense, there is no chance of even beginning a reform. [Jane Addams, *Democracy and Social Ethics* (Macmillan, 1902), 77–80, 82–90, 108–9, 116–7, 119–20, 124–6]

35. *The Marriage of Democracy and Christianity,* Vida Dutton Scudder (1861–1954)[8]

Vida Dutton Scudder was radical, both in her labor politics and in her private life. Prior to beginning her academic career, she joined the Companions of the Holy Cross, a semimonastic order of about fifty Episcopalian women devoted to prayer and social harmony. In 1912, as a young professor at Wellesley College, she supported the Industrial Workers of the World's (IWW) strike to organize the Lawrence textile workers. In 1919, she formed a personal household consisting of Florence Converse, Scudder's companion and former student (and author of a romance novel and a history of Wellesley College), and Converse's mother. In Socialism and Character *(1912), Scudder described herself as "a class-conscious, revolutionary socialist, if you will" but her socialism was part of a romanticized Christianity, as summarized in her contribution to Upton Sinclair's* Cry for Justice *(1915):[9]*

Deeper than all theories, apart from all discussion, the mighty instinct for social justice shapes the hearts that are ready to receive it. The personal types thus created are the harbingers of the victory of the cause of freedom. The heralds of freedom, they are also its martyrs. . . . Not for one instant can they know an undimmed joy in arts, in thought, in nature while part of their very life throbs in the hunger of the dispossessed. . . .

---

8. More biographical information on Scudder prefaces her selection in Chapter 1.

9. Upton Beall Sinclair (1878–1968) was a major figure in "muckraking" journalism. Of his ninety books, perhaps the best known is *The Jungle* (1906), a study of working and sanitary conditions in the slaughterhouse industry. Publication of *The Jungle* influenced the government's decision to pass the pure food laws. In 1934 Sinclair ran as the Democratic candidate for governor of California but was defeated.

So were they born: the children of the new age, whom the new intuition governs . . . men and women vowed to simplicity of life and to social service; possessed by a force mightier than themselves, over which they have no control; aware of the lack of social harmony in our civilization, restless with pain, perplexity, distress, yet filled with deep inward peace as they obey the imperative claim of a widened consciousness. By active ministry, and yet more by prayer and fast and vigil, they seek to prepare the way for the spiritual democracy on which their souls are set.[10]

In the following selection, taken from her textbook on English literature, Scudder views "spiritual democracy" as a many-faceted marriage of previously separated impulses, ideas, and ideals as well as of people.

—1898—

Socialism is no mere sentiment. It accepts as its starting-point the conviction that the individualist democratic state is a failure, but it seeks not to recede, but to advance. It believes in expressing through the actual constitution of society, that faith in the social organism as a living whole which we have seen so powerfully stirring in our authors. To this end, it holds the policy of collective control in all matters of collective concern. The recognition of a common duty toward productive labor; the demand for stable living conditions that shall remove from all classes the hideous pressure of material anxiety; the desire for opportunity equally shared, and hence for the diminution of inequalities in wealth; the reiterated plea for the better and more economical organization of labor through the agency of the state,—all these things enter the socialist spirit and find their home there. Above all, the synthesis of democracy with authority which we have seen the imagination imperatively seeking, and which has constantly baffled its search, finds at last in socialist hopes an answer; not through return to feudalism, but through the ideal of a social system more highly organized than any the past can show. Socialism has proved, indeed, to many paradoxes and perplexed contradictions, a House of Reconciliation. . . .

No one, it is obvious on the surface, could accept or imagine socialism who was still dubiously holding aloof from democracy, and chanting dirges over the dying aristocratic ideal. Only when democracy, recognized as the social destiny of the modern world, had actually forced the eyes of the dreamers from their longing gaze on the landscape of the past, did it reveal its own complex essence, and show within

10. Scudder, in Sinclair, *Cry for Justice* (1915), 289.

its large nature two antagonistic tendencies which, if developed, would lead to two social forms at least apparently opposed. Our fathers could not see this, but we see it. The socialistic principle, held in solution with individualism during the earlier phases of democracy, is recognized at last as a separate impulse, pulling away toward a sort of social organization which has never yet existed, and which promises results so strange that it is no wonder if men hold back. The question of this generation is not any longer the old controversy between democracy and aristocracy: it is the question between democracy social, bound together by laws more highly elaborated than any society that has yet been known, and democracy individualistic, a thing governed by principles inherited, unchanged, and hardly modified from the conditions of the natural world. Which of these two types of democracy shall be the social form of the future? This is the only question which the logic of events permits us. . . .

To complete political liberty and to rectify its grievous failures by the acquisition of liberty social and industrial will be as great a work as our generation, and perhaps the next, can accomplish; but once the summit won, we shall cry with Whitman:[11] "My spirit does but level that lift to pass and continue beyond.". . .

Far from the battle ground of theory, that spiritual instinct of wider brotherhood which we have traced in its wistful beginnings is finding free scope at last. The majority live untouched by it, many deride it; but positive, not negative factors are the significant elements in any progress, and it is certain that all around us earnest people are establishing a curiously untrammeled fellowship with all sorts and conditions of men. Such a fellowship means activity; eager and vigorous cooperation with the forces in the collective self making for righteousness. Yet however practical its manifestation, the governing instinct is as much contemplative as active. The mystic of former times, reacting against conventions and longing for simplicity of life, fled like Thoreau[12] into the wilderness; the mystic of the present, actuated by the same impulse, flees not from

---

11. Walt Whitman (1819–1892) was America's romantic poet of fraternity and democracy. His *Leaves of Grass* (1855) marked a watershed in American poetry and literature.

12. Henry David Thoreau (1817–1862) was an American transcendental poet and philosopher best known for his act of civil disobedience against slavery and for his book *Walden* (1854), a collection of essays that recounted his spiritual journeys and experiences while living alone at Walden Pond in Concord, Massachusetts.

but to the world, betakes himself, not to the woods, but to a crowded city district, and steeps his soul in the joy of the widest human sympathy he can attain. He is often misinterpreted and called a philanthropist, and the motive of compassion and service is doubtless strongly at work in promoting the new fellowship; yet deep in the heart is another impulse, a sense of need blending restlessly with the sense of power to help, and even more operative in driving men out from the conventions of class or clique into the fuller freedom. It is one of the practical outcomes of theoretical democracy that men begin to feel that there is literally no privilege in life, on its earthly side, so great as absolutely free and unlimited relations with their fellow men, and that actual conditions make this privilege rare. People are to be found in plenty who have never held any intercourse with wage-earners except either as employers or as benefactors. Such intercourse as this is not abnormal, but it is partial; it brings into relief only certain aspects of character on either side, and these not always the best. The craving for contact of the entire man with man, for full expression and reception of personality, is a pet theory with a poet like Whitman; but it remains theory to most of his readers. To realize or gratify this craving in all the rich relations of actual life by the constant extension of fellowship into new regions is no ignoble desire. . . .

What may be the result of this quickening of knowledge and sympathy between those naturally far apart is not yet apparent. The establishment of each tie is, in any case, a small result in itself, worthy of thanksgiving. Whether, beyond this immediate good, we may believe ourselves to be at the origin of a great movement, with a significant future, it is impossible to tell; but surmises are allowable and tempting. Looking forward ten years, we may be fairly sure that the big world of prosperous trade and decorous society will be going on its respectable way much as at present; but apart from it and opposed to it *in toto*, we may easily imagine that we see great groups of people, bound together by personal ties and by spiritual faith, and earnestly striving after a nobler civilization. Children of privilege and children of toil will be united in these groups; thinkers and laborers; women and men of delicate traditions and fine culture, mingled in close spiritual fellowship with those whose wisdom has been gained not through opportunity, but through deprivation. They will have found a deep union in a common experience and common desire, underlying all intellectual and social difference. They will realize in a measure the old dream of Langland,[13]—fellow-pilgrims of Truth, while they share life

---

13. William Langland (c. 1330–c. 1400) was the author of *Piers Plowman*, a medieval religious allegory.

and labor in joyous comradeship. And they will aim, like More,[14] at a reshaping and regeneration of all society, shutting themselves up in no small or isolated experiment; for they will realize that the fellowship they love can never be perfected except under conditions of a literally universal freedom. . . .

Democracy, which entered England hand in hand with Christianity, has become strangely separated from its companion during its long wanderings. The relation between the two was still close in Langland; in More, it had become chiefly theoretical; in the century of Swift,[15] it had ceased to exist. At this time, however, both democracy and Christianity were sleeping. During the nineteenth century, the two powers have been groping each for the other, hampered and well-nigh helpless on account of their separation, yet not knowing what they lacked. . . .

But this state of things could not continue, so long as the burning words of the Gospels were not blotted out from the New Testament daily read in the churches, and so long as the facts of the supreme Life of all history remained the great inheritance of the world. To trace the social awakening of the modern Church is to read one of the most interesting chapters of religious experience. . . .

The new social awakening came, as we have seen, in the secular world during the fertile period after 1880. And shame on shame indeed would it have been had the Church again held back, when that secular world, critical, artistic, practical, was all opening its eyes to see, its heart to feel, its hands to act. She has not held back. She has followed, if she could not lead; and this time, the impulse astir within her is a larger, fuller, deeper thing than it has ever been before. For it has been no affair of a party, or of a few solitary individuals. The desire to understand and to practice the social truths innate in Christianity is moving, in every religious communion, toward results which we cannot yet see. Who shall say, indeed, how potent is the influence of the profound radicalism of the Spirit of Christ, with its penetrating appeal to utter unworldliness, to the perfect love which is perfect service, even on the throngs, remote from any Church connection, who are sensitive to a

---

14. Sir Thomas More (1478–1535) was the author of *Utopia* (1516), a rumination on ideal government, and lord chancellor of England. He was charged with treason and beheaded for refusing to accept the claims of King Henry VIII over the Church.

15. Jonathan Swift (1667–1745) was an Irish-born Anglican author best known for his satires *Gulliver's Travels* (1726) and *A Modest Proposal* (1729).

quickening power? Even the most atheistic of socialists, even the many people who hold their religious and their social radicalism as inevitable parts of one attitude, yet feel and constantly say that Christ is Leader in their fellowship, and invoke the Gospels while they scoff at the Church. It is difficult, it is impossible, to define or describe a tendency of which we are all the disciples; but so much it is safe to say—that with the intellectual impulse toward the reconstruction of social theory, and the practical impulse toward the activity of social service, is blending more and more a spiritual impulse deeper than either of these, imperatively desiring and seeking the realization of the Kingdom of God on earth.

All around us, we can see in the religious world two tendencies rushing together: one is that intuition of the large misery of the disinherited, and their appeal for help, that great compassion, of which we have watched the beginnings; and the other is the stern religious desire for the subordination of earthly passion and of personal earthly joys. Either of these tendencies is imperfect alone. The purely humanitarian inspiration of the first too often, as experience shows, proves unstable. The purely ascetic inspiration of the other makes too often for self-centred morbidness and sterile spiritual pride. United, they become a power. Silently, unobtrusively, in many a crowded centre of wretched, suffering, sinning humanity, men and women, clergy and laity, swayed by the double force of these two impulses, are bearing their devoted witness, and finding the world well lost for the privilege of following directly in the steps of their Master. Sometimes, to these two inspirations from above and from around is added that intellectual desire to know, that enthusiasm for understanding, for interpreting our modern situation, which we have seen developing, quite apart from sentiment, all through the modern years. When this inspiration comes to supplement the other inspirations, human and religious, the resultant type is strong indeed. For then it is clearly seen that not rescue work alone, not alone the task of binding up the broken-hearted and the broken-bodied, is incumbent upon Christianity; but that the religion of Christ must undertake constructive work as well, and, however it shrink from the strenuous and perplexing labor, must find the way to help society to realize higher, purer, juster conditions than have yet been known, and to translate into fact the petitions of the divine prayer: "Thy Kingdom come, thy Will be done, on earth." [Vida Dutton Scudder, *Social Ideas in English Letters* (Houghton Mifflin, 1898), 283–6, 293–4, 296–7, 305–6, 313–5]

36. *Legislative Emancipation,* Florence Kelley (1859–1932)[16]

Florence Kelley and Jane Addams had a long and fruitful relationship, beginning with Kelley's thirteen years of residency at Hull House and the Nurses' Settlement in New York City. They published some of their books in the same "Citizen's Library" series edited for Macmillan by Richard Ely and worked on the same set of reform issues in Illinois. In 1912, Kelley and Addams helped draft The Progressive Party Platform *on social and industrial justice found in Chapter 9.*

—1905—

It is now generally accepted that that legislation has proved wholly beneficent which has, during the past half century, afforded to women and girls their present wide-spread opportunity for education. Indeed, we are so accustomed to it that we realize with difficulty the fact that such provision on so large a scale is new to human experience. As a result of this far-reaching movement there is present in the community an element of distinctive intelligence available for social and civic usefulness such as never before existed. That we are far from getting the full benefit of the virtue and intelligence stored up in the community; that the leisure and culture which have come to home-keeping women might be utilized on a far larger scale than we have yet attained; that an ethical gain has been made whenever the new intelligence of women has become available in the body politic; and, finally, that other important gains may reasonably be expected in proportion as its availability is extended by conferring the franchise upon women, it is the object of this chapter to indicate.

It has been urged by opponents of the enfranchisement of women, that there are other methods by which this intelligence may be utilized without active participation in political life, and this is not denied. Indeed, men who are faithful in the performance of their duty as voting citizens carry on, in addition thereto, many lines of social and civic activity. They do not, however, appear to believe that they would be more valuable in the performance of these voluntarily assumed tasks if relieved of their political duties. It is not members of philanthropic and civic committees who absent themselves from the polls; on the contrary.

---

16. More biographical information on Kelley prefaces her selection in Chapter 6.

Why, then, should not women follow both lines of activity and prove even more effective in their philanthropic and educational work, by reason of their added powers as voting citizens?

Does anyone believe that the efforts of the Public Education Association of New York would have been less effective during the past ten years, if they had been reinforced by the presence in the electorate of the mothers, the teachers, and the other interested women, including the members of the Association itself?

The fear lest the votes of ignorant women may outweigh those of the intelligent could be met by the imposition of an educational requirement such as is already in force in Massachusetts. The utterly unreasonable fear that the votes of the depraved may outnumber those of the righteous scarcely needs mention. The balance of virtue and depravity among women compares at least fairly with that of the present electorate. . . .

In general, the statement is true that in states in which women do not vote, they are not appointed to salaried positions on public boards and commissions, unless it is expressly provided in the statute creating the public body that a certain proportion of the members *shall* be women. Where the word *may* is used, there is a strong tendency towards the gradual replacement of non-voting women by voting men. . . .

By nature, by training, and by the accepted usage of the national life, women are chiefly occupied with the care, nurture and education of the young. Moreover, for reasons economic as well as pedagogic, the teachers in the public schools are largely women. It was, therefore, in following the line of least resistance that women have, in many places, become eligible for appointment or election to the school-boards; or enfranchised sufficiently to vote for the members of the boards of education. It is the belief of the writer that the results of such enfranchisement are conspicuously beneficial; that a broad line divides the communities in which women perform the duties of voting citizens in all matters relating to the schools, from those in which they are prevented from exercising those functions. It is the commonly accepted division of labor throughout the Republic that men are occupied with business and professional duties, and women take care of the children. . . . The consequences of this division, in communities in which women do not vote, are conspicuous. Business principles (keeping down the tax-rate), modified by political interest (corrupt awards of contracts, the spoils system in the appointment of teachers, etc.), exercise an undue influence,—greater than the consideration of the interests of the children, which do not readily become known to the businessmen who compose the boards of education. . . .

To the preponderance of the interests of business over the interests of the children, expressed in the majority of business men and the minority of women on boards of education, is due . . . the idiosyncrasy of the curriculum whereby the daughters of working-people are taught just those things which tend to make them valuable as stenographers, type-writers, cheap bookkeepers, clerks, copyists,—if they stay in school throughout the years of compulsory attendance. . . . But of the qualities which fit girls for home-making and intelligent motherhood, what preparation for the development of these have our business men been able to imagine and introduce into the curriculum? True it is that, in rare cases, a woman serving upon a school board has carried weight enough, by reason of unusual personality, to override the adverse pressure of other influences and secure the introduction of some slight beginnings of domestic science into the schools. But this has occurred in those schools which needed it least, *i.e.*, in the upper grades, which are not reached by the children of day laborers. . . .

It is the common experience that statutes of exceptional rigor for the protection of children are apt to remain dead letters, and this has been sadly true of child-labor laws, where powerful corporations have secured the removal of officials who were conscientious and efficient in enforcing such measures. How, then, is it to be accounted for that the county judge of Denver has for years enforced penalties upon saloon keepers, cigarette dealers (irrespective of their relation to the brewers, the whiskey trust and the cigar trust), telegraph operators (agents of two of the most powerful corporations, and the largest single employers of boys in the Republic); and has, nevertheless, not only not been retired from office but, on the contrary, was the only candidate upon whom every political party in Denver united at the last election? Citizens of Denver assert that this significant fact is due to the voting mothers, teachers and other interested women in Denver. It is a part of the recent history of the city that, when the corrupt political machine found Judge Lindsey unbending in his opposition, it dropped his name from the proposed list of nominees for the next election. But when the women of Denver heard of this, they held meetings and made known their will in such effective manner that, when the day came, no other name appeared as candidate for the office of county judge upon the ballots of any of the seven political parties which complicate elections in that lively city.

Opponents of the extension of the franchise to women have pointed out that political corruption in Colorado still exists, despite the fact that women have for ten years been admitted to the electorate. But in so doing, they mistake the direction in which ethical gain is to be expected to result from the enfranchisement of women. Political corruption is not a matter of sex; it results from the unethical basis of our business activities, and cannot be abolished until that basis is altered and made ethically sound. The ethical gain which may reasonably be expected from admitting women to the electorate is the extended activity of those members of the community who are primarily interested in the nurture and safeguarding of the young.

A suggestive comparison is that between the cherishing and nurture afforded to the children of Colorado by means of legislation due to the voting constituency of women, and the unsheltered state of the children of Georgia, where women are in every way excluded from public life, and where boys and girls at any tender age are wholly without protection from the demands and the cruel neglect of cotton-mill owners. . . .

Equally suggestive is the comparison of the defenseless position of girls in South Carolina, where women have no political power and the age of consent is ten years, with the careful safeguarding of girls in Colorado. It is not accidental that one of the first measures introduced into the legislature of Colorado after women were elected to that body, was the bill successfully carried by a woman senator, raising the age of consent to eighteen years, at that time higher than the corresponding law of any other state. Such a law affords protection to the boys and youths of the community which they are wholly unable to estimate. It saves them those temptations which beset youth in communities in which, as in North Carolina, the offense of tempting girls carries but a slight penalty, if any, with no certainty of enforcement against a white man. When the age of consent is raised to eighteen years, this is a protection not only to all the young girls and boys in the community, it is a protection to the community itself against the children of ruined girls. Denver needs no foundling asylum like that institution which confesses the disgrace of New York City. . . .

Never before in human history has the right of the young to pure living, the claim of the adolescent to guidance and restraint, the need of the child for nurture at the hands of father, mother, school and the community been recognized as in Colorado today. Never have the good influences of good homes received such reinforcement by means of legislation.

These gains have not been made because the subject matter ever developed political issues. Elections have not hinged upon them. But the accent has been shifted; the emphasis is different. It appears that, on the whole, the interests of children and youths are unusually well guarded in a community whose affairs are all carried on by men and women together. . . .

It is now more than twenty years since the writer printed in the *International Review* a paper on "The Law and the Child" in which it was pointed out that the two agencies which had chiefly modified the life of the children of the working class during the nineteenth century were the development of steam-driven machinery, which had made the labor of children available on a large scale in manufacture, and the emergence of women from the exclusively domestic life of former centuries to a participation, first in the education, and later in the philanthropic and educational work of modern times. During the intervening years since the publication of that paper the task of obtaining or promoting legislation on behalf of workingwomen, girls and children, or of securing its enforcement, has never ceased to be one of the deepest interest. The progress achieved, however, is so slight, the obstacles in the way of any real protection for young children are still so great, in all the industrial states, that it has become the settled conviction of the writer that, until women are universally admitted to the franchise, direct measures involve almost certain illusion and disappointment. This conviction is confirmed, not merely by the affirmative experience of Colorado, but by the negative experience connected with the effort to establish by statute the right to leisure of women and children in Illinois, where women vote only for the trustees of the state university. It is still farther confirmed by the overwhelming disparity between the advantages gained for themselves by workingmen who are voters, compared with the excessive difficulty involved in making any gain whatever, during the same period of twenty years, on behalf of workingwomen and children. . . .

It has been shown that in states in which women have been admitted to the electorate, certain substantial advantages have accrued to the schools and the children. It is entirely reasonable to infer that with a farther extension of the franchise to women, a similar gradual improvement in the lot of the minor wage-earners will come about, and that these improvements cannot be achieved so promptly or so lastingly in any other way.

While leisure has been increasing in the class of prosperous, home-keeping women, the need of their help, sympathy and protection has been growing among the young workers. Since the leisure of prosperous women is due largely to the labor of young wage-workers (who are engaged chiefly in the food and garment trades, the textile industries and that retail commerce which lives by the patronage of home-keeping women), it behooves the fortunate to assume their full share of the duty of making and enforcing laws for the protection of these young wage-workers. But this they can do only when they perform all the duties of citizenship, voting and serving on public boards and commissions when elected or appointed to them. It is because women are less under the stress of competitive business, because they do, in fact, represent children and youth, that their vote is needed. [Florence Kelley,

Some Ethical Gains through Legislation (Macmillan, 1905), 172–5, 178–9, 184–5, 192–5, 199–200, 205]

Further Reading

Baker, Paula, "The Domestication of Politics: Women and American Political Society, 1780–1920," *American Historical Review*, vol. 89 (1984): 620–47.

Davis, Allen F., *Spearheads for Reform: The Social Settlements and the Progressive Movement, 1890–1914* (Rutgers University Press, 1984)

——. *American Heroine: The Life and Legend of Jane Addams* (Oxford University Press, 1973).

Degler, Carl N., "Introduction," in Charlotte Perkins Gilman, *Women and Economics* (Harper & Row, 1966), vi–xxxv.

Fitzpatrick, Ellen, *Endless Crusade: Women Social Scientists and Progressive Reform* (Oxford University Press, 1990).

Flanigan, Maureen, "Gender and Urban Political Reform: The City Club and the Woman's City Club of Chicago in the Progressive Era," in Glenda Elizabeth Gilmore, ed., *Who Were the Progressives?* (St. Martin's, 2002).

Grimes, Alan P., *The Puritan Ethic and Woman Suffrage* (Greenwood, 1967).

Kraditor, Aileen, *The Idea of the Woman Suffrage Movement, 1890–1920* (Columbia University Press, 1965).

Ladd-Taylor, Molly, "Hull House Goes to Washington: Women and the Children's Bureau," in Noralee Frankel and Nancy S. Dye, eds., *Gender, Class, Race, and Reform in the Progressive Era* (University Press of Kentucky, 1991).

Lane, Ann J., *To "Herland" and Beyond: The Life and Work of Charlotte Perkins Gilman* (Pantheon, 1990).

Leach, William, *True Love and Perfect Union: The Feminist Reform of Sex and Society* (Basic Books, 1980).

McCarthy, Kathleen D., *Women, Philanthropy, and Civil Society* (University of Indiana Press, 2001).

Muncy, Robyn, *Creating a Female Dominion in American Reform 1890–1935* (Oxford University Press, 1991).

Nearing, Scott, and Nellie M. S. Nearing, *Women and Social Progress: A Discussion of the Biologic, Domestic, Industrial and Social Possibilities of American Women* (Macmillan, 1912/1917).

Parker, Alison, *Purifying America: Women, Cultural Reform, and Pro-Censorship Activism, 1873–1933* (University of Illinois Press, 1997).

Sinclair, Upton, ed., *The Cry for Justice: An Anthology of the Literature of Social Protest*, with an Introduction by Jack London (Pasadena, CA, 1915).

Sklar, Katherine Kish, *Florence Kelley and the Nation's Work: The Rise of Women's Political Culture, 1830–1930* (Yale University Press, 1995).

Skocpol, Theda, *Protecting Soldiers and Mothers: The Political Origins of Social Policy in the United States* (Harvard University Press, 1992).

9

Progressivism Triumphant in America

The election of 1912 marked the highpoint of Progressivism as a national political force. All three parties, but especially the Progressive Party—a newly formed confederation of like-minded Republicans—touted various aspects of a Progressive agenda. And although the victory went to Woodrow Wilson (a Democrat), the combined vote for Taft (3.48 million) and Theodore Roosevelt (4.13 million) exceeded the winner's by more than 1.3 million votes. The Progressive Party's nominating convention, discussed more fully below in the preface to its Platform, was itself a unique event, combining aspects of a religious revival, a prayer meeting, an academic public policy symposium, and a typical party convention with backroom deals, compromises, and bruised feelings. This highpoint was no accident: like the new industrial economy, the major institutions of Progressive ideas were thriving. Mass journalism, the new universities, citizen-oriented book series, women's clubs, and the infrastructure of reform organizations, churches, social workers, teachers, and professional and academic associations, each with their magazines and journals—all of these Progressive organizations and institutions were at the peak of their energies and morale.

The success of these Progressive institutions was mirrored in the flourishing careers of the leading Progressive spokespeople. Reformers in cities and states were increasingly elected to public office, as were ever-larger numbers of Senators and Congress members. Not only had such prominent Progressives as Jane Addams and Richard Ely become household names, they were also honored as exemplars of American civic ideals. Scholars who, after spending lonely years at German universities during the 1870s, had returned to find few academic positions available, were now considered to be the leaders of their academic professions (and their increasingly rich and powerful colleges and universities). After receiving his PhD in political economy in Germany, Edmund James spent six years teaching high school and freelance writing before becoming a founding member of the faculty at the Wharton School at the University of Pennsylvania. With Simon Patten (whose early career paralleled James' almost exactly), he founded the American Academy of Political and Social Science. James went on to become the president of the University of Illinois. Just as Jane Addams founded Hull House and Florence Kelley established the National Consumers

League, James and Patten created the institutional platforms on which they rose to fame and influence. In short, what began as something of a gray, dissident, and frustrated counterculture in the bosom of the Gilded Age had come to dominate America's civic culture and was soon to capture the citadels of national political power.

In this fluid and changing environment, energetic and talented individuals could have a huge impact on American society. Ida Tarbell's articles on the history of the Standard Oil trust were collected into a best-selling book and changed the popular discourse on trusts and monopolies. Working under Edward Devine (who had been one of Simon Patten's students at Wharton), Crystal Eastman (Franklin Giddings' former student at Columbia University) surveyed worker injury and deaths in Pittsburgh, Pennsylvania. By documenting the statistical incidence of industrial accidents—and the devastating effects those accidents had on the workers' wives and children—Eastman triggered a series of initiatives, first instituted by a few Progressive states in 1910, to establish workers' compensation laws. By 1920, forty-two of the forty-eight states had established similar laws.[1]

Eventually, the leaders of the business and financial worlds (and of the more traditional professions of law and medicine) began to surrender to the prestige, moral authority, and political power of the Progressive organizations and institutions. In 1900, fourteen national research universities incorporated into an association that monopolized the production of doctoral degrees and dominated the academic profession. Although the medical and legal professions faced much greater obstacles on the path to professional standards and national public service, they, too, eventually succeeded.[2]

The selections here, all written in the period 1912–1915, do not document the formation of Progressive ideas; rather, they are the late products of those ideas. Although none of the selections collected in this chapter are written by academics, all of the authors made their living as reform journalists and writers—the kinds of public figures we might call "pundits" or "public intellectuals" today. Walter Weyl and Walter Lippmann both were founding editors of *The New Republic* in 1914 under

---

1. Witt, *Accidental Republic* (2004).

2. The American Association of Universities (AAU) began in 1900 with fourteen charter members whose universities were producing 90 percent of American doctorates. Whereas the Association of American Law Schools (AALS) formed in 1900, it did not begin to control legal education until the 1930s. American medical education was effectively consolidated and monopolized by universities following the Flexner Report in 1910.

Herbert Croly, the founding editor-in-chief. This weekly magazine of opinion quickly became the most influential Progressive, and then liberal, publication in America.

37. *The New Democracy,* Walter Weyl (1873–1919)

The son of a German-Jewish wholesale milliner, Weyl was born in Philadelphia. He won a scholarship to the Wharton School of the University of Pennsylvania, where he attracted the attention of Simon Patten. After graduation, at the urging of Patten, Weyl spent four years studying in Germany. He then returned to the University of Pennsylvania for a doctoral degree in economics; he wrote his dissertation on the economics of railway passenger traffic. While holding down two early and brief government jobs related to his economics expertise, he tried his hand at writing; he was assisted in his literary endeavors by magazine writer and reform activist Bertha Poole, whom he had met at Hull House and married in 1907. Although Weyl and Poole both became respected and successful freelance magazine writers, it was Weyl's book, The New Democracy, *that brought him to the notice of such prominent Progressives as Herbert Croly and Theodore Roosevelt. According to Weyl's diary, Roosevelt once hailed* The New Democracy *as one of the "true books of the movement."*[3] *Weyl later wrote two books on American foreign policy and the war . He died soon after they were published.*

—1912—

The motive force of our modern ethics of social improvement reveals itself in a sense of disequilibrium between social wealth and a residual misery of large sections of the population. Two centuries ago, when population still pressed narrowly upon wealth, statesmen could look callously upon starvation, imprisonment for debt, and the hanging of vulgar rogues who stole a shilling and a penny. If fifty per cent and, in some years, seventy-five per cent of London babies died in the year, were there not too many people anyway? But today our surplus has made us as sensitive to misery, preventable death, sickness, hunger, and deprivation as is a photographic plate to light. The disequilibrium between social surplus and social misery colors all our thoughts. It is the

---

3. Quoted in Forcey, *Crossroads of Liberalism* (1961), 53.

basis of our social unrest. It causes the stirrings of uneasy social consciences.

It is also responsible for a more sober and searching social analysis. A salient fact about our modern social thinking is that we no longer so light-heartedly attribute to a personal delinquency the residual, persistent poverty of great masses of the population. We no longer so often hear the *dictum* that anyone who wants a job can get one; that no man need be idle; that all men can save against the rainy day, when they may be injured by industrial accident or discharged because of middle age. We have become more temperate in our social judgments and our social admonitions. . . .

Upon the wide democratic masses, the social disequilibrium exercises a far more direct and potent influence. With these classes, the theory that social wealth should be devoted to social uses—in ways to be determined by society—becomes axiomatic. It becomes a fixed idea. This impelling idea is all-conquering. By creating this idea, the growth of the social surplus lends to the democratic masses a vast new impetus to action. . . .

Our wealth is already so gigantic as to be almost incomprehensible. A billion dollars exceeds the fortune of any individual since the world began. It is like a "light-year" or some other convenient but unimaginable astronomical term. Yet in 1904 our national wealth was estimated by the census authorities at 107 of these billions of dollars. The present estimated wealth of New York State is twice the entire estimated wealth of the United States in 1850. We would sell under the hammer for fifteen times as much as we would have done a little over half a century ago.

The wealth of America, moreover, is not a secret hoard to which new billions are brought and added. It is a living thing, which grows at a stupendous rate as new millions of men pour into the land, and new machines, new scientific processes, new methods of organization, lay the continent wider open. From 1870 to 1900 our wealth increased at the rate of almost two billions a year; from 1900 to 1904 it recorded an apparent increase of almost five billions a year. During every eighteen months of those four years there was added to our possessions an *increment* greater than the whole estimated wealth of the country in 1850.

Everywhere are signs of a stupendous productiveness. The number of our horses, sheep, mules, swine increases; our production of wheat, corn, cotton, rice, has enormously grown. So also our mineral production. In 1840 we produced less than two million long tons of coal; in 1909 we produced four hundred and eleven millions. The mere increase in coal production in 1907 over that of the preceding year was about equal to the entire output of all the country's mines during the eighty-five years from the Declaration of Independence to the outbreak of the Civil War.

In 1870 we produced three million long tons of iron ore; in 1909, fifty-one millions. Our pig iron production, which never amounted to a million long tons before 1864, increased to almost twenty-seven millions in 1910. The production of steel, which remained below one million tons until 1880, rose to twenty-four millions in 1909. Enormously rapid, also, has been the increase in our output of gold, aluminium, cement, copper, lead, salt, stone, and zinc; while our production of petroleum, which averaged about a hundred million gallons a year during the Civil War, rose in 1909 to over seven and one half billions of gallons.

Our American agriculture has not only fed our growing population, but it still permits vast exportations of grain, flour, and meat products. Moreover, it has been carried on by a steadily lessening proportion of the capital and labor of the country. There has been simultaneously an almost bewildering increase in our manufacturing industries.

When we try to visualize the statistics of our American railroads, the mind sinks exhausted under the effort. The traffic increases incessantly and enormously. While our population has not quite doubled in thirty-three years, our railroad passenger and freight traffics have more than doubled in nine years. In 1909 our railroad freight mileage was equivalent to the work of our ninety-two millions of inhabitants carrying each a load of over four hundred pounds a distance of over thirty miles each day. This enormous traffic, like the tremendously increasing water carriage on the Great Lakes, reveals the actual and potential power of the machine-aided American nation. . . .

So much for the wonders of the past. But they are wonders only so long as we think solely in terms of the past. Actually our utilization of the continent has hardly begun. It has hardly begun to begin. . . .

A great social surplus, however, does not mean that a democracy is attained, but only that it is attainable. Without social wealth, a real democracy is not possible; with it, it is not inevitable.

The masses of the people, if they are to secure a democracy, must not fall or remain below the three levels of democratic striving. Below the economic level of democratic striving, men are for the most part too ill-fed, ill-clad, ill-conditioned, too depressed by want or sickness, too harassed by debt or insecurity, too brutalized by child labor or overwork, or too demoralized by recurring unemployment to maintain the *morale* required for the attainment of democracy. Below the intellectual level of democratic striving, most men are too credulous, too suspicious, too immersed in petty preoccupations, too narrow-viewed to perceive their

individual interest in the wider interest of group or nation, and they are
too near-minded to value the larger social gain of the future above the
smaller social or personal gain of the moment. Below the political level
of democratic striving, men are too unused to political weapons, or too
removed from them, to be able effectively to translate their economic
and intellectual powers into political facts. To achieve a real popular
sovereignty, the masses of the people must rise or remain above all of
these levels.

Of these three levels the economic and the intellectual are the more
important, for a voteless people with economic and intellectual
resources can better secure political representation than can an impoverished and ignorant people in full possession of political rights. All
these three levels are in a sense connected and all are related to the
social surplus. It is the social surplus which permits the economic
advance of the people, which in turn facilitates their intellectual enfranchisement, which in turn tends strongly in the direction of political representation. The lack of complete parallelism between these three
levels results in many of the worst abuses of our pseudo-democratic government of today. The possession of the vote by ignorant masses below
the poverty line leads to sluggish, reckless, or perverse legislation and
seems to justify the most hopeful fears of interested reactionaries. But
the true remedy for these evils is not what the reactionaries desire, a
change in the political level, but, on the contrary, a raising of the people to a higher economic and intellectual level. . . .

Thus, though the accumulations of the great industrial nations render democracy possible, and furnish a stake, motive, and ethical justification to democrats; though in America this social wealth is so
stupendously growing as to place, *beyond even the possibility of doubt*,
our ability, present and future, to pay for such a democracy,—still,
whether or not we shall achieve democracy depends upon these other
factors, upon the character of our population, upon its mean position
above or below the levels of democratic striving. Given the energizing
moral impulse of the startling disequilibrium between our social wealth
and our abiding poverty, it is still essential that the mass of the population have sufficient wealth or income, sufficient intelligence and clearness of perception, sufficient political power, political experience, and
political wisdom (as well as a high enough capacity for joint action), to
permit them unitedly to do their part in wresting a democracy from
men who have an interested attachment to present conditions. The
attainment of democracy depends upon the all-of-us, upon the qualities
and resources of the potentially overwhelming democratic masses. . . .

It is only when we attempt to apply the levels of democratic striving to our extremely differentiated population that we realize the vastness of the social spaces which separate groups which must be united in the bonds of solidarity. From the point of view of wealth the bulk of the democratic mass (bearing in mind the multitude of exceptions) do not stand either at the top or at the very bottom of Fortune's ladder. This mass excludes a majority of our business princes with dependents and hangers-on, as well as other men, who have no affiliation with the plutocracy other than a common lawlessness. The democratic mass also excludes a majority of men below the poverty line, the abjectly poor, who are also largely the defectives, dependents, delinquents, the illiterate, and the disfranchised. The democratic mass represents a residue of the population, after a majority of the very rich and of the abjectly poor have been drawn off. This residue seems to constitute or to be about to constitute a vast majority. If in the total absence of statistics or even of a statistical classification which would be applicable, we arbitrarily estimate at twenty millions the people who are debarred through excessive wealth or excessive poverty, ignorance, or political impotence from effectively willing a large measure of democratic reorganization, there would still remain of our ninety millions of people some seventy millions who may perhaps have the material, intellectual, and political means to strive for the attainment of a democratic civilization, and who have a perceivable interest in its achievement. . . .

But the question which presented itself at the beginning presents itself anew and with redoubled force. "Can these potentially democratic masses unite?" Will the Maine lumberjack, the Negro lawyer, the German saloon keeper, the Montana farmer—men of different race, religion, and language; of different political traditions, of different economic status, of different social outlook,—will these think alike and vote together? Can a group with widely diverse interests so compromise conflicting claims within the group as to unite an effective majority, and thus compel a permanent victory? . . .

In intercourse among social groups, as in intercourse among men, a common antagonism may be the beginning of a mutual understanding. Groups repelling the same group tend to attract each other.

The plutocracy is the chief objective of our social agitation. It, and it alone, unites in opposition factory workers, farmers, shopkeepers, professional men. The plutocracy creates between the few and the many a cleavage which for the time being obscures all other divisions. . . .

[T]he plutocracy is more and more opposed by an ever larger number of social groups and individuals; not only for what it does and for what it is, but for the deeper economic tendencies which it represents. Different men are arrayed against the plutocracy for different reasons.

While, however, such common hostility is a sufficient stimulus to an aggressive campaign, it is not a basis broad enough for a constructive program. Unless the opponents of the plutocracy have some common positive aim, their antagonism will dissipate itself in abortive assaults and waste heat, without permanent influence upon social conditions.

There exists, however, such a common aim. This aim, which holds together the opponents of an intrenched plutocracy, is the attainment of a common share in the conquered continent, in the material and moral accumulations of a century. When the trust raises prices, obtains valuable franchises or public lands, escapes taxation, secures bounties, lowers wages, evades factory laws, or makes other profitable maneuvers, it is diverting a part of the social surplus from the general community to itself. The public pays the higher prices, loses the franchises or lands, pays higher taxes, suffers in wages (and pays for the ill effects of low wages), and generally makes up dollar for dollar for all such gains. In all these things the people have a perceivable interest. The great mass is injured in its capacity of wage earner, salary earner, taxpayer and consumer. . . .

To secure their rights as consumers, as well as to secure other economic interests, less in common, the people unite as citizens to obtain a sensitive popular government. They attain to a certain political as well as economic solidarity. This solidarity is by no means a complete unification of interest. There remain differences in agreement and discords in harmony. The middle classes are as much opposed to the trade-union as are the trusts, and the professional man is as anxious to secure a docile and cheap housemaid as the farmer is desirous of getting high prices for his wheat and paying low wages to his farm laborer.

The elements of solidarity, however, being found in a common hostility to the plutocracy and a common interest in the social surplus, it becomes possible gradually so to compromise conflicting interests within the group as to secure a united front against a common enemy. The regulation of railroads in the interest of consumer and farmer may be extended to the protection of the railroad worker; the conservation of natural resources may be linked to a similar policy of human conservation, to a campaign against destitution, and to a progressive labor policy which will insure the health, safety, comfort, and leisure of all workers. By such internal adjustments within the wide democratic army the possibility of a sufficient, permanent solidarity is given. . . .

Today the democratic army, united by the loosest bonds, and subjected to the most attenuated discipline, is moving along three wide roads to a common but not clearly perceived goal. These three roads are the democratization of government, the socialization of industry, and the civilization of the citizen. These roads meet and cross and intertwine, and the various contingents join and separate, and again join and again separate, while, all the time, the army, stretching out far into the distance, approaches nearer to its goal. The men in the rear, marching partly through an inertia of motion, partly through imitation of the men ahead, occasionally desert and again reenlist. They see only vaguely the outlines of the country to which they are marching. But with each advance their view becomes clearer and with each new day the habit of marching and the instinct of fellowship with the men ahead increase. Occasionally great bodies, attracted by new leaders, branch off into side paths, which seem shorter and straighter, and some of these detachments are lost, and some, by occupying cross paths, obstruct the passage of the main army; while others, by still marching, once more strike the common road and thus rejoin their comrades. Gradually the army, though composed of many detachments led by many generals, becomes somewhat more unified. Gradually, as many men coming from many places converge on common points, the three broad roads of the march, the roads of democratic government, of socialized industry, and of a civilized people, become clearly marked highways.

The industrial goal of the democracy is the socialization of industry. It is the attainment by the people of the largest possible industrial control and of the largest possible industrial dividend. The democracy seeks to attain these ends through government ownership of industry; through government regulation; through tax reform; through a moralization and reorganization of business in the interest of the industrially weak. . . .

In attempting to secure political control, the democracy proceeds along five paths. These paths are (1) the democratic control of parties and of party nominations; (2) the democratic control of elections; (3) the democratic control of representatives already elected; (4) direct legislation by the people; (5) increased efficiency of the democratized government. . . .

The social goal of the democracy is the advancement and improvement of the people through a democratization of the advantages and opportunities of life. This goal is to be attained through a conservation of life and health, a democratization of education, a socialization of consumption, a raising of the lowest elements of the population to the level of the mass.

The most elemental phase of this social policy is conservation. . . .

This policy does not consider life solely from a quantitative standpoint. The demand for large populations is not democratic in origin. It is the despot who wants soldiers; the business prince who wants cheap labor; the jingo who believes in a swaggering, fighting nation. In

democratic countries, on the other hand, a decrease in the birth rate
has accompanied an improved education, a more diffused comfort, and
a rise in the general standard of living. The more advanced the country, the section, or the social class, the more marked in general has been
the tendency away from the old blind propagation of the species. The
democracy does not desire that life be given to so many that the gift
becomes of no value. It does not wish to see a swarming population
pressing upon the means of subsistence. It desires a full life for all who
are born, but it does not measure national success by the numbers who
are born.

This distinction between the number and the value of lives explains
one of the most curious anomalies of modern democratic policy.
Although the democracy is beginning to desire rather a lessened than
an increased birth rate, it demands absolutely that every child born shall
have a chance to live. The basis of democratic strivings toward human
conservation is an ethical belief in the sanctity of human life, and the
desire for an equality in this universal possession. Life is the one thing
which all have in common; and while the expectation of life is by no
means equal as between social classes, it is far more equal than is property, education, political power, or economic opportunities. . . .

The democratic policies of conservation, education, and the socialization of consumption have one element in common, a tendency to
promote equality of opportunity. The same element appears . . . in the
policy of extending the advantages of progress and democratization to
all groups in society. We may secure the life and health of the people.
We may educate them and promote a wise and beneficent consumption of the fruits of the nation's labor. One question, however, remains.
Who are to be the ultimate beneficiaries of all this progress? Who are to
be admitted to, and who are to be debarred from, the new civilization
which is preparing?

It would be an easy problem for democracy if, as standards rose, the
whole of the people would rise with them. Under such conditions
progress would be uninterrupted, equal, easy. Unfortunately, however,
society bears with it always the burden of the submerged. The ignorant,
incompetent, vicious, weak, the feeble-minded and feeble-willed we
have always with us. We drag behind us the chain and ball of the ruth-
lessness of the past. The democracy, even when successful against the
pretensions of privilege, finds itself opposed to the obstruction and dead
weight of the nether world. . . .

The democracy is thus compelled to cure the slum to prevent its own
destruction by the slum. Its instinct to live as well as its justice and
clemency impel the democracy to this course. No democracy can be

achieved, and no democracy, once achieved, can be maintained, except as the dead weight of the masses below the democratic levels is progressively lightened.

The policy of the democracy towards the submerged divides itself into three parts: first, the redemption of men who have fallen below the democratic levels; second, the utmost possible prevention of social failures, not by ending social contests, but by improving the contestants; third, the provision of a reasonably satisfactory situation for incorrigibles, and their effective isolation from the rest of society. . . .

For every wayward man and woman, society must be called to the bar. In other words, society must prevent crime by promoting education and happiness, or must accept the underlying responsibility for its default. It must not "punish" the criminal or hunt him forever within society, but must offer to him a life which, though dependent and below that of the rest of the population, is at least secure, reasonably eligible, and with as little constraint as is consistent with the safety of society and the education of the criminal. The democracy must not raise up enemies within its ranks.

What applies to the incapables and the criminals, applies with even greater force to special groups who are separated from the rest of the population and are hated or despised. In America we have a racial problem of more fearful portent than that of any of the nations of Europe. We are still paying the endless price of slavery. The South is psychologically cramped. The North is bewildered. The Negro problem is the mortal spot of the new democracy. . . .

If it be attempted to repress the Negroes, to show them their place, we may encounter the possibility of an inconceivably savage race war. If white men and black men were ever to fight on the old plantations of the South we should have an awakening of brutalities such as no war of modern times has evoked. Even so trivial a thing as a prize fight between a Negro and a white man led recently to a disgusting subemotional debauch of tens of millions of us, and to a violent recrudescence of the lynching spirit. If there were ever a reign of terror throughout the Black Belt, if a few thousand white men and women were to be slaughtered by hordes of enraged Negroes, there would be a backwash of civilization, a recurrence of barbarism, which would reach to the furthermost hamlets of Maine and Oregon.

And yet, if the democracy in America is to be a white democracy, and the civilization in America is to be a white civilization; if it is proposed to make of the Negro a thing without rights, a permanent semiemancipated slave, a headless, strong-armed worker, then let the white civilization beware. We may sunder the races if we can; we may preserve a race integrity if we can; we may temporarily limit the Negro's suffrage. If, however, we abate the ultimate rights, prerogatives, and privileges of either race, if we seek permanently to set up lower standards for one race, we shall plant the seeds of our own undoing. Our self-protection, as much as our sense of justice, must impel us towards the increase in the Negro's ability, *morale*, and opportunity. . . .

A somewhat analogous problem is presented by our increasing immigration. Here it is not a problem of racial hatred so much as it is one of economic and social adjustment. We need not claim a superiority over the people who throng in at Ellis Island. We may concede their splendid qualities, and still advance proposals for the stemming of this human flood.

The policy of a restriction of immigration does not involve a disbelief in America's future. It does not base itself on the belief that the country is "full up." Under proper economic and social conditions, we could easily take care of two hundred, or even more, millions of people. The crux of the difficulty, however, is that a too speedy and unregulated immigration tends to prevent the very adjustments which would make the prosperity of the greater millions possible. [From Walter Weyl, *The New Democracy* (Macmillan, 1912), 197–9, 203–8, 237–9, 244, 249, 253, 274–6, 298, 320–1, 334–5, 338, 342, 344–5]

38. *Drift and Mastery,* Walter Lippmann (1889–1974)

Lippmann was born in New York City into a German-Jewish family of wealth and leisure. From his undergraduate days at Harvard University, he was marked for greatness. William James,[4] Graham Wallas,[5] and George Santayana[6] all took an interest in Lippmann and sought to direct his talents. At twenty-three, Lippmann wrote an influential book, A Preface to Politics, in which he applied contemporary European theories of the unconscious to an exploration of the current American

---

4. William James (1842–1910), who taught philosophy and psychology at Harvard University, was a formative exponent of pragmatism. He is best known for his book *The Varieties of Religious Experience* (1902).

5. Graham Wallas (1858–1932) was an English Fabian socialist and the first faculty member in political science at the London School of Economics. He met Lippmann while visiting Harvard University.

6. George Santayana (1863–1952) was a Spanish-born professor of philosophy at Harvard University. A prolific author, he wrote many books on aesthetics, morality, and spirituality.

political scene. Theodore Roosevelt later described the twenty-six-year-old Lippmann as "on the whole the most brilliant young man of his age in the United States."[7] *A staunch national Progressive with little patience for those who would seek to restore the localized world of small business, states' rights, and isolation from Europe, Lippmann became an avatar of the "American Century."*[8] *Through his writings for* The New Republic, *the* New York World, *the* New York Herald Tribune, *and finally the* Washington Post *and* Newsweek, *Lippmann emerged as a nationally syndicated guru of the enlightened liberal ruling establishment. A thorough nationalist all his life, Lippmann distrusted populist attacks on the industrial and financial economy and, indeed, the other national institutions he thought well-managed by competent democratic elites. A short passage on antitrust laws in* Drift and Mastery *makes this point clearly:*

> I should not like to answer before a just tribunal for the harm done this country in the last twenty-five years by the stupid hostility of anti-trust laws. How much they have perverted the constructive genius of this country it is impossible to estimate. They have blocked any policy of welcome and use, they have concentrated a nation's thinking on inessentials, they have driven creative businessmen to underhand methods, and put a high money value on intrigue and legal cunning, demagoguery and waste. The trusts have survived it all, but in mutilated form, the battered make-shifts of a trampled promise. They have learned every art of evasion—the only art [populist] reformers allowed them to learn. . . . Revolutions are not stopped by blind resistance. They are only perverted. And as an exhibition of blind resistance to a great promise, the trust campaign of the American democracy is surely unequalled.[9]

In the following selection, Lippmann extends this argument to a call for a scientifically informed and tough-minded realism to achieve democratic ends.

—1914—

The American temperament leans generally to a kind of mystical anarchism, in which the "natural" humanity in each man is adored as the savior of society. You meet this faith throughout the thousand and one communistic experiments and new religions in which America is so abundant. "If only you let men alone, they'll be good," a typical

7. Levy, *Herbert Croly of the New Republic* (1985), 192.
8. Steel, *Walter Lippmann and the American Century* (1980).
9. Lippmann, *Drift and Mastery* (1914), 79.

American reformer said to me the other day. He believed, as most Americans do, in the unsophisticated man, in his basic kindliness and his instinctive practical sense. A critical outlook seemed to the reformer an inhuman one; he distrusted, as Bryan does, the appearance of the expert; he believed that whatever faults the common man might show were due to some kind of Machiavellian corruption.

He had the American dream, which may be summed up, I think, in the statement that the undisciplined man is the salt of the earth. So when the trusts appeared, when the free land was gone, and America had been congested into a nation, the only philosophy with any weight of tradition behind it was a belief in the virtues of the spontaneous, enterprising, untrained and unsocialized man. Trust promoters cried: Let us alone. The little business men cried: We're the natural men, so let us alone. And the public cried: We're the most natural of all, so please do stop interfering with us. Muckraking gave an utterance to the small business men and to the larger public, who dominated reform politics. What did they do? They tried by all the machinery and power they could muster to restore a business world in which each man could again be left to his own will—a world that needed no cooperative intelligence. . . .

There are thousands today who, out of patience with almost everything, believe passionately that some one change will set everything right. In the first rank stand the suffragettes who believe that votes for women will make men chaste. I have just read a book by a college professor which announces that the short ballot will be as deep a revolution as the abolition of slavery. There are innumerable Americans who believe that a democratic constitution would create a democracy. Of course, there are single taxers so single-minded that they believe a happy civilization would result from the socialization of land values. Everything else that seems to be needed would follow spontaneously if only the land monopoly were abolished. . . .

Men will do almost anything but govern themselves. They don't want the responsibility. In the main, they are looking for some benevolent guardian, be it a "good man in office" or a perfect constitution, or the evolution of nature. They want to be taken in charge. If they have to think for themselves they turn either to the past or to a distant future: but they manage to escape the real effort of the imagination which is to weave a dream into the turning present. They trust to destiny, a quick one or a slow one, and the whole task of judging events is avoided. They turn to automatic devices: human initiative can be ignored. They forbid evil, and then they feel better. They settle on a particular analogy, or a particular virtue, or a particular policy, and trust to luck that everything else will take care of itself.

But no one of these substitutes for self-government is really satisfactory, and the result is that a state of chronic rebellion appears. That is our present situation. The most hopeful thing about it is that through the confusion we can come to some closer understanding of why the modern man lacks stability, why his soul is scattered. We may, perhaps, be able to see a little better just what self-government implies. . . .

The desire for self-government has become vivid with the accumulation of a great surplus of wealth. Man today has at last seen the possibility of freeing himself from his supreme difficulty. It wasn't easy to think much of the possibilities of this world while he lived on the edge of starvation. Resignation to hardship was a much more natural outlook. But in the midst of plenty, the imagination becomes ambitious, rebellion against misery is at last justified, and dreams have a basis in fact.

Of course, there are immense sections of the globe where the hard conditions of the older life still prevail, and there the ideal of democracy is still a very ineffective phrase. But the United States has for the most part lifted itself out of primitive hardship, and that fact, more than our supposedly democratic constitution, is what has justified in some measure the hope which inspires our history. We have been far from wise with the great treasure we possessed, and no nation has such cause for shame at the existence of poverty. We have only our short-sighted selves to blame. But the blunders are not fatal: American wealth has hardly been tapped. And that is why America still offers the greatest promise to democracy.

The first item in the program of self-government is to drag the whole population well above the misery line. To create a minimum standard of life below which no human being can fall is the most elementary duty of the democratic state. For those who go below the line of civilized decency not only suffer wretchedly: they breed the poisons of self-government. . . .

Unfit for self-government, they are the most easily led, the most easily fooled, and the most easily corrupted. You can't build a modern nation out of Georgia crackers, poverty-stricken Negroes, the homeless and helpless of the great cities. They make a governing class essential. They are used by the forces of reaction. Once in a while they are used by revolutionists for agitation, but always they are used. Before you can begin to have democracy you need a country in which everyone has some stake and some taste of its promise. . . .

The only possible cohesion now is a loyalty that looks forward. America is preeminently the country where there is practical substance in Nietzsche's advice that we should live not for our fatherland but for our children's land.

To do this men have to substitute purpose for tradition: and that is, I believe, the profoundest change that has ever taken place in human history. We can no longer treat life as something that has trickled down to us. We have to deal with it deliberately, devise its social organization, alter its tools, formulate its method, educate and control it. In endless ways we put intention where custom has reigned. We break up routines, make decisions, choose our ends, select means. . . .

This is what mastery means: the substitution of conscious intention for unconscious striving. Civilization, it seems to me, is just this constant effort to introduce plan where there has been clash, and purpose into the jungles of disordered growth. But to shape the world nearer to the heart's desire requires a knowledge of the heart's desire and of the world. You cannot throw yourself blindly against unknown facts and trust to luck that the result will be satisfactory. . . .

It is a long and difficult process, one for which we are just beginning to find a method. But there is no other way that offers any hope. To shove our impulses underground by the taboo is to force them to virulent and uncontrolled expression. To follow impulse wherever it leads means the satisfaction of one impulse at the expense of all the others. The glutton and the rake can satisfy only their gluttonous and rakish impulses, and that isn't enough for happiness. What civilized men aim at is neither whim nor taboo, but a frank recognition of desire, disciplined by a knowledge of what is possible, and ordered by the conscious purpose of their lives. . . .

If the scientific temper were as much a part of us as the faltering ethics we now absorb in our childhood, then we might hope to face our problems with something like assurance. A mere emotion of futurity, that sense of "vital urge" which is so common today, will fritter itself away unless it comes under the scientific discipline, where men use language accurately, know fact from fancy, search out their own prejudice, are willing to learn from failures, and do not shrink from the long process of close observation. Then only shall we have a substitute for authority. Rightly understood science is the culture under which people can live forward in the midst of complexity, and treat life not as something given but as something to be shaped. Custom and authority will work in a simple and unchanging civilization, but in our world only those will conquer who can understand.

There is nothing accidental then in the fact that democracy in politics is the twin-brother of scientific thinking. They had to come together. As absolutism falls, science arises. It *is* self-government. For when the impulse which overthrows kings and priests and unquestioned creeds becomes self-conscious we call it science. . . .

For the discipline of science is the only one which gives any assurance that from the same set of facts men will come approximately to the same conclusion. And as the modern world can be civilized only by the effort of innumerable people we have a right to call science the discipline of democracy. No omnipotent ruler can deal with our world, nor the scattered anarchy of individual temperaments. Mastery is inevitably a matter of cooperation, which means that a great variety of people working in different ways must find some order in their specialties. They will find it, I think, in a common discipline which distinguishes between fact and fancy, and works always with the implied resolution to make the best out of what is possible. . . .

There is nothing in the scientific temper which need make it inevitably hostile to the variety of life. But many scientists have been hostile. And the reason for that is not so difficult to see. The first triumphs of the scientific mind were in mathematics, astronomy, and physics, out of which grows engineering. The habit of mind which produced such great results was naturally exalted, so that men began to feel that science which wasn't mechanical, wasn't science. They dreamt of a time when living bodies, consciousness and human relations, would be adjusted with the accuracy of a machine. But they were merely following an analogy, which a real scientist would abandon the moment it appeared that living organisms differ from the inert. I do not know whether any such distinction must be made, but there is nothing in the scientific temper which would preclude it. . . .

There is no question that science has won its way, in part, by insult and blindness, often by a harsh ignorance of the value of older creeds. It is associated with a certain hardness of mind and narrowness of feeling, as if it were a vandal in a sanctuary. But that also is not essential to the scientific mind; it is rather an accompaniment of the bitter controversy in which science grew up.

We can begin now to define the attitude of science toward the past. It may be summed up, I think, by saying that only when we have destroyed the authority of tradition can we appreciate its treasure. So long as tradition is a blind command it is for our world an evil and dangerous thing. But once you see the past merely as a theater of human effort, it overflows with suggestion. . . .

It may seem curious to approach a pretentiously scientific volume with the question: What is this man's dearest wish? The usual method is to regard that as of no importance, and to turn immediately to testing of logic or criticism of fact. It is no wonder that writers are not convinced by hostile reviews, or that editorials make so little impression on propagandists. Unless you go to the passionate source of ideas, you are a cat looking at a king. What does it matter to the suffragettes that they are called hysterical and lectured about their mistaken tactics? That is so much scrubby, withered stupidity fit only to set off vividly the grandeur of ideas it attacks. Or does anyone suppose that feminism is dependent on the logic of its supporters or opponents? Certainly not. Until you begin to see in feminism the opposition of attitudes toward life, drawn by hope and pushed by events, you are still the six-weeks convert who can rattle off her argument and repartee in a fusillade across the dinner-table.

Criticism will have to slough off the prejudices of the older rationalism if it is to have any radical influence on ideas. It is sophomoric to suppose that the emotional life can be treated as a decadent survival. Men's desires are not something barbaric which the intellect must shun. Their desires are what make their lives, they are what move and govern. You are not talking of human beings when you talk of "pure reason." And, therefore, anyone who deepens the conflict between thought and feeling is merely adding confusion to difficulty. The practical line of construction is to saturate feeling with ideas. That is the only way in which men can tap their own power,—by passionate ideas. There is, of course, no greater difficulty in thought than to attain a delicate adjustment of our own desires to what is possible. All important thinking achieves such an adjustment, and we recognize its success by the fact that it gives us control over brute things. That sense of control is the yielding of fact to intelligent desire. But if we try to ignore the desire that moves our thought, if we try in short to be "absolutely objective," we succeed only in accumulating useless facts, or we become the unconscious victims of our wishes. If thinking didn't serve desire, it would be the most useless occupation in the world.

The only reason, of course, for casting suspicion upon the emotional life is that it does so often falsify the world and build a fool's paradise in a human hell. But when you have faced this fully, there is still no reason for attempting the vain effort of jumping out of our human skins. The danger means simply that desire has to be subjected to criticism. It is a difficult task. But it is one that we are capable of beginning, for the great triumph of modern psychology is its growing capacity for penetrating to the desires that govern our thought. . . .

In the creative imagination no relevant fact is shirked; yet over all the things that are there hovers a feeling for what they might be. A sharp and clear sense of existence is shot through with the light of its possibilities. Each fact is a place where the roads fork. Each event is a vista. Each moment is a choice. To the man who lives without question from day to day, life is just one thing after another; to the mere dreamer it is harsh and unyielding. But to the creative imagination fact is plastic, and ready to be moulded by him who understands it.

That, I believe, is the spirit of invention: around each observation there gathers an aura of conjectures. The scientific discoverer can penetrate the crevices of fact with moving guesses; each experiment is suspended in pregnant hypotheses. It is the spirit of the working artist, embodied in the fine myth that the block of marble imprisoned a statue which the sculptor released. To the artist his material is not dead clay or a silent palette, but a living substance clamoring for its form. It is the dilettante who could do a fine work if it weren't for the hardness of the stone. It is the esthete who can do everything but write his poems. It is the amateur who complains about the conflict between matter and spirit. Not the producing artist: his medium is a friendly thing, the very substance of his dream. It is the spirit of education: not to produce a row of respectable automata, but to draw out of each child the promise that is in it.

It is the spirit of valuable statecraft: the genius among politicians is he who can deal in his own time with the social forces that lead to a better one. He does not ask for a world of angels before he can begin. He does not think his duty in life is merely to keep old institutions in good repair. He grasps the facts of his age, sees in the confusion of events currents like the union, the trust, the cooperative,—suffuses them with their promise, and directs them into the structure of the future. . . .

The method of a self-governing people is to meet every issue with an affirmative proposal which draws its strength from some latent promise. Thus the real remedy for violence in industrial disputes is to give labor power that brings responsibility. The remedy for commercialism is collective organization in which the profiteer has given way to the industrial statesman. The incentive to efficiency is not alone love of competent work but a desire to get greater social values out of human life. The way out of corrupt and inept politics is to use the political state for interesting and important purposes. The unrest of women cannot be met by a few negative freedoms: only the finding of careers and the creation of positive functions can make liberty valuable. In the drift of our emotional life, the genuine hope is to substitute for terror and weakness, a frank and open worldliness, a love of mortal things in the discipline of science. [Walter Lippmann, *Drift and Mastery: An Attempt to Diagnose the Current Unrest* (Mitchell Kennerley, 1914), 103–4, 107–9, 140–2, 147–51, 155–6, 161–2, 169–70, 173–4]

39. *The Progressive Movement,* Benjamin Parke De Witt (1889–1965)

A lifelong citizen of New York City, De Witt maintained an active role in the city's life. He graduated from New York University (NYU) and eventually obtained his doctorate and law degrees there. De Witt taught English and government at NYU for five years and served as assistant to the university's chancellor. It was during this period, when he was twenty-four, that he wrote his only book, The Progressive Movement: a non-partisan, comprehensive discussion of current tendencies in American politics. *He then turned to a career in law, serving first as assistant U.S. attorney for the southern district of New York and then as a partner in a private law firm. His book, an immediate success, later became a weapon wielded by historians as they sought variously to redefine or deconstruct the Progressive movement. Like many other books from which selections were taken for this collection,* The Progressive Movement *was part of the Macmillan "Citizen's Library" series edited by Richard Ely. The book remains the most comprehensive contemporary account of Progressivism. The selections here are taken from the first parts of the book. In them, De Witt defines the Progressive movement, shows how it has penetrated into all political parties, and hopes for the creation of two new political parties: one that would bring together all citizens who believe in government by the few, and one that would consolidate those citizens that believe in government by the people.*

—1915—

The progressive movement is broader than the Progressive party and, in fact, than any single party. It is the embodiment and expression of fundamental measures and principles of reform that have been advocated for many years by all political parties. Although differences in name, in the specific reforms advocated, and in the emphasis placed upon them, have obscured the identity of the movement, the underlying purposes and ideals of the progressive elements of all parties for the past quarter of a century have been essentially the same. To make clear this universal character of the progressive movement is one of the objects for which this book has been written. . . .

The breadth and extent of the movement are indicated partly by showing the large place it has filled and now fills in each of the important political parties, and partly by explaining in detail the issues and reforms of the movement as they apply to the nation, the state, and the city.

The point of view throughout has been non-partisan, but the spirit of treatment, it must be said, has been sympathetic. No one can study the progressive movement, no one can read the lives of its pioneers and advocates without feeling its strength and vitality and realizing that it is a potent force in our political and social life. War and business depression may divert the attention of people from progressive reforms for a time. But, sooner or later, that attention will return, more earnest and more intense, and the principles of the movement will receive a new emphasis and a wider application.

Whatever difference of opinion may exist concerning the meaning of the progressive movement, every thinking man and woman must be convinced that the nation today is passing through a severe political crisis. After a period of unprecedented industrial and commercial expansion, during which time little or no attention has been given to the problems of government, the people have suddenly realized that government is not functioning properly and that radical changes are needed. . . . Everywhere there are evidences that the nation has passed into a new political era.

In this widespread political agitation that at first sight seems so incoherent and chaotic, there may be distinguished upon examination and analysis three tendencies. The first of these tendencies is found in the insistence by the best men in all political parties that special, minority, and corrupt influence in government—national, state, and city—be removed; the second tendency is found in the demand that the structure or machinery of government, which has hitherto been admirably adapted to control by the few, be so changed and modified that it will be more difficult for the few, and easier for the many, to control; and, finally, the third tendency is found in the rapidly growing conviction that the functions of government at present are too restricted and that they must be increased and extended to relieve social and economic distress. These three tendencies with varying emphasis are seen today in the platform and program of every political party; they are manifested in the political changes and reforms that are advocated and made in the nation, the states, and the cities; and, because of their universality and definiteness, they may be said to constitute the real progressive movement. . . .

While the people were engaged in the search for corruption and its sources, the need of governmental interference to relieve social conditions became more and more pressing. In order to pass laws of this kind, the people had found it necessary to find and remove the corrupt influences which had so vigorously opposed any ameliorative measures. They now found it necessary, in order to keep out this corrupt influence and at the same time to make the government more responsive to their demands, to modify it in many important particulars. . . .

The point at which the government was most vulnerable under the attacks of special interests was in the elections known as the primaries. The primary elections, strangely enough, have always been considered secondary. They were, for a long time, uncontrolled by law. Some agency had to control them, and the extra-legal agency, the political party, acting through the political boss, with astonishing unselfishness, undertook the task which had been unprovided for by the law. These primary elections determined who was to control the party, who were to be the delegates to the various conventions which nominated men for office. The easiest and least expensive method of controlling the government was to control the man who controlled the [delegate] primaries. That man could control the selection of delegates; and, by consequence, the delegates themselves. The delegates controlled the nominations and therefore the nominees. The nominees—the governor, the legislators, the judges—controlled the government.

If the corrupting interests failed to dominate the primaries; if candidates, by some miracle, were nominated who were known to oppose them, the next step was to prevent the election of these candidates. The ways of accomplishing this result were many. If necessary, men could be bought to vote against the dangerous candidate. But such extremes were not always necessary. The newspapers could be induced to print scurrilous attacks upon the integrity of the candidate. His past record could be interpreted in a malign way. He could, in general, be discredited in the minds of people too little informed to know the real merits of the case and too busy to care.

But if the candidate, in spite of all his opponents could contrive, succeeded in winning, the special interests might be supposed to be at the end of their rope. Far from it. The next step was to prevent any law injurious to their welfare from passing through the legislature. As the student of American government knows, practically all important measures are referred to committees to be discussed and reported. To corrupt some member of the committee, to induce the committee by specious arguments advanced by well-trained and well-paid lawyers, to "kill the bill" by not reporting it, was not always impossible. If the committee and the legislature proved intractable and impervious to gold and favors, the governor might be induced to see things in the right light. Unfortunately, not even our governors have been wholly free from suspicion.

If by some accident the special interests lost in the primaries, in the elections, in the legislature, and in the governor's office, there still remained the courts. Under our peculiar system of government, courts have the power to declare laws unconstitutional. The state courts are first appealed to. If, after long litigation, they decide against the special interests, the case may, if the federal constitution is involved, be taken to the federal courts. The constitution of the United States has been twisted, mutilated, rendered almost absurd in some instances, to allow special interests to appeal from state to federal courts. The fourteenth amendment, an amendment primarily concerned with the Negro problem, has under the powerful alchemy of the well-paid corporation and railroad lawyers, been transformed into a bulwark of the corporations.

Special interests, then, have seized the government at these different points, and reformers before they can enact laws in the interests of the people must strengthen the government at these points. To wrest government from the hands of the bosses and corrupt interests and keep it free, it is proposed to use direct primaries, a system which allows the people directly to nominate their candidates for office. To diminish the power of the special interests to defeat a good candidate, corrupt practices acts are being passed. . . . To abolish the domination of the legislature by special interests, reform in legislative procedure has been suggested; and better still, in many states, the people themselves, whether the legislature wills it or not, are being given the power to pass laws which they desire and to reject those which they do not. The governmental device which gives the people the right to pass laws over the head of the legislature is called the initiative; that which enables them to reject laws is known as the referendum. If the legislators continue to display too great apathy toward the interests of the people and too great predilection for the special interests, a device known as the recall is used to expel the legislators. The recall may be used also to remove from office any executive officials who are tainted through too close contact with the privilege-seeking class; to control unfaithful judges; and, perhaps even more important, to recall judicial decisions that declare a law unconstitutional. . . .

Many persons think that the progressive movement proposes to usher in the millennium by legislation. Nothing could be farther from the minds of the men and women who call themselves progressive. What they do propose to do is to bring the United States abreast of Germany and other European countries in the matter of remedial legislation. They propose to regulate the employment of women and children in factories; to impose a maximum number of hours of work a day for men under certain conditions; to provide for workingmen in their old age and for their widows and orphans when their support is taken from them; to reduce or remove the tariff and substitute in its stead a system of taxation which will fall most heavily on those best able to bear it; to adopt a minimum wage law to strengthen the needy against temptation; to strike at poverty, crime, and disease; to do everything that government can do to make our country better, nobler, purer, and life more worth living. . . .

The great outstanding issue in the 1912 campaign was the same as it had been in the 1896 campaign, Who shall rule, a majority of the voters or the special interests of a minority? Both the Democratic and Republican parties were divided within themselves on that issue, the insurgent Republicans and the progressive Democrats standing for the same principles. In each case it was a fight to capture a party. Among the leading progressives of the two parties it was tacitly understood that the Democrats would try to nominate Wilson and the Republicans La Follette.[10] If both were nominated, the progressives would support the nominee of their respective parties. If only one were nominated, that one was to receive the support of the progressive elements in both parties. And in case neither was nominated, they would consider making a bolt and establishing a third party.

The Republican convention met in Chicago in June. There was a short, sharp struggle between the delegates sent there by the special interests and those that represented the people. And the invisible government, the government of the minority, won. Taft was nominated, Roosevelt bolted, and in the agony of defeat a new party was born. . . .

The campaign that followed was an extraordinary one. Wilson and Roosevelt were both progressive; Taft was an acknowledged reactionary. In spite of the fact that the progressive forces were thus split into two factions, Wilson was elected by a safe plurality. The significance of the 1912 campaign is not that the country went Democratic; for it did not. Roosevelt and Taft together received 1,316,917 more votes than Wilson. But the country for the first time had gone progressive, because the votes cast for Wilson and Roosevelt exceeded by almost seven millions those cast for Taft. For the first time, the people of the nation recognized that a select minority, and not they, had previously controlled government; and for the first time they voted consciously and deliberately to restore the government, misused and perverted, as it had been, to the control and use of the people.

----

10. Robert Merion La Follette (1855–1925) was governor of Wisconsin and a U.S. senator. He was the first state governor to tap a university's intellectual resources for the drafting of reform legislation and to provide legislative reference services.

[**The Democratic Party**] After a long period of preparation, followed by twenty years of development, the Democratic party as an instrument of progressivism is now entering upon a period of achievement. Already a Democratic Congress has revised the tariff, passed a currency law, and provided for additional regulation of trusts and monopolies. The President and Congress have put through a long program of progressive legislation. But it is doubtful whether the Democratic party as it is at present constituted can carry out the full progressive program. It may take the first step; by reducing the tariff, enacting a presidential preference primary law, a currency law, and a law providing for greater control over corporations, it may do something to take government from the power of special interests. But unless it changes its traditional position it cannot go far in using government to relieve economic and social distress. The Democratic party has always been the conservative party, it has always gone into power as the conservative party. It was returned to power in 1912 not because it was radical, but because Roosevelt and his party were more radical. Then there is further the problem of the Solid South. So long as men in the South are chosen for their color rather than their political creed, so long as a man may oppose a reduced tariff, income tax, control of corporations, and every other progressive measure and still be elected on the Democratic ticket to the United States Senate or the House of Representatives solely because of his stand on the Negro problem, so long will there be potential dissension in the Democratic party and inability to agree permanently on a fundamental program. . . .

[**The Republican Party**] Roosevelt, at the expiration of his seven years as President, in indorsing Taft as his successor, undoubtedly believed that he would carry to completion the measures for which he, Roosevelt, had so strenuously fought. Never did a man prove more disappointing. Although everyone, including Taft in his campaign speeches, interpreted the promise in the Republican platform as a pledge to revise the tariff downward, Taft allowed Congress to revise it upward, signed the bill and then in a speech at Winona had the effrontery, as his opponents put it, to declare the Payne-Aldrich tariff the best tariff bill ever enacted. . . .

It was the tariff session of 1909, however, which more than any other single factor, drew the line sharper between progressives and reactionaries and defined the progressive movement for the country. From the first, a small group of progressive Republicans . . . opposed the bill which the Payne-Aldrich forces planned to foist upon the people. All kinds of pressure were brought to bear upon these and other opponents of the measure to make them yield. They were invited to take breakfast with the President and talk it over; when persuasion failed they were threatened with loss of patronage, and in some instances the threat was carried out. When La Follette protested against these unfair tactics and asked that certain appointments be made, the President replied that he could not take the matter up "until after the tariff bill is passed."

Convinced that the time for an open break with the administration had come, a few progressive senators and members of the House of Representatives joined together to form the National Progressive Republican League. The object of the League was stated to be "the promotion of popular government and progressive legislation." The specific reforms advocated were:

1) The election of United States senators by direct vote of the people.

2) Direct primaries for the nomination of elective officials.

3) The direct election of delegates to national conventions with opportunity for the voter to express his choice for President and Vice-President.

4) Amendments to state constitutions providing for the initiative, referendum and recall.

5) A thorough-going corrupt practices act.

The formation of this League, which grew with astonishing rapidity and was largely instrumental in obtaining reform legislation in the early part of 1912, forms at once the culmination of the progressive movement in the Republican party and the beginning of the new Progressive party. It clearly showed that there was no room for real progressives in the Republican party as it was then constituted and forced the issue of regeneration of the old party or the formation of a new one. . . .

[The Progressive Party] From the beginning of the present century down to the presidential campaign of 1912, the two great political parties of the country, the Democratic and the Republican, divided less and less on clear-cut issues. . . . Within the parties, however, there were issues which, growing more and more definite, threatened to make the differences between the two factions within each party more pronounced than the differences between the parties themselves. . . . In the Democratic party an attempt was made to organize these men by forming the Democratic Federation and adopting a definite set of principles; and similar action was taken in the Republican party by organizing the National Progressive Republican League already referred to. . . .

For years, however, the progressive elements confined their efforts to an attempt to reform their respective parties from within. The tenacity with which men cling to parties and party traditions has always been a most formidable obstacle in the way of independent reform movements. Men will brook almost any treatment and accept any compromise to ward off the vengeance of the organization or to avoid being read out of the party. And so for years while special interests everywhere had long since ceased to recognize party lines and bribed the leaders of both parties without discrimination or favor; and while the machine forces of both parties secretly united while ostensibly opposing each other and thus played on party affiliations and affections, the rank and file of the parties were loyal and voted regularly under their respective party emblems.

Such a condition of affairs, however, could not continue. Little by little the progressive, anti-machine men of both parties realized that in order to accomplish anything they must abandon party lines as the reactionary machine men of both parties did, and combine. And, when the progressive Democrats and insurgent Republicans had combined a few times to defeat some obnoxious bill proposed by the representatives of special interests, they began to find that they had more in common with each other than with the other members of their own parties, and thus the foundation was laid for the construction of a new party standing for new principles and new ideals. . . .

The differences between the two [progressive] factions within the Republican and Democratic parties had greater opportunity to develop and manifest themselves in the early part of 1912 than in any previous presidential campaign by reason of the fact that a number of states held presidential preference primaries in that year. These primaries allowed the voter, in choosing delegates to the national convention, to pledge them to vote for designated candidates for President and Vice-President. The practical result of this system was to move forward by several months the contest for delegates and to force the fight before the people instead of within the four walls of a national committee room or convention hall. Consequently, in every state in which such primaries were held, the candidates of the various factions made speeches, distributed literature, and canvassed the voters; and, inasmuch as the issues between the conservatives and progressives in the two parties were more clear cut than issues frequently are between the different parties, it is fair to say that in almost every state where preference primaries were held there was waged a campaign that for intensity of feeling and warmth of argument rivaled most contests for the presidency itself. . . .

[At the Progressive Party convention] Roosevelt was nominated for President and Johnson for Vice-President by acclamation. The most significant incident connected with Roosevelt's nomination was the seconding speech made by Jane Addams of Chicago. This speech marked the entrance of women into national politics in a new sense, and, in addition to giving tremendous impetus to the suffrage movement, drew to the Progressive party the support of thousands of women in those states where women have the right to vote. . . .

[The Socialist Party] The progressive movement in the Socialist party differs from the progressive movement in the Democratic and Republican parties, not so much in the essentials of the movement as in the emphasis placed upon them. Progressives in the Democratic and Republican parties, although they appreciate the need of extending the functions of government, emphasize primarily the elimination of organized special influence and the modification of the structure of government with a view to making it more easily controllable by the people. The Socialist party, on the other hand, places the primary emphasis on the desirability of extending the functions and activities of government in the interests of the individual and looks upon the removal of corruption and the simplification of government as mere means to that end.

The progressive movement in the Socialist party differs from the progressive movement in the Progressive party, with which it is most readily compared, not so much in the emphasis placed upon any single phase of the movement as opposed to the other phases, as in the kind and amount of emphasis placed upon one phase; i.e., the extension of the activities of government. Both the Progressive and Socialist parties believe in freeing government from special influence, in making it more responsive to public opinion and in insisting upon its use to relieve social and economic distress. Both parties agree further in regarding the first two of these phases of the movement as subordinate to the third. But they differ fundamentally with regard to the extent to which, the purposes for which, and the methods by which the activities of government should be increased.

While the Progressive party and, in an even greater degree, the Republican and Democratic parties consider the normal state of society that in which the individual does all things for himself and look upon the government as a power to be invoked only when individuals cannot adequately take care of their own interests, the Socialist party regards the ideal and normal state of society that in which all functions are exercised by the state, and accepts the present condition of affairs as an unfortunate makeshift which must sooner or later be abandoned. The

Socialist and Progressive parties both have a place in the progressive movement, but they enter it from opposite directions. Socialists start with a complete system of social cooperation and accept particular measures that extend governmental activities, such as workingmen's compensation or mothers' pensions, as steps in the right direction, but nevertheless steps only. The Progressive party starts from complete individualism as a base and accepts any remedial legislation, not as a temporary expedient, but as an end in itself. With the Socialist party, the burden of proof is on the person who opposes an enlargement of governmental functions to show that it is not needed. With the Progressive party, the burden of proof is on the person who proposes the enlargement to show that it is essential. . . .

[The Prohibition Party] So far as issues other than the drink issue are concerned, the Prohibition party has always been abreast or ahead of the progressive movement in the other political parties. In the campaign of 1912 the national platform contained planks favoring woman suffrage, the suppression of traffic in girls, protection of the rights of labor, the direct election of United States senators, the abolition of child labor, the initiative, referendum, and recall, a non-partisan tariff commission, an income tax, an inheritance tax, and practically all the other important progressive measures. The progressivism of the party, moreover, is as old as the party itself. The first national platform, adopted in 1872, advocated woman suffrage and the direct election of President and Vice-President when the other parties were unwilling to take a definite stand on any of these questions. . . .

This very willingness of the Prohibition party to accept and support a number of fundamental debatable reforms has been one of the chief causes of its lack of success. . . .

Strange as it may seem, although the Prohibition party as a party has been at a standstill since it was established, the thing for which it chiefly stands; i.e., the prohibition of the sale of intoxicating beverages, has been gaining ground. A great wave of prohibition has swept over the country, especially in the middle West and South, resulting in state-wide prohibition in many instances and in local option in others. In every state where political action has been taken, it has been taken not by the Prohibition party but by the Democratic and the Republican parties. One reason why voters when they decide in favor of prohibition go to the Democratic and Republican parties to put it into effect is because they have an innate distrust of a party that makes political capital out of a moral issue, especially when that issue involves personal liberty. A second reason closely connected with the first is the unwillingness of voters to support so-called "Sunday-school politics." Because prohibition is so largely a moral and religious issue, many ministers have been prominent in the councils of the party; and these ministers, through lack of familiarity with political methods and an inevitable tendency toward narrow-mindedness, have alienated rather than attracted supporters. In the third place, many have believed that the sole issue for which the Prohibition party stands is the abolition of the liquor traffic and that the party has no policy with regard to the other problems of the day. . . .

[Conclusion] From the consideration of the development of the progressive movement in the Democratic, Republican, Progressive, Socialist, and Prohibition parties, it must be clear that present party lines are illogical and anomalous. Each of these parties has in it hundreds of members who hold the same beliefs and support the same measures and yet they are prevented from taking united action because of party lines. What is needed and what is slowly but inevitably coming is a realignment of the supporters of different political parties. Such a realignment should place in one of the great parties those who believe in government by the few, who fear any great addition to the power of the people, and who oppose the extension of governmental authority; and in the other there should be gathered those who believe that fundamental readjustments must be made, that the many are as competent to run the government in their own interests as the few are to run it for them, that substantial changes should be made in the structure of government to give to the people a large authority, and that government and not the individual must solve modern economic and social problems. [Benjamin Parke De Witt, *The Progressive Movement* (Macmillan, 1915), vii–ix, 4–5, 21–5, 41, 43–4, 68–72, 75–7, 85, 89–90, 104–5, 107–9]

40. *The Progressive Party Platform*

The Progressive Party Convention, held in Chicago in August 1912, was a curious affair—so curious, in fact, that newspaper reporters found it difficult to characterize. In the style of Protestant religious services, every delegate was given five minutes in which to offer political testimony. Theodore Roosevelt's address was entitled "Confession of Faith." Roosevelt was so popular with this crowd that the delegates substituted Roosevelt's name for Jesus' in singing an old revivalist hymn. The theme song of the convention was "Battle Hymn of the Republic." Following the keynote address by former Senator Albert Beveridge, the audience broke into "Onward Christian Soldiers" as they paraded through the hall—led by the head of the New York delegation, Oscar S. Straus, a prominent Jewish political leader. Despite this appearance of solidarity, real issues were contested. While the nationalists who followed the theories of Croly, Weyl, and Lippmann prevailed against more populist elements on the issue of industrial monopolies, strong antitrust sentiments remained. A second contentious issue was the "Negro question." Roosevelt, who had a strong black following in both the south and the north, wanted a national party; this idea was supported by many white southern Progressives. Those same southern Progressives thought that elite-managed segregation and voter restrictions were the southern blacks' best protections against violence and possible race war. Roosevelt and his most prominent black supporter, Booker T. Washington, both shared this view. The issue was complicated by the presence at the convention of Eleanor Garrison, granddaughter of the abolitionist William Lloyd Garrison, who was attending the convention as a delegate from Massachusetts. By portraying their party as the true heir of Lincoln's party, Garrison's group tried to force Roosevelt to recognize the rival slates of black delegates sent from three southern states and to adopt a strong plank against southern segregation. In the event, the platform was silent on the issue, and no blacks sat on southern delegations.[11] In other respects, however, the Platform documented the success of more than three decades of Progressive political and social thought. Especially successful were the planks on social and industrial justice, drafted largely by Florence Kelley and Jane Addams. Addams seconded Roosevelt's presidential nomination.

—1912—

The conscience of the people, in a time of grave national problems, has called into being a new party, born of the nation's sense of justice. We of the Progressive party here dedicate ourselves to the fulfillment of the duty laid upon us by our fathers to maintain the government of the people, by the people and for the people whose foundations they laid.

We hold with Thomas Jefferson and Abraham Lincoln that the people are the masters of their Constitution, to fulfill its purposes and to safeguard it from those who, by perversion of its intent, would convert it into an instrument of injustice. In accordance with the needs of each

---

11. On both of these issues and the convention generally, see Crunden, *Ministers of Reform* (1984), chapter 7, passim.

generation the people must use their sovereign powers to establish and maintain equal opportunity and industrial justice, to secure which this Government was founded and without which no republic can endure.

This country belongs to the people who inhabit it. Its resources, its business, its institutions and its laws should be utilized, maintained or altered in whatever manner will best promote the general interest.

It is time to set the public welfare in the first place.

THE OLD PARTIES. Political parties exist to secure responsible government and to execute the will of the people.

From these great tasks both of the old parties have turned aside. Instead of instruments to promote the general welfare, they have become the tools of corrupt interests which use them impartially to serve their selfish purposes. Behind the ostensible government sits enthroned an invisible government owing no allegiance and acknowledging no responsibility to the people.

To destroy this invisible government, to dissolve the unholy alliance between corrupt business and corrupt politics is the first task of the statesmanship of the day.

The deliberate betrayal of its trust by the Republican party, the fatal incapacity of the Democratic party to deal with the new issues of the new time, have compelled the people to forge a new instrument of government through which to give effect to their will in laws and institutions.

Unhampered by tradition, uncorrupted by power, undismayed by the magnitude of the task, the new party offers itself as the instrument of the people to sweep away old abuses, to build a new and nobler commonwealth.

A COVENANT WITH THE PEOPLE. This declaration is our covenant with the people, and we hereby bind the party and its candidates in State and Nation to the pledges made herein.

THE RULE OF THE PEOPLE. The National Progressive party, committed to the principles of government by a self-controlled democracy expressing its will through representatives of the people, pledges itself to secure such alterations in the fundamental law of the several States and of the United States as shall insure the representative character of the government.

In particular, the party declares for direct primaries for the nomination of State and National officers, for nation-wide preferential primaries for candidates for the presidency; for the direct election of United

States Senators by the people; and we urge on the States the policy of the short ballot, with responsibility to the people secured by the initiative, referendum and recall.

AMENDMENT OF CONSTITUTION. The Progressive party, believing that a free people should have the power from time to time to amend their fundamental law so as to adapt it progressively to the changing needs of the people, pledges itself to provide a more easy and expeditious method of amending the Federal Constitution.

NATION AND STATE. Up to the limit of the Constitution, and later by amendment of the Constitution, if found necessary, we advocate bringing under effective national jurisdiction those problems which have expanded beyond reach of the individual States.

It is as grotesque as it is intolerable that the several States should by unequal laws in matter of common concern become competing commercial agencies, barter the lives of their children, the health of their women and the safety and well being of their working people for the benefit of their financial interests.

The extreme insistence on States' rights by the Democratic party in the Baltimore platform demonstrates anew its inability to understand the world into which it has survived or to administer the affairs of a union of States which have in all essential respects become one people.

EQUAL SUFFRAGE. The Progressive party, believing that no people can justly claim to be a true democracy which denies political rights on account of sex, pledges itself to the task of securing equal suffrage to men and women alike.

CORRUPT PRACTICES. We pledge our party to legislation that will compel strict limitation of all campaign contributions and expenditures, and detailed publicity of both before as well as after primaries and elections.

PUBLICITY AND PUBLIC SERVICE. We pledge our party to legislation compelling the registration of lobbyists; publicity of committee hearings except on foreign affairs, and recording of all votes in committee; and forbidding federal appointees from holding office in State or National political organizations, or taking part as officers or delegates in political conventions for the nomination of elective State or National officials.

THE COURTS. The Progressive party demands such restriction of the power of the courts as shall leave to the people the ultimate authority to determine fundamental questions of social welfare and public policy. To secure this end, it pledges itself to provide:

1. That when an Act, passed under the police power of the State, is held unconstitutional under the State Constitution, by the courts, the people, after an ample interval for deliberation, shall have an opportunity to vote on the question whether they desire the Act to become law, notwithstanding such decision.

2. That every decision of the highest appellate court of a State declaring an Act of the Legislature unconstitutional on the ground of its violation of the Federal Constitution shall be subject to the same review by the Supreme Court of the United States as is now accorded to decisions sustaining such legislation.

ADMINISTRATION OF JUSTICE. The Progressive party, in order to secure to the people a better administration of justice and by that means to bring about a more general respect for the law and the courts, pledges itself to work unceasingly for the reform of legal procedure and judicial methods.

We believe that the issuance of injunctions in cases arising out of labor disputes should be prohibited when such injunctions would not apply when no labor disputes existed.

We also believe that a person cited for contempt in labor disputes, except when such contempt was committed in the actual presence of the court or so near thereto as to interfere with the proper administration of justice, should have a right to trial by jury.

SOCIAL AND INDUSTRIAL JUSTICE. The supreme duty of the Nation is the conservation of human resources through an enlightened measure of social and industrial justice. We pledge ourselves to work unceasingly in State and Nation for:

Effective legislation looking to the prevention of industrial accidents, occupational diseases, overwork, involuntary unemployment, and other injurous effects incident to modern industry;

The fixing of minimum safety and health standards for the various occupations, and the exercise of the public authority of State and Nation, including the Federal Control over interstate commerce, and the taxing power, to maintain such standards;

The prohibition of child labor;

Minimum wage standards for working women, to provide a "living wage" in all industrial occupations;

The general prohibition of night work for women and the establishment of an eight hour day for women and young persons;

One day's rest in seven for all wage workers;

The eight hour day in continuous twenty-four hour industries;

The abolition of the convict contract labor system; substituting a system of prison production for governmental consumption only; and the application of prisoners' earnings to the support of their dependent families;

Publicity as to wages, hours and conditions of labor; full reports upon industrial accidents and diseases, and the opening to public inspection of all tallies, weights, measures and check systems on labor products;

Standards of compensation for death by industrial accident and injury and trade disease which will transfer the burden of lost earnings from the families of working people to the industry, and thus to the community;

The protection of home life against the hazards of sickness, irregular employment and old age through the adoption of a system of social insurance adapted to American use;

The development of the creative labor power of America by lifting the last load of illiteracy from American youth and establishing continuation schools for industrial education under public control and encouraging agricultural education and demonstration in rural schools;

The establishment of industrial research laboratories to put the methods and discoveries of science at the service of American producers;

We favor the organization of the workers, men and women, as a means of protecting their interests and of promoting their progress.

DEPARTMENT OF LABOR. We pledge our party to establish a department of labor with a seat in the cabinet, and with wide jurisdiction over matters affecting the conditions of labor and living.

COUNTRY LIFE. The development and prosperity of country life are as important to the people who live in the cities as they are to the farmers. Increase of prosperity on the farm will favorably affect the cost of living, and promote the interests of all who dwell in the country, and all who depend upon its products for clothing, shelter and food.

We pledge our party to foster the development of agricultural credit and co-operation, the teaching of agriculture in schools, agricultural college extension, the use of mechanical power on the farm, and to re-establish the Country Life Commission, thus directly promoting the welfare of the farmers, and bringing the benefits of better farming, better business and better living within their reach.

HIGH COST OF LIVING. The high cost of living is due partly to worldwide and partly to local causes; partly to natural and partly to artificial causes. The measures proposed in this platform on various subjects such as the tariff, the trusts and conservation, will of themselves remove the artificial causes.

There will remain other elements such as the tendency to leave the country for the city, waste, extravagance, bad system of taxation, poor methods of raising crops and bad business methods in marketing crops.

To remedy these conditions requires the fullest information and based on this information, effective government supervision and control to remove all the artificial causes. We pledge ourselves to such full and immediate inquiry and to immediate action to deal with every need such inquiry discloses.

HEALTH. We favor the union of all the existing agencies of the Federal Government dealing with the public health into a single national health service without discrimination against or for anyone set of therapeutic methods, school of medicine, or school of healing with such additional powers as may be necessary to enable it to perform efficiently such duties in the protection of the public from preventable diseases as may be properly undertaken by the Federal authorities, including the executing of existing laws regarding pure food, quarantine and cognate subjects, the promotion of vital statistics and the extension of the registration area of such statistics, and co-operation with the health activities of the various States and cities of the Nation.

BUSINESS. We believe that true popular government, justice and prosperity go hand in hand, and, so believing, it is our purpose to secure that large measure of general prosperity which is the fruit of legitimate and honest business, fostered by equal justice and by sound progressive laws.

We demand that the test of true prosperity shall be the benefits conferred thereby on all the citizens, not confined to individuals or classes, and that the test of corporate efficiency shall be the ability better to serve the public; that those who profit by control of business affairs shall justify that profit and that control by sharing with the public the fruits thereof.

We therefore demand a strong National regulation of inter-State corporations. The corporation is an essential part of modern business. The concentration of modern business, in some degree, is both inevitable and necessary for national and international business efficiency. But the existing concentration of vast wealth under a corporate system, unguarded and uncontrolled by the Nation, has placed in the hands of a few men enormous, secret, irresponsible power over the daily life of the citizen—a power insufferable in a free Government and certain of abuse.

This power has been abused, in monopoly of National resources, in stock watering, in unfair competition and unfair privileges, and finally in sinister influences on the public agencies of State and Nation. We do not fear commercial power, but we insist that it shall be exercised openly, under publicity, supervision and regulation of the most efficient sort, which will preserve its good while eradicating and preventing its ill.

To that end we urge the establishment of a strong Federal administrative commission of high standing, which shall maintain permanent active supervision over industrial corporations engaged in inter-State commerce, or such of them as are of public importance, doing for them what the Government now does for the National banks, and what is now done for the railroads by the Inter-State Commerce Commission.

Such a commission must enforce the complete publicity of those corporation transactions which are of public interest; must attack unfair competition, false capitalization and special privilege, and by continuous trained watchfulness guard and keep open equally all the highways of American commerce.

Thus the business man will have certain knowledge of the law, and will be able to conduct his business easily in conformity therewith; the investor will find security for his capital; dividends will be rendered more certain, and the savings of the people will be drawn naturally and safely into the channels of trade.

Under such a system of constructive regulation, legitimate business, freed from confusion, uncertainty and fruitless litigation, will develop normally in response to the energy and enterprise of the American business man.

We favor strengthening the Sherman Law by prohibiting agreement to divide territory or limit output; refusing to sell to customers who buy from business rivals; to sell below cost in certain areas while maintaining higher prices in other places; using the power of transportation to aid or injure special business concerns; and other unfair trade practices.[12]

---

12. This controversial paragraph on antitrust was not included in the platform version given to the press and might have been left in the *Platform* through oversight. See Crunden, *Ministers of Reform* (1984), 222.

PATENTS. We pledge ourselves to the enactment of a patent law which will make it impossible for patents to be suppressed or used against the public welfare in the interests of injurious monopolies.

INTER-STATE COMMERCE COMMISSION. We pledge our party to secure to the Inter-State Commerce Commission the power to value the physical property of railroads. In order that the power of the commission to protect the people may not be impaired or destroyed, we demand the abolition of the Commerce Court.

CURRENCY. We believe there exists imperative need for prompt legislation for the improvement of our National currency system. We believe the present method of issuing notes through private agencies is harmful and unscientific.

The issue of currency is fundamentally a Government function and the system should have as basic principles soundness and elasticity. The control should be lodged with the Government and should be protected from domination or manipulation by Wall Street or any special interests.

We are opposed to the so-called Aldrich currency bill, because its provisions would place our currency and credit system in private hands, not subject to effective public control.

COMMERCIAL DEVELOPMENT. The time has come when the Federal Government should co-operate with manufacturers and producers in extending our foreign commerce. To this end we demand adequate appropriations by Congress, and the appointment of diplomatic and consular officers solely with a view to their special fitness and worth, and not in consideration of political expediency.

It is imperative to the welfare of our people that we enlarge and extend our foreign commerce.

In every way possible our Federal Government should co-operate in this important matter. Germany's policy of co-operation between government and business has, in comparatively few years, made that nation a leading competitor for the commerce of the world.

CONSERVATION. The natural resources of the Nation must be promptly developed and generously used to supply the people's needs, but we cannot safely allow them to be wasted, exploited, monopolized or controlled against the general good. We heartily favor the policy of conservation, and we pledge our party to protect the National forests without hindering their legitimate use for the benefit of all the people.

Agricultural lands in the National forests are, and should remain, open to the genuine settler. Conservation will not retard legitimate development. The honest settler must receive his patent promptly, without hindrance, rules or delays.

We believe that the remaining forests, coal and oil lands, water powers and other natural resources still in State or National control (except agricultural lands) are more likely to be wisely conserved and utilized for the general welfare if held in the public hands.

In order that consumers and producers, managers and workmen, now and hereafter, need not pay toll to private monopolies of power and raw material, we demand that such resources shall be retained by the State or Nation, and opened to immediate use under laws which will encourage development and make to the people a moderate return for benefits conferred.

In particular we pledge our party to require reasonable compensation to the public for water power rights hereafter granted by the public.

We pledge legislation to lease the public grazing lands under equitable provisions now pending which will increase the production of food for the people and thoroughly safeguard the rights of the actual homemaker. Natural resources, whose conservation is necessary for the National welfare, should be owned or controlled by the Nation.

GOOD ROADS. We recognize the vital importance of good roads and we pledge our party to foster their extension in every proper way, and we favor the early construction of National highways. We also favor the extension of the rural free delivery service.

ALASKA. The coal and other natural resources of Alaska should be opened to development at once. They are owned by the people of the United States, and are safe from monopoly, waste or destruction only while so owned.

We demand that they shall neither be sold nor given away, except under the Homestead Law, but while held in Government ownership shall be opened to use promptly upon liberal terms requiring immediate development.

Thus the benefit of cheap fuel will accrue to the Government of the United States and to the people of Alaska and the Pacific Coast; the settlement of extensive agricultural lands will be hastened; the extermination of the salmon will be prevented and the just and wise development of Alaskan resources will take the place of private extortion or monopoly.

We demand also that extortion or monopoly in transportation shall be prevented by the prompt acquisition, construction or improvement by the Government of such railroads, harbor and other facilities for transportation as the welfare of the people may demand.

We promise the people of the Territory of Alaska the same measure of legal self-government that was given to other American territories, and that Federal officials appointed there shall be qualified by previous *bona-fide* residence in the Territory.

WATERWAYS. The rivers of the United States are the natural arteries of this continent. We demand that they shall be opened to traffic as indispensable parts of a great Nation-wide system of transportation, in which the Panama Canal will be the central link, thus enabling the whole interior of the United States to share with the Atlantic and Pacific seaboards in the benefit derived from the canal.

It is a National obligation to develop our rivers, and especially the Mississippi and its tributaries, without delay, under a comprehensive general plan covering each river system from its source to its mouth, designed to secure its highest usefulness for navigation, irrigation, domestic supply, water power and the prevention of floods.

We pledge our party to the immediate preparation of such a plan, which should be made and carried out in close and friendly co-operation between the Nation, the States and the cities affected.

Under such a plan, the destructive floods of the Mississippi and other streams, which represent a vast and needless loss to the Nation, would be controlled by forest conservation and water storage at the headwaters, and by levees below; land sufficient to support millions of people would be reclaimed from the deserts and the swamps, water power enough to transform the industrial standings of whole States would be developed, adequate water terminals would be provided, transportation by river would revive, and the railroads would be compelled to co-operate as freely with the boat lines as with each other.

The equipment, organization and experience acquired in constructing the Panama Canal soon will be available for the Lakes-to-the-Gulf deep waterway and other portions of this great work, and should be utilized by the Nation in co-operation with the various States, at the lowest net cost to the people.

PANAMA CANAL. The Panama Canal, built and paid for by the American people, must be used primarily for their benefit.

We demand that the canal shall be so operated as to break the transportation monopoly now held and misused by the transcontinental railroads by maintaining sea competition with them; that ships directly or indirectly owned or controlled by American railroad corporations shall not be permitted to use the canal, and that American ships engaged in coastwise trade shall pay no tolls.

The Progressive party will favor legislation having for its aim the development of friendship and commerce between the United States and Latin-American nations.

TARIFF. We believe in a protective tariff which shall equalize conditions of competition between the United States and foreign countries, both for the farmer and the manufacturer, and which shall maintain for labor an adequate standard of living.

Primarily the benefit of any tariff should be disclosed in the pay envelope of the laborer. We declare that no industry deserves protection which is unfair to labor or which is operating in violation of Federal law. We believe that the presumption is always in favor of the consuming public.

We demand tariff revision because the present tariff is unjust to the people of the United States. Fair dealing toward the people requires an immediate downward revision of those schedules wherein duties are shown to be unjust or excessive.

We pledge ourselves to the establishment of a non-partisan scientific tariff commission, reporting both to the President and to either branch of Congress, which shall report, first, as to the costs of production, efficiency of labor, capitalization, industrial organization and efficiency and the general competitive position in this country and abroad of industries seeking protection from Congress; second, as to the revenue-producing power of the tariff and its relation to the resources of Government; and, third, as to the effect of the tariff on prices, operations of middlemen, and on the purchasing power of the consumer.

We believe that this commission should have plenary power to elicit information, and for this purpose to prescribe a uniform system of accounting for the great protected industries. The work of the commission should not prevent the immediate adoption of acts reducing these schedules generally recognized as excessive.

We condemn the Payne-Aldrich bill as unjust to the people. The Republican organization is in the hands of those who have broken, and cannot again be trusted to keep, the promise of necessary downward revision.

The Democratic party is committed to the destruction of the protective system through a tariff for revenue only—a policy which would inevitably produce widespread industrial and commercial disaster.

We demand the immediate repeal of the Canadian Reciprocity Act.

INHERITANCE AND INCOME TAX. We believe in a graduated inheritance tax as a National means of equalizing the obligations of holders of property to Government, and we hereby pledge our party to enact such a Federal law as will tax large inheritances, returning to the States an equitable percentage of all amounts collected.

We favor the ratification of the pending amendment to the Constitution giving the Government power to levy an income tax.

PEACE AND NATIONAL DEFENSE. The Progressive party deplores the survival in our civilization of the barbaric system of warfare among nations with its enormous waste of resources even in time of peace, and the consequent impoverishment of the life of the toiling masses. We pledge the party to use its best endeavors to substitute judicial and other peaceful means of settling international differences.

We favor an international agreement for the limitation of naval forces. Pending such an agreement, and as the best means of preserving peace, we pledge ourselves to maintain for the present the policy of building two battleships a year.

TREATY RIGHTS. We pledge our party to protect the rights of American citizenship at home and abroad. No treaty should receive the sanction of our Government which discriminates between American citizens because of birthplace, race, or religion, or that does not recognize the absolute right of expatriation.

THE IMMIGRANT. Through the establishment of industrial standards we propose to secure to the able-bodied immigrant and to his native fellow workers a larger share of American opportunity.

We denounce the fatal policy of indifference and neglect which has left our enormous immigrant population to become the prey of chance and cupidity.

We favor Governmental action to encourage the distribution of immigrants away from the congested cities, to rigidly supervise all private agencies dealing with them and to promote their assimilation, education and advancement.

PENSIONS. We pledge ourselves to a wise and just policy of pensioning American soldiers and sailors and their widows and children by the Federal Government. And we approve the policy of the southern States in granting pensions to the ex-Confederate soldiers and sailors and their widows and children.

PARCEL POST. We pledge our party to the immediate creation of a parcel post, with rates proportionate to distance and service.

CIVIL SERVICE. We condemn the violations of the Civil Service Law under the present administration, including the coercion and assessment of subordinate employees, and the President's refusal to punish such violation after a finding of guilty by his own commission; his distribution of patronage among subservient congressmen, while withholding it from those who refuse support of administration measures; his withdrawal of nominations from the Senate until political support for himself was secured, and his open use of the offices to reward those who voted for his renomination.

To eradicate these abuses, we demand not only the enforcement of the civil service act in letter and spirit, but also legislation which will bring under the competitive system postmasters, collectors, marshals, and all other non-political officers, as well as the enactment of an equitable retirement law, and we also insist upon continuous service during good behavior and efficiency.

GOVERNMENT BUSINESS ORGANIZATION. We pledge our party to readjustment of the business methods of the National Government and a proper co-ordination of the Federal bureaus, which will increase the economy and efficiency of the Government service, prevent duplications, and secure better results to the taxpayers for every dollar expended.

GOVERNMENT SUPERVISION OVER INVESTMENTS. The people of the United States are swindled out of many millions of dollars every year, through worthless investments. The plain people, the wage earner and the men and women with small savings, have no way of knowing the merit of concerns sending out highly colored prospectuses offering stock for sale, prospectuses that make big returns seem certain and fortunes easily within grasp.

We hold it to be the duty of the Government to protect its people from this kind of piracy. We, therefore, demand wise, carefully thought out legislation that will give us such Governmental supervision over this matter as will furnish to the people of the United States this much-needed protection, and we pledge ourselves thereto.

CONCLUSION. On these principles and on the recognized desirability of uniting the Progressive forces of the Nation into an organization which shall unequivocally represent the Progressive spirit and policy we appeal for the support of all American citizens, without regard to previous political affiliations.

Further Reading

Crunden, Robert, *Ministers of Reform* (University of Illinois Press, 1984).

Eisenach, Eldon, *The Lost Promise of Progressivism* (University Press of Kansas, 1994).

Forcey, Charles, *Crossroads of Liberalism: Croly, Weyl, Lippmann, and the Progressive Era* (Oxford University Press, 1961).

Levy, David W., *Herbert Croly of "The New Republic"* (Princeton University Press, 1985).

Steel, Ronald, *Walter Lippmann and the American Century* (Little, Brown, 1980).

Witt, John Fabian, *The Accidental Republic: Crippled Workingmen, Destitute Widows, and the Remaking of American Law* (Harvard University Press, 2004).

Zunz, Olivier, *Why the American Century?* (University of Chicago Press, 1998).

10

American Progressivism
Triumphant in the World

The Progressive vision of America's future was inseparable from its vision of America as the dominant force for justice in the world; thus, Progressive internationalism was an integral part of Progressive nationalism. From the start, the Progressive movement's German-educated social scientists were taught to place national states, societies, and economies in comparative perspective. Their textbooks were filled with comparative data from European and other advancing societies. Reformers of every stripe—social and settlement house workers and experts on municipal government, pension plans, workers' compensation, and public transportation—all drew upon materials from outside America's borders in their work.

The ecumenical foreign missionary activities of American Protestant churches provided another major source of internationalism. While an undergraduate at Cornell University in 1888, John R. Mott (1865–1955) founded the Student Volunteer Movement to recruit and train college students for one-year terms as foreign missionaries. Within a few years, six thousand students had signed on; by 1917, twenty thousand students had participated. The international YMCA and the World Student Christian Federation, both of which Mott led, were even larger in scale and scope.[1] By 1917, Mott's reputation and political power were such that President Wilson sent Mott on a diplomatic mission to Russia. During the war, Mott organized twenty-six thousand volunteer international aid workers through the YMCA to work with war prisoners and refugees. Mott helped found the World Council of Churches in 1946, the same year he won the Nobel Peace Prize.

W.D.P. Bliss' *The New Encyclopedia of Social Reform* (1908) stands as a literary monument to Progressive internationalism. The book's subtitle promises that the *Encyclopedia* is a compendium of "all social-reform movements and activities, and the economic, industrial, and sociological facts and statistics of all countries and all social subjects."

---

1. Eisenach, "Progressive Internationalism" (1999), 232–3. Protestant foreign missions in this period were largely oriented to social service rather than conversion; about 70 percent of the missionaries were non-clergy.

Although Bliss (the son of foreign missionaries) recruited contributors from all major countries, American Progressives were clearly given pride of place, with English reformers running a distant second. Florence Kelley, Edward Devine, Booker T. Washington, and Franklin Giddings were among the contributors to the *Encyclopedia*; Jane Addams, Richard Ely, and Theodore Roosevelt were given honorary contributory status because their writings were quoted so extensively. In a sense, *The New Encyclopedia* was something of a handbook for a Progressive-Social Gospel-Social Democratic Internationale. Although this Progressive internationale was headquartered in America, it maintained powerful centers throughout the English-speaking world and in the advanced states of Europe, especially Germany.[2]

Given this moral and missionary dimension of Progressive internationalism, it was no surprise that American Progressives—including most of those whose selections appear in this collection—took the lead in urging American preparedness and intervention when war broke out in Europe. What was surprising, however, was the extent to which the Progressives relied on "public opinion" and voluntarism in their efforts to mobilize for war. Such reliance was made possible by the extensive infrastructure of nationally oriented reform institutions and organizations that the Progressives themselves had largely created. The results were incredible. The initial funding for allied loans was offered voluntarily, with an initial subscription in June 1917, of $3 billion in "Liberty Loans," an amount that increased to $25 billion within two years to finance America's war costs. George Creel's Committee on Public Information, the government's propaganda agency, enlisted 150,000 volunteer academics, intellectuals, writers, and speakers to flood America with its messages of wartime preparedness. The 1,400 paid employees of Herbert Hoover's Food Administration directed a veritable army of 750,000 volunteer housewives in allocating and rationing the nation's food supply.[3] The war effort's crowning achievement, however, was military conscription. A staff of 429 paid federal employees coordinated 192,000 volunteer draft administrators. Two weeks to the day after Congress passed the Conscription Act, 9,500,000 men had presented themselves to local draft boards.

Woodrow Wilson, who headed the major party most opposed to

---

2. Kloppenberg, *Uncertain Victory* (1986) is especially good on the intellectual and cultural crosscurrents; Rodgers, *Atlantic Crossings* (1998) is especially strong on the international interchange of public policy ideas.

3. In the process, Hoover, by enlisting Jane Addams to play a prominent role, rescued her from public obloquy for her pacifist opposition to preparedness and war.

military preparedness and intervention in Europe, was speaking largely for a constituency that had rallied around the Progressive Party in 1912 when he said:

> Our participation in the war established our position among the nations . . . the whole world saw at last . . . a Nation they had deemed material and now found to be compact of the spiritual forces that must free men of every nation of every unworthy bondage. . . . The stage is set, the destiny is disclosed. It has come about by no plan of our conceiving, but by the hand of God who led us into this way. We cannot turn back. We can only go forward . . . to follow the vision. It was of this that we dreamed at our birth. America shall in truth show the way. (Speech to the Senate, July 10, 1919).

Although we now know that this burning triumphalism soon turned to ashes, both at home and abroad, it did not flame out until after a final surge of postwar reform idealism coursed through the Progressive ranks.

There is no satisfactory way to close this collection on Progressive social and political thought, because the aftermath of the war left Progressive reform so fractured, demoralized, and weakened at all levels.[4] The selections in this chapter try to capture only the nationalist-internationalist enthusiasm and hope that characterized Progressive social and political thought from the very start.

41. *The Americanization of the World*, William T. Stead (1849–1912)

The son of a Congregationalist preacher, Stead was born in Embleton, Northumberland, England. Stead began his career as a provincial journalist after grammar school but was soon called to London's Pall Mall Gazette to assist its editor, John Morley, who was a follower of—and journalistic successor to—John Stuart Mill. When Morley was elected to Parliament, Stead turned the paper into a crusading and innovative organ of liberal reform. Although the paper was best known for its attacks

---

4. The most dramatic example was the attempt to consolidate all religious and national reform forces through a vast ecumenical organization called the Interchurch World Movement for an American-led postwar world conquest of poverty, disease, oppression, and injustice. They wanted to raise 175 billion dollars in the first year, with a five-year goal of more than a third of a billion dollars. It began in 1920 with a paid staff of more than twenty-six hundred. Not even ten percent of its financial goal was reached, and it was soon dissolved. See Eisenach, "Progressive Internationalism" (1999), 242–3.

*on child prostitution, it also aimed to aid what Stead generally termed the
"submerged tenth, a grand and doleful army of criminals, paupers,
prostitutes, drunkards, tramps, the houseless, the homeless, in short the
great Army of Despair."[5] Stead then founded the* Review of Reviews, *a
monthly digest of the best writings from the English speaking periodicals
and daily press. The* Review's *American counterpart was edited by Albert
Shaw (1857–1947), a graduate of Grinnell (Iowa) College, with a PhD
in political science from Johns Hopkins University. Shaw had close ties to
Theodore Roosevelt and the broader world of municipal reform. Stead
came to Chicago during the World's Columbian Exposition in 1893.
There he met with Jane Addams and launched a journalistic investigation
of Chicago's own "submerged tenth." On November 12, 1893, Stead
called a civic meeting to discuss his findings. At the meeting he collected
$200,000 to fund an experiment in work relief. The Civic Federation of
Chicago, a reform and civic betterment group that is still active today,
was formed at that meeting. Drawing on his experiences in Chicago,
Stead wrote* Chicago Today *(1894) and* If Christ Came to Chicago
*(1894). The latter book was an imaginative portrait of what a thoroughly
reformed Chicago might become: the moral, industrial, political, and
financial capital of the world. Stead began his political life as a liberal
imperialist and strong supporter of William Gladstone (1809–1898), the
Prime Minister of Great Britain whom Stead's journalistic crusades had
helped restore to power. Although Cecil Rhodes, the famous diamond
magnate and imperialist, initially made Stead the executor of his vast
estate, Rhodes broke with Stead when the journalist opposed the Boer
War in 1898. It was Stead who convinced Rhodes to include America,
and not just British colonies, in his now-famous scholarship program. In
1912, Stead embarked on another trip to America, this time to give the
opening address on world peace at a meeting in New York of "Men and
Religion Forward," an ecumenical organization. Unfortunately, he
booked passage on the* Titanic. *Throughout his life, Stead dreamed of a
peaceful and progressive world led by an alliance of the English-speaking
community headed by the United States. The following selection is taken
from* The Americanization of the World, *one expression of this hope.*

—1901—

The United States of America owes no small portion of its exuberant
energies to the fact that there has poured into that Continent for the last

---

5. Stead, *Salvation Army* (1901), 14.

fifty years a never-ceasing flood of emigrants recruited for the most part from the more energetic, enterprising and adventurous members of the Old World. The United States has taken the place of the United Kingdom as the natural refuge of the political refugee. . . .

The crowded millions of the Old World who are born and live and die in the district in which they happen to be born represent the *vis inerticæ* of Europe. The nineteen millions who cross the Atlantic represent its aspirations and its energy. Many of them, no doubt, were driven westward by the scourge of starvation. But many millions who suffered as much as they, remained behind, lacking the energy necessary to transport them to another hemisphere.

The emigrant population, therefore, possesses preeminently this characteristic that it has sufficient life to have motion, sufficient faith to face the future, under the unknown conditions of a new world, and sufficient capacity to acquire the means requisite to transport them across the Atlantic. This emigration, which is often regarded by Americans as an element of danger, has probably contributed more than any other, except the Puritan education of New England, to the making of the Republic. . . .

The greatest thing which the Americans have done . . . has been the superintendence of this vast crucible. The greatest achievement was the smelting of men of all nationalities into one dominant American type, or—to vary the metaphor—weaving all these diverse threads of foreign material into one uniform texture of American civilization. . . .

The school to which his children were sent completed the operation. In one generation, or at most in two, the foreign emigrant became thoroughly Americanized, for the Americanization of the world is nowhere gaining ground more rapidly than in the Americanization of the citizens of the world, who from love of adventure, from sheer misfortune, or from any other cause, have transferred their residence from the Old World to the New. . . .

What type will ultimately issue from this crucible of the nations it is yet too early to predict. Into the crucible all the nations have cast of their best, and it would be a sore disappointment if this vast experiment in nation-making did not yield a result commensurate with the immensity of the crucible and the richness of the material cast therein.

If we in England, who from the point of view of politics and religion are much more American than we are Anglican, contemplate with satisfaction and even with enthusiasm the Americanization of the world, the process is naturally regarded with very different sentiments in other quarters. Even Anglican Englishmen can hardly refrain from a certain feeling of national pride when they see all the nations of the earth subjected to the subtle and penetrating influence of ideas which are at least conveyed in English speech, and which may in some cases be traced back to the days of the English Commonwealth. . . .

No such consolation, however, is vouchsafed to the nations of Europe, who find themselves subjected, against their will and without their leave being asked or obtained, to the process of Americanization. That the process is beneficial, that they will be better for the treatment, may be true; but they do not see it. At the same time it is well to discriminate between Europe and the Europeans that therein do dwell. To the majority of the Europeans the American invasion is by no means unwelcome, while a very large section would delight to see a much greater Americanization of Europe than anything which is likely to take place.

It is otherwise with the sovereigns and nobles, who represent feudalism and the Old World monarchical and aristocratic ideas which have as their European centre the Courts of Berlin and Vienna. . . .

The centre of resistance to American principles in Europe lies at Berlin, and the leader against and great protagonist of Americanization is the Kaiser of Germany. There is something pathetic in the heroic pose of the German Emperor resisting the American flood. It is Canute over again, but the Kaiser has not planted himself on the shore, passively to wait the rising of the tide in order to rebuke the flattery of his courtiers; he takes his stand where land and water meet, and with drawn sword defies the advancing tide. And all the while the water is percolating through the sand on which he is standing, undermining the very foundations upon which his feet are planted so that he himself is driven to Americanize, even when he is resisting Americanization.

There are no more Americanized cities in Europe than Hamburg and Berlin. They are American in the rapidity of their growth, American in their nervous energy, American in their quick appropriation of the facilities for rapid transport. Americans find themselves much more at home, notwithstanding the differences of language, in the feverish concentrated energy of the life of Hamburg and Berlin than in the more staid and conservative cities of Liverpool and London. The German manufacturer, the German shipbuilder, the German engineer, are quick to seize and use the latest American machines. The American typewriter is supreme in Germany as in Britain, and what is much more important than this, the American farmer continues to raise bread and bacon in increasing quantities for the German breakfast table. . . .

Against all these influences the Kaiser wages desperate but unavailing war. In resisting the Americanization of Germany, his first aim has naturally been to prevent the Americanization of the Germans who leave Germany. The ceaseless tide of emigration which sets westward from German shores flows for the most part to New York, the European gate of the American Continent. When once the German passes

Bartholdi's statue of Liberty Enlightening the World, he is lost to the German Empire. He may remain a German for a generation or two, cherishing his language, cultivating the literature of his country, but in ten years his children have picked up English, and in fifty years nothing but the name and family tradition remain to connect them with the Fatherland. Their descendants are no more Germans than President Roosevelt is a Dutchman. . . .

The dependence of Germany for her daily bread on shipments from overseas contributed greatly to strengthen the Kaiser's decision to double the German navy. "Our future," he declared, "lies upon the sea." The decision to double the strength of the German fighting fleet was significantly proclaimed in the ears of the world immediately after the threefold defeat of British arms in South Africa had severely shaken our prestige. That the new shipbuilding policy then announced by Germany was aimed against Great Britain was generally recognized abroad; but when the German Emperor visited London shortly afterwards he had a very different explanation to give of the increase of the German fleet. So far from being a menace to Great Britain, he is said to have protested, he regarded every new ship added to the German navy as an addition to the fighting force of the British fleet. For, he argued, it was inevitable that the United States, sooner or later would endeavor to grasp the supreme position on the sea at present held by Great Britain. . . .

In Berlin the German Industrial Union have expressed through their Secretary, Dr. Wilhelm Vendlandt, their views upon the subject. He declared that the time had come for some Bismarck to rise up and assemble the nations of Europe and throttle the American peril. Europe, he argued, could perfectly well be independent of the American market. Russia, by developing her cotton plantations in the Caucasus, had finally liberated the Old World from dependence upon the New. "I believe," he declared, "in fighting America with the same weapons of exclusion which America herself has used so remorselessly and so successfully. We propose to work for an all European Union. The commercial interests of the hour are paramount, and a discriminatory alliance of all European Powers, including England, will be the inevitable result of the American invasion."

This is all very fine and large, but what does it come to? So far it has come to nothing. The self-sufficing State which produces everything within its own frontiers has become an anachronism in the modern world. . . .

[A]lthough the Governments of the Old World may compel their subjects to pay high prices for goods which the Americans, if left unhindered, would supply more cheaply, they will thereby increase discontent and dissatisfaction, which will facilitate the Americanization of Europe. For the higher the tariff, the dearer will be food. Dear food means misery in the home. Misery in the home means discontent in the electorate, and discontent in the electorate means the increase of the motive force which will seek steadily to revolutionize the Old World governments on what may be more or less accurately described as American principles. . . .

Although the reaction against Americanizing influence finds most vigorous expression in Germany and Austria, the process of Americanization is going on steadily in all the other countries. In all the capitals and great cities from the Straits of Gibraltar to Archangel, American firms are establishing branches and the whole continent is patrolled by American commercial travellers. Berlin, Leipzig, and Dresden swarm with American students, while Paris has so large an American colony that the Chicago University [University of Chicago] is establishing an annex on the banks of the Seine. The finance Ministers of Europe are beginning to recognize more and more the influence of American commercial policy upon their revenues. Quite recently M. de Witte was provoked by a decision of the Treasury at Washington about Russian sugar to increase the import duties upon American iron and steel, and only the other day little Denmark was discussing whether or not it would be to her interest to indulge in a little tariff war with the United States.

The idea of a European solidarity of interest as against the United States is a vain dream. What difference does it make to the Austrian agriculturist whether his goods are undersold by the produce of Danish dairies or by the pork that is raised on the Western prairies? States that have a common budget may conceivably find it to their interest to protect the interests of their own taxpayers against the produce raised in a country which makes no contribution to their exchequer, but independent competing nations which have no common financial interest have no motive to discriminate between one foreign competitor and the other merely because of the difference of continent in which they dwell. . . .

It was not till the close of last century that the United States could be said to have secured the commercial primacy of the world.* But the fact

---

*The following figures condense into a nutshell the story of the last thirty years' material progress of the United States.

	[In millions]			
Products	**1870**	**1880**	**1890**	**1900**
Wheat (bu.)	287.7	459.4	309.2	522.2
Corn (bu.)	760.9	1754.8	1489.9	2105.1
Cotton (bales)	3.1	5.7	7.3	9.4
Wool (lbs.)	162.0	232.5	276.0	288.6
Petroleum (gals., 1877)	383.5	836.3	1476.8	2396.9
Bit. coal (tons, 1876)	28.9	38.2	99.3	172.6

that they would supersede us had long been foreseen by the more pre-
scient amongst us. Conspicuous among these was Mr. Gladstone, who
in 1878 and again in 1890 expressed in the clearest terms his conviction
both as to the inevitableness of the change, and also, what was more
important, his view as to the way in which it should be regarded by this
country:

> "It is America," he said, "who at a given time and probably will wrest
> from us that commercial primacy. We have no title: I have no inclination
> to murmur at the prospect. If she acquires it, she will make the acquisi-
> tion by the right of the strongest; but in this instance the strongest means
> the best. She will probably become what we are now—head servant in
> the great household of the world, the employer of all employed, because
> her service will be the most and ablest. We have no more title against her
> than Venice, or Genoa, or Holland has against us."

As to the fact that we could not possibly hope to hold our own against
the United States, Mr. Gladstone had no doubt whatever. He said:—

> "While we have been advancing with portentous rapidity, America is
> passing us by as if in a canter. There can hardly be a doubt, as between
> America and England, of the belief that the daughter at no very distant
> time (it was written in 1878) will, whether fairer or less fair, be unques-
> tionably yet stronger than the mother.". . .

The ingenuity of American mechanism, and the skill of American
engineers, have been employed for a generation past in reducing the
bread-bill of the British working man. Incidentally this has brought in
its wake agricultural depression among a minority of our people, but the
immense majority have fed and grown fat upon American harvests and
the beef and pork of American farms. If it is an evil thing to have cheap
bread, then the Americans were undoubtedly doing us an injury.

If, on the other hand, the very existence of our manufactures and our
capacity to command the markets of the world depends absolutely upon
cheap food, then the Americans have been of all people our greatest
benefactors. Imagine, for instance, if some great speculator were able to
effect such a corner in American foodstuffs as to absolutely forbid the
importation of a single carcase or a single cargo of grain, where should
we be? We should be face to face with famine, and the whole forty millions of us would be alternately filling the air with execrations against
the speculator who had cut off our supply of food from the United
States, or imploring him for the love of God to relax his interdict, and
allow our people once more to profit by drawing supplies from the
American store. . . .

The Americans have brought to us a host of ingenious inventions and admirably perfected machines which we are incapable of producing for ourselves. No one can say that in sending us the typewriter, the sewing-machine, the Linotype, the automobile, the phonograph, the telephone, the elevator, and the incandescent electric light, they invaded any British industry. These things were their inventions. After they were introduced, we imitated some of them or invented others on the same principle, but they first opened up the new fields. . . .

Mr. Chauncey M. Depew in his address to railway men at the Buffalo Exhibition gave some very interesting figures as to the growth of the American railroad. Railway freight rates in the United States were, he said, almost exactly one-third of what they were when he entered the service in 1866. At the same time the wages of the railway men have nearly doubled, the precise increase being 87.5 per cent.

As there are more than a million of them, the gain in the weekly wage bill of America from this source alone is enormous. Their annual pay bill for wages is £125,000,000, or 60 per cent of the cost of operating the lines. The United States with only 6 per cent of the land surface of the world has 40 per cent of the railroad track. Its 193,000 mileage is six times that of any other nation, and Mr. Depew declares that they haul more freight every year than is moved by all the railways and all the ships of Great Britain, France, and Germany combined. . . .

[A] very little observation will lead us to discover three of the American secrets which are capable of export. The first is Education; the second is increased incentives to Production; and the third is Democracy. . . .

It is little more than thirty years since education became compulsory in the United Kingdom; and it was in still more recent times that the school fees were abolished. But education has been universal, free, and compulsory in the United States of America from the very foundation of the New England Colonies. The first object of the Pilgrim Fathers was to found a conventicle in which they could worship God as they thought fit; but after the founding of the Church their first care was to open a school. Hence the average level of intelligence in the United States, despite the immense influx of nineteen millions of the uneducated European horde, is much higher than it is with us. In that vast Republic everyone can at least read and write, and upon that basis Americans have reared a superstructure of educational appliance which causes Englishmen to despair. Mr. Frederic Harrison, when he visited the United States last in 1900, was lost in amazement and admiration at the immense energy and lavish magnificence of the apparatus of education. "The whole educational machinery of America," he said, "must be at least tenfold that of the United Kingdom. That open to women must be at least twentyfold greater than with us, and it is rapidly advancing to meet that of men both in numbers and quality."

According to some statistics published this autumn by the *Scientific American*, there are 629 universities and colleges in the United States, the total value of whose property is estimated at £68,000,000. . . . The number of students pursuing undergraduate and graduate courses in universities, colleges, and schools of technology was 147,164. Of these only 43,913 were enrolled as students of the three professions—law, medicine, and theology. The number of students per million, which stood at 573 in 1872, rose to 770 in 1880, to 850 in 1890, whereas in 1899 it had gone up to 1,196—more than double in twenty-eight years. . . .

What is the conclusion of the whole matter? It may be stated in a sentence. There lies before the people of Great Britain a choice of two alternatives. If they decide to merge the existence of the British Empire in the United States of the English-speaking World, they may continue for all time to be an integral part of the greatest of all World-Powers, supreme on sea and unassailable on land, permanently delivered from all fear of hostile attack, and capable of wielding irresistible influence in all parts of this planet.

That is one alternative. The other is the acceptance of our supersession by the United States as the centre of gravity in the English-speaking world, the loss one by one of our great colonies, and our ultimate reduction to the status of an English-speaking Belgium. One or the other it must be. . . .

But here it is necessary to observe that, while on this side of the Atlantic there may be a great latent but powerful sentiment in favor of such reunion, it will come to nothing unless it is reciprocated by similar sentiments on the other side of the water. We may be willing to make great sacrifices of national prejudice and Imperial pride in order to attain this greater ideal, but will the Americans be equally fascinated by the ideal of race unity?

The United States, it is said by some, is quite big enough to take care of itself. It has no longer any need of a British alliance, which might entail considerable complications and involve the Republic in entanglements from which the Americans might not unnaturally recoil.

The subject is not one upon which the Americans can very well take the initiative. The suggestion has even offended some Americans, as indicating possibilities altogether beyond their reach. There is very little evidence, on one side or the other, as to what would be the probable attitude of the masses of the American people should this question be raised in a practical shape. . . .

It may be admitted by all, even those who are least favorable to the idea of complete reunion, that it would be well to keep the ideal of reunion before our eyes, if only in order to minimize points of friction and to promote cooperation in the broad field in which our interests are identical. Even if we cannot have the reunion, we might have the race alliance. This being the case, we may devote the concluding chapter in this book to a discussion of some of the suggestions which have been made for the promotion of a sense of race unity, whether or not we regard the ultimate goal as one that is within the reach of ourselves or of our descendants. . . .

The Americans are much better informed concerning English affairs than we are concerning the social, industrial and scientific movements of the United States. The news that reaches us from America is almost entirely confined to market quotations and political elections. The electoral struggles between parties in either country are as a rule the most uninteresting items of news that could be chronicled in the other.

When I was in Chicago seven years ago, I was much impressed by the immense superiority of the European news service of the Chicago papers to the American news service of the London papers. The Chicago citizen on Sunday morning would find as a rule three special correspondents' letters from London, one from Paris, and one from Berlin, telegraphed the previous night, each of the length of a column or more, giving a very intelligent, brightly written sketch of the history of the week. We have nothing approaching to that from the other side in any of our English papers. . . .

There remains the question of whether there should be an alliance, offensive or defensive, between the two States. When the United States was engaged in the war with Spain, the Americans relied very confidently upon the support of Great Britain, and to this day the belief is firmly fixed in the minds of the majority of the American people that the British Government went a great deal further than was actually the case in threatening to ally its fleet with that of the United States if the European powers ventured to intervene on behalf of Spain. . . .

Mr. Secretary Hay[6] declared in 1897 that: "It is a sanction like that of

---

6. John Hay (1838–1905) was Secretary of State under Presidents McKinley and Theodore Roosevelt. After graduating from Brown University, Hay apprenticed for the bar in a legal practice in Springfield, Illinois, next door to the office of Abraham Lincoln, and followed Lincoln to Washington as his private secretary. With John G. Nicolay, another of Lincoln's private secretaries, Hay wrote *Abraham Lincoln: A History* (1890), and edited Lincoln's *Complete Works* (1894).

religion which binds us to a sort of partnership in the beneficent work of the world. Whether we will it or not, we are associated in that work by the very nature of things, and no man and no group of men can prevent it. We are bound by a tie which we did not forge, and which we cannot break. We are joint ministers of the same sacred mission of liberty and progress, charged with duties which we cannot evade by the imposition of irresistible hands." . . .

Writing his book on the "Rise of the Empire," Sir Walter Besant[7] thus defined his conception of the great reconciliation which he believed would some day take place between the United States and the British Empire. "The one thing needful is so to legislate, so to speak and write to each other that this bond may be strengthened and not loosened. We want, should a time opportune arrive, to separate only in form. We want an everlasting alliance, offensive and defensive, such an alliance as may make us absolutely free from the fear of any other alliance which could crush us." . . .

The swelling phrase, "dominion of the World," is one at which long experience teaches us to look askance. It should be no ambition of ours to dominate the world save by the influence of ideas and the force of our example. The temptation to believe that we are the Viceregent of the Almighty, charged with the thunderbolt of Heaven, for the punishment of evildoers, is one of the subtle temptations by which the Evil One lures well-meaning people to embark upon a course of policy which soon becomes indistinguishable from buccaneering pure and simple.

But when all due allowance has been made for the danger of exposing the English-speaking man to the temptation of almost irresistible power, the advantages to be gained by the Reunion of the Race are so great as to justify our incurring the risk. . . .

I have now concluded a very rapid and most imperfect survey of some of the more potent forces which are Americanizing the world. There remains the great question whether the processes now visible in operation around us will make for the progress and the betterment of the world.

When Mr. Gladstone contemplated what he called "the paramount question of the American future" he expressed himself with the same sense of awe which filled the Hebrew prophet when he had a vision of the glory of the Lord and His train filled the Temple.

---

7. Walter Besant (1836–1901) was a British novelist and philanthropist best known for his work chronicling life in the East London slums.

"There is a vision," said Mr. Gladstone, "of territory, population, power, passing beyond all experience. The exhibition to mankind for the first time in history of free institutions on a gigantic scale is momentous."

With his inveterate optimism, he declared that he had enough faith in freedom to believe that it would work powerfully for good: —

"But together with and behind these vast developments there will come a corresponding opportunity of social and moral influence to be exercised over the rest of the world, and the question of questions for us as trustees for our posterity is, what will be the nature of this influence? Will it make us, the children of the senior race, living together under its action, better or worse? Not what manner of producer, but what manner of man is the American of the future to be? How is the majestic figure, who is to become the largest and most powerful on the stage of the world's history, to make use of his power?"

And then Mr. Gladstone went on in his accustomed style to ask various questions as to how the influence which the American would inevitably exercise in the world would be used.

"Will it," he asked, "be instinct with moral life in proportion to its material strength? One thing is certain, his temptations will multiply with his power, his responsibilities with his opportunities. Will the seed be sown among the thorns? Will worthlessness overrun the ground and blight its flowers and its fruit? On the answers to these questions, and to such as these, it will depend whether this new revelation of power on the earth is also to be a revelation of virtue, whether it shall prove a blessing or a curse. May Heaven avert every darker omen, and grant that the latest and largest growth of the great Christian civilization shall also be the brightest and best?"

To Mr. Gladstone all this pompous detail of material triumphs was worse than idle, unless they were regarded simply as tools and materials for the attainment of the highest purposes of our being. To use his own striking phrase: —

"We must ascend from the ground floor of material industry to the higher regions in which these nobler purposes are to be wrought out."

[William T. Stead, *The Americanization of the World* (Horace Markley, 1901), 145–7, 149, 151, 160–4, 166, 170, 176, 180–1, 342–3, 348–50, 369, 384–6, 396, 405, 418, 422, 427–8, 431–3, 437–41]

42. *Patriotism and Religion,* Shailer Mathews (1863–1941)

*Born in Maine, Mathews was educated at Colby College, Newton
Theological Seminary, and the University of Berlin. From 1894 to 1933,
he taught at the Divinity School of the University of Chicago; he also
served as dean of the school for most of this period. Although he was
never ordained into the ministry, he served as president of the Federal
Council of Churches from 1912 to 1916. Under Mathews, the Divinity
School became an educational center—first of Social Gospel
Christianity and then of theological modernism. His interest in these
movements was reflected in his books,* The Messianic Hope in the New
Testament *(1905) and* The Faith of Modernism *(1924). His strong
support for America's entry into war was tied to both movements. In this
selection, taken from lectures he delivered at the University of North
Carolina in 1917, Mathews criticizes Christian pacifism as strongly as
he criticizes religious creedalism and ritualism—both of which he saw
as linked to populist isolationism. Here Mathews tries to define a new
relationship between patriotism and religion that is inseparable from
Progressive ideals of social justice and internationalism.*

—1918—

As one attempts . . . to express the new devotion which has called our
nation to arms and has filled America with a militant loyalty, a sense of
companionship is at once detected. This passion of service, this readiness to sacrifice health and life for national ideals—what is it but a
counterpart of religion?

As we analyze this companionship, points of superficial similarity at
once emerge. There is the same symbolism in religion as in patriotism.
The rite or the doctrine or the shibboleth is a banner as truly as the Stars
and Stripes. If in our critical moods we trace unmoved its history and
analyze its purpose, we are bewildered when some one treats it as of no
heartfelt importance. It is a rare interdenominational meeting in which
one does not hear good-natured raillery at the expense of a rite or doctrine that characterizes one of the religious bodies there represented.
Such sallies meet with laughter, but the parties concerned are always a
little perturbed. It is disconcerting to have that for which one's fathers
died and by which we symbolize a faith turned into a joke. The rite or
doctrine in someway focalizes a social relationship that is precious—a
source of inspiration, a bond with the past, a challenge to the future.
Over against a religious inheritance as over against one's country the

individual feels dwarfed. He stands thankful, humble and proud before the land in which he was born and the church in which he was reared. Doctrines may be rejected, worship may be neglected, priests may be suspected, but when religion is really endangered even a Voltaire[8] will erect a temple to God. Many a man looks across the widening sea of disillusionment that sweeps between him and an earlier faith to find his heart growing tender as he thinks of that faith in which his fathers shared. Hope rises above debate, looking for that dear country, the home of God's elect.

But the deeper kinship of patriotism and religion lies far below passing emotions, and characterizes national policies as truly as the impulses of citizens. In these days as in the past it is a common origin of brutality and idealism, of aggression and sacrifice. To neglect this spiritual element of national personalities is to misunderstand national characters and to prophesy falsely of national destinies. Patriotism and religion alike are the expression of a nation's inner life. If the morale of an army is a key to victory or defeat, the national soul is the explanation of national futures and international struggles.

Patriotism and religions are both the product of social history. There can be no individualistic patriotism and no anti-social religion. . . .

Nothing was easier for [the] orthodoxy of the church than to express itself as a patriotism which centered about a divine monarchy. But a different situation arises in the days of democracy. Here we pass into a creative rather than an inherited patriotism. What fellowship has democracy with religion? Can it too, as the mood of a social mind, give form and terms to religious thought? Can theology describe a divine super-democracy? . . .

Democracy is more than an ideal. It is a discernible development of institutions. As such it should be regarded historically, not theoretically. And as a development of institutions it has not been symmetrical in different nations. In practice democracy must be described as the development of the rights of Englishmen into the rights of humanity. That which the Englishmen claimed as rights in England, our intellectual and idealistic development has made the basis of our conception of whatever democracy we actually enjoy. Not programs but genetic development has been the method by which such democracy as the world actually possesses has become the precious heritage of humanity. We

---

8. Voltaire was the pen name for François-Marie Arouet (1694–1778), a French Enlightenment philosopher and encyclopedist best known for his satirical novel *Candide* (1759).

are at war to preserve a real world in the making, not a Utopia that men have dreamed.

This actual democracy has been largely outside the range of economics and within the range of politics. The founders of the American Republic were not concerned with economic democracy. In fact, it is probable that if they had thought of it, they would have bitterly opposed it. To think of productive wealth in a collective fashion was something that obviously they never dreamed of. And this conclusion is enforced by the fact that they left in the American Constitution economic factors some of which plunged the nation into civil war, and others which are at present serving as the basis of a federal paternalism. What the future may have in store for a democratized world we cannot foretell. But in the light of our past experience we must believe that the process of extending popular rights by extending privileges enjoyed by some favored class, will continue. Already its direction is becoming apparent. Political rights inevitably involve economic rights. . . .

Sometimes men speak of the democracy of Germany. There is no democracy in Germany in the sense that there is a democratic movement in Anglo-American history. The very Socialism of Germany is not democratic. The political development of Germany has consciously been opposed to that which has characterized the Anglo-Saxon stock. The heart of Anglo-French and Anglo-American democracy is this: the people as such control their government; the authority of the state resides in the people, and sovereignty lies in the people and not outside the people. . . . The heart of the German conception is that the government derives its authority from God and not from the people. The democracy of England, America, and France has been worked out in revolutions in which the people dared face an oppressive government. Indeed, practically all constitutional governments have been born of peoples who dared revolt rather than lose their rights. The German blood of all Europe has never accomplished a successful revolution. Face to face with their government Germans have always quit the struggle for popular rights. German patriotism has never centered about the rights of individuals. There has never been a German democracy because Germans have never cared enough about democracy to organize a revolution.

This difference in political loyalties explains differences in the religious attitudes of autocracies and democracies. Democracy in America was the child of religious liberty. . . .

The real expression of democracy in religious thinking is outside the field of orthodox theology. We can no longer think of God as spatially separate from the world of action. He is with us till the end of the age. Most

of the constructive work now being done in the field of theology is by way
of extending Christian principles into social justice. By the process of
social reconstruction where democracy is working, lives are being fired
with the conviction that human beings have value as men and women.
The creative theological thinking of the past twenty-five years has been
done by men of the new patriotism—men in sympathy with the social
movements of the day. To them God is not an absentee monarch, but the
inner Life of the universe expressing His will in nature's forces and the
growing morality of the group-will. All recent books of theological significance have belonged to that new region into which prophetic souls are
entering where we have learned to see men and women as persons; where
we have learned to see that they have rights; and where we are learning
to give them and get them justice. Only where the spirit of democracy is
working is there creative religious thinking. Only there is the union of the
patriotism and the religion of tomorrow. For in democracy alone can the
immanence of God be expressed in the terms of human experience. . . .

In treating of a nation we thus have to deal with an entity which is
more or less logically arbitrary, but virtually real. It is more than a form
of government. France, as example, for centuries slowly evolved from a
group of feudal states at last to find a unity in a constitution. But France
to the Frenchman—and nowadays to the world!—stands for something
vastly more than a political unity. It has a place and a mission in the
world to which its government is almost incidental. Similarly in the
case of Germany. The German Empire as a political unity is vastly less
important than *das Deutschtum*.

So it comes to pass that loyalty to one's nation is far more inclusive
than loyalty to one's government. True, when, as in the case of Germany, a government is set forth as the state and makes its own ambitions
and policies a national program, it becomes the object of loyalty. But
the nation, whatever may be its constitutional aspect, is more than its
government. Loyalty to one's nation—or when government is imperfect
or lacking, one's people—is the only workable definition of patriotism.
On the one side it is a sort of property right in a social inheritance, and
on the other side it is an idealistic devotion to the mission which its citizens believe is the duty of a state to perform.

It follows that patriotism gets its highest moral values not from itself
as a state of soul. Patriotism no more than sincerity is a guaranty of wisdom. Its moral values are derived from the significance of the nation to
humanity. If this significance be morally indefensible, patriotism
becomes a menace. If the political, economic, and international policies of a nation tend to establish a better world order, patriotism is an
evangel of peace and justice. . . .

That international crimes have been wrought in the name of nationalism must be admitted. In the name of patriotism strong nations have oppressed the weak. National pride has given countenance to national aggression and brutality. National egotism made Continental Europe an armed camp and drenched the earth with the blood of helpless peoples. All this and more must be admitted as legitimate charges against nationalism and patriotism of a certain sort. . . .

Admitting, therefore, that there are dangers in patriotism and that nations are as yet competitive groups, we are all the more concerned with the purposes and ideals of nations. The danger of patriotism to the world-order lies in the sort of policies a nation represents. If nationality and patriotism are to be identified with German theories of the state, a German national loyalty will result. Nationality and patriotism are then undoubted evils which ought to be remedied. But a nation composed of persons who regard national welfare as consistent with the welfare of other nations is not a curse. Patriotism that prompts a nation to protect weaker nations from their stronger neighbors and seeks to lead in cooperative effort for the welfare of humanity is the promise of a new and better world-order.

Can patriotism thus be made a cooperative rather than a belligerent virtue? . . .

The nineteenth century saw this patriotism first worked out in the laboratory of Anglo-Saxon constitutional history on both sides of the Atlantic spread throughout the world. France after the Revolution increasingly embodied this idea of personal liberty in its national ideals, but until the last part of the nineteenth century no other great nation included within its patriotism similar ideals. Then for the first time in history there was to be seen the emergence of a democratic patriotism. Under Victor Emmanuel,[9] Italy joined the founders of the new epoch, and in the last decade of the nineteenth and through the twentieth century nation after nation has developed in Europe a patriotism of like character. . . . Only in Germany, in Austria-Hungary, and in Turkey has the old type of patriotism, which consists in loyalty to a divinely established irresponsible monarchy, persisted without serious modifications.

It is not of liberty that the German patriot boasts, but of his *Kultur*, defended and enforced by arms. And when *Kultur* is described by its evangelists it is seen to be a patriotism centering about a state relying upon military power rather than regard for personal rights.

Thus in our day there appear two types of patriotism, that of democracy

---

9. Victor Emmanuel II (1820–1878) was the first king of a unified and independent Italy.

and that of autocracy. By their morals as by their history shall they be judged!

The patriotism of the democratic power has never been militaristic and has taken up the present conflict with loathing. The patriotism of the German is essentially militaristic and regards war as an integral part of a foreign policy. The patriotism of democracy has never demanded that its government should conquer lands possessed of settled national life. It has respected the rights of organized nations and has increasingly recognized the fact that loyalty to one's country involves the recognition of the rights of other nations. The patriotism of Germany has excluded all such recognition and has centered itself vigorously upon aggressive conquest and an immoral disregard of other nations' wellbeing. . . . The demand of such a patriotism has been for the extension of national boundaries, the appropriation of other nations' territory, the laying of crushing indemnities. The patriotism of democracy has sought to extend constitutional rights even to those less organized peoples over whom its power has extended; the patriotism of autocracy has subordinated personal rights to the power of a state, deriving its authority from no other source than inheritance given sanction by an appeal to a German God. When the democratic patriotism has turned to God, it is to the God who rules over other nations, who is the God of law and justice. When the patriotism of Germany has turned to God, it has been to a national god whose chief aim is to inspire the courage of those who draw the flashing sword and give comfort to those who have perished in the extension of national power and the brutal imposition upon other countries of its own national civilization. . . .

The difference between the patriotism which thus lies back of the German policy and that which lies back of the Anglo-French-American policy is grounded in a difference in the recognition of international justice. Democratic patriotism has never sought to spread by conquest the blessings which the various democratic nations possess. The United States and Great Britain have been the outstanding representatives of the spread of Christian civilization through foreign missions. Enormous sums of money have been raised for the purpose of establishing schools and churches among non-Christian peoples. Such Anglo-American civilization has never been enforced by military power. In India the British have been particularly sensitive to the prejudices of the natives, and in the Philippines, where the United States has established itself by military power, the people have been encouraged and permitted to take over an increasing control of political affairs.

It cannot, of course, be claimed that such extension of the best elements of our civilization has been conducted without mistakes. We must admit whatever facts go to show that methods have been used which are not consistent with the ideals for which we have stood. And it must be added that the Germans also, though to a far less extent, have founded missions and schools among non-Christian people. But the great contrast lies in the general policy and tendency which the two types of patriotism have set forth—the one making central the German state and the other the furthering of human rights. The two types of patriotism are radically different and lead to radically different policies both at home and abroad. As to which will dominate the future no man of vision can doubt. . . .

Most of us did not see this in 1914. The outbreak of the war found us as unprepared in spirit as in armament. . . .

As Americans we felt that the war was born of conditions of such thoroughly continental pedigree as to make it strictly European. Whatever may have been our personal sympathies, we demanded peace and determined to avoid every act and expression that threatened peace. Christianity we felt was opposed to war and the choice between war and Christianity seemed absolute.

I do not need to dwell upon the bitterness of the awakening. Our eyes were gradually cleared to see the real meaning of the war. At last we were forced to realize that whatever may have been the occasions of the conflict, its fundamental causes involved us as truly as any other nation. But with the awakening came fundamental questions which continue to present themselves much to the disturbance of those souls which dislike to look at humanity as it is. For these fundamental questions focus in the challenge war makes to religion. . . .

If Christianity is to end war it must cure the world of its lust for conquest and bring economic expansion under the control of justice. To this I shall return in my final lecture. For the present let us look at the situation the present war illustrates, considering only the broad question of Christian duty in a war in which economic causes are not absent, but which has clearly become a struggle between two philosophies of the state, two national moralities. As events now stand, we must determine the call of duty with regard not to war in general but to a war in particular. . . .

On the one hand is the state philosophy which demands political control through military power, and a religion that worships a German God of battles; on the other is the policy that seeks commercial development through the maintenance of peace and an attempt, imperfect though it is, to supply Christian ideals to international affairs. . . .

The champions of the imperialistic and consequently the militaristic patriotism are not without argument. They appeal to the alleged law of biological necessity. They have the history of the past with its great empires of the East, of Alexander and of Rome. If social evolution has within it no idealistic creative power, if humanity is to be developed by the rigorous determinism of inherited conditions and animal evolution, it is indeed hard to see why war is not to be inevitable and permanent. . . .

One may even go further and say that it is not impossible that war has stimulated moral attitudes. Few modern nations have entered war without an appeal to noble sentiments and the protestation of loyalty to noble ideals. Out from such an attitude of mind have come noble examples of individual and social sacrifice and human hearts have been melted together by the fires of common agony. Our poetry is filled with war songs, and political leaders have very generally been soldiers.

But if thus war is not without its arguments, over against them must be others which modify the conclusions which have been drawn in favor of war. Not only does war plunge human life into the abysmal misery of fathers and mothers weeping for their children, but out from the acute hatreds of war have come persistent hatreds which have perverted the relations of nations and incalculably hindered the development of the finer things of life. Individualism has been lost in military organization; injury to nations and to individuals has been not only economic but moral; unworthy ambitions have been given new life; and social reforms have been obscured or abandoned because of military necessity. If it be true, as must be admitted, that out from war has come renewed confidence in immortality and in God, it must also be admitted that just as truly from war has come a lowering of moral habits, the loss of momentum in social reconstruction, a brutalizing of the thought of God, and a carelessness in the recognition of human rights. It is no wonder that the heart of a genuine Christian cries out against such an evil. . . .

Obviously the moral problems set a community which endeavors to put the principle of brotherhood into operation are vastly more complicated than the pacifist chooses to see. The development of civilization proceeds gradually, by the embodiment of ideals in human institutions. These institutions which guarantee personal liberty, the right of initiative, democracy in the sense of a people's right to control its own affairs, exist as an exceedingly precious heritage for succeeding generations. They increasingly embody the giving of justice, the social synonym of the love Jesus taught and embodied. They must be preserved if morality is to be preserved. To submit passively to their destruction is a violation of the fundamental principle of brotherhood. Society recognizes this clearly enough in its attempt to protect itself from evil minded men like thieves, adulterers, and oppressors of their kind. The decision as to whether a citizen shall undertake such protection is not a matter of individual likes and dislikes but of social obligation. The fact that as human society grows more responsive to ideals of justice and fraternity, the protection of the finer institutions of human welfare becomes increasingly conventional and so less in need of reliance upon force, serves only to obscure the fundamental necessity of a society's being able to offer protection to its members and successors if institutions born of justice are endangered. A refusal to undertake the duty of guaranteeing such protection, whatever may be its alleged ethical justification, is in reality an anti-fraternal act. . . .

So in the case of a nation that sees the world and itself attacked by another nation bent upon terrorizing its neighbors into subjection and destroying the most precious institutions of civilization. Pacifism under such circumstances is antisocial, a misguided idealism if not transcendentalized selfishness. The duty which a nation owes to a world as well as to itself and its future compels it to protect its institutions and its very existence against the assault of a national highwayman. And this duty must infiltrate the moral action of individuals. Christians are not insulated individuals; they are citizens.

This is the real spirit with which Christians must approach the question of a war. Against our likes, our hopes, our ideals, we fight because we love our race. War born of a perverted patriotism, war for the sake of national aggrandizement at the expense of other nations is un-Christian, no matter how much it may masquerade under appeals to the God of Gideon and of David. But the very essence of a Christian patriotism appears in the defense not of national institutions as such, but of institutions which are increasingly if not completely Christian. Love, which is the heart of the Christian message, cannot permit a nation to remain neutral while the well-being of other nations is endangered. The highest sacrifice which love demands is a frank recognition of the necessity of abandoning the ideals of peace when peace involves the suffering of others. The true Christian patriot at the present moment is in fact saying to certain ideals, "You must for the moment retire from the scene. I have a desperately nasty mess to clean up. I am not responsible for the situation but you are powerless to help. It is a choice between defending institutions which guarantee your existence and permitting these institutions to go down to destruction." And my own conviction is clear that such self-sacrifice in the interest of making permanent the achievement of peace and justice is the most idealistic service a man or a nation can render the world. . . .

Loathing war, determined to end war by the regeneration of the forces that shape national action, such patriots dedicate themselves to a national service which gets its value not from uncritical loyalty to a nation but from loyalty to a nation which has consecrated itself to the good of humanity. It is this sort of patriotism that we dare call Christian. "We hope," a well-intending body of Christians once said to Mr. Lincoln, "that God is on our side." "I am not much concerned," said Mr. Lincoln "to know whether God is on our side. What I want to know is whether we are on God's side." With this desire American patriotism may now face its terrible task. We pray for the victory of our arms, not because we demand that God shall give victory to our country whether we are right or wrong, but because we are convinced that the cause for which we struggle is more precious than a peace bought at the expense of the world's warfare; that the cause for which we fight is God's cause as we know it revealed both in the life and the ideals of Jesus and in the unmistakable tendencies of social evolution.

A religion which will keep its followers from committing themselves to the support of such patriotism is either too æsthetic for humanity's actual needs, too individualistic to be social, or too disloyal to be tolerated. . . .

The history of the international relations of democracies is a tribute to the change that is coming into our conception of Christianity. We have unfortunately to admit that this truer conception of the Christian faith is by no means universal. Too many of our churches are still in the control of professional churchmen whose vision is sectarian and who think that the gospel has no place in social affairs beyond the maintenance of individual respectability. Just at present forces of reaction are especially in evidence working mightily to keep Christianity within the confines set by the past, preferring an infallible Pope or an inerrant Bible to the spirit of Jesus and the ideals of the Kingdom of God. But never before were there so many evidences of the rise of a true Christianity. Denominations are ceasing their internecine strife and are organizing Federations and World Conferences. The bankruptcy of theological orthodoxy as an agency to prevent war forces thoughtful men to reconsider the real place of Christianity in our social order. We are repatriating Jesus in Christianity. Out of the Calvary of the present war will come the resurrection of a faith above shibboleths, born of a tested confidence in God, in Jesus, and human progress.

When we ask how this should and will affect patriotism as the expression of a national loyalty, we are passing from history to prophecy. Yet even here we are not at the mercy of hope unregulated by facts. Historical tendencies become our guide. Genuine religious faith does not attempt to rehabilitate the past, but to reconstruct the future.

Superficial optimism has no place in such forecasts, for the God we must worship is not the God of a finished world, but a God who cooperates with mankind in the production of a new world. From faith in such a God springs new confidence in the possible influence of a genuinely Christian spirit in national affairs. The new world has not been born, but there is still opportunity for the exercise of prenatal influences.

A religion fit for democracy will ennoble patriotism by giving moral direction to the spiritual life of a nation. . . .

As representatives of the democratic patriotism, Americans are in particular need of a Christianized public opinion. As already has been said, our democracy has been born of our religious liberty, and our active Christian conscience has played no small role in the maintenance of peace between ourselves and other nations. But we need to go further if our national life is to meet the crisis in world relations which will follow the war. National policy will embody our best ideals only as those ideals spring from our inner social life. International justice must be grounded in domestic justice. Social service in the sense of caring for the unfortunate through institutions of charity is possible in an autocracy, but social transformation through establishing a genuine fraternity is politically possible only where there is democracy. To recognize this possibility is to demand the spread of justice. If our nation is to be a plutocracy, it will be no more democratic than an autocracy. If the rights of our working men are to be gained only through more or less developed revolution which forces privileges from those who are unwilling to surrender them, our Christian morality is certainly weak. The center of Christianity is a sacrificial social mindedness. God and Christ sacrifice for men; men must sacrifice for each other. The gospel appeals to those who have enjoyed privileges denied their less fortunate fellows. The war in bringing us a clearer insight of our fundamental national unity is helping us to see that justice is the obverse of fraternity. Moral advance is increasingly seen to involve such concrete matters as the housing of the working man, the shortening of his working day, the increase of his opportunity for leisure and his larger share in the product of his own labor.

The last twenty-five years have shown that Christianity has a social power far beyond that of a mere incentive to social amelioration. Amelioration it is true is an approach to justice, but the creative religious teaching of the last quarter century has been reshaping patriotism itself into a devotion to human rights championed by national action. Sometimes this reconstruction has expended itself in denunciation of evils and unlimited criticism of our life and institutions. More than this, however, it has shown itself in an education in moral sympathies which has hastened the recognition by the capitalist class of its obligations to the people. It is true this process has still far to go before it reaches its goal. We still need to learn how to share privilege intelligently. The worth of the individual still needs to be more honored than class privilege and economic efficiency. Human motives, especially in the economic world, need inspiration for sacrifice in the interest of justice. During the last few months we have rapidly learned this lesson. We see clearly that our national ideals are worth fighting for. We are beginning to see that the virtues which we demand of a nation in its world affairs must rule a nation's inner life. If we are to make the world safe for democracy, we must make our own nation more than politically democratic. The ideals for which men die in war are ideals for which they must live in peace. [Shailer Mathews, *Patriotism and Religion* (Macmillan, 1918), preface, 4–6, 24–8, 31–2, 35–6, 40, 44, 62–5, 72–4, 78–80, 87–8, 90–3, 107–8, 111–5, 119–21, 131–3]

43. *The World State,* Mary Parker Follett (1868–1934)[10]

The democratic basis for Follett's arguments in The New State *was her ideal of the "group"—a communal, self-determining organization that would teach the most basic skills of social life to its members. The "group" was as important to Follett as the family was to other Progressives. Follett's belief that this "group" would help to spread democratic values, even beyond the boundaries of nation states, is evidenced in the following selection. When the impetus for political and social reform waned in the 1920s, Follett turned her attention increasingly to the management of business corporations and attempted to link group psychology to the Progressive values of expertise and efficiency. In that respect she was quite in tune with the attempts in the 1920s to turn large business organizations into quasi-public corporations concerned with the public welfare. Here, however, her stage is much larger.*

—1918—

No "alliances," no balance of power, no agreements, no Hague tribunals will now satisfy us; we know that it is only by creating a genuine community of nations that we can have stability and growth—world

---

10. More biographical information on Follett prefaces her selections in Chapters 2 and 4.

peace, world progress. What are the contributions of group psychology to the League of Nations?

There is no way out of the hell of our present European situation until we find a method of compounding difference. Superficial moralists try to get us to like some other nationality by emphasizing all the things we have in common, but war can never cease until we see the value of differences, that they are to be maintained not blotted out. The white-man's burden is not to make others like himself. As we see the value of the individual, of every individual, so we must see the value of each nation, that all are needed. The pacifists have wanted us to tolerate our enemies and the more extreme ones to turn the other cheek when smitten. But tolerance is intolerable. And we cannot dwell among enemies. The ideal of this planet inhabited by Christian enemies all turning the cheek does not seem to me a happy one. We must indeed, as the extreme militarists tell us, "wipe out" our enemies, but we do not wipe out our enemies by crushing them. The old-fashioned hero went out to conquer his enemy; the modern hero goes out to disarm his enemy through creating a mutual understanding. . . .

Internationalism and cosmopolitanism must not be confused. The aim of cosmopolitanism *is* for all to be alike; the aim of internationalism is a rich content of widely varying characteristic and experience.

Perhaps one of the most useful lessons to be learned from the group process is a new definition of patriotism. Patriotism must not be herd-instinct. Patriotism must be the individual's rational, self-conscious building of his country every moment. Loyalty means always to create your group, not to wave a flag over it. We need a patriotism which is not "following the lead" but involved in a process in which all take part. In the place of sentimental patriotism we want a common purpose, a purpose evolved by the common life, to be used for the common life. Some of our biologists mislead us when they talk of the homogeneity of the herd as the aim of nations. The nation may be a herd at present. What we have to do is to make it a true group. Internationalism must be based upon group units, not upon herd or crowd units, that is, upon people united not by herd instinct but by group conviction. If a nation is a crowd, patriotism is mere hypnotism; if a nation is a true federal state built up of interlocking and ascending groups, then patriotism is self-evolved. When you are building up an association or a nation you have to preach loyalty; later it is part of the very substance which has been built.

Then genuine loyalty, a self-evolved loyalty, will always lead the way to higher units. Nationalism looks out as well as in. It means, in addition to its other meanings, every nation being responsible to a larger whole. It is this new definition of patriotism which America is now learning. It is this new patriotism which must be taught our children, which we must repeat to one another on our special patriotic day, July 4th, and on every occasion when we meet. This new patriotism looks in, it looks out: we have to learn that we are not wholly patriotic when we are working with all our heart for America merely; we are truly patriotic only when we are working also that America may take her place worthily and helpfully in the world of nations. Nationalism is not my nation for itself or my nation against others or my nation dominating others, but simply my nation taking its part as "an equal among equals."

Shall this hideous war go on simply because people will not understand nationalism? Nationalism and internationalism are not opposed. We do not lop off just enough patriotism to our country to make enough for a world-state: he who is capable of the greatest loyalty to his own country is most ready for a wider loyalty. There is possible no world-citizenship the ranks of which are to be filled by those who do not care very much for their own country. We have passed through a period when patriotism among cultivated people seemed often to be at a discount—the ideal was to be "citizens of the world." But we see now that we can never be "citizens of the world" until we learn how to be citizens of America or England or France. Internationalism is not going to swallow up nationalism. Internationalism will accentuate, give point, significance, meaning, value, reality, to nationalism. . . .

The error of our old political philosophy was that the state always looks in: it has obligations to its members, it has none to other states; it merely enters into agreements with them for mutual benefit thereby obtained. International law of the future must be based not on nations as "sovereigns" dealing with one another, but on nations as members of a society dealing with one another. The difference in these conceptions is enormous. We are told that cessions of sovereignty must be the basis of an international government. We cannot have a lasting international union until we entirely reform such notions of sovereignty: that the power of the larger unit is produced mechanically by taking away bits of power from all the separate units. Sovereignty is got by giving to every unit its fullest value and thereby giving birth to a new power—the power of a larger whole. We must give up "sovereign" nations in the old sense, but with our present definition of sovereignty we may keep all the real sovereignty we have and then unite to evolve together a larger sovereignty. . . .

When the individual nations give up their separate sovereignty—as regards their armaments, as regards the control of the regions which possess the raw materials, as regards the great waterways of the world, as regards, in fact, all which affects their joint lives—the falling chains of a real slavery will reverberate through the world. For unrelated sovereignty, with world conditions as they are today, is slavery.

The idea of "sovereign" nations must go as completely as is disappearing the idea of sovereign individuals. The isolation of sovereign nations is so utterly complete that they cannot really (and I mean this literally) even see each other. The International League is the one solution for the relation of nations. Whenever we say we can have a "moral" international law on any other basis, we write ourselves down [as] pure sentimentalists.

There are many corollaries to this project. We do not need, for instance, a more vigorous protection of neutrals, but the abolition of neutrals. The invasion of the rights of neutrals in this war by both sides shows that we can no longer have neutrals in our scheme of union; all must come within the bond.

Further, diplomatic relations will be entirely changed. "Honor among thieves" means loyalty to your group: while to lie or to try to get the better of your own particular group is an unpardonable offence, you may deceive an outsider. We see now the psychological reason for this. Diplomatic lying will not go until diplomatists instead of treating with one another as members of alien groups consider themselves all as members of one larger group—the League of Nations.

Moreover, one nation cannot injure another merely; the injury will be against the community, and the community of nations will look upon it as such. Under our present international system the attack of one nation on another is the same as the attack of one outlaw on another. But under a civilized international system, the attack of one individual on another is an attack on society and the whole society must punish it. The punishment, however, will not consist in keeping the offender out of the alliance. If the Allies win, Germany should not be punished by keeping her out of a European league; she must be shown how to take her place within it. And it must be remembered that we do not join a league of nations solely to work out our relations to one another, but to learn to work for the larger whole, for international values. Until this lesson is learned no league of nations can be successful. . . .

To sum up all these particularist fallacies: live and let live can never be our international motto. *Laissez-faire* fails as ignominiously in international relations as within a single nation. Our new motto must be, Live in such manner that the fulness of life may come to all. This is "the ledge and the leap" for twentieth-century thought. . . .

The history of modern times from the point of view of political

science is the history of the growth of democracy; from the point of view
of social psychology it is the history of the growth of the social consciousness. These two are one. But the mere consciousness of the social
bond is not enough. . . . [W]e surely today have come to see in the
social bond and the Creative Will, a compelling power, a depth and
force, as great as that of any religion we have ever known. We are ready
for a new revelation of God. It is not coming through any single man,
but through the men and men who are banding together with one purpose, in one consecrated service, for a great fulfilment. Many of us have
felt bewildered in a confused and chaotic world. We need to focus both
our aspirations and our energy; we need to make these effective and at
the same time to multiply them by their continuous use. This book is a
plea for the more abundant life: for the fulness of life and the growing
life. It is a plea against everything static, against the idea that there need
be any passive material within the social bond. It is a plea for a splendid
progress dependent upon every splendid one of us. We need a new faith
in humanity, not a sentimental faith or a theological tenet or a philosophical conception, but an active faith in that creative power of men
which shall shape government and industry, which shall give form
equally to our daily life with our neighbor and to a world league. [Mary
Parker Follett, *The New State: Group Organization the Solution of Popular Government* (Longmans, Green, 1918), 344–8, 351–3, 359–60]

Further Reading

Bliss, William Dwight Porter, *The New Encyclopedia of Social Reform* (Funk &
Wagnalls, 1908).

Eisenach, Eldon, "Progressive Internationalism," in Jerome Mileur and Sidney
Milkis, eds., *Progressivism and the New Democracy* (University of Massachusetts Press, 1999).

Kennedy, David M., *Over Here: The First World War and American Society*
(Oxford University Press, 1980).

Kloppenberg, James, *Uncertain Victory: Social Democracy and Progressivism*
(Oxford University Press, 1986).

Knock, Thomas, *To End All Wars: Woodrow Wilson and the Quest for a New
World Order* (Oxford University Press, 1992).

Perkins, Bradford, *The Great Rapprochment: England and the United States,
1895–1914* (Atheneum, 1968).

Rodgers, Daniel T., *Atlantic Crossings: Social Politics in a Progressive Age* (Harvard University Press, 1998), Chapters 7 and 9.

Rosenberg, Emily S., *Spreading the American Dream: American Economic and
Cultural Expansion, 1890–1945* (Hill and Wang, 1982).

Schaffer, Ronald, *America in the Great War: The Rise of the War Welfare State*
(Oxford University Press, 1991).

Stead, William T., *The Salvation Army* (Review of Reviews, 1901).

Steel, Ronald, *Walter Lippmann and the American Century* (Little, Brown, 1980).

Tonn, Joan C., and Mary P. Follett, *Creating Democracy, Transforming Management* (Yale University Press, 2003).

Vanderlip, Frank A., *The American "Commercial Invasion" of Europe* (Scribner's, 1902).

Vaughn, Stephen, *Holding Fast the Inner Lines: Democracy, Nationalism, and the Committee on Public Information* (University of North Carolina Press, 1980).

Wynn, Neil A., *From Progressivism to Prosperity: World War I and American Society* (Holmes & Meier, 1986).

Index

Abbott, Lyman, 183
abolitionism/abolitionists, xiii, 5–6, 11–2, 17, 256, 273
absolutism, 188–9, 258
Adams, Henry Carter, 43, 79, 84, 117, 123, 155, 210
Addams, Jane, 13–4, 16, 33, 38, 78–9, 84, 100–1, 111, 132, 225, 231, 237, 242–3, 270, 273, 288, 290
administration/administrative commissions, ix, xiv, xx, 22, 78–9, 102, 112–5, 118, 123–4, 127, 131–3, 136, 146, 154, 207, 210, 221, 271, 276, 279, 288. *See also* regulation
agriculture, 5, 47, 52–3, 63, 110, 158, 203, 247, 277, 281, 294–5
American Academy of Political and Social Science, 65, 85, 211, 243; and *Annals of the American Academy of Political and Social Science*, 65, 211
American Association for Labor Legislation, 50
American Economic Association, 39–45, 65, 85, 117, 123. *See also* political economy
American Philosophical Association, 72
American Psychological Association, 72
American Sociological Society, 14, 25, 94, 100; and *American Journal of Sociology*, 25, 33, 58, 64, 114, 117, 213. *See also* sociology
anarchism/anarchy, 115, 205, 255, 259

androcentrism, 220, 222–41
Anglo-Americans, 29, 303, 305–6
antialcohol. *See* Prohibition
Antin, Mary, 183
antislavery. *See* abolitionism
antitrust laws. *See* Sherman Anti-Trust Act
arbitration, 49, 156, 206
aristocracy, 3, 73–5, 77, 89–90, 178, 203, 232–3, 292; judicial/legal, 124, 128
artisans. *See* tradesmen
autocracy, 169, 174, 180, 303, 306, 311

Bacon, David Francis, 2, 4
Batten, Samuel Zane, 177–8, 181, 190, 208
Beard, Charles, 40, 112–3, 146, 157, 212
Beard, Mary, 212
Beecher, Henry Ward, 213
Beecher, Lyman, 16, 213
Besant, Sir Walter, 82, 299
Beveridge, Albert, 272
Bible, 176, 181, 195, 310; Gospels, 83, 153, 176, 187–92, 235–6, 310–1; New Testament, 176, 235, 301
Bliss, W.D.P., 10, 50, 177, 208, 213, 287–8, 316
boss/bosses, 37, 109, 112, 221, 264–5
Breckenridge, Sophonisba, 58
brotherhood, xvi, 79–80, 195, 228, 233, 308
Brotherhood of the Kingdom, 177, 190
Bryan, William Jennings, xix, 157, 256

Acknowledgments

I thank Brian Balogh, David Ciepley, James Kloppenberg, Kevin Matt-son, Sidney Milkis, Dorothy Ross, and Jeffrey Sklansky for their advice and encouragement during the early stages of this project. I thank Jean Yarbrough for getting me interested in the project in the first place. The process of finding, copying, scanning, refining, and editing the selec-tions was made immeasurably easier with the help of what became an increasingly efficient team: the circulation and interlibrary loan staff of McFarlin Library, my department secretary Toy Kelley and her band of work-study students who manned the copying machine, the library duplicating service that produced digital versions, and, especially, my wife, Valerie, who magically transformed these versions into clean and uniform copy. Eric Saulnier, my undergraduate research assistant for the entire length of the project, deserves special thanks for his help on the biographical research and for serving as an intelligent reader.